P9-BZK-470

HOW TO SETTLE YOUR OWN
AUTO ACCIDENT
CLAIM Without A Lawyer

By Benji O. Anosike

Printing History
First edition   October 1993
Second Printing   March 1994
New edition,revised,June 1998

Library of Congress Cataloging-in-Publication Data

Anosike, Benji O.
    How to settle your own auto accident claim without a lawyer / by
    Benji O. Anosike
      p.   cm.
    Includes bibliographical references and index.
    ISBN 0-932704-46-8 (paperback)
    1. Insurance, Automobile--Law and legislation--United States-
-Popular works. 2. Insurance, Automobile--Adjustment of claims-
-United States--Popular works. 3. Liability for traffic accidents-
-United States--Popular works.   I. Title.
    KF1218.Z9A56   1998
    346.73'086092--dc21   98-4093
                                                           CIP

Printed in the United States of America
ISBN: 0-932704-46-8
Library of Congress Catalog Number:

Published by:
Do-It-Yourself Legal Publishers
60 Park Place #1013,
Newark, NJ 07102

ACKNOWLEDGMENTS

The author is deeply grateful and indebted to many persons and entities without whose help the research and writing of this book would not have been possible. They are responsible in large part for the book's truths, but for none of it's errors.

Special thanks are due to Ms. Norma Feld, reference librarian, for her generous provision of access to the rich facilities of the Benjamin Cardoza Law School Library, New York. Appreciation is also extended to the library staff of the College Of Insurance, New York, whose excellent library enabled me to mount the kind of extensive search that became necessary of the meager published literature concerning the adjustment and settlement of insurance claims.

Special mention need to be made of, and expression of indebtedness extended to, the authors and publishers of the following works which were, among others, considerably consulted during the course of the research for this manual: Professor H. Laurence Ross, author, <u>Settled Out Of Court</u> (Aldine De Gruyter, New York); Daniel G. Baldyga, author, <u>How To Settle Your Own Insurance Claim</u> (The McMillan Company, New York); John Guinther, author, <u>Winning Your Personal Injury Suit</u> (Anchor Press/Doubleday); Edward Siegel's <u>How To Avoid Lawyers</u> (Ballentine Books, New York); Packard Thurber & Packard Thurber, Jr., edited text, <u>Claims Medical Manual</u> (Pacific Book Publishers, Palo Alto, California); Michelle Saadi's <u>Claim It Yourself</u> (Pharos Books, New York); Joseph Sindell, author, "What Price Personal Injury?" *(3 Practicing Law, 37)*, and "The Sindell Folio (Lawyers and Judges Publishing Co.); and the American Insurance Association, Washington, D.C., editors, <u>Summary Of Selected State Laws & Regulations Relating To Automobile Insurance</u>.

All of the above-named (and many others too numerous to mention) have, in one way or the other, by their courage, pioneering work, and research in the field — and by their unselfish readiness to share and disseminate the fruits of that— inspired and encouraged the present author, and made the present undertaking both more purposeful and easier for the author and the present publisher.

Included among those to whom appreciation must be extended are a number of persons — attorneys, insurance company adjusters and executives, and former claimants — who offered invaluable and frank opinions and insights on aspects of the claims settlement system but only on the guarantee of anonymity. Those persons know, however, who they are, and to them many thanks, nevertheless. Last, but by no means the least thanks are reserved for Amy R. Feigenbaum and Suzanne Feigenbaum for their skilled and dedicated work in the typesetting, designing and editing of this book. Their untiring efforts in undertaking the seemingly endless revisions called for in the process of turning out the book, is in large part responsible for whatever textual readability the final product possesses.

The Publisher's Disclaimer

✴ *Praise For* ✴

"HOW TO SETTLE YOUR OWN AUTO ACCIDENT CLAIM WITHOUT A LAWYER"

Here are what the EXPERTS *say:*

"The ASPON (Anosike 8-Step Strategic Program of Negotiations) formula developed by the author, is [in deed] a systematic approach to negotiating the claim, from start to finish…a great asset in the [auto accident] claims negotiating process…comprehensive, orderly and systematic…a tremendous help for a consumer involved in an auto accident."

—**Wendy Reiboldt, Ph.D.,** in American Council on Consumer Interest's
ADVANCING THE CONSUMER INTEREST Dec. 1993

"A handy how-to guide…Anosike offers extremely practical and digestible information and advice…to familiarize the uninitiated with the often confusing maze of paperwork and the [mechanics of processing insurance claims]"

—**American Library Association's**
BOOKLIST Oct. 1993

"The wealth of details, checklists, explanations and advice are well worth the extra expense."

—**The Midwest Book Review's**
BOOKWATCH Oct. 1993

"The work is clear and complete…readers [relying on] the book's advice are likely to secure a larger net recovery than they would get with [lawyer] representation."

—**Prof. H. Laurence Ross,**
America's top insurance industry sociologist and eminent author

"Tired of handing 50 percent of your accident settlements to attorneys? Think $96 billion is too much to pay each year in legal fees? Then you need [this book]…[it] provides 'the essential equalizer' for dealing with the insurance adjusters."

—*AUTOWEEK* June 28, 1993

TABLE OF CONTENTS

INTRODUCTION: WHAT THIS BOOK IS ALL ABOUT

HOW TO USE THIS MANUAL

CHAPTER 1
SETTLING YOUR AUTO ACCIDENT "TORT" CLAIMS:
WHEN & WHY YOU SHOULD DO IT YOURSELF WITHOUT A LAWYER

CHAPTER 2
SOME FEW FIRST STEPS YOU MUST TAKE IMMEDIATELY FOLLOWING THE
ACCIDENT TO PROTECT & MAXIMIZE YOUR RIGHTS

CHAPTER 3

THE WINNING FORMULA: START YOUR INFORMATION GATHERING HOMEWORK RIGHT AWAY, RIGHT FROM THE MOMENT OF THE ACCIDENT

CHAPTER 4

GATHERING DOCUMENTATIONS FOR CLAIMING YOUR MONEY DAMAGES

CHAPTER 5

THE CHECKLIST FOR USE IN COMPILING YOUR MONEY DAMAGES

CHAPTER 6

YOUR BODILY INJURY: A CRASH COURSE IN THE COMMON MEDICAL
TERMINOLOGY & TYPES OF INJURIES ENCOUNTERED IN AUTO ACCIDENT CASES

CHAPTER 7

THE LAW OF FAULT, NEGLIGENCE, & ACCIDENT LIABILITY, VERSUS HOW THE "SYSTEM" ACTUALLY WORKS IN THE REAL WORLD OF CLAIMS SETTLEMENT

CHAPTER 8

DO YOU HAVE AUTO INSURANCE COVERAGE? WHAT TYPE & WHAT PAYMENTS DOES IT ENTITLE YOU TO? WHICH INSURANCE COMPANY DO YOU FILE CLAIM AGAINST?

CHAPTER 9

EVALUATING THE WORTH OF YOUR CASE. HOW TO FIGURE OUT

WHAT AMOUNT YOU'RE TO ASK FOR.

CHAPTER 10

EVALUATION OF THE SETTLEMENT VALUE IN MORE

"SERIOUS" CASES: THE MODIFIED SINDELL METHOD

CHAPTER 11

CONDUCTING YOUR OWN FINAL SETTLEMENT NEGOTIATIONS:

THE ANOSIKE 8-STEP STRATEGIC PROGRAM OF NEGOTIATIONS — ASPON

SECTION A

SECTION B

THE ANOSIKE 8-STEP STRATEGIC PROGRAM OF NEGOTIATIONS, ASPON

CHAPTER 12
IF ALL ELSE FAILS, HOW TO PICK THE RIGHT ATTORNEY TO PRESS YOUR CLAIM WHILE SQUEEZING THE BEST DEAL OUT OF HIM

APPENDICES

LIST OF TABLES, CHARTS & FORMS:
WHERE TO FIND THEM

INTRODUCTION
WHAT THIS BOOK IS ABOUT

What This Book Is All About

This book is primarily concerned with the NON-LAWYER and the non expert; it is concerned with providing the ordinary citizen who falls victim to an automobile accident, with the essential "tools" and knowledge to successfully file for and negotiate his (or her) own personal injury claims himself, while coming away with a fair and reasonable settlement. It is concerned, not with the "formal law" (the law as it is ideally supposed to operate) of the world of auto liability claims settlement; but with the "law in action" of that world — the auto liability claims system as it actually operates in the day-to-day lives of the average citizen. And in this, the principal institution of the "law in action" is not the written law, or court trials or procedures, but out-of-court negotiations and settlements between parties.

Of course, the book is primarily meant for the non-expert. However, the claims professional — namely, the insurance claims manager, the adjuster, the claims or "negligence" attorney, etc. — can also definitely use this manual in his or her daily work, and with equal profit to himself just as well; the essential principles and procedures are no more or less different, after all.

The Unprepared Claimant Faces A Two-Fold Problem Financially, One With The Lawyer, And The Other With The Adjuster

The stark reality, much of it amply documented in this manual, is crystal clear regarding the nature of the main handicaps that an injured motorist or auto accident victim who seeks to file liability claims for damages confronts vis-a-vis the lawyer or the insurance adjuster. **They are basically two-fold:** *If he goes and hires a lawyer to press his claims for him, he stands to receive far less in "net" compensation (some 40% or more, LESS) for his claims; and if he were simply to handle it on his own directly with the insurance company adjuster, as most claimants are apt to do —i.e., without the benefit of being adequately informed and knowledgeable on the basics of claims settlement— he, again, stands to receive far less compensation from the adjuster than he is fairly entitled to.*

Most Claimants Already Go It Alone, Without A Lawyer

Indeed, apparently, the American automobile accident victim already knows, even if intuitively, that he (or she) can — and should — handle his own claims himself, without using a lawyer; that it is (or must be) , in some way, better or easier for him to deal directly with the claims department of the insurance company or it's adjuster! Little wonder, then, what the record shows: THAT THE VAST MAJORITY OF AUTO ACCIDENT VICTIMS AND CLAIMANTS CONSISTENTLY GO IT ALONE, WITHOUT USING AN ATTORNEY!

Already, in the overwhelming majority of claims all across the nation — up to 70% or more, according to some studies[1] — neither the claimant nor the defendant motorist (meaning, generally, the insurance company) is represented

---

[1]Field studies of records of major American insurance companies made by Ross, showed that 7 in 10 claims were concluded without attorney representation. And a famous and probably the best known study of its kind in the field, known as the Michigan Study, found that only 12,000 of 81,000 auto accident victims hired a lawyer. These same studies showed that hiring a lawyer is strongly correlated with the size of the claim (and living in a city), with almost 50% of the "seriously injured" victims in the Michigan Study hiring lawyers. The studies found, however, that claims of "serious" type, involving serious tragedy, (disfigurement, paralysis or death), and economic loss exceeding $10,000 in 1958, are rare (only 2% to 3% in the Michigan Study); and that, rather, most accidents fall under the "routine," relatively non-serious types, involving trivial losses (60% of the cases in the Michigan Study involved losses of less than $500) and minor injuries: cuts and bruises, a sore neck, and at most a day or two at home from work. [See, for example, Ross, Settled Out Of Court, pp. 24, 64-70; Conard, et. al. Automobile Accident Costs & Payments: Studies In The Economics Of Injury Reparations (Univ. of Michigan Press, 1964), esp. pp. 152-155, 183.]

by lawyers.

Rather, the claims in such cases are processed and settled directly between the insurance adjuster and the unrepresented claimant. And, even among that 25 to 30 percent of cases in which an attorney is hired, only an infinitesimal fraction of them get to be filed as a court case, or get to trial. (In New York City, for an example, a city with a reputation for being an unusually "litigation conscious" jurisdiction, 98% of all bodily injury negligence claims are terminated without adjudication by a court).[2]

But it's not simply out of a touch of intuition or personal proclivity that the American claimants have overwhelmingly opted to handle their own claims by themselves. There is, to be sure, a much more fundamental but pragmatic reason for that: the average motorist is quite aware, even if vaguely, of the dynamics and economics of claims settlement when the claimant is represented by a lawyer. ***To put it simply, the overwhelming fact, widely documented and verified even in this manual,[3] is that an automobile accident claimant filing his claims without using an attorney potentially stands to gain several tangible benefits*** — he gets to keep a much larger share of his "net" settlement money (he's spared the lawyer's average "contingency fee" of 33 1/3% to 40%, and, by some empirical studies, a total charge of up to 46%, of the gross compensation); he gets to receive his money in his pocket much faster, and gets to do so with considerably less bureaucratic redtape or delay, among other benefits!

The Claimant's Traditional Handicap In Handling His Own Claims: Lack Of Basic Knowledge & Information

The point is that, whether it is for some objective reasons, or merely by some intuition, the American auto accident claimants have already declared their overwhelming preference: the wish and preference to handle their claims settlements on their own. That's fine! UNFORTUNATELY, THOUGH, THERE'S ONE FUNDAMENTAL PROBLEM: *the average claimant is totally lacking in one critical prerequisite — he or she lacks the basic knowledge and information about the insurance claims process work, and how to utilize the claims system to secure himself a fair and reasonable settlement at the hands of the insurance adjuster.* Primarily, he lacks, not so much some fancy or sophisticated doctrines of law relating to claims settlement; but rather, the requisite basic procedures and information about the claims settlement and adjustment process — the nature of his rights, for example, the nature and extent of his bodily injuries and of his "special" as well as "general" economic damages, a reasonable idea of the value of his possible recovery, the method by which to evaluate the fair settlement value of his claim, and an understanding of the basic rules and tactics involved in claims negotiations.

The description by University of Denver's Professor H. Laurence Ross, a rare breed of specialist as an insurance industry sociologist whose empirical study of the auto insurance establishment remains one of only a handful in the field, accurately sums up the handicaps under which the "unsophisticated" claimant — meaning, one who is unprepared and uninformed in the procedures of claims settlement — typically labors:

> "The [unsophisticated and uninformed] claimant's understanding of his rights and obligations is generally vague and imprecise. When he makes a claim, he is looking for payment of his actual losses plus… "a little gravy." He desires a simple, mechanical payment of his claim, and views any delay as a hardship deliberately imposed by the insurance company. He does not understand the [legal] rule of contributory negligence, and when this is explained to him he strongly disagrees with it. His understanding of, and liking for, the rule of negligence are only slightly greater. The claimant is often uninformed in evaluation and unskilled in negotiation…
>
> [He] has a less precise idea of the ultimate value of his possible recovery, and thus is less able to make appropriate demands. His demands may be too low as well as too high. He is ignorant of the accepted principles according to which his demands can be rationalized. He does not know which, if any, threats may be effective in the situation, and he is incapable of making deliberate commitments to support these threats… [Hence, because he] attempts to negotiate with these handicaps [he] runs a strong chance of accepting an unusually low settlement…"[4]

---

[2]Marc A. Franklin, Robert H. Chanin, and Irving Mark, "Accidents, Money and the Law: A Study of the Economics of Personal Injury Litigation," in Walter E. Meyer Research Institute of Law (ed.). *Dollars, Delay and the Automobile Victim: Studies in Reparation for Highway Injuries and Related Court Problems* (Bobbs-Merrill Company, 1968), pp. 39-40, also cited in Ross, Settled Out Of Court, p.4.

[3]See pp. 8-17, for example.

[4]Ross, Settled Out of Court, pp. 70-71, 169-170.

Strangely, Legal Expertise Is Largely Irrelevant!

BUT HERE'S THE FASCINATING ANGLE: Oddly enough, conventional wisdom notwithstanding, the credible evidence is that it is not in the least the law degree or knowledge of "the law" that the self-representing claimant (or, for that matter, the claims lawyer) actually needs, or actually suffers from not having! That rather, what the claimant actually needs and suffers from not having, is *simply knowledge and information* of more basic nature — the claims adjustment and settlement process, the requisite practical "tools" of the process.

The weight of empirical research and evidence, a lot of which is documented in the manual (see, for example, pp. 8-9), shows that auto accident liability claims cases fall under a distinct "world" or category among all personal injury tort cases, in that they (auto claims) are, as a class, uniquely easier and simpler to process, and are ideal for ordinary citizens and non-lawyers to process on their own. Among the characteristics found, which are particular to auto liability claims, making them ideal for the non-lawyer to directly undertake, are that:

- they are highly routine and ordinary in character;
- by and large, they involve relatively modest or minor injuries;
- they largely involve low financial stakes and minor economic losses;
- because of their high volume and the stability of the relevant law and procedures, such cases are processed in highly routine, assembly-line format;
- they are characterized by stable, predictable outcomes and awards;
- the parties in the disputes are ordinary citizens, rather than institutions;
- auto accident claims work largely requires no major or specialized legal expertise to undertake; and
- *that this category of cases constitutes the easiest kinds of cases such that the average citizen and the non-lawyer can — and often do —handle the settlement of the cases themselves, without a lawyer's involvement.*

No Claim Is Without Some Worth. But You've Got To Have The "Know-How" To Be Able To Secure That "Worth"

The credible research data and evidence is crystal clear on the issue: In the real world of the "law in action" of insurance claims settlements — which is vastly different from the world of "formal" or theoretical law, concerned with things as they are supposed to work — all claims are worth certain reasonable value in the light of the facts and circumstances of a case, and practically no claims whatsoever, even those of extreme questionable liability on the part of the claimant, is without merit or totally lacking in some value. [See pp. 102-4 of the manual, for example].

THAT REALITY, ALONE, OR EVEN YOUR KNOWLEDGE OF THAT, IS NOT NEARLY ENOUGH FOR YOU, THOUGH, FOR YOUR PURPOSES AS A CLAIMANT! Not at all! Far more important, as a claimant, is that you become fully prepared, informed and knowledgeable, about the way the claims "system" works. And, then, you've got to be predisposed to go out there and to aggressively but properly make your claims for your rightful compensation.

Being "Determined" & Knowledgeable In The Claims Process, And Not Knowledge Of "The Law," Is The Key

The records amply show that the average claimant, assuming he's the "determined" or "sophisticated" or "knowledgeable" type in claims negotiations and settlement procedures, will fare just as well as a claimant who is represented by an attorney[5] in the settlement awards he is able to extract from the adjuster. AND THAT, INTERESTINGLY ENOUGH, THOSE ARE JUST ABOUT ALL THE ATTRIBUTES THE CLAIMANT NECESSARILY NEEDS TO HAVE. THAT HE NEEDS NOT, IN OTHER WORDS, NECESSARILY BE LEARNED IN THE LAW OF TRAFFIC OR NEGLIGENCE, MUCH LESS POSSESS A LAW DEGREE! *To put it simply, it is knowledge of the basic information about how the claims process actually works, and of the claims negotiation procedures, and not so much knowledge of some sophisticated doctrines of law, that gives the claims attorney or the insurance adjuster the qualitative "edge" in the claims settlement process. And, it is precisely that some knowledge, too, that will give the claimant — the one who cares to acquire and possess it -—an essential edge, as well.*

---

[5]See, for example, pp. 159-160 of the manual; Ross, pp. 130-1; 169.

As one study concluded:

> "[The apparent advantage of the claimant represented by an attorney, in contrast to the unrepresented and uninformed one], is understandable, less in the light of the attorney's knowledge of the formal law than in the light of his negotiation power... knowledge of formal law [is not] the key to the attorney's advantage,.... Negotiation power, on the other hand, is present throughout the range of liability and injury combinations [in the claims settlement]. The attorney, as compared with the unrepresented claimant, understands the rules of negotiation; he knows that payment will be made on a 'danger' or 'nuisance' value basis in nearly any bona fide claim, provided that the insurance company believes that the claims will be pressed, and the attorney can credibly threaten to take any claim to court. He may also credibly threaten to accumulate testimony favorable to liability and to magnify the appearance of an injury."[6]

Forget The Popular Stereotype; Claims Adjusters Are A Fair And Principled Bunch Who Will Deal Fairly With You When You Can "Document" & "Justify" Your Case & Damages

An underlying implication which follows from the above-stated premise, can be interpreted as follows: that if you can, as a claimant (or a lawyer), display knowledge and understanding of the requisite claims negotiations skills, and of your rights and the basic workings of the insurance claims process, then you should expect to be treated fairly and decently at the hands of the insurance adjuster, and, probably, to be given a fair settlement.

Does this proposition or corollary actually materialize, in practice? To be sure, you might not be "guaranteed" that you'll necessarily get a fair or even decent settlement even with your possessing those attributes. But this much can be granted: You stand the best chance of your getting such a treatment and such a result under such a circumstance! A more fundamental but relevant point, however, is that by every credible research in the industry, most insurance claims adjusters are primarily dedicated to fairness and are ordinarily not out to "chisel" the claimant or to pay less for the economic losses and legitimate injuries of the honest claimant — conventional thinking and common stereotype, notwithstanding. To be sure, and as is probably to be expected, the average adjuster has a somewhat natural dose of job-induced distrust and cynicism regarding claims and the accounts of events presented by claimants, and are pre-disposed to resisting claims. But, by and large, they are, in the final analysis, fair and principled professionals whose main concern is not really to "save" their company money by paying you less than you deserve, but who would just as quickly pay you and "close the file" — if only you can document and justify to them the legitimacy of your claims.

The adjuster's main concern is, in a word, to be able to "justify" a settlement, to satisfy himself and his conscience that he's paying you "what the claim is worth," and, quite importantly, to be able to demonstrate to his claims supervisor that payments made by the company are "documented" and "justified" by the case file and records — i.e., by such types of proofs and documentations as are outlined in Chapters 3, and 4 of the manual. To put it another way, adjusters are simply a group which, as a professional class, have a great respect for the claimant who can show that he is honest, informed, determined, and well prepared and organized.

Again, Professor Ross' characterization, honed from his exhaustive empirical field study on the subject, sums up the reality as well as any other in the field:

> "As succinctly put by one man, 'Closing files, two words, describes our [the adjuster's] job in the ultimate — closing files!'
>
> A consequence of the pressure to close files is that claims men often seem to search for a way to make a payment on the claim. *Contrary to common impression, the typical adjuster is not fixated upon the goal of denying claims; his fixation is rather on terminating them, and in most cases the easiest way to do so is to make a payment. The adjuster may prefer denial, but when faced with a*

---

[6]Ross, Settled Out Of Court, pp. 195-196.

situation in which the file can be made to support a payment, and which the adjuster is convinced that a denial would not close the file, he desires to make a payment: 'I find it the easier way to adjust a claim... to look for a way to pay it, rather than wait'

The principal problem in paying and thus closing claims is to be sure that the payment can be substantiated, i.e., to produce a file that will satisfy the supervisor that the claim deserves payment, and that enables the adjuster to close the case....

Adjusters are therefore not — stereotypes to the contrary — resisters of claims. Their goal is not to deny or pay the lowest settlement possible, regardless of other considerations. Rather, the claimsman may be envisioned as a sharp but decent buyer of commodities. His orientation is above all to consummate the purchases, with prices being a secondary consideration. He is willing to buy various qualities of goods, to be sure on different terms, but there are relatively few items for which he is unwilling to make some small payment. His goal is a low price per item, but a fair price, and one that will be high enough to avoid frequent delays in the sale. ***Rather than resisting the transactions, he wants them to be supported by documents that will provide him and his superiors with evidence of value received. If the intangible claim can be nailed down with doctor bills, statements from employers, and similar documents, the adjuster's a willing buyer.***"[7] [Emphasis added by the writer].

Heed The Central Message: Give The Adjuster What He Needs, Using The "Tools" In This Manual

There you have it! ***THE CENTRAL MESSAGE TO A CLAIMANT IS CRYSTAL CLEAR: Get Going!*** *Get to the point — the* ***relevant*** *point!! Get informed on the facts and details of your case; know what to realistically ask for and how to negotiate for it; get prepared and organized; supply the adjuster with the documentation and proof to establish your claim. And, if you can only do these, you can be almost sure of walking away from the negotiation table with as fair a settlement as possible —and it wouldn't have mattered a bit that you had no lawyer!*

The essential "tools" of doing precisely that, are exactly what this manual provides you. Here it is. I humbly commend it to you, the ordinary citizen (and claims adjuster and lawyer) of America, who must file an auto liability claim, or contemplates filing one. Utilize them (the book and the tools). Enjoy it!

— Benji Anosike
June 15, 1993

---

[7]Ross, <u>Settled Out Of Court</u>, pp. 61 & 66.

HOW TO USE THIS MANUAL

A few words about how to use this book. The "heart and soul" of this book, especially for a reader who is primarily concerned with processing a claims settlement case, are probably **Chapters 9 & 10**, which deal with the methods by which to evaluate the worth or determine the value of a claim. There is a common agreement among experts, that for the average claimant, being able to determine the fair or approximate value of a claim is the single most central problem and need.* And because of the considered centrality of the issue of claim valuation, we have provided in the manual two distinctive methods of claims evaluation commonly used in the trade — one (Chapter 9), for doing the supposedly less serious, more "routine" types of cases, and the other (Chapter 10), for doing the more "serious" types of cases, involving crippling and permanent injuries and bigger financial stakes, though generally far fewer in number and rarer in occurrence.

The issue of **"liability"** in an accident, an all-important issue in claims matters, is addressed in **Chapter 7;** primary attention should be paid by the reader to the sections devoted to the insurance industry 'short-cuts' and 'rules-of-thumb' in determination of liability. Also, because much about claims settlement often revolves around medical and **"injury"** issues, and because of the perceived need, therefore, for some ability to read and interpret one's medical records, an unusually substantial amount of information of medical nature (common types of bodily injuries encountered, common kinds of disabilities associated with various injuries, body structure and physiology, etc.) is provided in **Chapter 6.** This material is further supplemented by **Appendices D, E and F,** providing the reader with an extensive dictionary of medical words and terminology, and the principal "short hands" used by doctors in medical reports and records.

Chapter 11, which lays out a systematic method of conducting the final settlement negotiations with the adjuster through the *Anosike 8-Step Strategic Program Of Negotiations (ASPON),* is the centerpiece— "the glue" — which finally ties together the whole book into a programmatic "system" for filing and processing a claim, from start to finish.

Granted, Chapters 9 and/or 10 are pivotal, as it's critical that you have some idea of the worth of your claim; and Chapter 11 is very important, as it provides you a systematic roadmap, from incident to negotiations and settlement. But, as the reader will quickly discover in reading through the book — or, more importantly, in actually processing a claim following the book's guidelines — for you to be able to evaluate a claim under Chapter 9 & 10, or to be able to negotiate a claim under Chapter 11, you would need to have mastered the background materials contained elsewhere in the rest of the chapters.

So, the advice is this: First of all, to begin with, read and master all "background" chapters — **Chapters 1 to 8**, and, possibly the Appendices to the book, if necessary — before anything else. Next, you may go to **Chapters 9 & 10**, to get a sense of the value of your claim. And, finally, go to the chapter that ties it all together for you, **Chapter 11**, and SYSTEMATICALLY AND ORDERLY follow, step-by-step, the ASPON program outlined therein to file for and negotiate your claim with your adjuster.

A lot of times, you would probably not need all or some of the information provided in a given chapter; some information may be irrelevant or inapplicable in your particular situation. It's all here, though, just in case you need it!

---

*"Most people don't realize that determining the value of a bodily injury claim is neither a province of nor a prerogative restricted solely to lawyers and claimsmen ... Yet, more than any other factor ... this initial step of assessing the worth in dollars of his bodily injury is what keeps the layman from dealing directly with the insurance company." (Baldyga, How To Settle Your Own Insurance Claim, p. 3).

CHAPTER 1
SETTLING YOUR AUTO ACCIDENT "TORT" CLAIMS: WHEN AND WHY YOU SHOULD DO IT YOURSELF WITHOUT A LAWYER

A. Auto Accidents Are All Around Us

"Courtrooms are like hospitals," said Edward Siegel, a long-time Jacksonville, Florida lawyer and author, "They're o.k. if you don't have to go there. Unfortunately, if you drive an automobile, your chances of landing in one or both places [a courtroom or hospital] increase every day."[1]

Siegel is absolutely right. It is commonly estimated that for most lawyers in the United States, cases involving auto accidents constitute almost one fourth of all their courtroom litigation, and that more than 5 million people are involved in auto-related injuries each year. According to the National Safety Council and the Insurance Information Institute, in 1990, for example, there were 33.3 million motor-related accidents, involving 5.5 million injuries and 46,300 deaths, and a total estimated loss of $96 billion dollars. And, as Siegel notes, "whether you agree or not, most of these accidents don't "happen", they're caused."

Consequently, in realistic terms, chances are that you could, at one time or the other in your life, probably find yourself involved in an auto accident. THE CENTRAL QUESTION IS: *if this should happen with you, what should you do? Should you try to handle the accident, or more specifically, the "tort" claim that arises out of it, by yourself? Or, use a lawyer? This is the central issue addressed by this book.*

B. What is a Tort Claim?

The term "tort" is one which you're all too likely to hear much about from lawyers and other court operatives dealing with auto accident and personal injury cases. A tort has been defined as a civil (i.e. private) wrong or injury which results from a breach of a legal obligation—any wrongfully inflicted injury or harm, in short. To put it simply, whenever you or your property has been wrongfully harmed or injured by someone else's actions, you are generally said to have suffered a **tort**, with the wrongdoer being termed the **"tortfeasor."** Under the legal doctrine of tort, it is held that under any given circumstance, each and every individual owes the other a legal duty, which exists by virtue of society's expectations regarding interpersonal conduct, rather than by contract or other private relationship. And that when someone commits a "breach" of this duty — that is, fails to observe or respect another's entitlement to this duty—then such a person has committed the civil wrong of "tort" against the deprived or wronged party.

A tort could take several forms: ranging from a wrongful arrest and imprisonment, to wrongful dismissal from a job, sexual harassment, wrongful injury to you or damage to your property. For the purposes of the book, however, a tort should be thought of simply as financial "damages" (a claim) generally for bodily pain and injury to you and/or physical

---

[1]Siegel, "How to Avoid Lawyers," (Ballantine Books) p.1.

damages to your automobile which came about from a motor vehicle-related accident stemming from someone else's "negligence" (see pp. 93-106 for more detailed treatment of the doctrine of "negligence").

C. Kinds of Financial Damages Applicable in Auto Accident Cases

In automobile and liability torts, you are entitled to some rewards, in the form of money, the general theory being that you need to be compensated for the harm done to you and/or your property (automobile). The following are the types of harm or losses ("damages") for which one may be compensated in an auto accident situation: value of earnings and time actually lost; value of wages and time likely to be lost in the future; medical and hospital expenses actually incurred, and those likely to be incurred in the future; all miscellaneous out-of-pocket expenses made (for household help during disability, for medication, rental cost of substitute car, etc.); estimated compensatory monetary value of the pain, suffering, and inconvenience you suffer from injuries arising from the accident; and cost of repairs or the value of the damaged property.

D. When Should You Use a Lawyer for Your Claims?

Supposing you find yourself a victim in an auto accident, should you always automatically run out and get a lawyer? The answer is an emphatic NO! In the vast majority of auto liability cases, the claims are clear-cut in terms of the legitimacy of the claims and who is at fault, with the fault almost 90% or so that of one or the other party involved. Also, most such cases typically fall under the so-called "bread-and-butter" type of injury situations — injuries such as the "concussion" or "cuts and bruises" types. In such situations, you can usually handle the claims settlement yourself quite satisfactorily with just about the same result, but with better monetary compensation accruing to you than you would get using a lawyer.

Indeed, as is more fully explained elsewhere, a careful analysis would indicate that only in one situation would it be strictly advisable to use the lawyer: if and when your claim involves serious or major injuries involving long hospitalization, a lifetime of medical care, serious multiple fractures, or the probability of permanent disability, or when the accident is such that it will leave you severely handicapped or disfigured.

E. Why it May Generally Pay You Better To Do it Yourself

The following are some of the major reasons why it will generally be to your ultimate best interest to seek to settle your own claim, for the most part:

1. MOST AUTO ACCIDENT CASES ARE ROUTINE AND ORDINARY.

A widely respected body of empirical research[2] which has looked at the nation's tort system and the personal injury liability cases, for example, makes this finding of great usefulness for our purposes: that the nations's personal injury tort system, rather than being simply a single monolithic tort system, is actually THREE different tort "worlds" (systems), with each "world" having its own distinct class of characteristics, growth rates, jury verdict trends, legal dynamics and cost and compensation profiles.[3] The research found that when contrasted against each other among these three completely different categories or "worlds" of personal injury tort cases, the auto accident types of claims are generally the most routine and most ordinary of all three categories, that the auto claims are, as a class, uniquely easier and simpler to process, and are most ideal for ordinary citizens and non-lawyers to process on their own. (See chart below for the comparison of the characteristics)

---

[2]See "Trends in Tort Litigation," Deborah R. Hensler, Mary E. Vaiana, James S. Kakalik, Mark A. Peterson (Rand Institute of Justice, Santa Monica, CA: 1987) esp. pp. 30-34.

[3] The Lawsuits fall under three categories: ordinary personal injury suits (e.g. auto lawsuits); "high stakes personal injury suits" (e.g. product liability, malpractice and business torts); and "mass latent injury" cases (e.g. mass or class action suits over asbestos, and other suits arising from mass exposure to drugs, chemicals or toxic substances.)

TABLE 1-1

The Evolving Worlds of Tort-Litigation: Case Profiles

- Auto and other ordinary lawsuits
  - High volume
  - Stable law
  - Routinized
  - Increasing ADR
  - Modest stakes
  - Little deterrence potential
  - Slow growth in frequency, outcomes, costs

- Product liability, malpractice, business torts
  - Low volume
  - Evolving law
  - Increasingly specialized
  - Heavy pretrial procedure
  - Little ADR
  - Large $ potential per case
  - Deterrence is factor
  - Faster growth in frequency, outcomes, costs

- Mass latent injury cases
  - Concentrated in time and place
  - Problematic law
  - Small, highly specialized bar
  - Discovery critical
  - Procedural innovation
  - Enormous $ stakes for parties
  - Deterrence is key issue
  - Highly uncertain in number, outcomes, costs

Source: *Trends in Tort Litigation:* The Story Behind the Statistics (R-3583-IJC), by Deborah R. Hensler, Mary E. Vaiana, James S. Kakalik, and Mark A. Peterson (Rand Institute for Civil Justice)

Here is how the researchers at the prestigious Rand Institute for Civil Justice summed up the distinctive characteristics that mark the auto accident category of cases:

> "Auto accident cases epitomize this [routine personal injury torts] category. There is a high volume of such cases, about half a million filed annually nationwide…little recent change in the substantive law relating to them…Because of their high volume and stability of the law, it has been possible to routinize their processing and their resolution…most of these cases involve relatively modest injuries and small amounts of money, and the parties of the dispute are ordinary citizens rather than institutions. Except in cases of very serious injury, there is little basis for large awards and the attorneys who handle them are generally not high stake litigators…[and such cases have] stable, predictable, outcomes…
>
> In sum, this world of tort litigation is the least problematic by most standards. It also remains the world in which the average citizen is most likely to become a participant"[4]

TRANSLATION: By and large, auto accident claims cases are relatively routine and ordinary, generally require no great or particularly specialized legal expertise, and constitute the easiest kinds of cases such that ordinary citizens and non-lawyers can — and often do — handle the settlement of such cases as easily and successfully as the lawyer!

2. YOU GET TO KEEP MORE OF THE SETTLEMENT MONEY

A second important reason why it may be more generally advisable for you to undertake your claims settlement yourself and not hire a lawyer to do it for you, is that, as one analyst summed it up, "in a great many cases [the role of a lawyer in an auto accident case] can be an unnecessary one…in the average case, a lawyer is not only unnecessary, but the claimant receives less money after all [legal] expenses are deducted and [the lawyer's] fees are paid than if he had settled with an insurer privately."[5]

---

[4]"Trends In Tort Litigation: The Story Behind the Statistics," op. cit. pp. 30-32. Those research findings and conclusions are widely supported in the relevant literature, by the way. See, for example, Ross's "Settled Out of Court," pp. 73-83. Ross, citing several other well-known studies, such as Jerome E. Carlin's Lawyers on their Own (Rutgers Univ. 1962), and Hunting and Neuwirth's Who Sues in New York City (Columbia Univ. Press, 1962), finds that "a large proportion (of the lawyers who handle automobile cases) appear to come from near the bottom," and that they are akin to the category of lawyers described by Carlin in his famous study . Ross adds: "[their] education is non-elite,…their legal skills are marginal, their rewards in money and prestige are minimal, and their orientation to the ethics of the bar, is, at best, pragmatic…much of this work is not professional in the traditional sense, but is closer to brokerage" (Ross, pp. 74-5)

[5]Eugene Sullivan, Where Did the $13 Billion Go? (Prentice Hall, Englewood, N.J. (1971) p. 100.

Except for America's trial lawyers and their handful of apologists who defend the so-called "right to sue" by Americans, almost every expert generally agrees, and research on the matter generally demonstrates, that the "tort system," of which, of course, the auto accident claims settlement system is the prime example, is, as one assessment put it, "not set up to serve consumers well."[6] A major reason why the lawyer's involvement in the average auto accident claims case is often more detrimental to the best interests of the claimant's financial health, relates to the **legal fee structure** in such matters. To put it simply, *BY THE TIME THE LAWYER SHALL HAVE FINISHED TAKING HIS "CONTINGENT FEE" (TYPICALLY A CUT OF 33 1/3 TO 40%) OUT OF THE CLAIMANT'S AWARD, AND BY THE TIME HE IS DONE WITH DEDUCTING HIS LEGAL EXPENSES AND THE COURT COSTS FROM THE AWARD ON TOP OF THAT, THE CLAIMANT IS OFTEN WORSE OFF THAN HE OR SHE WOULD HAVE BEEN IF HE HAD SIMPLY NEGOTIATED WITH THE INSURANCE COMPANY DIRECTLY — WITHOUT THE LAWYER'S INVOLVEMENT.*

"Sadly, in many cases, after the attorney has taken his fee, the claimant ends up with less than if he had negotiated directly with the insurance company," said Daniel Baldyga, an insurance claims authority and author with a vast practical experience in the field. "I have seen it happen in so many instances that I have become dismayed, discouraged, and disenchanted. Because the [lawyer's] contingency, or percentage fee, has reached into the claimant's settlement so profoundly, he simply doesn't get all that should be coming to him."[7]

Such an assessment is widely borne out by the bulk of studies and research in the field. The following table, reproduced from a 1970 study of the U.S. Department of Transportation's Auto Insurance Compensation staff, probably the most comprehensive of any such study ever attempted or available on the subject, will amply illustrate this point.

TABLE 1-2

RATIO OF AGGREGATE PAYMENTS, NET OF ATTORNEYS FEES AND OTHER
LITIGATION EXPENSES, TO AGGREGATE ECONOMIC LOSS TO DATE OF
SETTLEMENT SIZE OF LOSS AND ATTORNEY REPRESENTATION

Economic Loss to Date of Settlement	Attorney Representation		
	No Attorney	Attorney – No Suit	Attorney – Suit
$1 – 500	2.8	2.6	2.0
501 – 1,000	2.1	1.9	2.0
1,101 – 1,500	1.8	2.0	2.1
1,501 – 2,500	1.9	1.5	2.0
2,501 – 5,000	2.0	1.4	1.6
5,001 – 10,000	1.6	1.1	1.3
10,001 – 25,000	1.4	.8	1.1
Over $25,000	.9	.4	.2
Total	2.2	1.7	1.5

Source: Table V-22, U.S. Department of Transportation, Automobile Personal Injury Claims, Vol. I (July 1970)

These data show the "net" payment/loss ratios received by the claimant — i.e., the amounts that the claimant finally gets AFTER the deduction have been made for attorney's fees and other "legal" or "court" expenses. Having estimated that the attorney's fees average 35.5 percent of the gross-settlements, and that the average expense involved in a case amounted to 3.2 percent of the gross settlement, for a total of 38.7 of the gross settlement amount from the insurance companies, Table 1-2 reflects the NET settlement actually received by the claimant, meaning what the claimant actually gets in his pocket after all the fees and expenses shall have been deducted.

These figures indicate the ratio of payments for economic loss to amounts actually lost. Simply stated, the figure 2.8

---

[6]"Everyday Law Series," The Legal Reformer (HALT), vol. 9, No. 4 (July-Sept. 1989), p. A-5.
[7]Baldyga, How To Settle Your Own Insurance Claim, (The Macmillan Co. (1968), p. 3.

in the column headed "No Attorney" means that victims with losses in the range of $1-$500 recovered 2.8 times their actual economic loss, while the figures 2.6 and 2.0 in the same column headed "Attorney—No Suit" and "Attorney Suit," means, on the other hand, that victims with losses in the same $1-$500 range, correspondingly recovered 2.6 times their actual economic loss (when no suit was filed), and 2 times the actual economic loss (when suit was filed). In a word, in virtually all cases illustrated—indeed, except for the sole case involving the claimant who lost between $1001 and $2500 and had retained an attorney and also filed suit—claimants **without** attorneys received the highest ratio of net benefits to economic loss in every other instance, and recovered more than their counterparts with attorneys in just about every instance![8]

Still on the same issue, a more recent empirical research study by the prestigious Rand Corporations Institute for Civil Justice in Santa Monica, California, overwhelmingly confirms the general thesis of this book. It found that accident victims as a whole who filed claims in federal and state courts in the United States in 1985 were awarded about $21 to $25 billion of the $29 to $36 billion in total national expenditure made on all tort lawsuits in that year, but that after having deducted the lawyer's fees and their court and related costs from that, the victims wound up going home with a "net" compensation of just $14 to $16 billion. In other words, for the victims to actually receive this $14 to $16 billion compensation in their hands, the "tort litigation system" alone — meaning the plaintiffs' and defendants' fees,[9] and other expenditures, such as court costs and the value of the time spent by litigants and their employees — had eaten up $16 to $19 billion by itself! To put it still another way, out of the total amount paid in compensation, the injured party only received approximately 56 percent of that, while the so-called "litigation system" got the rest—44 percent!! (See Figure A-1 below). In deed, if the value of the time spent by the plaintiff and defendant parties is added, the study found that the "net" compensation received by the injured plaintiff sinks to a mere 46% of the total national expenditure for that year!! (See Figure A-2 below).

And, with specific respect to the torts cases involving ONLY motor vehicles, the researchers found that the legal fees and expenses paid by the injured plaintiffs (the victims) as a percentage of their total compensation were 31 percent, and the "net" compensation the injured plaintiff is left with as a percentage of the total expenditures, is only 52%. (See Fig. A-3 below).

---

[8]It should be emphatically made clear here that in no way should the data be construed to mean, nor does the present author imply, that this data (or any other data known to the present author) is either saying that accident victims should never retain attorneys , or that self-representation results in higher net compensation to claimants always or under all circumstances. What the data can be construed to mean, though, is that the system of auto claims settlement leaves much room, at least in substantial number of cases involving small or moderate values, for the ordinary individuals to file their own claims themselves, and with reasonable expectation of good, if not better results. Indeed, in all fairness, proponents of the usefulness of attorney involvement in auto tort matters could well argue that the group of claimants represented by attorneys who receive settlements, at all, probably contain a higher percentage of persons who may never have received anything at all were it not for their use of counsel — such as cases, for example, where the question of liability may be hotly contested by the insurance company. That may be so. However, it is also obvious, even from the above table, that far from being hotly contested, the vast majority of such cases are not contested, again making the services of a lawyer superfluous.

Admittedly, large value cases and cases involving more substantial and serious injuries—the types substantially not represented in the above Table—are more likely to attract attorney involvement and to be contested by lawsuit. However, even allowing for this, the fundamental thesis of this book would still remain valid since it is basically for the small value and less-serious-injury cases that the do-it-yourself approach of claims settlement is primarily advocated anyway.

Finally, it should be pointed out that in further fairness to those who extol the supposed virtue of using the attorney in claims making, there is some support in the literature for the view that the presence of a lawyer is a major influence on the outcomes in bodily injury claims, and that claimsmen generally assign higher settlement values to attorney-represented claims than nonrepresented ones. However, a major shortcoming of such body of literature is that while much of this literature has been able to demonstrate that the lawyer's representation would often result in winning higher settlement figures from the claimsmen, it has not shown—or even made much effort to show—that such higher or better settlements have translated into higher or better "net" recovery to the claimant who files claim without a lawyer. (See for example, the following on the differential effect of lawyer involvement in claims settlements: Ross, Settle Out of Court, pp. 193-8. Among the array of other authorities cited by Ross as "strongly supporting" his thesis, are the following: Conard, Morgan, Pratt, Voltz and Bombaugh Automobile Accident Costs and Payments: Studies in the Economics of Injury Preparation, p. 154; Linden, The Report of the Osgoode Hall Study on Compensation for Victims of Automobile Accidents (privately printed, 1965.), chap. IV, p. 27; Morris and Paul, "The Financial Impact of Automobile Accidents," Univ. of Pennsylvania Law Review 110: 913, 1962; and Franklin, Chanin and Mark, "Accidents, Money, and the Law: A Study of the Economics of Personal Injury Litigation," Columbia Law Review, 61:1, 1961.)

[9]The combined lawyers fees alone constituted a whopping $11 to $13 billion of the total tort litigation system amount.

FIGURE A-1

FIGURE A-2

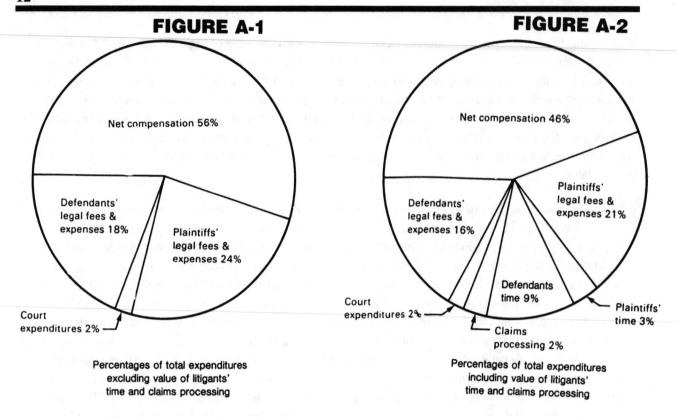

Figure A-1

Net compensation 56%

Defendants' legal fees & expenses 18%

Plaintiffs' legal fees & expenses 24%

Court expenditures 2%

Percentages of total expenditures excluding value of litigants' time and claims processing

NOTE: Totals may not sum to 100 due to rounding.

Figure A-2

Net compensation 46%

Defendants' legal fees & expenses 16%

Plaintiffs' legal fees & expenses 21%

Defendants time 9%

Court expenditures 2%

Claims processing 2%

Plaintiffs' time 3%

Percentages of total expenditures including value of litigants' time and claims processing

Costs and compensation paid for the average tort lawsuit terminated in 1985.

FIGURE A-3 Auto Torts

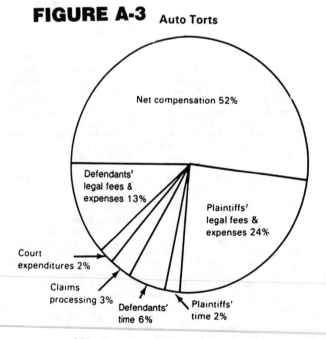

Net compensation 52%

Defendants' legal fees & expenses 13%

Plaintiffs' legal fees & expenses 24%

Court expenditures 2%

Claims processing 3%

Defendants' time 6%

Plaintiffs' time 2%

NOTE: Percentages are based on the average of two estimates, and may not sum to 100 due to rounding.

—Costs and compensation paid for the average auto and other tort lawsuit terminated in 1985

Source: The Rand Institute For Civil Justice (1986).

Lawyers Take Their Contingency Fee Right Off the Top!

What compounds the financial dynamics and makes it an inescapable losing battle for the claimant, is that the lawyer will often deduct his contingency fee FIRST and right off the top — from the gross award of your compensation, rather than deducting the legal expenses first, and then basing his contingency fee percentage on what is left over thereafter. And then, out of the balance you are left with after the lawyer shall have first deducted his fee, you will then pay the reimbursement for the lawyer's out-of-pocket legal expenses, and whatever balance is left after that is finally what you get — your "net" compensation!

What this practice (of first deducting the lawyer's contingency fee right off the top) means for you, as a claimant, could often be substantial in financial terms: it directly translates into thousands of dollars *LESS for you, and a corresponding thousands of dollars MORE in the lawyer's pocket!*

To illustrate, let us assume you're using a lawyer, and that the final settlement award you get is $20,000. The lawyer is representing you on a one-third contingency-fee basis. His out-of-pocket legal expenses come to a total of $3,000.

Observe the difference in your "net" award, depending on the point at which the lawyer repays himself his expenses:

CONTINGENCY FEE FIRST

Total Award	$20,000
Less: lawyer's fee (1/3 of $20,000)	- 6,666
Remainder	$13,334
Less: reimbursement of expenses	- 3,000
NET TO YOU	$10,334

EXPENSES FIRST

Total Award	$20,000
Less: reimbursement of expenses	- 3,000
Remainder	$17,000
Less: lawyer's fee (1/3 of $17,000)	- 5,666
NET TO YOU	$11,334

In other words, merely by the lawyer's device of taking the contingency fee first, you suffer additional financial "woes" over and above what you were already suffering by employing a lawyer — to the tune of ADDITIONAL $1,000 in the above example.

But that's not all. There's an additional but even more profound implication to read from the above illustration — in terms of whether or not it will pay you, financially, to use an attorney in your case, and at what point it may begin to pay. HERE'S WHAT THE FIGURES FROM THE ABOVE ILLUSTRATION ARE ALSO TELLING US: that even if all you were able to secure is just a settlement award of merely $10,334 (or even slightly less, to allow for possible court expenses), you would just have about "broken even" with a lawyer who gets you as much as $20,000 in gross award; and that if you merely secure by yourself anything ABOVE $10, 334, you're already doing financially better for yourself relative to how you would fare using a lawyer! To put it another way, what this means in practical terms to YOU, is that an award of approximately $10,000 won by yourself, is worth (is as good as) an award of $20,000 won with a lawyer; that a nominal award of $1 with a lawyer, would translate into only 50¢ in YOUR POCKET. Which is to say, that if you were, on your own, to merely secure even 60¢ or 70¢ (or more) on a $1 — i.e., 60 or 70% — of what your reasonable award ought to be, you would have been doing pretty well, even better, than you ordinarily would using an attorney!!

3. YOU GET YOUR SETTLEMENT PAYMENT FASTER

A third major advantage in doing your claims settlement yourself, as against using a lawyer, is this: you get your compensation considerably faster, with a minimum of bureaucratic redtape or delays. Studies by the U.S. Department of Transportation (DOT) and others have attempted to examine this issue. As can be seen from Tables 1-3 and 1-4 reproduced below from the DOT study, the data clearly establish that the time required to settle claims vastly differ for claimants who retain an attorney as compared to those who do not, with the claimants who do not retain an attorney securing their settlements much more rapidly. According to the DOT study, the most significant factor in delayed settlements at the hands of the lawyer is the tendency of the lawyer to engage in the litigation process.[10]

TABLE 1-3

CUMULATIVE PERCENTAGES OF CLAIMS SETTLED BY ATTORNEY
REPRESENTATION AND ELAPSED TIME BETWEEN ACCIDENT AND SETTLEMENT

Elapsed Time Between Accident and Settlement	Cumulative Percentage of Claims Settled			
	No Attorney	Attorney	Attorney - No Suit	Attorney - Suit
30 days	38.7%	1.1%	1.6%	.2%
60	58.1	3.1	4.6	.5
90	69.6	6.9	10.5	.7
180	86.0	24.9	36.7	4.1
365	95.3	53.5	73.6	18.0
550	97.9	68.0	87.6	33.4
998	99.6	84.9	97.8	62.3

Source: Table VII-6, U.S. Department of Transportation, Automobile Personal Injury Claims, Vol. I (July 1970)

TABLE 1-4

CUMULATIVE PERCENTAGES OF LOSS DOLLARS SETTLED BY ATTORNEY
REPRESENTATION AND ELAPSED TIME BETWEEN ACCIDENT AND SETTLEMENT

Elapsed Time Between Accident and Settlement	Cumulative Percentage of Loss Dollars Settled			
	No Attorney	Attorney	Attorney - No Suit	Attorney - Suit
30 days	13.1%	.3%	.6%	—
60	23.9	1.0	1.8	.2%
90	34.1	2.4	4.8	.2
180	57.7	11.8	22.7	2.1
365	80.2	34.3	57.6	13.7
550	91.2	52.6	78.5	29.6
998	98.9	77.5	95.8	61.1

Source: Table VII-7, U.S. Department of Transportation, Automobile Personal Injury Claims, Vol. I (July 1970)

A similar pattern is also shown in another study done by a body called the Closed Claims Sub-Committee of the Insurance Industry Advisory Committee, which included the 10 largest automobile insurance companies in the country, in cooperation with the U.S. Department of Transportation Automobile and Compensation Study Group. As shown by Table 1-5 below, almost half (46%) of all claimant cases in that study in which the claimant dealt directly with the insurer were settled within 30 days of the reporting of a claim; over three-fourths (76%) of all such no-attorney claimant cases were settled within 100 days and only 3% remained unsettled within 400 days from the reporting of the claim.

In contrast, for the claimants who retained an attorney, there's immediately evident a dramatically greater length of time from the filing of the claim report to the date of settlement. For example, for cases in which legal suit is instituted, only 1% of the claimant cases are settled within 30 days (as compared to 46% for claimants who retain no attorneys), a minuscule 3% of the cases are settled within 100 days (as compared to 76% for cases involving no attorney), and a whopping 73% of the cases still remain unsettled after 400 days from the report of the claim, as compared to a mere 3% for claimants who retained no attorneys!

---

[10]The pattern of delays is found to be consistent even when allowances is made for the fact that lawyers ordinarily handle a large proportion of permanent or more serious injury cases and that such cases should therefore be ordinarily expected to take longer to settle than cases generally. For example, permanently disfigured claimants who retained attorneys were found to have disproportionately larger number of cases and dollar amounts still unsettled more than 998 days after the accident, and that by the time 550 days have elapsed, claimants with no attorneys have settled cases representing 91.2 percent of their dollar losses, as compared to only 52.6 percent for claimants with attorneys. (See DOT study, Tables VII-8 and VII-9 on pp. 93-94).

TABLE 1-5
PERCENTAGE OF CLAIMS SETTLED WITH/WITHOUT ATTORNEY
AND LAPSED TIME BETWEEN CLAIM AND SETTLEMENT

TIME*	NO ATTORNEY	ATTORNEY NO SUIT	ATTORNEY SUIT	ALL
(up to)				
30 days	46% (248)	4% (11)	1% (2)	26% (261)
100 days	76% (409)	20% (58)	3% (6)	47% (473)
400 days	97% (520)	81% (238)	27% (45)	80% (803)
700 days	99% (532)	94% (277)	48% (80)	89% (889)
1,000 days	100% (536)	98% (288)	65% (109)	93% (933)
Unlimited	100% (539)	100% (294)	100% (167)	100% (1,000)

Notes: * Claim Report to Settlement Date
%'s are of all claimants in that column
(#) Successful claimants out of every 1,000

Source: U.S. Department of Transportation, Automobile Personal Injury Claims, Vol. I (July 1970)

Fred Utz, an expert court testimony specialist with over 30 years experience in auto accident claims practices who generally favors the use of lawyers in claims settlement, quite pointedly sums up the reality with respect to the lawyer-associated delays, this way:

> "What attorney representation [in insurance claims cases] does not usually provide is **speed** (don't hire him if you want your claim handled **faster**, and don't threaten an adjuster by saying you'll get a lawyer if he doesn't settle quickly because he will laugh all his way home!). Also, don't use a lawyer to get yourself just a little more money (15% to 30% more) because his fee will eat up the difference. *Use attorneys when you must resolve real legal questions and make sure they specialize in this field.* All we can add to this lengthy compendium of advice are the mere words—Good Luck!"[11]

4. YOU'RE BETTER MOTIVATED AND TEMPERAMENTALLY EQUIPPED TO DO THE JOB THAN THE AVERAGE LAWYER

Another key reason why it may often be to your greater advantage to undertake your claim settlement work yourself is that, according to research and claims experts and practitioners, you, the non-lawyer layperson, are frequently better motivated and temperamentally better equipped to do the job than your average hired lawyer, especially as regards the undertaking of the less appealing but essential aspects of the claims processing work.

Recall that, as has been amply documented in different sections of this manual (see for example, pp. 8-9), the reality of the claims settlement business is that most attorneys who handle auto accident claims cases possess neither specialized nor great legal expertise, and are not required or expected to particularly demonstrate high legal skills or professionalism in much of their claims settlement work. Auto liability claims work is, as has been established elsewhere (pp. 8-9, 159-160), by and large a simple, routine, assembly-line type of work largely resolved by negotiation and settlement out of court. Experts and serious students of the system have noted that when one talks about the bodily injury claims settlement cases, in general, or auto accident claims cases, in particular, it is largely irrelevant and misleading to talk about "the law" and the formal operation of the legal system in the conventional sense of the terms. Such terms and concepts, experts say, do not quite apply in the claims settlement world for this reason: The overwhelming majority of bodily

---

[11]Fred Utz, <u>Collision Course</u>, pp. 17-18.

injury claims cases (98% even in a "high litigation" jurisdiction like New York City, for example) are settled and resolved not through adjudication within the judicial (i.e., court) system, but outside the judicial system, and through private negotiations and adjustments between the parties. Consequently, as one expert summed it up, "if the handling of the great mass of injury claims is to be improved [or addressed], it's the [private, negotiated] adjustment process rather than the judicial process which will have to be addressed."[12]

To put it another way, looked at in terms of the lawyer (or, for that matter, in terms of any operative) engaged in claims settlement work, the most relevant skills, tactics and attributes he really needs and must possess to be successful and to secure the best results for a claimant, are not so much the traditional skills and attributes associated with conventional lawyering and legal practice. Rather, they are those skills and attributes, and an outlook, that are consistent with human relations, negotiations and private settlement of affairs among parties — an approach which, as one analyst put it, "[requires and] employs different tactics, uses different skills and facilities, and produces different results from litigation."[13] It is not, in other words, for his great knowledge of the law or great expertise in courtroom skills that a lawyer can be effective in securing for the claimant the best possible settlement in an auto accident case; rather, it is for possessing other types of 'skills' and attributes — the skills and ability, essentially , to make patient, painstaking investigations, to gather information and document a claim, and to conduct reasoned negotiations and "haggling."

BUT HERE, THOUGH, LIES THE PROBLEM: *lawyers, unfortunately, by and large precisely lack those same essential skills and attributes! By training and professional tradition, they lack the necessary discipline and temperament, the appropriate motivation to do a good job of the kind called for in accident liability and claims negotiations.*

Daniel G. Baldyga, the widely acclaimed insurance claims expert, has found that one distinct, critical way this professional deficiency has been manifested among lawyers (and insurance claimsmen as well), is in their handling of the investigation and data-gathering aspects of claims settlement work—tasks like finding a critical eye-witness, searching out a passenger present in a car accident, digging up a key photographer or photograph that may 'make or break' a claimant's case, and the like. A great many lawyers, Baldyga found, either simply neglect or totally fail to devote much interest or attention, not to speak of passion, to the kinds of tasks which, though tedious and possessing little "sex appeal," are often the crucial elements in claims settlement work. Baldyga cites as a case in point the typical attitude of lawyers (and claimsmens) in an issue like tracking down or securing potentially critical photographs of accident scenes or bodily injuries that might possibly have been taken by others but are essential in establishing a claimant's case. "Generally speaking, in the business of securing photographs, many lawyers and claimsmen fail badly," Baldyga asserts. "[Yet], photographs are one of the most potent, and, in my judgement, the <u>second</u> most critical part of your [claims] file. (next to being able to dig up a favorable eyewitness)." Baldyga sums up the central point this way:[14]

> "It's a tragic misconception, but the laymen is under the impression that when he gave the lawyer his case in the first place he did so on the assumption that the large percentage fee the lawyer would eventually extract was in exchange (and some sort of guarantee) for **skilled and professional** representation. Well,…they [often] suddenly learn differently… But, now [by then] it's too late!
> We know that all lawyers have passed rigorous examination, so we have to assume that when it comes to the proper execution of legal documents and knowledge of the law, surely they know what they are doing. *But how to properly investigate a client's automobile accident case and how to intelligently create that particular client's file, is unfortunately not a skill that all lawyers have and/or ever develop.*"

[12]Ross, <u>Settled Out of Court</u>, p. 6, quoting Conard, et al., pp. 3-4.
[13]Ross, <u>Settled Out of Court</u>, p. 21.
[14]Baldyga, <u>How To Settle Your Own Insurance Claim</u>, p. 34.

The reverse, though, is often the case with regard to the nonlawyer claimant. While the average lawyer may not possess such essential skills and attributes that are fundamentally required in the claims settlement process, you, the layperson claimant, often may. Or should. You typically have an inherent advantage over the lawyer! As a claimant whose own case and self- interest are at stake, you are better equipped, better suited, and better motivated in doing whatever is necessary for you to prevail, including the undertaking of the tedious non-lawyer-like tasks that often form the core of the claims settlement process. As Baldyga starkly posed the issue: "will your lawyer, [for example], make it his business to find a crucial witness right at the beginning [of your case]? Will he leave his office to go to the scene and at least try? The answer to these questions are too often 'No!'"[15]

But it should not be so with you, the CLAIMANT, on the other hand, though! Your own answer to the above question, as a claimant, would well be 'YES!' Hence, you have one significant way in which — and significant reason why—you are better off doing your own claims settlement yourself, rather than hiring a lawyer to do it for you!

5. A Lawyer Can't Do Much for you Anyway When the Other Driver Carries Only the Minimum Insurance Coverage

Finally, there's one notable situation when it's almost guaranteed that you'll be better off filing the claim on your own: In instances when you're certain that the other driver has only the minimum required amount of insurance coverage, and that he has no independent assets, wealth or resources of his own. Indeed, this may be one situation where you can still get excellent results on your own even if your case involves major, serious or disabling injuries of the type we said you should ordinarily not attempt to undertake by yourself. (Section D above).

The figures for the minimum required dollar limit for insurance coverage varies in each state. [See Table on p. 110]. A typical state minimum today, as could be seen from the figures on p. 110 given by the Insurance Information Institute, would be bodily injury coverage that pays up to $20,000 for each person hurt in an accident, but no more than $40,000 in total compensation per accident, and property damage liability coverage of $10,000 per accident.

In any event, let's assume that you happen to find yourself in a situation where you've made all the necessary verifications and you're absolutely certain that the other driver carries only the "minimum" required insurance coverage under the state law. And let's further say that the injuries you sustained are clearly worth more than the insurance limit of the insurance coverage. Then, in such a situation, in all probability, you should have no trouble getting the other driver's insurance company adjuster to pay you the full policy limit, or something very close to it, without using an attorney. But, first make absolutely certain that the other driver actually has the <u>minimum</u> state insurance coverage, and no more (demand to physically see the policy), before you make this deal or sign the release.

---

[15]Baldyga, Ibid. p. 34

CHAPTER 2
SOME FEW FIRST STEPS YOU MUST TAKE IMMEDIATELY FOLLOWING THE ACCIDENT TO PROTECT & MAXIMIZE YOUR RIGHTS

As a general rule, the first few hours and days following an accident are, in many respects, frequently the most crucial in protecting and enhancing your rights to ultimately get a decent settlement in the end. Here in this chapter, we shall cover, largely in a summary way rather than exhaustively, a few very important procedural things you must *promptly* do, as *immediately* as possible following the accident, and the general attitude you must adopt, if you are to maximize your potential for securing the best possible settlement in the end.

This chapter should be read — and the recommendations thereof undertaken — in conjunction with the steps in chapters 3 and 4, as they are largely supplementary and complementary to one another.

HERE THEY ARE, SOME OF THE STEPS YOU MUST PROMPTLY TAKE, AND THE GENERAL ATTITUDE YOU MUST ADOPT, **IMMEDIATELY** FOLLOWING YOUR ACCIDENT:

1. Write Down, Record, or Otherwise Preserve Everything

This is of crucial importance: make it a duty and a habit, write down and otherwise make a record of everything you possibly can about the accident — the location and its surroundings, the parties involved, the economic losses and physical damages incurred, the eye-witnesses, the passengers, the injuries, etc. etc. And make this record by any and every means available to you — by written notes, photographs, video, tape recording, etc. [See Chapters 3 & 4 for detailed procedures].

2. Begin Immediately To Assemble Your Documentations

Documentations — adequately and timely assembled documentations — are the essential KEY to a successful claims settlement process. You should begin IMMEDIATELY, right after the accident, to assemble any and all letters, notes, financial documents, medical records, tapes, photos, newspaper clippings, pieces of paper, etc., you generate from the accident. And, just as importantly, you should organize such documentations into proper categories — i.e., separate and arrange the documents and records by category, so that all items for each category are kept in a separate folder or file and properly labelled in such a way that it can be easily identified and differentiated. [See Chapters 3 & 4 for detailed procedures of documentations].

3. Promptly See a Doctor

A common reality not often understood by the average person involved in an accident is the absolutely critical and indispensible necessity of seeing a doctor and getting medical attention IMMEDIATLEY after an accident. By all accounts by expert claimsmen, this decision — as to whether medical attention is obtained, from whom it is obtained, and the timeliness of it — often spells the critical difference between getting a handsome settlement in the end, or going home merely with a paltry "nuisance" settlement just to close a case.

Like it or not, it is the operative rule of the game in insurance claims settlement; *A CLAIM OF BODILY INJURIES BY A CLAIMANT CARRIES LITTLE OR NO CREDIBILITY WITH INSURANCE CLAIMSMEN **UNLESS** IT IS VERIFIED BY REPORTS OF MEDICAL DOCTORS WHO CAN ATTEST TO THE CLAIMANT'S CLAIMS!*

Here's how Edward Siegel, a lawyer and expert in claims settlement matters, sums up how and why it's of such great importance that the claimant gets prompt medical attention:[1]

> "....you should have him (a doctor) examine you as soon as possible. Even if your aches are minor, don't try to treat them yourself. An aspirin and some rest may be all you really need, but it is just as likely that you have some injury you're not aware of. *Just as important — from the standpoint of being paid for your damages — is the fact that your injuries will be worth much more, in the adjuster's eyes, if they warrant going to a doctor (even if the doctor can't find anything seriously wrong with you).*
>
> *If you don't see a doctor, but you still try to claim you had cuts and bruises, or pains, and that you lost time from work, you won't get much of an offer for your injuries. But if you do see your doctor, and have him write a report, the settlement value of your case improves tremendously.*
> When your injury is mild, your doctor will probably see you two to six times, on the average (occasionally more), without any complicated treatment. You can expect, in the typical situation, to be x-rayed, given some pills, told to rest for a few days, and possibly advised to take some heat therapy.
>
> If the injury is more serious, you may have to wear a cervical collar (a neck brace) for a few weeks. This can be uncomfortable, and literally, a "pain in the neck," but it will help the value of the claim and hopefully your recovery). Your doctor may also refer you to a specialist, such as an orthopedist (bone doctor) or a neurologist (specialist in nervous system disorders)......
>
> You should not consider trying to settle your case until the doctor discharges you. This could take only few days, or several months. ***Regardless of the cost, though, you should consider the report (from a doctor) as indispensible to your claim, since you will generally only get a "nuisance" type of settlement (under $500) without a report.***"

Siegel added:[2]

> "The value of a claim necessarily does have some relationship to the amount of your (medical) bills. Why? Because a claim with doctor bills of $500 will be worth more than a claim with bills of $50. The adjuster will normally reason that if you were hurt badly enough to run up $500 worth of medical expenses, then your injuries must be fairly substantial. But if you only see a doctor once or twice, and your bills are about $50, then they figure you can't be hurt too seriously...[that's] why you should go for [medical] treatment as often as [necessary] ...you may be accused of padding the (medical) bills, or malingering, but its an unfortunate fact of settlement negotiations that the more doctor visits, the higher the claim value."

---

[1]Siegel, <u>How to Avoid Lawyers</u>, pp.5-7.

[2]Ibid. pp.9-10.

To summarize: ALWAYS SEE A PHYSICIAN IN ANY AND EVERY ACCIDENT, ANYWAY, REGARDLESS. Get as much medical attention as you can or find necessary — even if you have to pay for the medical treatment, it will still be all worth it for you in the end, both in terms of the fact that you will generally be repaid for medical expenses and in terms of the far higher value that would be placed on the "pain and suffering" component of your injuries. Also, you are not only to see a doctor, but you must see him **promptly,** as soon after the accident as possible. And, furthermore, as much as possible, you should endeavor to be treated by medical practitioners and institutions belonging to the "mainstream Western medicine" family — physicians (M.D.s), hospitals, medical research institutions and clinics — as opposed to "nontraditional" practitioners, such as physical therapists, acupuncturists, chiropractors, herbalists, and non mainstream doctors. As one report put it, "One of the insurance industry's strong prejudices is in favor of mainstream Western treatment...Any medical bill you have incurred at [their] hands...no matter how outrageously expensive, will be considered legitimate by almost any insurance adjuster...[while] the often much less costly but equally effective treatments of non-physician providers, on the other hand are often multiplied by lower numbers."[3] [See Chapter 3, Section C (pp. 41-44), Chapter 4, Sections IV & V (pp. 54-7) for the procedures of assembling your medical records, and Chapter 6 (pp. 69-92), for the types of common injuries often encountered in accident cases].

4. Promptly Notify The Insurance Companies

Immediately following the accident, one of the first things you should do at the earliest time possible, is to notify the insurance companies of the respective parties about the accident. Obviously, at this point, it shall not have been possible to determine who exactly is really responsible . Hence, at this point the emphasis should be on giving preliminary notice of the accident to EVERY party who may have even the slightest responsibility for or connection with the accident.

Essentially, you should send notifications to :

- the Claims Department of the insurance companies of: the drivers and the owners (if they're different from the drivers) of all vehicles involved in the accident; or directly to the drivers and owners themselves, if identity of the insurance companies is unknown at this time.
- the insurance company of your own vehicle, whether you have a "fault" or a "no fault" insurance coverage, but especially if you have a no-fault coverage (look at the provisions of your policy); or if you plan or expect to make a claim under your own uninsured motorist or medical payments coverage or collision coverage [see pp. 107-125 for more on the various types of insurance policies that may apply].
- the employer of a driver of any vehicle involved in the accident which might have been either a government vehicle or is engaged in the business of a company at the time of the accident.
- any persons who may have contributed in any way to the accident (or their insurance companies, if known), such as the property owner of an object constituting an obstruction on the roadway.

Notification should be in the form of a simple one-page letter that basically informs the parties (as applicable in the case) of the occurrence of the accident, and of your intention to file some sort of claim. It should provide only the basic informational data — the time, place, date of the accident, the vehicles and parties invoved, and the like. **But it should**

---

[3]Mathews, How To Win Your Personal Injury Claim, p. 5/8.

strictly refrain from any discussion of details — who is at fault or responsible for the accident, injuries or physical damages sustained, the amount of claims you are to make, and matters of that sort. When you send the letter(s) to the parties, <u>always</u> retain a copy for your file. [See samples of 3 notification letters on pp. 23-24].

If your letter is to an individual or business rather than to an insurance company, ask the party to refer the matter to the appropriate insurance carrier for the individual or business and/or to promptly provide you, by return mail, the name and address of the carrier; and if the letter is to your own insurance company, provide the company also with any basic identifying information you may have on the other driver(s) or vehicle(s) — their names, phone numbers, the names of their insurance companies, insurance policy numbers, license plate numbers of their vehicles, and the like.

> <u>NOTE</u>: In many states, if you are involved in an accident of some magnitude in terms of its level of physical injury or the property damage sustained, you are required to file a report of the accident with the state's department of motor vehicles. If this applies to you in your case (check this with your insurance company and/or the local department of motor vehicles), be sure to give a brief statement providing the basic informational data only — your name, address, the date and place of the accident, the vehicles and parties involved. DO NOT DISCUSS, MUCH LESS ADMIT TO LIABILITY FOR THE ACCIDENT. Most such states have a pre-printed form for furnishing the information. If the form asks for details of your injuries, simply enter something to this effect: "EXTENT OR NATURE NOT FULLY DETERMINABLE AT THIS TIME UNTIL COMPLETE EXAMINATION BY MY DOCTOR." (You do not want the insurance company to later get a hold of any details you may enter there and use it to clobber you!)

5. The First Contacts With The Insurance Adjuster: Don't Tell Him Much

Typically, in an accident, even by the time you get home from the accident your phone may be ringing. The insurance adjuster may already be calling. Or, if not quite then, you can be sure it will be right as soon as they shall have received your initial notification letter. The adjuster will often try to get you to "give a statement," to give an oral or written statement about the accident and any injuries or damages sustained, and will usually pull every trick in the book and stop at nothing to get you to do so. He'll try to give you the impression that he's all out for you, all on your side working in your own best interest; and that your immediate provision of a statement to him is for the purpose of working out a fast offer of a fair and equitable settlement for you.

And what should be the proper reaction on your part? DON'T! ABSOLUTELY DON'T!! Tell him nothing; provide him with as little information as possible — basically, just your name, address, telephone number, and the kind of work you do for a living, and nothing more at this time. Why? Because the insurance adjuster is just too smart a professional for you to play around with at this juncture; he might just induce or trick you into making what lawyers call "incriminating" statements that might later be interpreted or slanted to make it look like you have some liability for the accident! [See Chapter 7 on page 93 for more on this]. Do not write or sign anything — anything whatsoever — for the adjuster (or for anybody or any insurance company) either then or later, no matter what the adjuster or the person says. Instruct your household and relatives not to talk to anybody whatsoever about you or your accident, either. You do not have to provide the insurance company with the identities (or the statements or accounts) of any eye witnesses you have, or go out of your way to help them with any information at all. *Turn down any invitation to discuss the accident or your injuries. (Simply respond that you're still engaged in your investigations and the gathering of evidence and would provide the adjuster with every information he needs "at the appropriate time"). In fact, in the first contact with an adjuster, make it absolutely clear to him that you do not wish any further phone discussions with or contacts by the adjuster, and ask that he only communicate with you in writing until such a time when he gets your written demand for settlement negotiations. Bluntly tell the adjuster that he should expect you to be ready with your written demand [see Section D of Step 2 on p. 165] only after you have completed your medical treatment and fully recovered from your injuries. DON'T BE IN A RUSH. NEVER SHOULD YOU BE IN A HASTE TO SETTLE. NEVER!*

Take notes each time, of the details of every conversation you have with the insurance company officials. On each occassion, get the name, title, and phone number of the person with whom you spoke, and the person or company he represents, and put down the substance of the discussions or contact.

Why do you have to take all these precautions not to say too much too early to the insurance company? There are many very important reasons why this is absolutely necessary. For one thing, it's essential to guard against the typical adjuster who will often call constantly day and night and will pull all stops and resort to all tricks in the book to try to pressure you into making a quickie settlement for a meagre amount — before you can ever know fully what the nature and extent of your injuries are and how much your claim is really worth. More importantly, in the immediate aftermath of the trauma and excitment of an accident, accident victims are all too often very excitable and vulnerable, and insurance adjusters know this. You can be easily manipulated by a sweet-talking but skilled adjuster into making statements which may seem perfectly harmless at the time but may later be interpreted or slanted as an admission of some fault on your part, or be employed to limit the seriousness of your injuries. In deed, at worse, adjusters (some unscrupulous ones) have been known to put down some information from claimants inaccurately, and all too often, as a layman, you're unlikely to catch the mistake or subtle slanting until it's too late — frozen in the insurance adjuster's notes or records as "evidence"! Furthermore, not having had the time to think about and through the accident or to fully investigate the case, and not having known fully what your injuries are or had the opportunity to recover from your injuries, you are not at all in the position yet to give accurate, definitive and complete information in answer to the adjuster's questions. And, as a rule, if you rush to give inaccurate or incomplete information to the adjuster, you can bet your last dollar that the insurance company will use that to its maximum advantage later to "impeach" (challenge as less than true) the evidence or facts you submit.

Hence, it's a lot better and 'safer' for you that you simply say nothing and not engage in any discussions of any kind with the adjuster until you've done all your homework and are fully prepared and ready finally to discuss your settlement [Chapter 11, especially pp. 161 & 175]. *In a word, keeping silent until you're really ready to talk is easily one of the key ways a claimant can retain "control" of his case, to his great advantage, as any experienced claims lawyer or negotiator will readily tell you* . [See Chapter11, especially pp. 161-183]. [See also, Chapter 7, Section J, (pp. 105-106), "A Cautionary Note: Avoid Talking to the Adjuster to Minimize Complicating Your Liability Position," for more on this issue].

6. Diligently Guard Your Medical Records

There are two things you should be sure not to do relating to your medical records: never sign any authorization for or otherwise agree for the doctor (your doctor or any doctor) to release medical reports to the insurance adjuster; and never agree to be examined by a doctor affiliated with or recommended by the insurance company.

As to the doctor's report, the far better practice is to let it come to you first. This way, you'll have an opportunity to review its contents first, and if it is a fair and accurate report, you can then forward a copy to the adjuster; and if it's not so fair or complete a report, you'll still be in a position to call the doctor's attention to any inaccuracies or ommissions and ask for some possible revisions before you may then submit it to the adjuster. And, with respect to not agreeing to an examination by an insurance company doctor, very often the adjuster will tell you he wants you to be examined by a doctor of the insurance company's choice before he can consider your demand. As a general rule, be very wary of such a request: doctors picked by the insurance company are notorious for frequently finding nothing wrong with the claimant, or, for often finding "no objective basis" for the claimant's complaints — i.e., failure to find any symptoms that they could physically see or specifically measure. Not having had the benefit of seeing you often or over an extended period of time, as your own regular doctor might have, and being agents or affiliates of the insurance company which pays them, it's somewhat natural for such doctors frequently to lean towards the insurance company, especially in circumstances where there is some element of doubt or no clear-cut answer about your condition!

In any event, the important thing here for you to remember is that **you do not have to agree to be examined by the insurance company doctor;** you have a right to see only the doctors of your choice and the insurance company has no right to make you submit to their doctor — unless your claim actually becomes a formal court case involving a lawsuit.

ACCIDENT NOTIFICATION LETTERS

FORM 2-1

SAMPLE LETTER TO THE CLAIMANT'S OWN AUTO INSURANCE COMPANY WHERE CLAIMANT CARRIES A REGULAR INSURANCE POLICY

Claimant: John Doe
Address: 127 Hand Street
New York, NY 10001
Date: _____

TO: Claims Department
XYZ Insurance Company
10 Main Street
New York, NY 10025

RE: Insured Party: John Doe
Policy No.: WW1-7864-A
Date of the Accident: ___ 199___

Dear Claims Intaker:

This is to inform you that I was involved in an automobile accident on _____ 199___ at the intersection of 2nd Avenue and Apple Street in Brooklyn, New York, and sustained bodily injuries and damages to my car.

The other person involved in the accident was Mr/Mrs _____ whose full address is _____. He was driving a car bearing a New York license plate number ___, whose make, year, and body color, are as follows: _____

_____.

Please be advised that, as of this time, I intend to proceed against Mr/Mrs _____.

I reserve the right however, to file a claim under my own medical payments or collision coverages, If I should so determine.

Thank you very much.

Yours truly,

John Doe

FORM 2-2

SAMPLE LETTER TO THE CLAIMANT'S OWN AUTO INSURANCE COMPANY WHERE CLAIMANT CARRIES A NO-FAULT POLICY

Claimant: John Doe
Address: 127 Hand Street
New York, NY 10001
Date: _____

TO: Claims Department
XYZ Insurance Company
10 Main Street
New York, NY 10025

RE: Insured Party: John Doe
Policy No.: WW1-7864-A
Date of the Accident: ___ 199___

Dear Claims Intaker:

This is to inform you that I was involved in an automobile accident on _____ 199___ at the intersection of 2nd Avenue and Apple Street in Brooklyn, New York, and sustained bodily injuries and damages to my car.

The other person involved in the accident was Mr/Mrs _____ whose full address is _____. He was driving a car bearing a New York license plate number ___, whose make, year and body color, are as follows: _____

_____.

Please be advised that, as of this time, I intend to proceed under my Personal Injury Protection coverage and further reserve my rights to proceed as well against the others responsible for the accident, if warranted.

Please confirm by return letter that you have received this notice.

Thank you very much.

Yours truly,

John Doe

FORM 2-3

Sample Letter of Inquiry to Insurance Commissioner for Insurance Information About Other Driver

Your (Claimant's) Name: _____

Address: _____

Date: _____

TO: Insurance Commissioner
       Financial Responsibility Section

    RE: Date of Accident: _____
         Location of Accident: _____
         Party Being Inquired About: _____

Dear Commissioner/Director:

 I was involved in an automobile accident on the above date and at the above location. Please advise me as to whether the other driver, as named below, carries liability and other pertinent insurance, or has otherwise complied with the financial responsibility laws of your State and if so, how?

The other Driver's Name: _____

His/Her Address: _____

His/Her License Number is: Year _____
                          Number _____
Thank you for your assistance in this matter.
      Yours truly,

_____

FORM 2-4

SAMPLE NOTIFICATION LETTER TO AN INDIVIDUAL WITH WHOM CLAIMANT (JOHN DOE) HAD AN AUTO ACCIDENT

(CLAIMANT):   JOHN DOE

ADDRESS: 127 HAND STREET
                 NEW YORK, NEW YORK 10001

DATE: _____

TO: David Damages
       14 Accident Street, Apt. #4
       New York, New York 10001

Dear Mr. Damages,

You and I were involved in an automobile accident on October 6, 199X and the intersection of 2nd Avenue and Apple Street, Brooklyn, New York. I just need from you the name, address, and telephone number of your insurance carrier, and the policy number of your insurance policy. Will you please send that to me. Also, I enclose herewith a copy of this letter which I hereby request that you send to your carrier concerning insurance coverage on the accident.

Yours truly,

John Doe

CHAPTER 3
THE WINNING FORMULA: START YOUR INFORMATION-GATHERING HOMEWORK RIGHT AWAY, RIGHT FROM THE MOMENT OF THE ACCIDENT

I. The Key Winning Formula in Any Claims Case

The formula is rather simple. That is, the ultimate "winning formula" to prevail in claims negotiations and settlement. *If you want to be in the best possible position to eventually secure the best possible settlement for your claims, you had better got one fundamental point unmistakably clear:* THE PROCESS THAT *UNDERLINE ULTIMATELY* LANDS YOU THERE STARTS (MUST START) RIGHT FROM THE VERY TIME AND PLACE OF THE ACCIDENT! Simply put, it's much like you would do when you're intent on building a house you'd intend to be strong. You'd start right from its very foundation, from the very first block laid or the very first concrete poured! Likewise, the time and place you start building the "foundation" for filing a solid claim for your auto accident claim is directly *from the time and place of the accident occurrence!* And, use of the ASPON strategy of claims negotiations set forth in this book for negotiating your settlement (see chapter 11), is totally predicated on the premise that you shall have thoroughly done your background homework.

Essentially, you do this by promptly starting the process of building a file of information and documentations on your case. Or, if you momentarily can't do this yourself due to initial disability, you should have someone else immediately start working on it for you in the meantime. It is of the utmost importance (in deed, this cannot be emphasized enough) that YOU, the accident victim, or a temporary helper thereof, start obtaining and assembling the facts surrounding the accident just as **IMMEDIATELY AFTER THE ACCIDENT** as possible. For one thing, if you should delay, human memory is amazingly short, and it generally doesn't take long for the facts and details to begin to disappear and for memory to actually fade away. MAKE NO MISTAKE ABOUT THIS. TAKE IT FROM THIS OBSERVER: this reality hardly ever fails to be vindicated—when it is not heeded! Furthermore, and equally very important, a physical record of an event (whether it is made in writing, or by audio or video recording, and the like), would generally command legal validity and credibility in claims settlement, or even court proceedings, when such record is taken as close as possible to the time and date of the event's occurrence.

II. Categories of Information to Gather

The following are the categories of information and data you should begin to put together as promptly as possible:

        a. Detailed account of the accident and its occurrence

        b. The witnesses and their statements

        c. The bodily injuries

        d. The property damage

e. Photographs

f. Diagram of the accident scene

g. The police or investigating officer's report

h. Weather report

i. Uninsured motorist information

A. Compiling Your Personal Account of the Accident & its Occurrence

As soon after the accident as possible, promptly make a detailed written statement, or a voice or video recording thereof, of your own version of the accident—what happened, how it happened, who in your opinion was at fault, who and who did what immediately leading to the occurrence of the accident, who and who were at the scene or did or said what, etc etc. As emphasized at the beginning of the chapter, YOU MUST DO THIS PROMPTLY AND WITHOUT DELAY—as soon after the accident as is physically possible when memory is still fresher and the facts and recollections more likely to be accurate.

If you are personally unable to do so yourself because of physical impairment in the meantime, then verbally detail the facts and information to someone else and have him (or her) record or write them down for you—in the tiniest and most complete details.

NOTE: If you take the trouble to develop this record, and to properly do so, you'll find that this statement may prove to be a most invaluable and useful tool to you, probably the single smartest thing you did in the entire claims process, when it comes time later down the road for you to negotiate your claim with the insurance adjuster, or even to proceed in a court case.

A Checklist of Personal & Other Related Information to Gather

Here is a suggested CHECKLIST of the kinds of information to include in your personal statement and factual record:

1. Date, time and location of the accident

2. Your destination—where you were going and for what purpose

3. Names, addresses and phone numbers (business as well as home) of persons with you in your vehicle (each and every one of them)

4. Names, addresses and phone numbers (business and home) of <u>ALL</u> the persons involved in the accident—either as drivers of the other vehicle or vehicles, or as passengers or pedestrians. [Get also the names, addresses and business and home phone numbers of the parties' relatives or close friends who will always know the parties' whereabouts].

5. Additional information to obtain from he persons involved in the accident (persons named under item #4 above):
- Who was the driver at the wheels of the other vehicle (or vehicles) at the time of the accident?
- For passenger(s) in the involved vehicle, the relationship to the driver (and/or owner) of the car the passenger was in; and, the same questions for the driver(s) with respect to their passengers.
- Your exact sitting arrangement and positions immediately before the accident
- What is the exact nature of the trip, for what purpose was it being made, at whose invitation and for whose benefit?
- Who, exactly, invited the passenger(s) for the ride? (May be of help in determining whether passenger(s) would be considered a 'guest' under the laws of a given jurisdiction).
- Ever rode with the driver before?
- Did any passenger voice out (or merely harbored) any complaints, comments, concerns, or observations concerning the driver's driving style during the course of the ride?
- What was the complainant's or commentator's previous knowledge of the driving ability or record of the

person driving? Did he or she feel the driver drove carefully or properly on this particular trip?
- Did any person in the vehicle, particularly the driver, imbibe alcoholic drinks, or any narcotics during the trip? And, if so, who and who, and in what amounts and at what times and places?
- And was the driver (and any other person or persons) intoxicated or seemingly so to the observer?
  NOTE: The usual and most practicable procedure with respect to the driver, and often the passenger(s) as well, is to obtain this information from them at the scene of the accident. For the rest of the persons concerned, you may usually obtain the information from them either directly at the scene of the accident, or if not immediately possible, then later on at their private locations but as promptly as possible.

6. Description of the weather conditions at the time of the accident.
- was it snowing, frosting, raining, brightly sunny, windy, etc?
- was there sleet, fog, mist, tornado, flooding, hail?
- was the windshield steamed up or frosted? Was the windshield wiper working?
- was the sun ray in the driver's face?

7. Description of the traffic conditions of the road
- was it dry, wet, slippery, icy, etc?
- was it smooth, rough, bumpy, full of potholes, etc?
- what is the width of the street, the number of lanes; was road marked or not, and if marked, what special markings?
- were there any obstructions, parked vehicles, trees, shrubbery? (if so, describe them).
- description of all marks, gouges, or debris on the road
- was road crowned or flat, straight or curved?
- was road paved or unpaved? If paved, then with what material (macadam, asphalt, concrete, cobblestone, brick, gravel, dirt, etc)?
- was the street under road construction? Did it contain ditches and trolley tracks? (If applicable, then give the width, depth, and general nature of any ditches, the width, construction and type of shoulders).
- were there any debris lying at the scene (auto parts, glass, stones, oil stains, etc)? And if applicable, then give details as to material, quantity and locations.

8. Description of the traffic control signals and personnel
- was a police officer directing traffic at or near the accident scene?
- details of any traffic lights, signals or warning signs at the location of the scene. (What lights or signs, specifically; the exact locations, whether or not they were in proper operation, etc.)
- details of speed limit signs posted, if any.
- if within a hospital or school zone, describe exactly the signs posted, if any; and if none was posted, then so state.

9. The lighting condition in the area
- was it daylight, dusk, night, moonlight, cloudy, foggy (including the position of the sun and in what direction it was shining)?
- Headlights (bright, medium, dim, parking, fog lights?)
- Nature and impact and power of the approaching headlights (was it blinding or just normal).
- Nature, impact and power of the road or street lights.
- Details of any flares and local lights, if any was needed.

10. Some detailed description of the area.
- Was it residential, industrial or business district?
- Was it city, urban, suburban?

11. Description of road skid marks (the exact locations, measurements, direction).

12. Names, addresses and phone numbers (business and home) of any witnesses, aside from the persons listed in paragraphs 3 & 4 above. Get also the names, addresses and phone numbers of relatives or close friends who will always know each party's whereabouts.

13. Details of what happened upon impact or fall; the physical sensations you felt, if any.

14. Description of any conversations you had with (or comments made by) relevant parties (the other drivers, passengers, pedestrians, witnesses, a police officer, etc.) at the scene of the accident.

15. Description of the condition of the other driver's vehicle (its body, color, year and make, and general care and condition, brakes, lights, horn, directional signals, tires, tail lights, steering, etc.)

16. Details of when the other vehicle was last checked and inspected by the official state-designated authority, and where and by whom (you may generally locate such information in the stickers posted on the vehicles' windshield or door). And note that this information is especially essential if and when it's strongly believed or suspected that some defects of a mechanical nature, such as the ones listed in paragraph 15 above, may have substantially caused or contributed to the accident.

17. Description of the medical treatment you may have initially received on emergency or other basis following the accident, if applicable, plus the names, addresses, job titles and phone numbers of all the persons who attended to you.

18. If you were removed from the accident scene by ambulance, you shall have interviewed the attendants and driver and taken down their statements or comments. Now, state in details their statements as to the location of the accident-related vehicles, skid marks, position of injured persons, admissions of or statements made by the other driver and others in the other vehicle, etc.

19. If vehicles were removed by a wrecker or a wrecking or towing company, interview the wrecker's driver and take down his statements. (What did he have to say, if any, on the after-accident details — skid and drag marks, location of debris, condition of the vehicles' brakes, lights, horns, tires, etc, nature and extent of damage to the vehicles, statements or admissions of drivers or others, etc.)

20. Names, addresses and work and home phone numbers of the negligent party or parties. Also, the same particulars for their relatives and/or close friends who will always know the parties' whereabouts.

21. Detailed description of the negligent party's comportment, actions, reactions and inactions, and of any statements or utterances he may have made, and to whom and whose hearing it was made.

22. Name, address, and phone numbers of the negligent party's (the other driver's) insurance carrier.

23. File number designated by the police for the Police Report on the accident, if any report was made.

B. Get Your EYE WITNESSES and their Statements

1. WITNESSES COULD BE CRUCIAL

One of the most important sources of help in digging up information and assembling a record of the accident, are the eye witnesses to the accident and/or to the surrounding events, and their accounts and recollections as to what happened. Of particular weight and significance would be to secure detailed written statements (and/or recorded or video statements) from such witnesses, if there were any — eye witness persons, such as passengers in your own and the other vehicles, pedestrians, onlookers and bystanders at the scene and time of the accident, and even the driver of other vehicles not involved in the accident. In the view of claims experts experienced in the claims settlement process, the testimony (statements) of eye witnesses could be of such critical importance that "it can make or break a case." Accounts of such witnesses often serve as highly valuable evidence to support ("corroborate") your own statements and claims (and, in many instances, could be admissible evidence in court trials as well).

One widely experienced and respected practitioner in insurance claims settlement operations, gives a sense of the crucial importance attached to a claimant having a witness:

> "A witness can make or break a case. For those of you who have had the opportunity (and if you have been able to keep your wits about you) the very first thing you do *immediately* after the accident has occurred, is to look all about you and try to find somebody who saw the accident. If you do spot someone, don't be bashful. Go right over to him and ask if he saw the accident. If someone did, then jot down their name and address. If they get into a car and drive away before you can get them, then jot down that automobile's registration number [and try to get their name through the department of motor vehicles office…]."[1]

In short, no amount of trouble is too much to take in trying to secure an eye witness to an accident and his testimony as to the events!

2. LOCATING AND UTILIZING WITNESSES

How do you actually go about the task of securing the relevant witnesses? Or their testimonies or cooperation? To begin with, you should know this: *it is a wiser strategy on your part if you should try and talk to the witnesses FIRST before the insurance adjuster ever gets to or speaks to them. This way, you'll stand the best chance of getting them committed to your account of the events or your side of the case.* Briefly speaking, you should contact each witness to the accident (identified from the list of persons you shall have compiled at the time of the accident or from the police report, or possibly from the insurance claims adjuster), and talk to them about what they may have known or seen about the accident. The ideal procedure is to get them to write out, in great detail, what they saw in their own words, their own personal account of what happened. But if they are not willing (or able) to do this, then write out a statement (or merely jot down on a pad) in as great a detail as possible, some notes of what each witness tells you and have each person sign the paper, and date it. Ask wide-ranging questions covering the major aspects of the accident which you think are relevant or significant, seeking to know their accounts, recollections, impressions and observations of what happened. [The sample forms on pp. 33-40 pretty much summarize the kinds of questions to be covered, for a passenger witness, or a driver or pedestrian witness, respectively].

---

[1]Baldyga, How to Settle Your Own Insurance Claim, p. 8.

Upon completing the interview of each witness and taking down his (or her) statement, you should first have the witness read the statement (or, if the witness is illiterate and is unable to read or write, have a third party read it to him or her). Then have the witness (and the reader or interpreter, if applicable) sign and date the statement, with their home address and phone numbers included).

The ideal situation is to have a direct, person-to-person interview with the witness. However, it's not unusual to find many witnesses who either are shy of being "interrogated" or afraid of being "involved" and may be reluctant to give you a direct personal interview. If a given witness will not consent to a personal interview, try requesting him to let you "talk to" him (or her) over the phone and send him a statement of his answers (and a diagram of his description of the scene of the accident) for him to review and then sign for you. Thereupon, you should type up the questions you asked the witness and his answers to them (and if necessary, draw up as well a diagram of the described scene of the accident), then mail or give this to the witness to sign, date it, and return it (the original copy) to you. (Always enclose a self-addressed, stamped, return envelope for the witness to facilitate his returning of those documents to you). Also, if you are unable to directly reach or communicate with a particular witness, a good practice is to simply mail the STATE-MENT OF WITNESS form (pp. 36-7) to the witness's known address, with a brief letter attached [see sample of such letter on p. 31] requesting him to complete and return the form, and also enclose a self-addressed, stamped return envelope for the witness's convenience.

> **NOTE:** For simplicity and convenience, you may simply use one of the three versions, as applicable, of the STATEMENT OF WITNESS forms on pp. 33-40, or your own adapted version thereof, to collect your information from the respective parties. You may also employ THE WITNESS ACCIDENT SCENE DIAGRAM form (sample on p. 32), and THE LETTER TO WITNESS REQUESTING STATEMENT (sample on p. 31), for your convenience as necessary. Simply mail (or personally present) these forms as necessary, to the appropriate witnesses with a self-addressed, stamped return envelope attached, and the letter of request that they complete and sign the forms and return them to you promptly.

3. LOCATING A MISSING WITNESS

As it often happens, you may, on occasion, be unable to directly contact or locate the whereabouts of a witness whose home address or phone number you may have obtained. Americans are known to be one of the world's most mobile people, and the witness may have moved in the meantime, or the address at your disposal may have been the wrong one in the first place. To locate a witness or his/her whereabouts whose statement or testimony may be of great importance to your case, there are a few helpful steps you can take.

They include the following:

1. Send a certified or registered letter to the witness, addressed to his last known address with the "Return Receipt Requested" and the "Addressee Only" boxes checked off. This way, if you should receive back from the post office the return receipt signed by the witness or filled out by the post office, you should find fully entered therein the current address of the witness.

2. Search through the phone and city directories of the area of the person's last known residence, and of the likely localities you think he might have moved to.

3. Contact the following parties and inquire from them about the witnesses' whereabouts, address or phone numbers, or any possible leads thereof: his (or her) known relatives and friends, if any; his last known employer; the Department of Motor Vehicles (ask for his most current known address on record); the city/county tax assessor; the local registrar of voters; the janitor and landlord of the last known address; any fraternal, veterans union or other organizations to which the witness may have belonged, if any; local churches and/or church organizations; the local parochial and public schools, if party has or seems to have children of school age; utility and telephone companies; and the area's welfare agencies.

FORM 3-1

LETTER TO WITNESS REQUESTING STATEMENT & DIAGRAM OF ACCIDENT

My Name: _____

Address _____

_____ Zip _____

Date _____

To Mr/Mrs _____

Address _____

     RE: Date & Time of Accident: _____

               Place of Accident: _____

Dear Sir/Madam:

    *I am informed that you were a witness to the above accident.

    *Pursuant to that, please find enclosed a "STATEMENT OF WITNESS" form (and "WITNESS DIAGRAM" form) which I'd greatly appreciate your completing and promptly returning to me, duly signed.

    I would be most greatful to you for your prompt response and assistance in this matter, as your statement (and diagram) will be of great help to me in my claim for injuries and other damages I sustained.

    Please use the enclosed self-addressed, stamped envelope for your convenience.

Thank you.

Yours Very truly,

*NOTE: Or, if perchance, you have spoken to the witness by phone or in person and he had consented to furnish you such a statement, or to sign a statement if you write out one based on your interview with him, then you can substitute something like this for paragraphs one and two: *"It was a great pleasure speaking with you on this matter on the ___ day of _____ 19___. Pursuant to our conversation, please find enclosed the "STATEMENT OF WITNESS" and "WITNESS DIAGRAM" forms which I'd appreciate your signing and returning to me."*

FORM 3-2

Witness Accident Scene Diagram Form
(by a Driver, Passenger, Pedestrian or other)

Instructions: Please show in the diagram below how the accident occurred, and then sign the form below. (Or, if diagram was drawn by another person from your description of the events, then simply examine the diagram and sign below to confirm its accuracy). Label each street or highway by its proper name or other designation.

Indicate north by arrow and letter "N,"
South by arrow and letter "S," and so on.

Show vehicle thus:

Show pedestrian thus:

Mark one vehicle "A"
Mark other vehicle "B"
Mark a third vehicle "C" and so on.

North ("N")

West ("W")

East ("E")

South ("S")

I have carefully looked over this diagram, and as a witness to the auto accident at issue, and, under pain of perjury, I hereby certify that it is a true and accurate depiction of the said accident to the best of my knowledge.

Signed: _____
Full Name is: _____   Witness to the Accident

Street Address: _____ City or town: _____ State: _____ Zip: _____

Today's Date: _____

FORM 3-3

𝔖tatement of 𝔓assenger in 𝔄utomobile 𝔄ccident

Your Full Name (the Passenger's): _____ Phone #(H)_____ Job # _____

Address: _____ City _____ State _____ Zip _____

Your Occupation _____ Age: _____

Are you related to the drivers or any of the persons involved in this accident? _____

If so, explain the nature of the relationship _____

_____

What was the date of the accident? _____ 19 _____ Time of day/night _____ M.

Place of accident _____

In which vehicle were you a passenger (make, style, year, license #)? _____

Name & Address of the driver of vehicle in which riding _____

_____

Where in the vehicle were you seated? _____ How many other passengers were in

the vehicle?_____ What are their names & address: _____

_____

What was the destination or purpose of the ride or travel? _____

Why were you in the car for that ride? _____

What was the condition of the streets (wet, dry, icy, snowy, slippery)? _____

Describe weather conditions (snowing, raining, windy, flooding, brightly sunny, foggy, misty)_____

What were you doing just before and at the time of the accident:? Give full details _____

Did you actually see the accident occur? _____ If so, describe what you saw: _____

_____

How many vehicles were involved, in your best observation?_____ Describe the vehicles involved

(make, style, year, license plate, color; for simplicity of understanding, please designate the vehicles by letters: "A," "B," "C," "D," etc.)

_____

_____

Assuming you were a passenger in vehicle "A", in what direction was vehicle B going? _____

Its approximate speed? _____

In your honest opinion, would you say that one of the vehicles was unduly speeding (or both) at the time of the

accident? _____ Which vehicle or vehicles?_____

Were the traffic lights lit and in operation? _____

Was any pedestrian struck? _____ If yes, in what direction was the pedestrian going? _____

Was the pedestrian walking or running? _____

Name and address of the pedestrian (if known): _____

If at night, did both (all) vehicles have their headlights on? _____ If not, which one(s) had lights on? _____

Signed: _____

Signature of witness (passenger)

(please continue on next page)

Page 1 of 3 pages

Statement of Passenger (Cont.)

If the accident occurred in an intersection, were any obstructions at corners to block views of either driver?_____

What obstructions (parked cars, trees, shrubbery, road construction) & against which driver(s)? _____

Which vehicle reached the intersection first?_____ Any traffic lights, signs or signals at the intersection? (describe): _____

Which vehicle had the green light or the right of way? _____ Was vehicle "A" on the right side of the road? _____ How about vehicle "B"? _____ Did either driver give a signal? _____

If so, please explain how _____

In what position and at what place on the road was your car when you first observed the other car or cars with which you were involved in the accident? _____

Did you warn or alert your driver of the movement of the other car? _____

What did your driver do to avoid the other car, if any? _____

How far did vehicle "A" move after the collision? _____ And vehicle "B"? _____

What was the position (direction & location) of each vehicle after the accident? _____

Which vehicle struck or hit the other? _____

What part of vehicle "A" struck other vehicle, object or person? _____

What part of vehicle "B" struck other vehicle, object or person? _____

Did you hear (or overhear) any comments made by any of the drivers? _____ If so, what was said and by which driver? _____

What did you observe of the general attitude, behavior, or comportment of the drivers following the accident?

Describe in full for vehicle A, B, C, etc. _____

_____

Did any of the drivers appear to be intoxicated or tipsy or "under the influence of," in your observation? Give full details _____

_____

Did you or other passengers, or the driver of your car have any alcoholic drinks or use any drugs before or during the ride?_____ If so, please give details _____

In your opinion who was at fault for the accident and why? _____

_____

Do you consider both parties at fault? _____

Signed: _____

Signature of witness (passenger)

(please continue on next page)

Statement of Passenger

Was anyone injured? _____ State names of persons injured (or, if not known, simply describe them), and give the nature and extent of the injuries: _____

_____

Please give names and addresses of any other witnesses or observers you may know of: _____

_____

Please describe the accident in detail, stating how it happened, who in your opinion was to blame and why and mentioning any statement made by yourself or others (the passengers, drivers, other witnesses, onlookers, the police, etc.) after the accident: _____

_____

_____

_____

_____

_____

Date: _____ 19 _____

Signed: _____

Signature of Witness (passenger)

FORM 3-4

Statement of Pedestrian or Other Witness

Your Full Name (the Witness)` _____ Phone # (H) _____ Job # _____

Address _____ City _____ State _____ Zip _____

Your Occupation _____ Age _____

Do you know the driver (s) or any of the persons involved in this accident? _____

If so, whom? _____ Are you related to the car owners, drivers, passengers or

any of the persons involved in this accident? _____ If so, explain the nature of the _____

relationship _____

What was the date of the accident? _____ 19 _____ Time of day/night _____ M.

Place of accident _____

Where were you at the time of the accident? _____

What was the condition of the streets (icy, wet, dry, snowy, slippery)? _____

Describe the weather conditions (snowing, raining, windy, flooding, brightly sunny, foggy, misty)? _____

Did you actually see the accident occur? _____ If not, how soon after its occurrence did you arrive at

the scene? _____

How many vehicles were involved in your best observation? (Please designate the vehicles by letters:

"A," "B," "C," "D," etc) _____

Describe the vehicles involved (make, style, year, color, license #): _____

_____

In what direction was vehicle "A" going? _____ Its approximate speed? _____

In what direction was vehicle "B" going? _____ Its approximate speed? _____

In your opinion would you say that one of the vehicles was unduly speeding (or both) at the time of the

accident? _____ Which vehicle or vehicles? _____

Were the traffic lights lit and in operation? _____

Was any pedestrian struck? _____ If yes, in what direction was the pedestrian going? _____

Was the pedestrian walking or running? _____

Name, address of the pedestrian, if known: _____

If at night, did both (all) vehicles have their headlights on? _____ If not, which one(s) had lights? _____

If the accident occurred in an intersection, were there any obstructions at corners to block views of either

driver? _____ What obstructions (parked cars, trees, shrubbery, road construction, etc.) & against which driver?

_____

Which vehicle reached the intersection first? _____ Any traffic lights, signs or signals at the

intersection? (describe) _____

Which vehicle had the green light or the right of way? _____ Was vehicle "A" on the right side of

the road? _____ How about vehicle "B"? _____ Did either driver give a signal? _____

Signed: _____

Page 1 of 2 pages

Signature of Witness (pedestrian)

(please continue on next page)

Statement of Pedestrian or Other Witness (Cont.)

If so, explain how _____

How far did vehicle "A" move after the collision? _____ And vehicle "B"? _____

What was the position (direction & location) of each vehicle after the accident? _____

Which vehicle struck or hit the other? _____

What part of vehicle "A" struck other vehicle, object or person? _____

What part of vehicle "B" struck other vehicle, object or person? _____

Did you hear (or overhear) any comments made by any of the drivers? _____ If so, what was said

and by which driver? _____

What did you observe of the general attitude, behavior, or comportment of the drivers following the accident?

Describe in full for vehicle A, B, C, etc. _____

_____

Did any of the drivers appear to be intoxicated or tipsy or "under the influence of," in your observation? Give

full details _____

_____

In your opinion who was at fault for the accident and why? _____

_____

_____

Do you consider both parties at fault? _____

Was anyone injured? _____ State names of persons injured (or, if not known, simply describe

them), and give the nature and extent of the injuries: _____

_____

Please give names and addresses of any other witnesses or observers you may know of:

_____

Please describe the accident in detail, stating how it happened, who in your opinion was to blame and why,

and mentioning any statement made by yourself or others (the passengers, drivers, other witnesses,

onlookers, the police, etc.) after the accident: _____

_____

_____

_____

_____

Date: _____ 19 _____

Signed: _____

Signature of Witness (pedestrian)

Page 2 of 2 pages

FORM 3-5

Statement of Driver in Automobile Accident

Your Full Name (the Driver's) _____ Phone # (H) _____ Job # _____

Address _____ City _____ State _____ Zip _____

Your Occupation _____ Age: _____

Which vehicle were you driving (make, style, year, license #)? _____

Name & Address of the owner of the vehicle you were driving: _____

_____

Did you have the owner's permission to drive the vehicle? _____

If so, how and when? _____ Are you related to the driver, the passengers, or any of the persons

involved in this accident? _____ If so, explain the nature of the relationship _____

What was the date of the accident? _____ 19 ___ Time of day/night: _____ M.

Place of accident? _____

Where in the vehicle were you seated? _____ How many other passengers in your vehicle? _____

What are their names & addresses: _____

_____

What was the destination or purpose of the ride or travel? _____

For what use or purpose was the vehicle being employed at the time of the accident? _____

When was the vehicle last inspected? _____

Are there any driving restrictions on your license? _____ If so, what restrictions and why?

_____

What was the condition of the streets (wet, dry, icy, snowy, slippery)? _____

Describe weather conditions (snowing, raining, windy, flooding, brightly sunny, foggy, misty) _____

What were you doing just before and at the time of the accident? Give full details _____

Did you actually see the accident occur? _____ If so, describe what you saw _____

_____

How many vehicles were involved, in your best observation? _____ Describe the vehicles involved

(make, style, year, license plate, color; for simplicity of understanding, please designate the vehicle by letters: "A," "B," "C," "D," etc.)

_____

_____

Assuming you were driving (or a passenger) in vehicle "A," in what direction was vehicle "B" going? _____

Its approximate speed? _____

In your honest opinion, would you say that one of the vehicles was unduly speeding (or both) at the time of

the accident? _____ Which vehicle or vehicles? _____

Were the traffic lights lit and in operation? _____

Was any pedestrian struck? _____ If yes, in what direction was the pedestrian going? _____

Was the pedestrian walking or running? _____

Name and address of the pedestrian (if known): _____

Signed: _____
Signature of Witness (Driver)

Page 1 of 3 pages   (please continue on next page)

Statement of Driver in Automobile Accident(Cont.)

If at night, did both (all) vehicles have their headlights on?_____ If not, which one(s) had lights? _____

If the accident occurred in an intersection, were any obstructions at corners to block views of either driver?_____

What obstructions (parked cars, trees, shrubbery, road construction) & against which driver(s)?_____

Which vehicle reached the intersection first?_____ Any traffic lights, signs or signals at the intersection?

(describe): _____

Which vehicle had the green light or the right of way? _____ Was vehicle "A" on the right side of the

road?_____ How about vehicle "B"? _____ Did either driver give a signal? _____

If so, please explain how _____

In what position on the road and at what place was your car when you first observed the other car or cars with which

you were involved in the accident? _____

Did you give any signals? What signal, if any?_____

Did the other car(s) give any signals? _____

What action did you take to avoid the other car?_____

What action did the other car(s) take to avoid you?_____

What did your driver do to avoid the other car, if any?_____

How far did vehicle "A" move after the collision? _____ And vehicle "B"? _____

What was the position (direction & location) of each vehicle after the accident? _____

Which vehicle struck or hit the other?_____

What part of vehicle "A" struck other vehicle, object, or person?_____

What part of vehicle "B" struck other vehicle, object, or person?_____

What part of your vehicle was damaged?_____

What is the nature and extent of the damage?_____

Did you hear (or overhear) any comments made by any of the drivers or witnesses?_____

If so, what was said and by which driver?_____

What did you observe of the general attitude, behavior, or comportment of the drivers following the accident?

Describe in full for vehicle "A," "B," "C," etc. _____

_____

Signed: _____

Signature of Witness (Driver)

(please continue on next page)

Statement of Driver in Automobile Accident(Cont.)

Did any of the drivers appear to be intoxicated or tipsy or "under the influence of," in your observation? Give full details _____

Did you or any passengers, in your car have any alcoholic drinks or use any drugs before or during the ride? _____ If so, please give details _____

In your opinion, who was at fault for the accident and why?_____
_____

In your opinion, was this accident avoidable?_____

Or was it unavoidable? Please fully explain _____
_____

Was anyone injured? _____ State names of persons injured (or, if not known, simply describe them), and give the nature and extent of the injuries: _____
_____

Please give names and addresses of any other witnesses or observers you may know of: _____
_____

Please describe the accident in detail, stating how it happened, who in your opinion was to blame and why, and mentioning any statement made by yourself or others (the passengers, drivers, other witnesses, onlookers, the police, etc.) after the accident:_____
_____
_____
_____
_____
_____

Date: _____ 19 _____

Signed: _____
                                              Signature of Witness (Driver)

C. Compile An Account / Record Of Your Bodily Injuries

When an accident occurs, it is almost automatically presumed that some physical (i.e. bodily) injury will be involved, including, as well, generally some "pain and suffering" of some sort from the injury. *IN DEED, GIVEN THE PRACTICE WITH THE INSURANCE CLAIMS INDUSTRY, THIS MUCH CAN BE SAID: you had better made pretty sure that there are some physical injuries from your accident, or there won't be much by way of compensation for you to collect, as in such a case the insurance industry would consider the level of your "damages" minimal, perhaps even totally non-existent!*

Given that reality, it becomes most important, therefore, that you keep a detailed, comprehensive account of your bodily injuries — your own personal version of it. This way, you will, among other things, avoid the possibility of having some minute details that often become critically important forgotten, or some significant facts or aspects of the injuries completely overlooked, especially later down the road when the brunt of the pain and discomfort from the injuries may have been forgotten.

The Two Components Of Your Bodily Injuries

There are TWO basic components of the bodily injury issue, both of which your account should equally and adequately capture and reflect—

i) the actual physical harm and injuries you sustained; and

ii) the mental and emotional pain, discomfort and suffering that is caused you from and by those injuries.

Your report and account should, in a word, describe in detail and in your own words, the bodily injuries you have or feel you have (what anatomical parts or areas of your body you are unable to use or feel are broken, where and when and how you feel discomfort or pain in your body when you perform certain activities, to what degree of severity, etc.), as well as give details of the "intangible" dimensions of such injuries — the pain, suffering, inconvenience and/or mental anguish you experience from them.

1. THE RECORD / ACCOUNT OF THE "INJURIES" COMPONENT

Primarily, the most important account and description of the actual physical injuries you sustain will have to come from your doctor and your doctor's medical report and records. It is his reports and records (along with, perhaps, those of other medical experts, where applicable) that will primarily detail the physical bodily injuries you received, the treatments administered, and the probable future effects and consequences, etc. Nevertheless, you still should build and keep your own independent record of your injuries — to the extent you can develop one as a lay person.

On your own part, not being a doctor or a medical expert, your description or record of the bodily injuries will be somewhat limited in scope as that subject matter is apt to be viewed by claims negotiators and lawyers as a "technical" question, the exclusive province of a qualified medical "expert" or doctor requiring only an "expert opinion". You need not yourself be particularly too detailed or elaborate in your description or report of the injuries; look to the official medical records and your doctor's reports to provide that. You'll only need to keep a record of your own general impressions; your general feelings of harm and hurt, preferably on a daily, even minute-by-minute basis, starting as early as possible from the time of the accident.

Of perhaps greater importance in this connection, is the need for you to generally familiarize and educate yourself with, and be knowledgeable about, the types and nature of the injuries and disability you have, the nature of the medical treatments and care you received, and the basic medical terminology you'd need to have to be able to interpret your doctor's medical reports or to extract necessary information from your medical and hospital records. [See Sections IV & V of Chapter 4, pp. 54-7, and Chapter 6, pp. 69-92, as well as Appendices D, E, & F]. Just as importantly, with such familiarity, you'd also be in a position to "coach" your doctor on the kinds of descriptive language, words or terms you'd like him to use in his reports in his description of your condition [see Section V of Chapter 4].

AS A CLAIMANT, THE CRITICAL IMPORTANCE OF AMASSING EVERY POSSIBLE DOCUMENTATION, INFORMATION OR DESCRIPTION OF YOUR BODILY INJURIES (THEIR NATURE AND EXTENT, THEIR USUAL OR ACTUAL EFFECTS ON THE INJURED PARTY, ETC) CANNOT BE OVEREMPHASIZED. For now, suffice it to say, simply, that such information — the nature and extent of your proven injuries and the supporting documentations thereof — is the principal element which directly determines how much value is assigned to the "pain and suffering" component of your medical special damages claims.[2] Or, to put it another way, the degree of "pain and suffering" that gets assessed to you from your injuries, is directly a factor of the nature and degree of your bodily injuries.

> **NOTE:** Unfortunately, quite often doctors get so busy that they simply do not have the time to write a complete or elaborate report about the injuries sustained or found. As a way of getting around such a problem, we provide a MEDICAL REPORT FORM in the manual which covers many aspects of significance for claims purposes (see pp. 60-61). For your convenience, you could send this to your hospital and/or attending doctor to request your medical report or records.

2. THE RECORD / ACCOUNT OF THE "PAIN AND SUFFERING" COMPONENT

In attempting to build a record of the pain and suffering you claim, your method will be primarily to describe and depict in as much detail as possible the pain itself — its frequency, its location or locations in your body, and your emotional state as a result of it. You can describe activities in your daily life that have became painful for you, activities such as sitting in a chair, lying in bed or on your back, turning your neck, bending down, lifting an object, walking, taking a bath, climbing stairs, cooking, eating, having relations with your spouse, getting up at your normal times in the mornings, playing your usual game or sports, etc.

Use of Daily Diary to Compile your Record of Pain & Suffering

The rules are basic. Be brief, direct, and simple in the record (written, audio or visual) that you keep. Avoid employing medical or technical terms. State matters honestly, without falsification or over exaggeration. In deed, experts strongly recommend the *use of a daily "pain" diary* as the best mode of keeping one's pain-and-suffering record. The point of it all is to attempt to convey a mental and visual picture, as strong and vivid an image of the pain and suffering you experienced as possible to the claims adjuster (or the jury, if applicable) who reads, views, or hears the record.[3]

---

[2]As one expert put it, highlighting the crucial interconnection between the claimant's injuries and the value assessed to his pain and suffering, "The degree of pain and suffering undergone by the claimant and its reflection on the value of claim are approximated by considering the type of injury involved, the age and prior physical condition of the claimant, the response of the claimant to treatment, and the disability... Naturally, the severity of the injury is the basic factor involved in determining pain and suffering,...the nature of the injury [further] determines the amount of hospitalization, and the type of medical care needed, factors which reflect pain and suffering." Foutty, "The Evaluation and Settlement of Personal Injury Claims." 492 The Insurance Law Journal, 5 (1964) p.9.

---

[3]The use of a daily diary or a running program of detailed, comprehensive record-keeping system of the sort recommended in the manual, could be likened to the use of so-called "day-in-the-life of" videotapes in some contemporary court cases, as one method of evidentiary technique to establish the extent of a plaintiff's pain and suffering, the primary object being to visually show the various restrictions that are often imposed in injured plaintiffs, especially a seriously injured one's daily activities (See, for example, Strach v. St. John Hosp. Corp., 160 Mich. App. 251, 408 N.W. 2d 441 (1987), wherein a videotape was allowed to be shown in evidence in order to demonstrate plaintiff's difficulty in getting out of bed, grooming, and getting out of the house.)

By way of summarizing the process, here is how one expert summed up the manner of employing such a diary and the uses to which it can be put in depicting one's pain and suffering.[4]

> "In it [the diary], note — in as much details as you can and as soon as you can, while your memory is fresh—both the pain and your mental state, beginning with the date of your injury and continuing throughout the entire litigation. Jot down descriptions of the pain: "sharp," "dull," "arthritic," and so on. When symptoms begin to appear only sporadically, note the date and length of each recurrence and what you were doing when the pain appeared.
>
> Also include in your pain diary, adverse reactions to medication or to physical therapy. The medicine, for example, may have numbed the pain but caused you an upset stomach; the reaction is a form of pain and suffering for which you have a right to be compensated. Similarly, exercises you are required to undergo as therapy for your injury can often be as painful or more painful than the injury itself, and that pain too is compensable...
>
> Offer precise descriptions...*It is, for instance, much more effective to be able to say* "at least four times this past year the pain became so bad that I had to ask my husband to carry my purse for me," than to have to say, "sometimes I have difficulty holding on to things." Similarly when you can say, "The pain recurs most sharply during the early spring and late fall, when the weather is changing," you have given the jurors (or insurance adjuster) a meaningful fact, but haven't when you can only say, "the pain comes and goes." In describing the pain itself, try to use vivid terms: "The pain was like a continuous toothache" is much more likely to be remembered by the jurors (or the adjusters) when they are making your award than if you had said "the pain was awful." (Do not, incidentally, be tempted into giving descriptions of pains that haven't occurred; the defense has its medical experts who might be able to prove you couldn't have suffered the pain you claim.)
>
> In describing your pain...it is also a good idea to point to places on your body where the pain occurs. [Also], never overstate your case."

Another expert, also an advocate of the use of a daily diary, offers more or less similar advice on how to make a proper record or account of your bodily injuries:

> "Be honest. Don't exaggerate your injury. One of the keys to receiving a reasonable offer from the claims adjuster is your honesty and sincerity. Keep a diary on a daily basis of all physical and mental pain. When recounting your complaints and injuries, start with a description of your pain, as you remember it, at the scene of the occurrence.
>
> Next, move on day by day, describing everything that hurts. Begin with your head and go down through all parts of your body in detail. Explain any problems with each part of your body, such as shooting pain, throbbing pain, or loss of feeling. Include in your record all discomfort since the injury. Medications given at the hospital and afterwards for pain or nervousness should be noted.
>
> Next, relate your injuries, aches, pains, and discomforts to the way you live your life. Take a normal day from the time you rise and shine until the time you go to bed and explain in detail the ways in which the injury has affected or changed your life. For example, describe the changes in the way you put on your clothes, get in and out of bed, take a bath or shower, or move yourself around during the day (or note that you are unable to get around at all)."[5]

[More information related to compilation of bodily injury documentations are further outlined in parts IV & V of Chapter 4, at pp. 54-7, and should also be consulted.]

---

[4]Guinther, <u>Winning Your Personal Injury Suit</u>, pp. 139-140.
[5]Kaplan and Benjamin, <u>Settle It Yourself</u>, p. 19.

NOTE This point is of utmost importance and should be strictly noted by anyone filing claims: the actual and potential significance of a detailed and comprehensive personal account of the bodily injury, such as the kind anticipated by this Section, cannot be emphasized enough. If properly done and secured, such a report will prove a great resource to you throughout the entire claims process. Months, or years later, at settlement negotiations with the claims adjuster or at trial, a review of this record will bring back to your mind many otherwise forgotten or faded facts of the injury, especially the pain-and-suffering component. Thanks to the availability of such a record (or diary), upon its review at any time, your memory of events will be sharpened and you may discover patterns to the pain which you had previously been unaware of, thereby enabling you to offer precise and persuasive descriptions of the events.

D. Compile an Account/Record of Your Auto Body & Other Property Damages

We'll assume that you suffered a property damage as well in your accident—that your automobile (or other personal property items) sustained a damage in the course of the accident, for which you are making a claim. In that event, it is most essential that you take stock of your property loss or damage and prepare a complete and accurate description and account of the items damaged and their economic worth. "Take your time," advised one property insurance claims adjustment expert of over 40 years practical experience in the field. "Itemize, itemize, itemize! This cannot be stressed strongly enough."[6]

True, insurance adjusters generally use a number of published guide books as their primary basis in determining the "actual cash value" of a used car, and they may in the end probably use one of such guide books to determine the value in your present case.[7] Nevertheless, it is still important that you develop a credible itemized list of the property values in question, and the nature and extent of the damage. This is necessary because, generally speaking, the insurance companies are habitually skeptical of claims and values that are not "documented."

The rules for valuation of the damages are fairly straightforward. In general, where the repair costs for the vehicle are LESS than the vehicle's fair market value, (if your damaged vehicle is not completely wrecked and can still be repaired), your reimbursement for the damage in such a situation will be equal to what it will cost or has cost (the estimated or actual cost) to repair it. But where, on the other hand, your repair costs (estimated or actual) EXCEED the vehicle's fair market value, your reimbursement will be equal to only the fair market value of the vehicle at the time of the accident.

THE CENTRAL POINT OF IMPORTANCE HERE IS THIS: that you need to begin immediately, right **from the time of the accident,** to assemble the necessary data and documentations. The insurance company will require certain factual materials from you for the purpose of determining the likely condition of your vehicle before its loss or damage or destruction, and would require you to "document" what the appropriate reimbursement ought to be for the cost of the damaged vehicle's repairs or its market value. Relevant purchase receipts, credit records of any kind for recent improvements to the car (e.g., new paint job or body work), invoice, or cancelled checks, as well as repair estimates, service station receipts, towing service charges, and bills for repairs already made, receipts for loss of use (e.g., rentals of substitute vehicle), should be located and assembled.

Some Points Regarding Procedures For Filing Claims For Property Damages

If you are filing a claim against a party without an insurance coverage, should you do anything special about your

---

[6]Dumas, Claim Paid, pp. 49-50

[7]In recent times, there has appeared on the market a growing number of such guidebooks. They include: "The Used Car Book." (Harper Collins, $11) by Jack Gillis, and "The Consumer Reports Used Car Buying Guide (Consumer Reports Books, $8.95), both of which provide some general guidelines on used car prices. More specific price information updated frequently during the year, including average prices that a consumer can expect to pay or receive for a car produced in the last decade, and the value that specific optional equipment adds to used car, are produced by a guide published by Edmund Publications Corp. of Concord Mass. (800-253-1089) and one from Pace Publications Inc. of Milwaukee (800-272-0246). Cost of each is $4.95. Still another such used-car guidebook, published for the first time in 1992, is the one issued by The National Automobile Dealers Association, a trade group based in McLean, Virginia, cost $9.95. (800-248-6232).

One of the oldest guides used in the insurance industry is the "Kelley Blue Book," which lists all cars by year, make and model. If the car is less than 6 years old, it will be listed in the "Blue Book" with the "high value" (the average retail price) and the "low value" (the average wholesale price). By adding up any "extras" your car might have, and making deductions for excessive mileage you arrive at an appropriate "actual cash value" of your car.

damaged vehicle? In practice, the overwhelming number of vehicles are covered by collision insurance, which means basically two things: 1) that you have the right to make claims for the car (and other property) damage by filing the claim against your own company, providing you pay the "deductible," commonly just $50 or $100; and 2) that the sum at issue that really matters to you in the property damage claim (i.e. the only amount it will cost you) is the deduction amount. Your insurance company will have you sign a **"subrogation agreement"** allowing them to be reimbursed ("subrogated") upon your settling your claim with the other driver's insurance company.

Typically, you are required (or, at least, expected) to submit to the insurance company two or more estimates for the car damage, preferably from reputable auto body repair shops.

Finally, a word about the use of standard 'guides' often used by insurance adjusters to determine your car's **"actual cash value."** It's important to remember one relevant fact regarding this: the figures arrived at using these guides are merely a GUIDE. If the value being given from a "guide" seems too low to you in a specific instance, you may refuse to accept that; you may instead, suggest to the adjuster, for example, that the guidebook figure be averaged with the prices of indentical vehicles on a used car lot and any advertised price in the want ads. Listen to this advice from an eminent property insurance claims expert:

> "Always remember that these tables [from the guide] are merely guides. They are not set in concrete and there is no law that requires that you accept the values set forth in these tables.
>
> In an insurance settlement, depreciated values are reached by using common sense, negotiation, and mutual agreement. *You should never permit an adjuster to force you into accepting his value of an item "because that's what the book says."* What is important in obtaining an equitable settlement is to determine what it would cost you today to duplicate as nearly as possible the property lost or destroyed, taking into account the age and amount of use of the property. Because ascertaining value is a subjective exercise, with your opinion just as valid (perhaps more so since you owned the article) as that of the adjuster, this area affords the greatest opportunity to question any proposed settlement. Don't be afraid to bargain, dicker, or even argue with the claims representative about the value of an article. It is your money you are talking about."[8]

E. Take Photographs And/Or Otherwise Secure Them

1. Photos Could Often Play a Critical role

Chances are that you shall have probably heard of the old saying "a picture is worth a thousand words." You shall have probably heard of that saying even a thousand times! And, you better believe that that saying rings true! For, in the insurance compensation world, they religiously do. They view a good photograph of an accident or related matters as precisely the best evidence, the best proof a claimant could possibly have.

---

[8]Passage quoted from Dumas, Claim Paid, p. 53.

"I can't emphasize enough the importance of photographs for your file" said Daniel Baldyga, claims author and one of the nation's most knowledgeable insurance claimsmen, lending his considerable professional weight to the common thesis. Baldyga adds: "Photographs are one of the most potent and, in my judgement, the second most critical part of your file. (The first being the ability to dig up a favorable witness!)"[9]

To sum it up in a nutshell, details and documentations are of the utmost importance in insurance claims settlements. And vivid photographs (or videos) of the accident scene, or of the damaged vehicles or other property, or bodily injuries, are often the most graphic and convincing presentation of your story that you can make to the insurance company in claims negotiations. Hence, that's why IT'S SO VITAL; YOU MUST DILIGENTLY ENDEAVOR TO GET GOOD PHOTOGRAPHS (AND/OR VIDEOS) OF THE EVENT, IF AND WHEN IT IS AT ALL POSSIBLE.

2. HOW TO TAKE THE PHOTOGRAPHS

What do you do? If you happen to have a camera with you at the time of the accident, or if you can borrow one, take your own snapshots anyway. And/or, if at all possible, also have a professional photographer (you will find one in the yellow pages) came to the scene and take the photographs for you. Photographs should be taken of the scene of the accident, all the vehicles involved in the accident, or packed in the adjoining area, and of the injured persons and their injuries and the damaged vehicles.

Usually, at least two sets of photos are sufficient—one for you and one for the insurance claims people. (Always retain the negatives yourself just in case you should need more copies later or the originals get lost.) Baldyga, the claims expert, advises that the pictures of each scene or object be taken from at least three different views and angles: get a general view of the area or object from 20 to 40 feet away; then a "medium" shot from about 10 to 15 feet way, and a "close-up" shot from about 3 to 6 feet away. All three different photographs for each scene or object, he suggests, should have "one common point of orientation." If, for example, you are taking the photograph of a skid mark on a paired, concrete street surface, firstly, such photograph of the skid mark in such a situation should be taken from such an angle as to clearly show where the skid mark is in relation to some prominent and permanent landmark (e.g. in relation to a street sign, a building, a fire hydrant, and the like). And next, still on the skid mark, another photograph should then be taken of a closer view of the skid mark showing the skid mark in detail but also attempting to include this readily identifiable object or landmark (the street signs, building, etc.)

Baldyga gives this important WORD OF CAUTION: A person engaged in the task of taking the photograph of an accident scene or object should be careful and ensure that he is not undertaking it with a casual, hasty or careless attitude, and one that tends to leave it to the camera to do the thinking for him. Rather, the photographer ought to first apply some thoughtfulness to the process itself and take the undertaking very seriously. You should analyze the scene and thoughtfully determine how many photos will be required and from what angles, if the photos produced are to have the maximum usefulness for you.

You should take photos of the following, as applicable, each from different views and angles: of the accident scene; the intersection where the accident occurred; shots of the immediate surroundings, shots of relevant skid marks, traffic signs, etc as applicable. As much as possible, when you take the photographs have all involved cars (and people) in the

---

[9]Baldyga, How to Settle Your Own Insurance Claims, p. 34. Baldyga adds that a photograph is "by far the best witness you can have and…also the most perfect record" for the reason that it records every detail within the range of its vision.

final positions they were after the collision, since establishing the stopping place of the cars can often be important in determining the facts of the accident. Skid marks can be a valuable piece of evidence as well, since they can often indicate the speed of the car at the time of the accident and are therefore useful in establishing fault. Take note also of the impact marks on the roadway, dividers, and other vehicles.

If your accident causes any bodily injuries that are visible (such as burns, deep cuts, bruises, swellings, lacerations and dislocations), it is even more important that you have some photographs of such injuries taken immediately. Color photos (take them in close details from different angles) are particularly recommended for injuries, especially for graphic injuries, as they can often be quite dramatic and can add to the ultimate settlement value.

A good practice is always to make a brief notation on the backs of photos, entering thereon a brief account, what or who the photo is showing, the date it was taken and by whom.

3. SECURING NEWSPAPER PHOTOS OR REPORTS, IF ANY

One further but related guideline suggested by claims experts for potentially securing a relevant photograph (and other useful information) that might otherwise be available, is for you (the accident victim) to check through to see if there were possibly any newspaper accounts reporting on the accident. If there were any, it is suggested, you should clip out the relevant articles, or simply the headline or the mere mention of the accident, and save it. The area's local newspapers may also be checked for the possibility that they might have published a synopsis of the weather for the day of the accident. Upon clipping out such items, you should make a notation on them indicating the name of the newspaper, and the date and page of its publication, and file the material away as an important part of your records.

Furthermore, a photograph may be contained in any of the newspaper articles. If that is so, you should simply go down to the newspaper office (or make a telephone call to it) and make an order of an 8 x 10 glossy print of the photo from the article's reporter or photographer. It is even possible at times, upon making an inquiry, to find that a newspaper or television photographer has available a relevant photo that had been taken but wasn't used on the article, and which he could make available to you for a nominal charge.

NOTE: Aside from the obvious, conventional reasons for having a photograph, there are at least two other "by-products" noted by experts for which photographs can additionally be useful to you in your claims settlement undertaking. One by-product is the very real possibility that, upon your closely studying an available photo, you could very well spot a witness that nobody ever knew existed. (And with such a photo in hand, you could then canvass the area and, hopefully, search out the witness). Or, as another by-product, you might, for example, possibly be able to pick out from the photos the registration numbers of other vehicles packed in the accident area at the time but were not involved in the accident. And, again, from such piece of information, you can get the police or the motor vehicle department to give you the names and addresses of the parties to whom the registration number belongs, thereby once again yielding you the possibility of potentially locating a critical witness for your case!

F. Develop A Diagram Of The Accident Scene

Assuming you had a camera (or had an individual or a photographer who had one), and that you were able to take the needed photographs of everything necessary as outlined in Section E above, that would fairly much settle that important issue. But if you don't have a camera (and couldn't otherwise get the pictures), drawing a simple diagram of the scene and the events thereof can also be very useful, especially in cases where the police are late in coming or never came. In deed, even if photographs were taken alright, a diagram depicting the accident scene and location or the street intersection where the accident occurred, can still be very useful as it will better put the photograph in perspective. On the other hand, where the taking of photos has not been possible, the diagram can also be useful since the insurance adjuster can easily determine from it (the diagram) the sequence of movement of the vehicles prior to the incident.

In drawing the diagram, draw as complete a diagram of the accident scene as possible. Indicate all compass points for the accident, fully indicate the location of any traffic control signs, and give a full description of the surrounding area, and the weather and visibility conditions. Give the measurements and locations of all pertinent objects as best as you can determine them — the position of all vehicles before, during, and after impact, measurement of the street, and traffic lanes; distance from curb or shoulder, skid marks, distance from lights and intersections, positions of all skid marks and debris on the road or shoulders, and so on. And, equally important, don't forget to mark in the diagram the spot where the accident happened.

With respect to the skid marks, inspect the direction and length of such marks and mark them on the diagram. Also, note the impact marks on the roadway, dividers, and other vehicles.

Note that at times the police makes its own diagram as part of its police report. Many police reports, however, though expected to contain a detailed diagram of the accident, among other things, have been described as often being "sketchy at best."

NOTE: Adapt the WITNESS ACCIDENT SCENE DIAGRAM form on p. 32 as a sample for use in drawing up an accident location diagram.

G. Secure The Police Report On The Accident, If Any

A frequent advise to motorists involved in automobile accidents is: 'always call the police whether or not someone is hurt, but especially if someone has been hurt!' It's generally maintained by motorists and experts alike that, except of course, for very minor accidents, it's almost always a good idea to call the police when there's an accident, and that it's to the claimant's advantage to do so and to have a police report filed. In any event, in most states the police are required, by law, to be promptly notified whenever an accident occurs, especially when there's serious injury or the damages to the vehicle exceed some fixed amount, say $300.

In any case, whether the police are called to the accident scene by you or by someone else, or merely venture upon it on their own, by law the police must file a formal report upon being there. (The city or county police will usually have the jurisdiction in the given area of the accident's occurrence, unless the accident occurs on a state highway.)

a. What the Police Report Will Typically Show

The police, upon arriving at the scene of the accident, will question the persons involved and interview the witnesses with a view to making an official assessment of the contributing factors to the accident. Thereafter, after completing their investigations, the police writes up a POLICE REPORT and keeps it on file with the appropriate division of the police department.

Customarily, the report will show the names and addresses of the parties and witnesses to the accident (although they often omit listing the key witnesses); name of the insurance company; the weather and road conditions at the time of the accident; a diagram of the scene of the accident; and other pertinent details, such as some comments on their assessment of what caused the accident or who was at fault.

b. When/Where & How to Apply For the Report

About a week or so after the police takes down the report, the report will usually be available for issuance to the public at the police department and you can (and should) secure a copy of the report by requesting a copy and paying a nominal charge generally about $1 to $5 in most states. If the accident occurs in a state highway, you apply for the police report from the state's Highway Patrol's office, and if the accident occurs anywhere else, you should apply for the report from the city or county police or sheriff's police department that investigated your accident (Adapt REQUEST FOR POLICE REPORT Form on p. 49 to make such an application).

FORM 3-6

POLICE ACCIDENT REPORT REQUEST

My Name: _____

My Address: _____

_____

Phone # _____

Date: _____

To Police Dept. _____
Street _____
City/Town: _____
State _____ Zip _____

RE: <u>REQUEST FOR POLICE REPORT</u>

Dear Sir/Madam:

Please provide me with a photostatic copy of the police report for the accident described below. You'll find enclosed my check (or money order) for $_____ to cover the cost of the service.

Date & Time of the Accident: _____
Place (Street, City, State, etc): _____
My Name (Party involved in the Accident): _____
Year, Make, License Plate of my Vehicle: _____
Names of the other party (or parties) involved: _____

Thank you for your cooperation.

Yours truly,

Signed: _____

Generally speaking, you should first telephone the particular arm of the police investigating office you think investigated the accident. (If you had been at the scene when the police took the report, you would have had all of that information as to where and who exactly to call, since you would have, we presume, obtained their names, phone numbers, and other particulars when they interviewed you on that occasion!) Upon contacting the appropriate police department by phone, you will give the necessary identifying information to enable them trace your case (your name and address, the name and address of the driver or registered owner of the other vehicle, the location or area where the accident took place, and the date of same), and then request information as to whether the police report was available and on file in their records. Assuming that is the correct police department and that the report is available there, you should obtain from them the address to write to (or to go in person) for a copy of the report and the cost thereof. You may then adapt the REQUEST FOR POLICE REPORT sample form on p. 49 to make your application for a report.

> **NOTE:** Aside from the ordinary and obvious uses which you can make of the police report, there are other less than obvious but equally fruitful uses which you can make of the report. For example, upon obtaining a copy of your police report, you could scan it for a witness the police may have included therein. You could discover from the report that the police have taken some useful photographs and that they are willing to sell you the reprints. And you may find from it, especially in severe accidents involving, say, alcoholism, that there is in existence some special police reports or highly detailed diagrams on the accident. You can inquire with the investigating officers who prepared the report (you simply phone the names listed on the bottom of the reports) as to whether there was any professional photographers they may have seen or observed at the scene and his identity thereof, thereby yielding you yet another source for potentially helpful photographs or witnesses!

H. Secure the Weather Reports, if Relevant

If the weather or the weather conditions shall have played a significant part in the accident, you may be well advised to obtain a weather report, and the successful handling of a claims case may often depend on the revelations of such a report. For one thing, such weather conditions at the time of the accident may render the actual physical facts subject to change, thereby revealing or confirming the other party's negligence. Let's say, for example, that the facts show that on the day and at the time of the accident it was snowing, or sleeting or raining and that the other driver was driving within the speed limit quite alright, but that he was going too fast for the snowy or rainy conditions. Then that will constitute a significant piece of information in your favor pointing to the other driver's negligence, or that in any event he is the one seemingly "at fault."

You may obtain from the United States Weather Bureau a weather report for the day of the accident published for your particular locality by that agency. The local station of the bureau in your area will furnish you such a report for a nominal charge.

The report generally contains information covering conditions of cloudiness or sunshine, precipitation (rain or snow conditions), wind velocity, the temperatures at various hours of the day, as well as the average temperature for each day, and other important details.

I. Secure Information on Uninsured Motorist, If Applicable

Suppose the other motorist involved in the accident has no (liability) insurance, what do you do? For one thing, don't give up. There are still a number of helpful things you may do—like gathering some basic information.

The general rule in most states is that whenever the other motorist is either uninsured or a hit-and-run driver who you cannot identify, you may make your claims (whether for damages or for personal injury) with your own insurance company. The rule applies, whether you're in a fault or a no-fault state. This is achieved in some states by requiring that your own insurance company include an "uninsured motorist" clause in your policy. In other states, however, where there is no such requirement, you will still be able to get the same benefit if you happen to carry a type of insurance coverage called the Uninsured-Motorist or Underinsured Motorist policy. Basically, uninsured motorist insurance coverage will pay (reimburse) you for any bodily injury and medical expenses—but not for any **property** damages that you or anyone in your vehicle may sustain from accidents caused by a drive who has no insurance, a hit-and-run driver, or a driver of a stolen car. In deed, in general, you're entitled to claim everything (except property damage) that you could if the other motorist had insurance——time lost from work, medical expenses, pain and suffering, disfigurement, etc. In other words, in this instance, you get reimbursed by **your own** insurance company, rather than looking to the other motorist's policy to do so!

An important question of relevance, though, is: how do you make a claim for such uninsured motorist benefits? The practices and particular details may differ in terms of particular insurance companies, but, generally, your insurance company would want to have some sort of proof or verification that the other motorist does not, in fact, have an insurance coverage (i.e., that he was, in deed, an uninsured motorist) as of the date of the accident. While some companies may on their own make their own verification to satisfy themselves of this information, others may ask that you obtain such proof yourself and file it with your insurance company.

If your insurance company (or its adjuster) should put the burden of having to obtain proof of the other motorist's non-insurance upon you, here's what you do. Simply send the STATEMENT OF UNINSURED MOTORIST (sample is below) to the uninsured motorist in question (presumably you should have obtained his or her identity and other particulars from all the background work you shall have done from the preceding passages in this chapter.) Request him or her to sign and return this statement to you as promptly as possible. The sample cover letter on p. 31 could be properly adapted and used to make your request. Always enclose a stamped, self-addressed return envelope for the convenience of the other party. [See, also, the SAMPLE LETTER OF INQUIRY on p. 24; you can use this letter to request insurance information on a motorist from the State Insurance Commissioner].

FORM 3-7

STATEMENT OF NON-INSURANCE BY UNINSURED MOTORIST

STATEMENT

I, the undersigned party, do herewith certify that on the date and at the place given below, I was involved in an automobile accident or collision with Mr/Mrs ——————————————— , who was driving a vehicle whose make, year, color, and license plate number were as follows _____

_____

I further certify that at the time of this accident I did not have public liability insurance on the vehicle I was driving, nor did I have public liability insurance on any other vehicle.

(Uninsured Motorist's)
MY Full Name: _____ Date of Birth: _____

My Home Address: _____ Phone # _____

Work Address _____ Phone # _____

Date of Accident: _____ Time: _____

Place of Accident: _____

Make of My Vehicle: _____ Year: _____ License Plate No.: _____

My Driver's License No.: _____ State of Issuance: _____

Signed: _____

Date: _____

CHAPTER 4

GATHERING DOCUMENTATIONS FOR CLAIMING YOUR MONEY DAMAGES

I. The Two Main Categories of Damages

In automobile accident liability claims actions, the types of bodily harms and losses ("damages") for which the accident victim is monetarily compensated are grouped into two broad categories: *"special damages"* and *"general damages"* (also called *"compensatory* damages"). [It's worth noting, for now, that in general, while virtually every claimant is almost automatically entitled to an award of some sort of *special damages* in every case, whether at all a given claimant gets *general damages*, on the other hand, and in what amounts, are wholly dependent on the facts and circumstances of each case]

A. Special Damages

Special damages ("specials," as lawyers and claimsmen often call them) refer to those items which, by legal practice and precedent, are required to be documented (i.e., "specially" proved) before you can collect compensation for them. **They include items like:**

- The value of time and earnings you lost from work (lost wages)
- Medical and hospitalization expenses you incur as a result of the injuries caused you
- All miscellaneous out-of-pocket expenses you incur as a result of the injuries you sustained. (Expenses for housekeeping and household help during disability, medication, rental cost of substitute car, ambulance service and nursing care expenses, emergency room care expenses, cost of help needed in your business for the self-employed who is unable to work, cost of trips to the doctor or hospital, cost of wheelchair or crutches and braces, etc...)
- Value of damaged or lost property or cost of repairs or replacing them.

NOTE: Use the CHECKLIST on pp. 63-8 to compile the actual dollar figures for your special damages (as well as other damages).

B. General Damages

General damages are apparently "general," as the term would seem to imply, in the sense that by their nature they can't be precisely documented in dollar terms: there is no mathematical system by which a price tag or an exact dollar amount can be placed on one's "pain and suffering" from an injury, for example.

They include items like:

- The pain and suffering (discomfort) caused you by injuries from the accident and any accompanying mental anguish (fear & worry)
- Disfigurement from the injuries (if any)
- Value of medical expenses you are likely to incur in the future
- Value of wages and time you are likely to lose in the future
- Aggravation of pre-existing injury or ailment (if any)

> • Disability from the injuries, (if any)
> • Impairment of your future earnings.

NOTE: Use the CHECKLIST or pp. 63-8 to compile the actual dollar figures for your general damages (as well as other damages).

II. How Critical it is to Compile Documentation for Your Money Damages

It is not enough simply to make a claim maintaining that you supposedly incurred losses or damages for which you ought to be compensated. The far more important part—indeed, the critical part—is what the claims industry people commonly call the "documentation" of the claim. In a word, whatever your claims or contentions as to the nature and size of your damages, you had better be fully ready with the necessary documentary proofs and verifications sufficient to support those claims; you had better assembled adequate and proper supporting documentations to establish each item of loss, costs and expenses being claimed—verified bills and receipts, medical reports and hospital records, time-and-earnings-lost verification letter from employer, auto repair estimates from auto appraisers, doctor's report of his findings, treatment, diagnosis and prognosis etc. *In deed, as stressed elsewhere in his manual (see, for example, pp. 18 & 25), the critical importance of documentations in claims adjustment management can hardly be stressed enough. IT IS NOT JUST __EVERYTHING__.; IT'S JUST ABOUT __THE ONLY THING__ in claims settlement matters!*

III. Documentation to Get For Time Lost From Employment or Business

For any time and earnings you might have lost from your job, business, or trade, here are the documentations and verifications to get. Have your employer complete for you a TIME LOST VERIFICATION form (see samples on p. 58, along with a letter of request with which to ask for it on the same page). Or, if on the other hand you are self-employed or own your own business, then you should complete the TIME LOST AFFIDAVIT OF SELF-EMPLOYMENT. (see sample on pp. 59). Under the law in most states, you're still entitled to compensation for lost time and earnings even if you have no actual loss of money, as, for example, when your salary is paid by your own insurance or by taking sick leave or a like arrangement.

If **self-employed**, you may include also as part of the value of time you lost, the cost of additional help you hire while you are undergoing medical treatment or recuperating. Attaching copies of your prior year's federal (and state) income tax returns for yourself, or for your business, may be helpful to the claims adjuster for "verification" of your figures. And, if necessary and available, copies of your Social Security tax payments, and of the unemployment tax, may also be attached.

If the type of job you are engaged in is such that commissions, tips or even overtime income constitute a substantial part of your earnings, have your employer include that fact in his letter of employment for you, spelling out exactly the earnings you normally make (or made the previous year) for the number of days in question in comparative seasons.

Finally, it is very important to recognize that if you are a full-time **housewife** — that is, a housewife with no other occupation and no employment outside the home—you, too, may be entitled to monetary compensation for lost earning capacity. You can do this by verifying from your local labor department office, just what the fair market value (the current hourly wage rate, for example) of a non-live-in full-time domestic servant is in your own particular region, or the minimum national wage rate currently in effect. (As additional documentation, it's strictly advisable to keep a running daily diary detailing how many hours during each day of your medical disability, and for how long, you were confined to bed or in the hospital or were otherwise unable to physically function, in part or in full.)

For any wages and time you are likely to lose in the future (let's say your doctor predicts future surgeries or other continuing future medical treatment or conditions from the injuries you sustained), in such a situation you need to further obtain from your treating doctor a medical report, or letter specifically detailing, among other things, his medical opinion of the prognosis for you — i.e., his opinion of what the future holds for you in terms of your expected medical or health condition. In a situation such as this, particularly, the **"prognosis"** part of such a report — the part dealing with the doctor's prediction about your future condition and the future disability and pain you are likely to suffer — is one of the most important parts of the report by your doctor. A doctor's report which states, for example, that you'll keep having some pain, difficulties or discomfort for a few more weeks or an indeterminate period of time in the future, or that your condition remains "guarded", will be better for you for purposes of your claims, than if the report were to simply say there's "no permanent disability"!

NOTE: You should not request this report (a medical report) until <u>AFTER</u> you've been discharged by the doctor.

IV. Documentations To Get For Medical and Hospitalization Expenses

This documentation, it should be noted, should be obtained only <u>afterwards</u>—after the treatment and hospitalization, if applicable, has ended.

For medical and hospitalization expenses that you shall have either actually incurred or are likely to occur in the future, request from each of the doctors who treated you for your injuries two basic documents—medical reports of your treatment and condition, and itemized bills of your treatment. As a rule, you will usually have to give them or the record department of the institution a <u>written</u> authorization (see sample letter, AUTHORIZATION TO RELEASE MEDICAL RECORDS/REPORT, on first part of p. 60) before they may release the medical reports to you or to others.

The Doctor's Report

The medical reports part of one's records are extremely important as a necessary proof in establishing one's injuries and its extent, and the associated expenditures thereof. As with most such documents, it is most essential that the report expressly and specifically outline the following: the doctor's findings regarding the diagnosis (i.e., details or analysis of the type and nature) of the injuries, the treatments given, and the prognosis (his prescription on the future disability or pain, therefrom, if any). The diagnosis part of the medical report is probably the most important aspect of the report, though the prognosis has also been assigned high significance by some expert. As one expert account summed it up, *"The final and most crucial part of a medical report is the diagnosis. This is the single most important factor in determining a settlement figure...The diagnosis portion of a medical report may be only one line, but it is the most important line."*[1]

If your doctor's report indicates, or your doctor thinks, that you will be getting additional or continuing medical treatment or hospital care in the future (i.e., meaning that you are likely to incur further medical expenses in the future), then have your doctor give you a statement (or add that information to the medical report he gives you) **expressly** stating the necessity of such future medical care, a detailed description of the nature of the planned or anticipated future medical

---

[1]Saadi, <u>Claim it Yourself</u> p. 37.

procedures (e.g., plastic surgeries, physical therapy), and indicate whether or not it will require hospital care or outpatient care, the estimated costs of such service, and the duration or recuperation period.

> <u>NOTE:</u> Make sure you request these records only AFTER you shall have been discharged by your doctor. Secondly and just as important, here's an important caution you should keep in mind: NEVER SIGN ANY AUTHORIZATION FOR THE DOCTOR TO RELEASE YOUR MEDICAL RECORDS TO THE ADJUSTER (OR ANYBODY ELSE). The best practice is for you to send for the records and have them come to you first, before you may then forward a copy to the adjuster. *First preview the doctor's report yourself.* This way, you'll have the opportunity of first examining the records and your doctor's report and getting them corrected or revised by the doctor, if there appears to be a legitimate need for such, before giving them to the adjuster.

V. Documentations To Get For Pain and Suffering, Disfigurement, Disability, or Aggravation of Pre-existing Condition.

Your Doctor's Report is Probably the Single Most Important Document

The contents of your doctor's report, especially what it shows or says about how serious, permanent, disabling, or aggravating your injuries are, or are likely to become, and/or what it shows about the nature and scope of the medical treatments you received or are projected to receive, are easily the single most powerful piece of documentation you can get in substantiation of a claim of some serious pain and suffering, disfigurement, disability, and the like. [Note: further see pp. 41-44 for more on the documentation and verification of bodily injuries and pain and suffering].

Let's say, for example, that you claim—and your medical records or doctor's report support the assertion—that you sustained a fractured finger (which, certainly, could be considered a "disfigurement"). That, certainly, constitutes a credible indication that you might have endured some degree of "pain and suffering." That means that your claim should justify a higher settlement than, say, simply a pulled muscle injury. Likewise, medically substantiated injuries of more permanent type, such as scarring (a scar resulting from the accident or surgery hereto), the loss of the use of an arm or hand, or skin discolored form a burn, presume more "pain and suffering" than, say, a quick-at-healing type of injury like, say, cuts, bruises and sprains.

HERE'S THE CENTRAL POINT: If we are to sum it all up in one word, the one common but central denominator (the "bottom line," if you like) that underlies the documentation of anything relating to a claimant's bodily injuries, or the "pain and suffering" relating to that, should not be mistakable: *the doctor's report, and the details, language and scope of coverage thereof, is the most fundamental piece of "documentation" with the greatest weight and credibility that you can provide.* And, it should also be added, a report produced by a respected specialist in the field or one having good professional reputation for integrity and competence, will command more weight and credibility with the insurance company adjusters than one from a doctor or an institution of lesser or dubious professional reputation. The expressed LANGUAGE of your doctor's report — what it says about your injuries or medical condition and how serious and disabling it is portrayed to be — will pretty much determine its value as a claims evaluation tool in the eyes of the claims adjuster. The more expressive and elaborate or detailed the report, the more meaningful and helpful it will be for your purposes.

You Have A Right to Ask Your Doctor To Amend or Correct the Report, if Necessary

The implication of the above paragraph? It's a very important one. *What it means is this: that you, the claimant, have a special obligation to yourself to take the initiative on the matter, if and when it should seem necessary for you to do so, and that you have an obligation to take an aggressive, rather than simply a passive role in the area of the development of your medical documentations.* You can, for example, talk to your doctor about the contents of the report he gives you, if need be. First of all, you should always make sure, anyway, that what the doctor tells you verbally, or the general impressions he gives you, about your medical condition or the status of your injuries or future prospects, are exactly and actually what is stated in the written report he gives you. And, if you should find that the report omits what the doctor had verbally said to you or led you to believe, or that it states them less strongly, you should immediately speak up. It's perfectly within your legal right, by the way, for you to do so!

Let's say, for example, that your doctor tells you during an examination that you will have some pain or discomfort for a few months, and that you will have to "learn to live with it." However, when you get the written report, you find no mention of this, but find, instead, just a rather optimistic conclusion: "there's no permanent disability." In this instance, what you should do is to immediately call or visit the doctor and remind him (tactfully) of what he had told you privately in his office or clinic. Ask him to revise his report and to include the statement of future pain and his opinion that you'll learn to live with it. (This one revised sentence alone, if added to this report, will considerably raise the value of your settlement!)

Or, let's say that the doctor told you that your lower back condition will be permanent or recurring and will require surgery and more time away from work; or, say the doctor told you that your injury will produce some kind of "permanent" scarring (a disfigurement), even if minor. If so, your doctor's written report must include mention of these facts or statements, and should be as expressive and detailed as possible. And, if the doctor's report does not, you should be certain to get after your doctor immediately to have him make the necessary corrections and additions.

Potential Areas Where Your Medical Report May Need To Be Amended

True, ordinarily much of your doctor's report will perhaps primarily focus on the purely "medical" aspects of your case — the physical injuries you received, the treatment administered, the probable future consequences to you, and the like. It would often not expressly say too much on what could be called the "pain-and-suffering" dimension of your injuries. Hence, this may be one area concerning which you can take an active part in convincing your doctor to include in his report some appropriately expressive and elaborate statements. Your doctor, for example, will be perfectly within permissible and legitimate professional bounds to express his "expert opinion" **in your report** about the nature and frequency of the pain that an injury such as yours will likely cause. Or, to give a description of the pain symptoms you described to him in the course of your medical treatment. Or, to give a description of any pain-killing medications you were given, their purpose, any adverse reaction you had to them, and the time periods over which you took them.

Disfigurement, Disability, Etc.

Another point of relevance to the topic at hand. It's perhaps of more relevance to cases where claims of "disfigurement" or "disability" are made. Here's the point: in cases particularly involving "disfigurement" and disability claims, because of lack of precise formula by which to measure such "damages", coupled with the extreme difficulty in being able to do so, quite often other extraneous factors assume a great deal of weight in the determination of the value of such damages — factors such as the personality or the occupation or social status of the injured claimant, the type of people he meets or deals with in his professional life, or the degree to which the injury seems to interfere with the way the given claimant earns his living, or even what part of the body a particular claimant sustains his injury relative to another claimant.

For example, a one inch scar on the top of the claimant's foot would not count for as much "disfigurement" as, say, a scar on his face; and if you were to be, say, a professional modeler of shoes, the same one inch scar on the foot would count for (and be worth) considerably more "disfigurement." Likewise, a fractured hand by a housewife with minor children and a husband to care for would count for more "disability" than the same fracture on the hand of, say, a fifth grade student; and if the housewife or the fifth grader were to be, say, a professional piano player for whom a fractured hand would be considered an interference with her ability to earn her living, the very same injury would count for (and be worth) considerably more "disability"! A cut on the head which would leave some scar may be worth nothing (or relatively little) to a truck driver, for example, but worth a good deal more if he's a salesman who has to meet the public to make his living, or a woman who runs a beauty and charm school.

NOTE: Use the CHECKLIST on pp. 63-68 for compilation of the actual dollar figures for your special and general damages.

Refer to the following passages in the manual for more detailed information on the subject matter of the chapter: Chapter 6 "Your Bodily Injury: A Crash Course in the Common Medical Conditions Encountered in Auto Accident Claims Cases", pp. 69-92; and Section O therein, titled "Medical Disability, the Definition & Types," pp. 91-92, and Appendices D, E and F, respectively, are intended to aid you in the reading, comprehension and interpretation of your doctor's and other medical reports.

FORM 4-1
TIME LOST FROM WORK VERIFICATION

Date: _____

To: _____
    Employer

Address _____

RE: Employee: _____
    Address: _____
    Social Security #: _____

Gentlemen/Ladies:

    I'm making a claim pertaining to my accident which occurred on _____ 19 ___ and my absence from work as a result of that. Would you please complete the attached TIME LOST VERIFICATION form set forth below, and return it directly to me in the enclosed self-addressed stamped envelope.

    Thank you very much.

                    Yours truly,

                    Signed: _____

- -

TIME LOST VERIFICATION

Name of Employer _____

Address _____ Phone # _____

Name of Employee _____

Address _____

Date Employed _____ Present Title _____

Employee was absent from work
(regardless whether or not employee was paid)   FROM _____ TO _____ inclusive
                                          Date

Average Wage/Salary $ _____ Per _____

Bonus, Commissions or overtime lost, if any $ _____

Employee Regular Duties _____

Comments _____

_____

                    Signed _____

                    Title _____

                    Date Signed _____

FORM 4-2
Time Lost Affidavit of Self-Employment

STATE OF ————)
)   SS

COUNTY ————)

AFFIDAVIT OF SELF-EMPLOYMENT

I, MR/MRS. _____, being first duly sworn, depose and state as follows under oath:

1.   That I reside at: _____

_____;

2.   That on _____ I was involved in an accident which occurred at this location: _____;

3.   That as a result of the said accident, I was unable to work from

_____ to _____;

4.   That at the time of the accident, I was self employed as _____,

under the business name of _____

located at _____

and my earnings per week were $ _____

5.   That for the reason that I was unable to work, I lost income for the said period of unemployment and disability of $_____.

_____
Signature

DATE: _____

Subscribed and sworn to
before me this_____ day
of ————— , 19 — .

_____
Notary Public

Medical Report Form

_____
Date

Authorization To Release

Dear Doctor,

     Please furnish me directly, on the form set forth below, a report regarding my medical condition. Pursuant to that, I hereby authorize you to furnish me, and none others, with the said medical report and records; I enclose a check for $_____ to cover your fee for this report.

Signed: _____

My Full Name/Address: _____

— —

Note: Physician detach form from this point before sending it out.

— —

MEDICAL REPORT

Patient's Name _____

Address: _____ **Date of Birth:** _____

History of Condition

Date & Nature of Accident _____ Complaints and History as Described by Patient _____

_____

Give a description of the pain symptoms and inconvenience (its nature and frequencies, disabilities, etc), complained about by patient in the course of your medical treatments.

Date of first treatment: _____ Date of last treatment: _____

X-ray (and/or other diagnostic & Laboratory tests)

Date taken _____ Where taken _____ Findings _____

Diagnosis (please describe and locate character, nature and extent of injury, physical findings, including all rating factors & laboratory reports, etc).

_____

_____

Patient's subjective symptoms _____

_____

Objective Findings on patient: _____

_____

(Continued next page)

𝔐𝔢𝔡𝔦𝔠𝔞𝔩 𝔑𝔢𝔭𝔬𝔯𝔱 𝔉𝔬𝔯𝔪 (𝔠𝔬𝔫𝔱.)

Contributing Factors

In your opinion is disability solely as a result of above described accident? —————— If answer is "no' then please explain ——

——

In your medical opinion are there any pre-existing conditions or factors which were aggravated by the patient's injuries? —————————————————— If so, please explain in full: ——————————————————

Treatment

What treatments were administered, why, and for what durations? ————————————————

——

What medications were prescribed & in what amounts and for how long? ————————————

What symptoms or medical problems are such medications meant to relieve? ——————————

——

Any adverse reactions shown by patient? (Describe them)————————————————————

——

In your expert medical opinion, what is the nature, extent and frequency of the pain that an injury such as the patient's will likely cause? —————————————————————————————————————

——

——

Prognosis (including information on patient's progress, part played by pre-existing condition, if any, future temporary total and permanent disability, residual impairments, etc) ————————————————

——

——

——

Total Disability

Weeks ————————————— **Days** ————————— **Ended** ————————————

Partial Disability

Weeks ————————————— Days ————————— Ended ————————————

Recommended or anticipated future or further treatment ———————————————————

What is your opinion regarding the present or future temporary total and permanent disability of patient?

——

——

Signed: ————————————————————
(Doctor's Signature)

Full name of Doctor: ——————————————————

Official Address: ——————————————————

City or town ——————————— State ———— Zip ————

Date Signed: ——————————————————

Page 2 of 2

CHAPTER 5
THE CHECKLIST FOR USE IN COMPILING YOUR MONEY DAMAGES

The following Damages Checklist form contains detailed listing of each individual "damage" component and related factors that often go into calculating what to ask for in a damage claims case. Each major damage category is broken down into individual items. The total of these individual damage components may then be recorded in the appropriate boxes provided at the end of each category. The sum of damages, when totalled for each major category, yields the total damage amount for **SPECIAL** as well as **GENERAL** damages.

If properly filled out (and updated, if and as necessary), the checklist should provide a rather thorough summary of your damages to aid you in compiling your damages data and in your settlement negotiations.

Note, however, that not all damage categories or components may apply to your particular case, as this checklist is purposefully designed to be somewhat all-inclusive. Hence, be careful to just pick out the individual damage components and items that are properly applicable to your given case and situation.

| Pointer: | By and large the following segments of this CHECKLIST would be more applicable and relevant and should suffice, for the needs of the average users of this manual:

Sections I, II, and III. Sections IV may frequently apply, but only as a by-product of the preceding Sections and the overall case evaluation determination.

FORM 5

PERSONAL INJURY DAMAGES CHECKLIST

I. MEDICAL AND RELATED EXPENSES

A. PAST MEDICAL EXPENSES (ALREADY INCURRED)[1]

1. Physician, Hospital, and Related Medical Expenses

Description	Charge/Cost
Names of Physicians & Surgeons (Services rendered)	

Hospital Charges (Specify names of hospitals & for what services)

Diagnostic Tests
X-rays/CT Scan

Laboratory Services: (Urinalysis, blood test, serological tests, EKG, EEG, Ultrasound, etc. specify)

Ambulance Services/Emergency Room Care Svcs:

Description	Charge/Cost
Prescription Medications:[2]	

Dentists (Names/Services Rendered)

Chiropractors (Names/Services rendered):

Medical Consultants (Names/Services rendered):

Ambulance Services/Emergency Room Care Svcs:

Other Past Medical Expenses:

2. Past (Post-Injury) Rehabilitative Care

Physical Therapy(Name of therapist & for what services) [3]

---

[1]In completing this form, enter all costs even if an item had been or will be paid for by your insurance company.

[2]Note that the size of this item (i.e., the amounts expended on various prescription medications actually used in the treatment of the claimant's injury), even if monetarily insignificant when compared with other items of the claimant's medical expenses, nevertheless may sometimes be used as a basis to seek other damages, such as those for pain and suffering. See, for example, Hinnen v. Barnett [144 Ill. App. 3d 1038, 495 N.E. 2d 141, 147 (1986)], where the Court reversed a special jury verdict that had awarded no damages for the plaintiff's pain and suffering despite an award of $2,500 for past medical expenses which included expenses for pain medications and physical therapy

[3]May include in this category, especially with certain types of injuries, such as those involving serious disability, physical therapy for scarring, or for disfigurement, or various types of psychiatric treatment.

Description	Charge/Cost		Description	Charge/Cost

Prosthetic Devices & Related Equipment:[4]

_____

_____

_____

_____

Other Rehabilitative Expenses:

_____

_____

_____

3. Expenses Related to Medical Care[5]

Private Nursing Care (where received, for what service)

_____

_____

_____

Travel Expenses:

_____

_____

_____

_____

Lodging Expenses:

_____

_____

_____

_____

Telephone Expenses:

_____

_____

_____

Baby Sitting Expenses:

_____

_____

_____

Rental Equipment:

_____

_____

_____

Specially Equipped Vehicles:

_____

_____

Other Expenses Related to Past Medical Care:

_____

_____

_____

_____

TOTAL PAST MEDICAL EXPENSES:
(Subtotal) $ _____

B. FUTURE MEDICAL EXPENSES[6]

1. Physician, Hospital, and Related Medical Expenses

Description	Estimated Charge/Cost

Physicians & Surgeons (Names/Services to the rendered):

_____

_____

_____

Future Hospitalization (for what services & expected duration):

_____

_____

Future Diagnostic Tests & Medical Treatments:
X-rays/CT Scan: _____

_____

_____

---

[4]Includes items like: prosthetic arms or leg, hearing aid, braces, crutches, wheelchairs, and orthopedic devices used by injured party.

[5]This category of damages includes a variety of other expenses which, although not truly medical, are related to injured party's medical treatment. For example: costs for private nursing care, personal attendants (e.g. cost of hiring a driver to assist in transporting a disabled person), travel to seek medical care or rehabilitative treatments, telephone and lodging expenses incurred for arranging medical treatment, rental vehicles, baby-sitting expenses; and the cost of, say, specially equipped vehicle to provide for transportation need [e.g., specially equipped hydraulic lift van], a wheelchair. commode chair, weight and exercise equipment, in the case of severe disability.

[6]Note: the items under this subdivision ("Future Medical Expenses") are especially significant or mostly applicable usually in cases involving serious permanent injury or disability requiring long-term medical attention or care of the claimant in the future, and may not generally or necessarily be applicable to routine, ordinary auto accident case with which this book is primarily concerned. If not applicable, skip this subdivision and go onto the next one. As with the "Past Medical Expenses" category covered in subdivision A of this form, the principal components of this category includes the estimated costs for doctors and physicians, future surgeries, (including operations, costs of hospitalization, and anesthesiologists' fees), hospitalization, treatments, medications, medical supplies, and special equipment (wheelchairs, hydraulic lifts for bathtub and bed, leg braces, alternating pressure mattresses, special orthopedic stockings and sheets, etc.), future dental treatments and physical or psychiatric therapy, future nursing and home attendant care, etc.

Description	Estimated Charge/Cost

Laboratory Services: (Urinalysis, blood test, serological tests, EKG, EEG, Ultrasound, etc. specify)

———————————————— ————————
———————————————— ————————
———————————————— ————————
———————————————— ————————

Medical Treatments: ————————

———————————————— ————————
———————————————— ————————
———————————————— ————————

Future Prescription Medications:

———————————————— ————————
———————————————— ————————
———————————————— ————————
———————————————— ————————

Future Medical Supplies & Equipment:

———————————————— ————————
———————————————— ————————
———————————————— ————————
———————————————— ————————

Future Medical Consultants & Specialists:

———————————————— ————————
———————————————— ————————
———————————————— ————————

Other Future Medical Expenses:

———————————————— ————————
———————————————— ————————
———————————————— ————————
———————————————— ————————

2. Future Rehabilitative Care[7]

Future Physical Therapy:

———————————————— ————————
———————————————— ————————
———————————————— ————————

Future Prosthetic Devices & Related Equipment:

———————————————— ————————
———————————————— ————————
———————————————— ————————

Future Psychological & Psychiatric Treatment:

———————————————— ————————
———————————————— ————————
———————————————— ————————
———————————————— ————————

Description	Estimated Charge/Cost

Other Future Rehabilitative Expenses:

———————————————— ————————
———————————————— ————————
———————————————— ————————

Total Future Medical Expenses (Subtotal) — $ [   ]

Section I: Total Past Medical Expenses & Total Future Medical Expenses = $ [   ]

II. LOST EARNINGS

A. LOST PAST EARNINGS AND WAGES

1. Lost Past Earnings Due to Total (Temporary) Disability[8]

Description	Amount

Lost Past Wages & Earnings:

———————————————— ————————
———————————————— ————————
———————————————— ————————

Lost Vacation Time or Sick Leave:[9]

———————————————— ————————
———————————————— ————————
———————————————— ————————

Other Lost Earnings from, say, deprived opportunity for advancement or promotion from the injury, foregone bonuses, etc.

———————————————— ————————
———————————————— ————————

2. Lost Past Earnings Due to Partial(Temporary) Disability[10]

Lost Past Wages & Earnings: ————————

———————————————— ————————
———————————————— ————————

Other Lost Earnings: ————————

———————————————— ————————
———————————————— ————————
———————————————— ————————

TOTAL LOST PAST EARNINGS AND WAGES (Subtotal) = $ ————————

---

[7]This category (Future Rehabilitative Care), typically include: costs of physical therapy, special equipment, a variety of psychological and psychiatric treatments and therapy, the costs of periodic future monitoring of further medical complications arising from the principal injury; cost of future psychological treatments necessitated by the plaintiff's actual fear and anxiety over the increased possibility of later developing some medical complication or condition.

[8]The period of TOTAL TEMPORARY DISABILITY is that period in which, immediately following an injury, the victim typically is rendered completely incapable of performing any gainful employment whatsoever resulting in at least a temporary period during which there had been a total loss of earnings. This type of disability contemplates that the injured person, at some future time, will be able to regain at least a portion of his former physical earning capacity.

[9]This item (the value of Lost Vacation Time or Sick Leave) will apply in a situation where the victim continues to receive a paycheck during the period of total employment disability but is forced to lose accumulated vacation time or sick leave.

[10]Refers to later, following that initial period immediately following an injury in which there is a temporary total disability and total loss of earnings, when the victim's condition improves, and he (she) is able to return to work but only at a reduced level of performance and a corresponding reduction in his level of earnings and total compensation. This is the period of Partial (Temporary) Disability, a term used to convey the fact that the victim, although injured, is not totally disabled and, further, that even this partial disability is not necessarily expected to remain a permanent condition.

B. LOST FUTURE EARNING CAPACITY[11]

Source	No. Years

1. Life Expectancy

Natural Life Expectancy:[12]

_____   _____

_____   _____

_____   _____

Work Life Expectancy:[13]

_____   _____

_____   _____

_____   _____

_____   _____

2. Lost Future Income

Description	Amount

Lost Future Earnings:[14]

_____   _____

_____   _____

_____   _____

Lost Future Employment Benefits:

_____   _____

_____   _____

_____   _____

_____   _____

LOST FUTURE EARNING CAPACITY   = | $ |
(Subtotal)

C. ADJUSTMENTS TO LOST FUTURE EARNINGS

1. Present Value Reductions   [   ]

2. Future Inflation Adjustments   [   ]

3. Future Income Tax Adjustment   [   ]

ADJUSTMENTS TO LOST FUTURE
EARNINGS (Subtotal) | $ |

Section II: Total Lost Past Earnings
(Total) and Wages, plus Total Lost   =   [   ]
Future Earning Capacity

---

[11]This represents wage losses that are reasonably anticipated to continue for some period beyond the actual settlement (or trial) date. This aspect of damages for lost earnings is often referred to also as the victim's impaired earning capacity as it relates to the future earnings potential which had been diminished because of the injury. Unlike lost past earnings, which must be specifically asked for in order for it to be recovered, the impairment of a claimant's future earning capacity is ordinarily regarded in most courts as something which is presumed to flow naturally from the mere occurrence of a permanent disabling injury. Secondly, damages for the impairment of a plaintiff's future earning capacity may be recoverable even if the claimant didn't work previously, or if a claimant is otherwise capable of substantially higher earnings at the time of the injury, regardless of the actual "amount" of past or present earnings.

Finally, note that what the claimant is entitled to recover (i.e., his impairment or loss of earning capacity) is this: the difference between what was actually being earned at the time of the injury and the amount the claimant was reasonably capable of earning in the future had the injury never occurred — and not what the claimant would have continued to earn had the disabling injury not occurred. [See, for example, Wactor v. Picken Lumber Co., 505 So. 2d. 815, 820 (La. Ct. App. 1987), "award for impairment of earning capacity…encompasses the loss of one's earning potential — the loss or reduction of a person's capacity to do that which he is equipped by nature, training, or experience;" and Lewis v. Pruitt, 337 Pa. Super. 419, 487 A. 2d 16, 21 (1985), "the test for impaired earning capacity is whether the economic horizon of the disabled person had been shortened because of injuries sustained…" To make such determinations of the claimant's proper "loss of earning capacity," consideration must be given to a variety of individual factors, such as: the type of work involved, the previous employment history, the availability of reasonable employment opportunities for which the claimant is suited by education, experience and physical capacity, claimant's age, life

expectancy, work life expectancy, health, lifestyle, occupation skill, experience, and previous training, prospects of rehabilitation, probable future earning capacity, loss of future earning capacity, loss of earning ability, the nature and extent of the injuries and the diminished earning capacity, and the inflation factor. [See, generally, Dunaway v. Rester Refrigeration, Serv. 428 So. 2d 1064, 107 (La. Ct. App. 1983); McPherson v. Buege, 360 N.W. 2d 344 (Minn. Ct. App. 1984); and generally Restatement (Second) of Torts 924 commend (1979).

[12]The two important considerations, among others, in estimating the actual amount of a claimant's loss of future earning capacity, are: both the extent of claimant's physical impairment and the length of time during which the impairment can reasonably be expected to continue. (Standard mortality tables, chief among them being the American Experience Table, are commonly used by expert economists and the courts to project individual claimants' life expectancy to calculate such future damages as pain and suffering or physical disability).

[13]The majority of Americans courts compute impairment of earning capacity on the claimant's entire life or work life expectancy as if the injury had not occurred. Work life expectancies can be projected from worklife expectancy tables derived from Labor Department tables.

[14]To prove the loss of future earnings, you need only prove the impairment of earning capacity to a reasonable degree of certainty—i.e., the estimated amount of the future earnings must be both reasonably related to the claimant's injury and reasonable in amount, and be established to be reasonably certain to be incurred. *Proof of an impaired earning capacity typically requires the use of expert testimony, however.*

III. RELATED ECONOMIC LOSSES

A. COINCIDENT PROPERTY DAMAGE OR LOSS[15]

Description   Amount

Vehicles (replacement or repair cost):

_____   _____
_____   _____
_____   _____

Clothing:

_____   _____
_____   _____
_____   _____
_____   _____

Jewelry:

_____   _____
_____   _____
_____   _____
_____   _____

Cash:

_____   _____
_____   _____
_____   _____
_____   _____

Other Items of Personalty:

_____   _____
_____   _____
_____   _____
_____   _____

TOTAL OF COINCIDENT PROPERTY DAMAGE
(Subtotal)   = | $ |

B. LOSS OF USE

Description   Amount

Vehicles (car rental or alternative transportation):

_____   _____
_____   _____
_____   _____

Other Personalty:

_____   _____
_____   _____

TOTAL LOSS OF USE
(SUBTOTAL)   = | $ |

C. OTHER INDIRECT ECONOMIC LOSSES

Description   Amount

Vehicle Towing, Storage & Rental Costs:

_____   _____
_____   _____
_____   _____
_____   _____

Handicap Accommodation Expenses:
Special Clothing: _____

_____   _____
_____   _____
_____   _____

Other Expenses:

_____   _____
_____   _____
_____   _____

Other Indirect Expenses (lost opportunity for job interviews, scheduled sales meeting, etc.)

_____   _____
_____   _____

TOTAL OF OTHER INDIRECT ECONOMIC LOSSES
(Subtotal)   = | $ |

Section III: Total Coincident Property
(TOTAL) Damage, plus Total Loss of
use, plus Total Other Indirect
Economic Losses.   = | $ |

---

[15]This category concerns all personal property items that get damaged or are rendered unusable in the accident, aside from the damaged auto. Such items as the following are includable in this category: the repair or replacement value of the auto, repair or settlement costs of any other personal property items (clothing, jewelry, etc.) that was actually destroyed in the accident, reasonable and necessary expenses for loss of the property's use (e.g. for a rental of other vehicles while your car is being fixed), etc. To determine values of the property, use the documents (the purchase receipts, cancelled checks, charge account invoices, etc); or, if unable to find such documentations, you may simply obtain independent evaluations, in writing from such stores, businesses, or organizations that sell the type of products damaged or lost, specifying the property's retail or replacement value.

IV. DISABILITY

A. PERMANENT DISABILITY

Permanent Impairment   Amount

_____   _____

_____   _____

_____   _____

Permanent Disability Subtotal…   [$]

B. TEMPORARY DISABILITY

Percentage Impairment   Amount

_____   _____

_____   _____

_____   _____

Temporary Disability Subtotal…   [$]

C. TOTAL DISABILITY

Duration   Amount

_____   _____

_____   _____

_____   _____

TOTAL DISABILITY SUBTOTAL…   [$]
(Subtotal)

D. PARTIAL DISABILITY

Duration   Amount

_____   _____

_____   _____

_____   _____

PARTIAL DISABILITY SUBTOTAL   [$]

V. DISFIGUREMENT DAMAGES

A. VISIBLE SCARRING

Description   Amount

_____   _____

_____   _____

_____   _____

Visible Scarring Subtotal   [$]

B. PHYSICAL DEFORMITIES

_____   _____

_____   _____

_____   _____

Physical Deformities Subtotal   [$]

Section V [Add up V-A & V-B]   TOTAL =   [$]

VI. PAIN AND SUFFERING

A. Physical Pain and Suffering

Description   Amount

_____   _____

_____   _____

PHYSICAL PAIN & SUFFERING   =   [$]
(Subtotal)

Section VI   TOTAL: [$]

Section IV [Add up IV-A, B, C, & D]

TOTAL =   [$]

CHAPTER **6**
YOUR BODILY INJURY: A CRASH COURSE IN THE COMMON MEDICAL TERMINOLOGY & TYPES OF INJURIES ENCOUNTERED IN AUTO ACCIDENT CASES*

A major, even critical, component of any auto accident claims case, in general, or personal injury damage case, in particular, are often medical and related expense and cost items. In this chapter, we attempt a discussion, in as simple a layman's terms as possible, of the general types of bodily injuries commonly encountered in auto accident cases, and the kinds of disabilities associated with various injuries. The discussion here should be recognized, however, for its inherent limitations: it is, and can only be, a synoptic overview of the subject, meant only to impart a general knowledge, and not a medical text or encyclopedia on the subject.

To supplement the medical material in this chapter, particular pains are also taken to provide in Appendices D, E, & F, an extensive dictionary of medical words and terminology, roots, and principal abbreviations ("short hand") commonly used in medical reports and/or commonly encountered in personal injury claims. The primary objective is to provide the reader with sufficient medical information to enable him to reasonably read, and interpret his doctor's and other medical records and reports.

Types of Bodily Injuries Covered in the Manual

The following types of bodily injuries commonly encountered in auto insurance claims will be discussed in that order:

           Whiplash Types of Injury
           Disc Herniation
           Fractures
           Dislocations
           Back Injuries
           Injuries of the Spine
           Fractures and Dislocations of the Vertebrae or Spine
           Fractures or Dislocations of the Intervertebral Disc
           Injuries to the Nervous System, (the Head, Brain, etc...)
           Injuries to the Female Genital System

---

*Much of the material in this chapter is summarized from the following sources, to whose authors and publishers the present writer is most grateful: Baldyga, How To Settle Your Own Insurance Claim, esp. pp. 63-85; Thurber, Claims Medical Manual; and Automobile Personal Injuries Claims, U.S. Department of Transportation (July 1970) Vol. I.

A. The 'Whiplash' Types Of Injury

The so-called "whiplash" injury is a sprain in the cervico-dorsal (neck) area. The whiplash phenomenon has been described as the backward and forward snapping of a person's head, the kind which one gets from sudden acceleration or deceleration of an automobile, and which can result in the stretching of the neck muscles and ligaments which sometimes produces muscle spasm. This type of injury frequently occurs with rear end automobile accidents, though it may be caused also by other external forces. It can be a serious and painful injury that often doesn't bother you until two or three days after the accident.

a. Misconceptions and Misuse of the Term By Claims Professionals

Medical experts and analysts have, for long, contended that claimsmen and people within the insurance claims industry have often misused the term "whiplash" and the concept it's meant to embody, and that such parties have created unnecessary misconceptions and a bad and suspicious image about it which, they say, one should be aware of. Insurance claimsmen, critics say, have often used the term, quite unfairly, to denote a specie of alleged injuries that are either insignificant or of doubtful validity. Among the major complaints made about the "infamy" with which the concept has commonly come to be viewed in the claims world, are:

- That the original intent of Dr. Harold E. Crowe, the Los Angeles orthopedic surgeon who first coined the term 'whiplash' around 1933, was merely to employ the term **descriptively**, and never diagnostically; that it was intended only to describe the sudden and inadvertent snapping movement, backward and forward, of the head, and to designate certain accident facts which produced injury in the cervical area in 8 specific patients he had examined who responded poorly to treatment. That, in other words, the term as used or intended by Dr. Crowe, only described a motion, and not an injury; and that at no time, whether then or now, did the expression have any medical connotation which would properly bring it within the area of medical diagnosis.

- That the term whiplash, as original used and intended by Dr. Crowe, only described the manner in which a so-called "cervical sprain" (neck injury) was acquired and that while there may or may not be a clear-cut or objective finding associated with the claimant's subjective complaints, this can only be independently deter mined by medical diagnosis.

Whiplash types of injury constitute a substantial part of the claimsman's everyday work life, being that it makes up a great proportion of the total bodily injury claims business. *And the point of relevance to emphatically stress here is that, as a claimant, you must make sure to insist on your whiplash injury being viewed and assessed in the original and proper conceptual context of the term, and not fall prey to possibly being blackmailed or intimidated into a downgrading of the true nature or seriousness of your injury.* Claimants have, for long, been at the mercy of the claimsmen and the insurance industry on the use of the term "whiplash," as they have often employed it in a loose, ill-defined and unspecific manner designed to work to the claimant's disadvantage.

One critic, Daniel G. Baldyga, sums up the significance of making sure that one keeps the proper perspective, this way:

> "Without a question, there are oftentimes actual (and sometimes severe) injuries that involve the cervical region of the spine; but with the misuse of the term 'whiplash', it automatically makes the insurance company suspicious because in the great bulk of such cases we find that the term, to the honest thinking person, means a wall behind which ignorance stalks and, to the dishonest thinking person, the term means a "medical smokescreen" which is used to confuse, delude, and defraud."[1]

In other words, the term is like a double-edged sword; it is one that can just as easily be used manipulatively in the hands of the dishonest insurance company adjuster and other operatives to short-change you as a claimant — unless, of course, you (the informed claimant) take steps to ensure compulsion of honest and correct use of the term by the claimsmen!

b. Nature of the Whiplash Injury

Medical experts say that the so-called whiplash — otherwise known as "cervico-dorsal" sprain, or simply neck injury — is the type of injury that frequently occurs in rear-end automobile accidents, although such may also be caused by other external forces. They assert that the individual sitting in a car seat (especially with the head unsupported), upon receiving an unexpected impact in the rear, is subjected to a tremendous "hyperextension force" (backward bending of the neck) — the kind of force which, the experts add, has been shown by engineering studies and slow-motion picture produced under testing conditions, to be considerably more than the average person would expect it to be. This phenomenon is said to be due to the unique anatomy of the neck (the dorsal portion of the spine), in comparison to that of the rest of the vertebrae column (the cervical spine portion).

The common results of the cervical-dorsal or neck type of injury arise from:

1. Muscular strain

2. Stretching or tearing lingaments

3. Compression effects upon the vertebral arteries, occipital nerves, and at times possibly on the nerve roots. (And, to some degree, the symptoms reflect responses from the sympathetic nervous system of the area that essentially induces subjective or psychosomatic complaints).

4. Fractures, dislocations, true subluxations of tissue injury, and actual intervertebral disc damage are rarely encountered.

In any event, in any and every instance whatsoever, the degree of injury or the structures involved, can only be determined by proper medical diagnosis by a physician before one should draw any definitive conclusions as to the degree of injury, and is not necessarily correlated with the amount of automobile damage incurred.

c. The Symptoms

The more common symptoms of a whiplash type injury encountered in patients (beginning with the highest frequency) are as follows:

1. NECK PAIN, which should appear within a few hours after injury, if not immediately.

2. NECK STIFFNESS is a frequent accompanying symptom and may derive from muscle spasm, or (in later stages of convalescence) from too long a period of immobilization (not engaging in much activity). Most people with these symptoms may also complain of headache.

---

[1]Baldyga, How To Settle Your Own Insurance Claim, pp. 69-70. Another critic states: "The term 'whiplash' should be discarded because it is in no way medically diagnostic. Although it has gained popularity as a way of describing the mechanism of an injury, it in no way reflects the degree of injury or the structures involved. Proper medical diagnosis should be requested and obtained before one draws any conclusions as to the degree of injury." (Thurber, Claims Medical Manual, 4th ed., p.76.)

3. DIZZINESS. A fair percentage of people would also complain of this. (It is found, however, that upon detailed questioning the supposed dizziness is seen not to be true vertigo — a true symptom of dizziness, e.g., the sensation that objects or individuals are turning in space — but rather a feeling of unsteadiness at intervals, indicating that there's probably a disturbance of circulation to the brain or vascular instability.)

4. VISUAL DISTURBANCE is sometimes complained of also, but in these cases an eye examination usually shows that there is no relation to the injury.

5. EMOTIONAL RESPONSE of the injured person. This is a rather important factor that must be taken into consideration. This symptom varies quite substantially from one individual to another. It includes numbness, nervousness and other related symptoms. Depending on the particular patient involved in a given case, the patient's emotional response may intensify the other symptoms and at times even lead to rather bizarre or "wild" symptoms (i.e., psychosomatic or subjective complaints or symptoms) for which there's no possible physical explanation.

Finally, some patients complain of discomfort in the shoulders, or even down the arms and legs, with possible associated complaints of disturbances of sensation.

d. Your Doctor's Role

In those patients examined by the physician soon after such an injury (within 7 to 10 days of the accident), there will be some objective finding — if a practical degree of injury was incurred. This will consist of muscle spasm and limited neck motion.

X-rays (typically consisting of flexion and extension views of the spine) will generally show nothing abnormal since the damage is to the "soft" tissue, and, typically, will not show on the x-rays. Objective findings of damage to the nervous system are relatively rare.

The problems of muscle spasm and limited neck motion tend to resolve in the period of convalescence in an overwhelming majority of the cases. If degenerative joint disease (arthritis) is present in the spine at the time of such injury, one can expect a longer convalescence than in the individual with apparent normal tissues.

e. Prognosis

With the right medical treatment (basically temporary splinting, by means of a collar, accompanied by heat and massage, and medications) and proper psychotherapy, one should expect steady improvement after the first two or three weeks, (unless, definite skeletal or neurological damage can be established), and insofar as the physical structures are concerned, recovery should usually be obtained in a period of three to four months. Except in only a tiny minority of cases (i.e. those involving very severe trauma), complaints and supposedly permanent effects of the injury do not generally persist past closure of litigation.

B. The Disc Herniation Type Of Injury

There are, of course, many other types of neck (and back) injuries a person can sustain in an auto or other accidents. One of these, probably the biggest one, is the HERNIATED INTERVERTEBRAL DISC injury. Simply described, if it is in the neck, the disc herniation usually occurs between the fifth and sixth (or at the sixth and seventh) cervical vertebrae; and in the back, the disc herniation usually occurs in the lower portion of the back, generally between the fourth and fifth lumbar vertebrae and sacrum. The symptoms are pain in the area down the arms and legs, as well as the neck (and the lower part of the back, when the back is affected), and must be differentiated from such conditions as tumors, infections, muscle inflammation and neck sprains.

FIGURE 6-1: The Human Skeleton

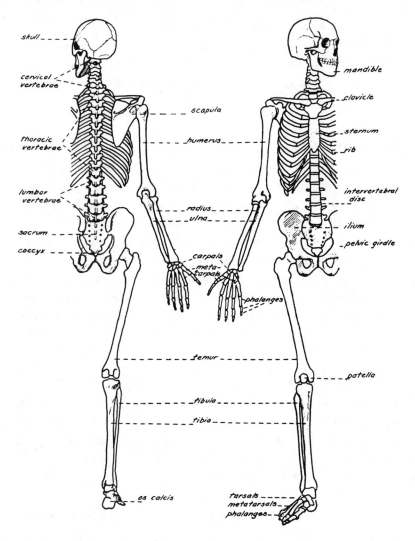

Physical examination usually consists of checking flexes and the muscle strength down the arms and legs, as well as the neck and lower portion of the back (e.g., the so-called "straight leg raised" and "big toe weakness" tests), the objective being to determine the "areas of localized tenderness" (areas of pain) and the "dermatome patterns" (the section of the skin that receives pain signal from the nerve which supplies that segment or limited area), and thereby correlate the affected muscle with the nerve root which is affecting that particular area, thereby indicating the places that need to be given medical treatment.

Several other diagnostic procedures[2] could be employed by doctors to attempt to determine the nature and extent of the problem. However, once finally determined and properly located, such injury is usually treated by a surgical procedure called "laminectomy" — removal of a portion of the vertebral arch called the "lamina." The period of convalescence may extend beyond 12 weeks, for the back related injury, and almost three months, for the neck related injury.

---

[2]They include x-rays, myelography (doing a spinal puncture and inserting radio-opaque dye into the spinal canal to detect an indentation in the sac which might be caused by a herniated disc); cineradiography (moving pictures of dye through the spinal cord); electromyography, which gives a determination of muscle strength and muscle activity, and discography, an x-ray study using radio-opaque dye injected into the vertebral disc to detect abnormalities of the disc.

SUMMARY: To put it simply, what it all boils down to is that if you should find yourself confronting a so-called 'whiplash' type of neck or back injury (or, for that matter, any type of injury at all), you should simply throw it in the laps of a competent medical practitioner to make the diagnosis and the determination. Submit yourself to his (her) thorough examination and diagnosis. Leave it only to him to draw any conclusions that are to be drawn as to the nature and degree of the injury sustained, and so on. This way, you stand the best chance possible to at least dampen the often negative effect of the common "infamy" with which the term "whiplash" has long been associated in the personal injury claims settlement world!

C. Dislocations

A dislocation can be described as a disruption of a normal joint structure that results in displacement of the normal contact of one bone with another. Dislocations may be divided into two major groups — INCOMPLETE dislocations and COMPLETE dislocations. An incomplete dislocation is one in which the displacement of the bone has only partially occurred, but with still a portion of one bone end in contact with the other.

A complete dislocation is one in which normal contact of one bone with another is entirely lost and one bone is completely separated from any joint contact with the other bone. Dislocations may also be **"compound,"** and at times, both fracture and dislocation occur in the same area, which increases the scale of disability considerably. In a dislocation there is also often damage to the nerves and blood vessels passing beside the joint as a result of stretching or subsequent compression and bruising. *These factors should always be fully examined and taken into consideration as well, since they will influence the rate of recovery to a considerable degree.*

D. Fractures & Their General Structure

The human bones differ in terms of age and gender. Bones of adult persons, for example, have been found to be more subject to injury than those of young persons. The reason for this lies in changes which take place in the solid portions of the bones. Almost 70% of bone solids are made up of mineral salts which make bones hard. But an all-important 30% consists of white fibrous tissue which loses its elasticity and bones become brittle. Doctors have found, for example, that when children's bones break they are apt to suffer a special type of fracture which medical experts call a "green stick." This is a kind of splintering and bending which occurs in a green twig rather than the sharp break of a dry stick. There are more "young" bones than "adult" ones — an adult has 206 bones, but was born with at least nine more, or 215. Early in life some of the separate spinal vertebrae became fused, giving you, as an adult, 24 although you started out with 33.

In terms of differences in the bone structure of men and women, a women's skull, for example, is relatively longer than a man's, but her neck is shorter. Her torso accounts for a greater portion of her body height, so that a seated woman is relatively taller than a seated man. A woman's thumb is shorter than a man's, but her index finger is relatively longer and her wrist swivels with more ease, which (thankfully for males!) explains why she is apt to have more manual dexterity than her all-thumbs male counterpart.

E. Types Of Fractures

A fracture is defined as an interruption in the normal continuity of a bone. Fractures are classifiable into various types. They include the following:

1. SIMPLE FRACTURE

This is a *single* break in the continuity of bone, such as you will get, for example, in a break one ordinarily gets by breaking a stick into two pieces. (See Fig 6-2 below) In a simple fracture the broken bones remain inside the flesh.

FIGURE 6-2

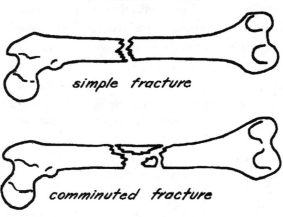

simple fracture

comminuted fracture

2. COMMINUTED FRACTURE

This is a fracture in which there are multiple breaks within a given bone resulting in more than two bone pieces or fragments. (See Fig. 6-2 above)

3. COMPOUND FRACTURE

This is one in which there is a wound, caused either by bone end puncturing the skin, or by external force. In a compound fracture, the broken bone piece (or pieces) pierce through the skin or into an opening in the body (as differentiated from a "simple" fracture, for example, where the broken bones remain *inside* the skin.)

4. IMPACTED FRACTURE

This is one in which the bones are driven together and held solidly.

5. COMPRESSION FRACTURE

The bones are violently forced together.

6. DEPRESSION FRACTURE

The bone is driven inward, usually in the skull or face.

7. GREEN STICK FRACTURE

A crack or break not extending completely through the bone.

8. SPRAIN FRACTURE

The bone is torn off by a tendon or ligament.

9. PATHOLOGICAL FRACTURE

Fracture caused by bone weakness, usually a disease.

F. The Process By Which A Fracture Occurs

Bones can give way under any of the following four forces.

1. Tension (Impact)
2. Compression
3. Torsion
4. Shear

1. TENSION (IMPACT)

Tension (or impact), which can be a pulling or pushing force, is the most vulnerable manner by which fractures can occur. If a claimant's bone is hit by a car bumper it can break on the side where the bumper strikes it but it can also be broken on the opposite side where the bone tissue is being pulled out of shape, stretching in an attempt to let the bone arch and ride with the blow — the way a stick will break when you stomp on it with your foot. (In children this type of break is usually called a **"greenstick fracture".**)

Because of this susceptibility to tension, bones can be broken by the pull of muscles attached to them, particularly the soft bones of children. A young baseball pitcher trying to get his curve ball to "break" can exert so much tension in the bone with his muscles that small chips of bone are detached from his elbow. Have you ever heard of the ballplayer bothered with "bone chips" in his elbow? Well, that's it!

2. COMPRESSION

Though rarer than tension breaks, the compression fracture — resulting from bones pressed violently together — is common enough, especially in the spine where the vertebrae sometimes come under truly great pressures.

3. TORSION

The classic fracture caused by torsion, a twisting force, is the typical ski break. A leg bone twisted too far as the body above falls to one side and the foot below it remains fixed on the ski.

4. SHEAR

Pressure in two opposite directions. This very rarely breaks a bone, but it sometimes does.

G. Treatment Of Fractures: The "Reduction" Method

One basic method of treating fractures is by a procedure called **"reduction."** Reduction refers to the setting of broken bones, or replacing of a dislocated joint, back (as near as possible) to the normal condition. There are two types of fracture reductions, the closed reduction and the open reduction.

Closed Reduction: This is a method of accomplishing this (of doing the setting of the broken bones) by manipulation or traction, without opening the site of the fracture. (**"Traction"** is defined as an arrangement of weights and pulleys to counteract the unsettling pull of muscles attached to a bone, usually used to hold broken pieces of bones firmly in place.)

Open Reduction: This is a method of accomplishing this (of doing the setting of the broken bones) through a cutting operation to get the bones back into place. This may include wiring, insertion of metal plates, bone grafting, or the tying together of the bones. An open reduction makes a simple fracture a compound one. Prompt reduction gets the bones back into place and gives nature a better chance to start the healing process.

Fractures of long bones of the body (e.g., the forearm, the hand, the thigh, and leg area) are generally more easily reduced than fractures at or near joints, and fractures into the joints cause more difficulty and longer disabilities because joints are composed of ligaments, tendons, cartilages and lubricated surfaces, and hence have much poorer blood supply, and damage to joints seems to develop adhesions and formation of callus.[3]

H. Healing Of Fractures By "Union" Method

The term "union" describes the process of healing and certain stages which such process goes through. The process of healing ("union") goes through certain stages.

The first stage after the injury is one of blood clot formation between bone ends. This clot is subsequently invaded by the fibrous tissue cells, which cause healing in all tissue by scar tissue formation. Subsequently, there is an invasion of bone-forming cells which convert this tissue to hard bone substance. (The new bone in its formation is referred to as a **callus**). In the adult, the repair process, under the best of circumstances, requires 10 to 12 weeks before union is solid and strength is fully regained.

---

[3]Readers should also note these similarities with respect to the structures of bones in some other parts of the body and the degree to which they respond to healing. The structure of the forearm and the hand (the upper and lower extremities), for example, has been described as "probably the most complicated mechanical apparatus of the body from a practical standpoint." In human anatomy, whereas the upper extremities are used primarily for "prehension" (handling objects), the lower extremities , on the other hand, are primarily used for weight bearing and locomotion. Fractures and other injuries involving the forearm, the hand, and the finger, potentially create greater disabilities than equal injury to the leg, since the leg area is less complicated mechanically. Another fact of importance is that the small bone of the leg (the fibula) does not sustain weight; and for this reason, fractures of this bone usually do not disable a patient from weight bearing for any considerable period, and should normally result in little, if any, permanent disability.

There are different kinds of union. They are:
1. Good Firm Body Union describes the normal healing of a fracture.

2. Fibrous Union is one where nature heals the fracture partially but the line and bone cells do not harden the union and solidity, resulting in an unsatisfactory healing wherein the member, say the arm-leg, is not of much use and will not support weight.

3. Delayed Union is a situation where the soft union does not harden in the average time (four or five months), but finally solidifies. To put it differently, if solid union has not occurred by the end of four to five months, it is referred to as delayed union.

4. Partial Union is a situation where new bone does not form to bridge adequately the fracture site.

5. Non-Union describes a situation where no bone structure reforms to span the area between the two bone fragments of the fracture, often resulting in a condition where only scar tissue holds the bone ends together.

6. Mal-Union describes the condition where the fragments heal in a poor functional position, or considerably at variance with the normal bone contour.

Prognosis on Fracture Injuries

Laymen, it should be noted, often consider a fracture and a break to be two separate conditions of different severity. But it is important that it be emphasized that in medical practice there is no such differentiation.

The extent of the fracture, the rapidity of healing, the asociated soft tissue injury, good or poor reduction, the quality of the "after case" and the cooperation of the patient, are all things which will influence the final results. Furthermore, and just as important, patients should take note of this medical fact: in any fracture whatsoever, there shall also have been some surrounding soft tissue damage to muscles, blood vessels and nerves, and in most instances these damages (injuries) are of more severity and of more serious nature than the fracture itself. And it is believed that the presence or rapidity of union (the setting of the broken bone), is dependent upon the damage done to the local circulation in the region of the fracture at the time of the injury, and not upon the general body physiology of the individual in most cases. Also, it is important to note that the location of the fracture is very relevant as healing depends on circulation.

The following Table (Table 6-A) gives some estimates of how much "TOTAL" and/or "PARTIAL" disability you can expect from uncomplicated common fractures and dislocations. (NOTE that this is only for first estimates purposes and are only average figures for large groups of cases and not individual figures for multiple injuries in a given individual.)

TABLE 6-A
DISABILITY FOR COMMON FRACTURES
AND DISLOCATIONS (UNCOMPLICATED)
FOR FIRST SURGICAL REPORT ESTIMATES

Type		Temporary Disability	Permanent Disability
(1) Skull	(a) with concussion	4-8 weeks	Possible subjective complaints
	(b) without concussion	1-3 weeks	Probably none
	(c) with brain damage	2-6 months	Variable
(2) Cervical spine	(a) without cord injury	4-6 months	Mild to moderate restriction of neck motion
	(b) with cord injury	6-10 months	May have upper (and/or lower) extremity involvement in form of weakness, motion loss, paralysis, subjective complaints
(3) Dorsal spine	(a) compression fracture	3-5 months	Possible subjective complaints
(4) Lumbar spine	(a) compression fracture:		Mild motion loss
	(i) slight	2-5 months	and variable
	(ii) moderate	6-10 months	subjective
	(iii) severe	8-12 months	complaints

Type		Temporary Disability	Permanent Disability
(5) Sacrum and coccyx		2-5 months	Probably moderate subjective complaints
(6) Shoulder	(a) dislocation	6-10 weeks	Possible slight motion loss
	(b) fracture	3-5 months	Moderate motion loss
(7) Clavicle	(a) simple fracture	10-12 weeks	Usually none
(8) Humerus	(a) simple fracture	3-4 months	Mild motion loss in shoulder and elbow
(9) Elbow	(a) dislocation	3-5 months	Moderate motion loss
	(b) fracture	6-10 months	Moderate to marked motion loss
(10) Olecranon	(a) Usually needs surgery	3-5 months	Mild motion loss
(11) Head of radius	(a) May need surgery	3-5 months	Mild motion loss, minimal rating of 5% if head removed
(12) Forearm	(a) one bone	3-5 months	Mild to moderate elbow and wrist motion loss
	(b) both bones	6-10 months	Moderate to marked motion loss in elbow, forearm, wrists, and possibly in hand-grasp loss
(13) Colles'		3-5 months	Mild to moderate wrist motion loss
(14) Carpal	(usually scaphoid)	3-6 months	Mild to moderate wrist motion loss, possible subjective complaint, grasp loss
(15) Metacarpal		6-10 weeks	Possibly slight finger motion loss
(16) Phalanx	(a) Proximal	3-4 months	Moderate finger motion loss
	(b) Middle	3-4 months	Mild to moderate finger motion loss
	(c) Distal	4-6 weeks	Little if any
	(d) Dislocation	4-8 weeks	Moderate finger motion loss, possible subjective complaint

Any upper extremity injury may result in ratable degree of grasp loss.

Type		Temporary Disability	Permanent Disability
(17) Pelvis		2-4 months	Possible mild subjective complaint
(18) Hip	(a) Dislocation	3-6 months	Mild hip motion loss
	(b) Fracture	6-12 months	Mild to moderate hip motion loss, possible thigh atrophy
(19) Femur		5-8 months	Possible hip motion loss, mild to moderate knee motion loss, possible shortening and/or thigh atrophy
(20) Knee		5-8 months	Moderate knee motion loss, possible atrophy and/or instability
(21) Patella		2-4 months	Slight motion loss, possible subjective complaints

Type		Temporary Disability	Permanent Disability
(22) Tibia		5-8 months	Mild to moderate knee and ankle motion loss, possible atrophy and shortening
(23) Tibia and fibula		7-10 months	Mild to moderate knee and ankle motion loss, possible atrophy and/or shortening
(24) Fibula		6-10 weeks	Little if any
(25) Potts'	both bones at ankle joint	4-6 months	Moderate to severe ankle motion loss, mild to moderate subjective complaint, possible atrophy
(26) Os calcis	(or astragalus)	10-16 months	Loss (usually marked) of lateral ankle motion, slight loss of dorsi-plantar flexion, ankle thickening, mild to severe subjective complaint, possible atrophy
(27) Other tarsal bones		4-8 months	Slight midtarsal and/or ankle motion loss, possible subjective complaint
(28) Metatarsal		2-4 months	Probably moderate/complaint
(29) Phalanges		3-5 weeks	Possibly slight toe motion loss

(Table 6-A)   Source: Thurber, Claims Medical Manual, 4th ed.

NOTE: if a fracture is compound, comminuted, enters a joint, or is multiple in the same area, add 50% to the above estimates. If there is a nerve damage, or severe soft tissue damage, double the above estimates.

I. The Back Injuries

There are an estimated half a million disabling back injuries in the United States each year. Doctors who treat these cases today trace a good many of these injuries to the CARTILAGINOUS DISCS—plates which act as shock absorbers between the bones of the vertebrae along the spine.

J. Anatomy Of The Spine

As an aid to help understand the analysis in this discussion, we shall undertake a brief description of the anatomy of the SPINE. Basically, the spine is composed of 26 vertebrae, as follows (see the illustrations below):

a. Seven upper vertebrae, called **"Cervical"**; this part is located in the neck.
b. Twelve DORSAL (or thoracic) vertebrae; this part is located in the upper back.
c. Five LUMBAR vertebrae; located in the lower back.
d. The SACRUM, which joins the whole spine to the PELVIS.
e. The COCCYX (or tail bone) located in the distal end of the Sacrum.

Fig. 6-3.
Verterbral Column—Left Side

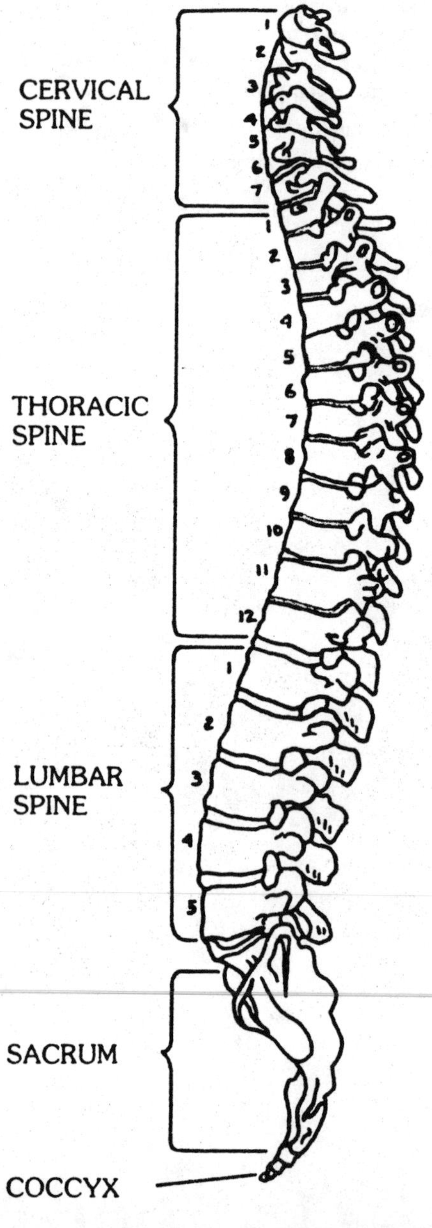

CERVICAL SPINE

THORACIC SPINE

LUMBAR SPINE

SACRUM

COCCYX

Fig. 6-4
The Bones of the Trunk—Anterior View

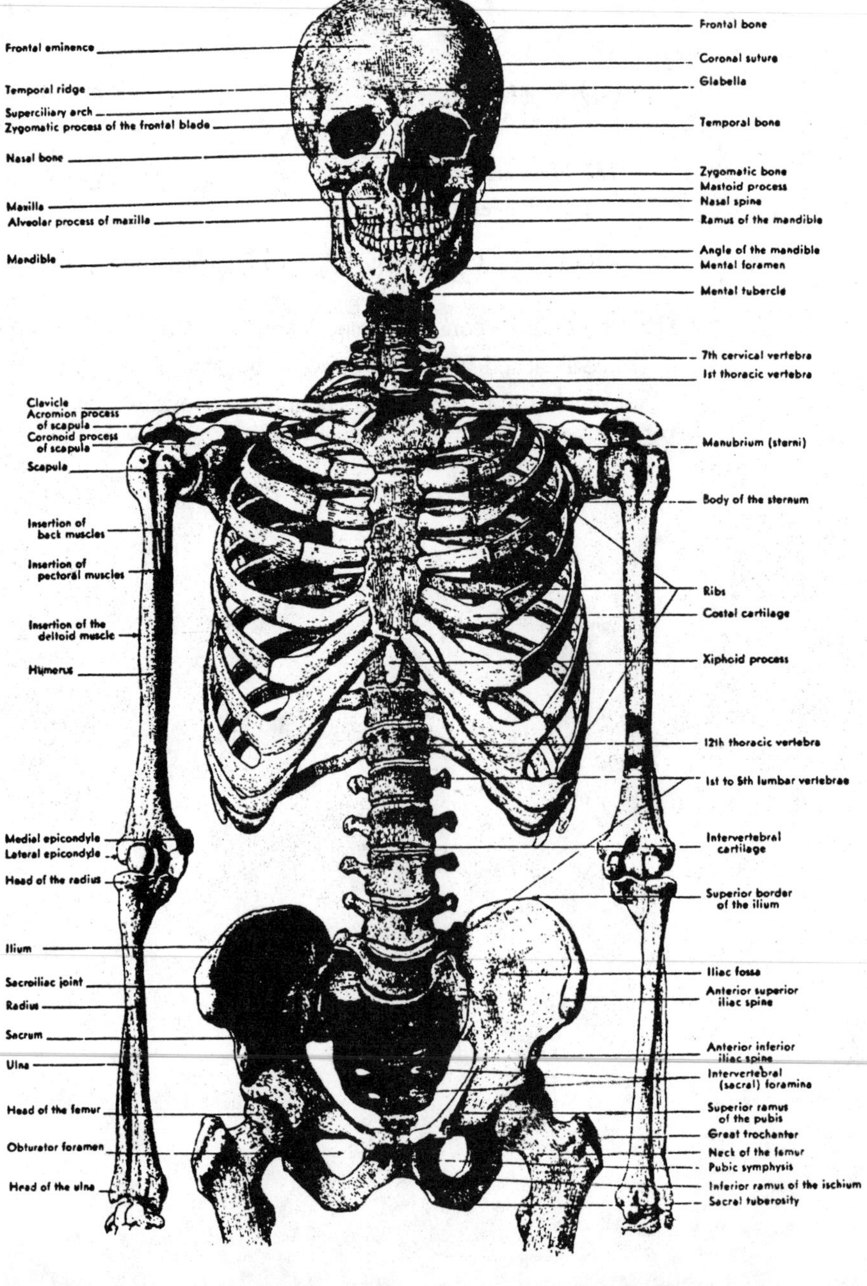

Frontal eminence
Temporal ridge
Superciliary arch
Zygomatic process of the frontal blade
Nasal bone
Maxilla
Alveolar process of maxilla
Mandible

Clavicle
Acromion process of scapula
Coronoid process of scapula
Scapula
Insertion of back muscles
Insertion of pectoral muscles
Insertion of the deltoid muscle
Humerus

Medial epicondyle
Lateral epicondyle
Head of the radius

Ilium
Sacroiliac joint
Radius
Sacrum
Ulna
Head of the femur
Obturator foramen
Head of the ulna

Frontal bone
Coronal suture
Glabella
Temporal bone
Zygomatic bone
Mastoid process
Nasal spine
Ramus of the mandible
Angle of the mandible
Mental foramen
Mental tubercle

7th cervical vertebra
1st thoracic vertebra
Manubrium (sterni)
Body of the sternum
Ribs
Costal cartilage
Xiphoid process

12th thoracic vertebra
1st to 5th lumbar vertebrae
Intervertebral cartilage
Superior border of the ilium
Iliac fossa
Anterior superior iliac spine
Anterior inferior iliac spine
Intervertebral (sacral) foramina
Superior ramus of the pubis
Great trochanter
Neck of the femur
Pubic symphysis
Inferior ramus of the ischium
Sacral tuberosity

One usual form of back problem or injury that could be brought about by an automobile related accident is **HERNI-ATED OR SLIPPED DISCS** (discs which bulge beyond the edges of the vertebrae and press against spinal nerves) It is usually brought about by an automobile accident caused by repeated unequal pull from the back muscles, such as that which happens to the body in an automobile accident.

K. Fracture Or Dislocation Of The Verterbrae Or Spine

Fracture of the body of a vertebrae (i.e., of any part or parts of the 26 vertebrae, as in he diagram on p. 80), is generally called a broken or injured back. Crushing fractures of the vertebral bodies and fracture dislocation in the neck may cause the injury to the spinal nerves or spinal cord, resulting in permanent total paralysis. When there is a fracture of the body of a vertebra or a protruding disc sufficiently severe to require operation, there will be about a year's disability.

The spine (all or part of the spinal cord), may, on the other hand, be **dislocated** or partially dislocated, as opposed to being **fractured.** *In sofar as dislocation is concerned, the danger in dislocation is injury to the spinal cord in that damage to the spinal cord does not heal and is permanent. And even worse, if the cord should be severed, there will be complete and permanent paralysis of the lower extremities, loss of control of the bladder and rectum below the point of the severance.* With respect to the neck, permanent total disability with a short life-expectancy almost always results from major damage to the spinal cord in the neck.

Only partial paralysis results when there is minor damage to the cord or spinal nerves. (Needless to say, however, that claimants should not delay whenever a permanent spinal injury or nerve damage is involved, but should promptly call in a competent neurologist to undertake a thorough medical diagnosis and treatment.)

L. Fractures Or Dislocations Of The Intervertebral Disc

The **intervertebral disc** is a plate (disc) lying between each of the vertebrae. It has a central core (the **nucleus polposus**) of a rather firm, jelly-like material. The disc is fairly resilient and acts as a cushion between the vertebrae in the presence of motion, sudden shock, or compressive forces.

To a degree, there is always a certain amount of constant compression being applied to the disc, due to the surrounding muscle holding the vertebrae together. If degeneration occurs in the fibers surrounding the central core of the inverterbral disc (the nucleus polposus), then the surrounding jelly-like substance may be forced outward through the border of the disc by these compressive forces. When it bulges out, there are disturbances in the form of pain or numbness or weakness or atrophy. Such an occurrence usually takes place in the lower lumbar region (particularly the fourth or fifth lumbar interspaces), or in the cervical region where it is usually around the fifth or sixth cervical interspace. When it does occur in the lumber region, its effects are usually evident in the lower part of the body, When it occurs in the cervical region, the effects are usually seen in the upper parts of the body.

It is pretty well agreed that all ruptured disc syndromes are due to a degenerative process of the structures of the intervertebral disc, which precedes by a long period the onset of symptoms. This entails a slow deterioration until it has weakened enough to allow the jelly-like substance through the wall. It is also felt that quite probably there are instances where this occurs in a spot so located that no vital structures are affected and therefore no clinical symptoms develop.

BUT THEN, MR. JONES CRASHES INTO YOU! Now trauma becomes the aggravating or precipitating factor in the development of these symptoms in that, in the presence of a disc (which is weakened almost to the point of rupturing), an unusual increase in force (due to strain) results in the actual "trouble" occurring at an earlier time than it would have in its normal process of degeneration. A good comparison might be that old adage (slightly revised) "the straw that broke the claimant's back"—in which a slight additional force created an immediate breakdown. (Note: note that, in such instances the traumatic incident is usually very minimal in nature, as differentiated from compression fractures, where force upon the disc must be maximum.)

The sensory and motor changes due to ruptured disc are usually limited to one side, right or left, and should confine to the area supplied by the particular nerve root involved. Pain radiating down the lower extremity, particularly the lateral side accompanied by numbness in a similar area, reflex change, and possibly by atrophy (in the more prolonged case), strongly indicates the presence of a ruptured disc.

As a rule, a fair percentage of these cases will be relieved by conservative treatment consisting of absolute bed rest, leg traction and possibly physiotherapy measures. However, upon giving the patient the benefit of such treatment for a reasonable period of time of from three to five weeks, if there has not been definite improvement by the end of this time (and the diagnosis is reasonably certain) then, in most doctors' opinion, surgery is indicated. To delay surgery for many months may mean a poor end-result, both because of the psychological problems (such as neurosis) which may arise, and from the fact that the longer the nerve remains in a damaged condition the poorer are its chances for a complete recovery.

There are various schools of thought as to whether a procedure called **spinal fusion** should be done at the time of the surgical removal of a disc, but the most logical approach is probably one in which a fusion is done if there are indications that the disc is not the sole cause of the complaint and that some mechanical instability of the back is a contributing factor. As can be seen from the following table, the addition of a spinal fusion extends considerably both the outlook as to hospital stay and temporary stability.

The following Table (Table 6-B) lists the average disabilities and hospital stays the patient is likely to undergo for operative (surgical) procedures:

TABLE 6-B

AVERAGE DISABILITY IN COMMON SURGICAL CONDITIONS (UNCOMPLICATED) FOR FIRST SURGICAL REPORT ESTIMATES

Operation	Temporary Disability	Hospitalization	Permanent Disability
(1) Hernia	1–3 weeks	1–2 days (local anesthesia)	None
		5–7 days (general anesthesia)	
(2) Bursa excision	2–4 weeks	3–5 days	None
(3) Tendon repair (a) extensor	6–8 weeks	1–4 days	Possibly slight motion loss
(b) flexor	8–12 weeks	3–7 days	Moderate motion loss, probable grasp loss
(4) Knee cartilage	10–12 weeks	7–10 days	Possibly slight knee motion loss—watch atrophy!
Arthroscopic excision	5–6 weeks	3–5 days	
(5) Shoulder dislocation	2–4 months	1–3 days	Slight motion loss
(6) Head of radius excision	2–3 months	3–7 days	Mild motion loss, minimum rating 5%*
(7) Patella fracture (a) repair	3–4 months	1–2 weeks	Possibly slight motion loss—watch atrophy!
(b) excision	4–6 months	1–2 weeks	Mild to moderate motion loss, atrophy minimum rating 5%*

AVERAGE DISABILITY IN COMMON SURGICAL CONDITIONS (UNCOMPLICATED) FOR FIRST SURGICAL REPORT ESTIMATES

Operation	Temporary Disability	Hospitalization	Permanent Disability
(8) Hip nailing	6–10 months	3–5 weeks	Mild to moderate motion loss in hip
(9) Ruptured disc	4–6 months	3–5 weeks	Mild to moderate motion loss, mild to severe subjective complaint
(10) Spinal fusion	6–10 months	2–3 months	Mild to moderate motion loss, possibly mild subjective complaint
(11) Bone graft	Varies with type of fracture	2–3 weeks	Varies with type of fracture
(12) Skin graft	6–20 weeks	2–3 weeks	Varies with location and size of defect
(13) Ganglion excision (wrist)	4–6 weeks	3–5 days	Little, if any
(14) Amputation (a) fingers	6–8 weeks	3–5 days	Varies with location of amputation
(b) major	4–6 months	2–3 weeks	Varies with location of amputation
(c) stump revision or neuroma removal	3–6 weeks	3–5 days	Varies with location of amputation; subjective factors usually improved

*State of California.

Source: Claims Medical Manual, ed. Thurber

Automobile Occupant Injuries by Nature of Injury and Part of Body, 1988

Part of Body	All Injuries	Nature of Injury						
		Contusion	Laceration	Abrasion	Strain	Fracture	Concussion	Other, Unknown
All Injuries....	100.0%	40.7%	18.2%	14.0%	10.8%	6.8%	3.9%	5.7%
Total........	100.0%	100.0%	100.0%	100.0%	100.0%	100.0%	100.0%	100.0%
Head, skull.....	11.7	9.3	13.5	4.9	0.0	3.9	100.0	11.7
Face..........	21.6	18.3	42.4	28.2	0.2	24.2	0.0	15.3
Neck³........	8.6	0.8	0.9	1.7	69.1	2.4	0.0	4.1
Shoulder.......	4.3	5.7	1.5	3.5	1.6	6.8	0.0	10.4
Arm, upper.....	1.8	2.2	2.3	1.8	0.2	2.2	0.0	0.6
Elbow........	2.0	2.2	2.4	3.8	0.0	0.0	0.0	1.9
Forearm.......	2.4	2.8	2.3	3.4	0.6	3.3	0.0	0.5
Wrist, hand....	5.3	3.0	10.0	6.3	0.0	9.3	0.0	12.6
Upper limb³....	1.0	1.0	1.3	2.1	0.2	0.4	0.0	1.0
Back³.........	4.1	1.2	1.2	1.8	24.8	4.6	0.0	2.3
Chest.........	6.7	10.8	1.4	3.0	1.2	17.8	0.0	4.8
Abdomen......	3.3	4.7	2.3	1.9	0.2	0.0	0.0	11.4
Pelvis, hip.....	2.9	4.4	0.5	2.1	0.1	7.1	0.0	3.6
Thigh.........	2.9	5.0	1.3	2.2	0.4	3.8	0.0	0.2
Knee.........	11.6	16.6	8.2	20.4	0.1	1.4	0.0	6.1
Leg, lower.....	4.0	4.8	4.2	6.1	0.4	4.9	0.0	0.9
Ankle, foot.....	2.7	2.2	1.7	2.7	0.2	7.4	0.0	10.0
Lower limb³....	1.3	1.4	2.2	1.9	0.0	0.4	0.0	1.1
Whole body....	1.5	2.9	0.3	1.7	0.0	0.0	0.0	0.2
Unknown region.	0.4	0.5	0.1	0.5	0.7	0.1	0.0	1.2

Source: National Safety Council analysis of National Highway Traffic Safety Administration, National Accident Sampling System, Crashworthiness Data System, 1988
³Back includes thoracolumbar spine. Neck includes cervical spine. Upper and lower limbs include whole or unknown part only.

TABLE 6-C: As cited Accident Facts, 1991, p. 75.

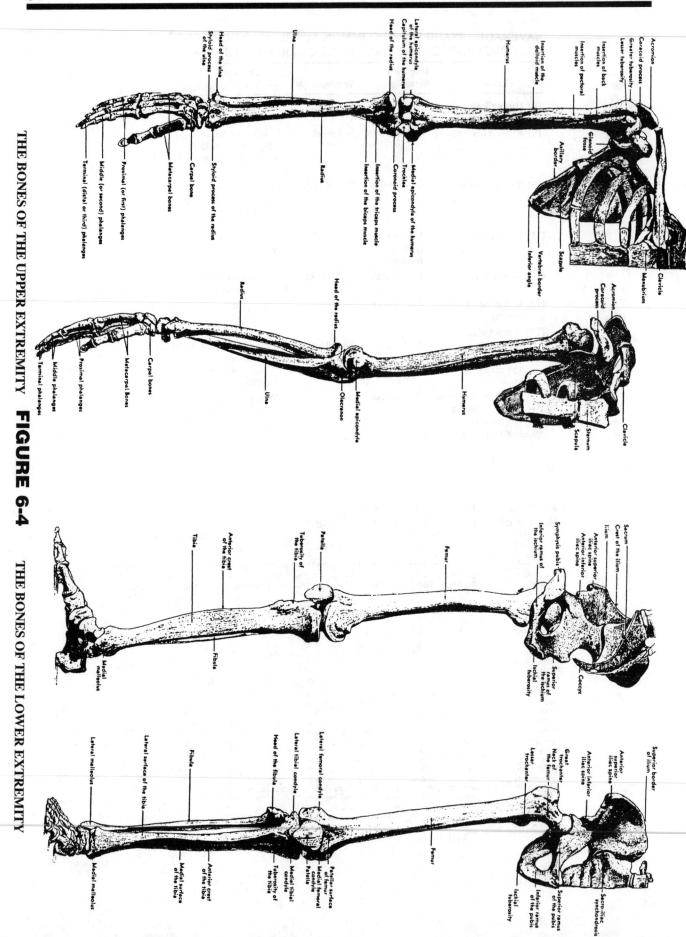

THE BONES OF THE UPPER EXTREMITY **FIGURE 6-4** THE BONES OF THE LOWER EXTREMITY

M. Injuries To The Nervous System

Head Injuries: Among the most common injuries sustained to the head are lacerations to the scalp—a tear or wound in the soft tissue or skin. These scalp lacerations may or may not mean that there is also any underlying injury to the skull or brain. Transverse **lacerations** — a tear in which the tissue or skin is torn in a crosswise fashion — will, as a rule, undoubtedly cause severance of some of the nerves of the scalp, which may cause the patient to suffer indefinitely or permanently from a numb area of the scalp. These patients will often complain of a headache; however, when they are closely questioned, the headache is subsequently described as a dull, cold, peculiar feeling at the site of the laceration, which is tolerated well in many individuals but gives distress in others.

1. FRACTURES OF THE SKULL

The most common type of skull fracture is the **basal skull fracture** in which there is clinical evidence of bleeding from one or both ears. Following such a fracture, there is often a permanent disturbance of hearing, and the patients often complain of a continuous ringing in their ears. Other fractures of the skull may come under the heading of **linear skull fractures** in which there is no depression of the skull. As a rule, these fractures do not cause any significant damage unless they happen to cross some of the blood vessels on the inner surface of the skull. When such a fracture crosses one of the arteries on the inner surface of the skull, bleeding outside the brain covering (extradural hemorrhage) will result. **Depressed skull fractures** are those fractures in which bone fragments are driven in to the intracranial cavity. They may cure a laceration of the brain and its covering membrane or they may not. **Compound fractures of the skull** are those fractures in which there is direct communication with the external scalp. **Complicated fractures** are those which involve the paranasal sinuses or the orbital cavities. These complicated types of fractures may cause the loss of the sense of smell from involvement of the cranial nerves, or loss of vision; the possibility of brain abscess must also be considered when one of these fractures implicates the paranasal sinuses.

2. INJURIES TO THE BRAIN

a) **Cerebral Concussion:** Cerebral concussion may be classified into four degrees. The first degree of concussion usually passes undetected and is manifested only by a paralysis (a condition of loss of function) of short duration. (This is the type of concussion often seen in prize fighters or in football players, who are rendered unconscious for a few moments). This is usually followed by acute dizziness, sometimes followed by nausea and vomiting, but as a rule, recovery is not long delayed.

The second degree of cerebral concussion is one in which the injured individual is only dazed or stunned and does not completely lose contact with his environment. The surface or cortex of the brain is affected with immediate onset of paralysis of movement functions, but the center of consciousness is only mildly disordered. There may also be acute dizziness. The immediate symptoms are very transitory, although a typical post-concussion syndrome may ensue.

The third degree — this type represents the state generally considered as concussion, in which there is a transitory loss

FIGURE 6-5

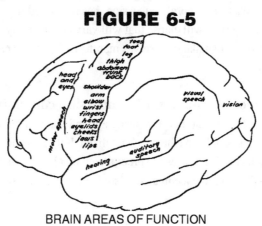

BRAIN AREAS OF FUNCTION

of consciousness. The duration of unconsciousness may last for several minutes or for longer; however, there is usually progressive improvement.

The fourth degree—in this group are patients who regain consciousness more slowly after an interval ranging from one to six hours in length. While there may be some slight degree of bleeding between the surface of the brain and its covering membranes, the brain itself is not grossly damaged. There may be some localized disturbances in the electroencephalogram. No localizing residuals tend to occur. This state is, therefore, still considered a pure concussion.

b) Cerebral Contusion: Cerebral contusion has a period of unconsciousness sufficiently prolonged so that gross lesions of the brain, as well as fractures of the skull, may be present. Such patients may survive or die, depending upon the severity of the associated lesions. Cerebral contusion implies swelling and bruising of the brain with associated intracranial pressure. Some of the individuals may die within a short interval after cranial injury. There are degrees of cerebral contusion which result in sudden death.

In sum, it may be said that in **concussion**, in its mildest form, the surface or cortex of the brain alone is disturbed, usually with minimal and transitory phenomena of paralysis, either weakness in movement activities or sensory disturbances. With a slightly greater degree of force, not only the surface or cortex of the brain, but also the upper midbrain and subthalamus are affected with the resulting impairment of consciousness in the form of a dazed state. This state is characterized by retention of consciousness and orientation with one's surroundings, but with an inability to focus one's attention and initiate action, regardless of how urgent the need for such action may be. In more severe degrees of concussion, consciousness is completely lost for progressively longer intervals of time indicating that the function of the nerve cells of the center have been more or less profoundly disordered even though this effect is reversible.

In general, it may be stated that patients suffering from cerebral **concussion** will not have any permanent changes demonstrable; but, in contrast, those patients who have sustained a cerebral **contusion** will, on the other hand, demonstrate gross lesions, such as inflammation and hemorrhage (bleeding) of the membrane surrounding the brain, bruising, or laceration of the cerebral tissue with damage to some of the more central structures within the brain or brain stem.

c) Cerebral Hemorrhage: Cerebral hemorrhage, following injuries, may be (1) **extradural** (outside the brain covering), in which laceration of the vessels between the coverings of the brain and the skull will produce a progressive pool of blood which will cause increasing and progressive compression of the brain. This condition is often preceded by a loss of consciousness, followed by a return of consciousness, followed by a progressive stupor with increasing evidence of neurologic involvement. The treatment is immediate surgery. Or, it may be (2) **subdural** hemorrhage (inside the brain covering), which may be acute or chronic. This is usually due to bleeding between the coverings of the brain and the brain itself. In these instances, the patient may again regain consciousness for short periods of time and then gradually lapse into deepening stupor and unconsciousness. The symptoms may occur from a few hours to several days to as long as several weeks.

3. THE POST-CONCUSSION STATE

After an individual who has sustained a true cerebral concussion, has recovered from its acute effects and begins to assume his normal activities, an interval of time will elapse that will vary considerably from individual to individual, following which divergent symptoms begin to make themselves manifest. Not every patient is affected to the same degree.

The following are among the most common post-concussion complaints:

1. Headaches. These vary from one patient to another in severity and in localization, but certain features are fairly typical. The patients complain of two types of headaches: a generalized dull ache, and a sharp, shooting, stabbing pain having its origin at the point of impact. The headaches are precipitated by changes in posture, physical effort, fatigue, emotional upsets. They are aggravated by indulgence in alcohol and excessive exposure to heat. These headaches tend to become less severe as time goes on. Any headache that is not precipitated by physical effort, or that is not promptly relieved by complete physical rest, and tends to become worse without intervention of some complication, should be looked upon with suspicion as to its alleged traumatic origin.

2. Nervousness: Nervousness may include anxiety and fear, restlessness, irritability, sleeplessness, forgetfulness, mental confusion, inability to concentrate, emotional instability, sensitivity to noise, excitability, etc. All of these reactions are, as a rule, foreign to the patient's former status. The patient often finds it impossible to understand them. The patient sleeps poorly and often has dreams referable to the accident. The patient is forgetful and absent-minded and finds it difficult or impossible to concentrate. The patient becomes fatigued after physical effort of even moderate degree.

3. Dizziness: The complaint of dizziness in the post-concussion period is seldom a true dizziness, that is, with subjective or objective sense of rotation. The symptom is usually described as a feeling of light-headedness, a weaving sensation, or an uncertainty in walking. Occasionally, it may be described as a feeling of faintness. At times sudden change of position may provoke short, acute episodes of true dizziness. Undue physical effort, changes in position, exposure to the sun, or indulgence in alcohol tend to exaggerate these symptoms.

4. Disturbance of Vision: The most common complaint is that of blurred vision, which may or may not be associated with headaches or physical activity.

5. Fatigue: This symptom is a fairly common complaint in the post-concussion syndrome. It is sometimes described as a weakness. This symptom tends to disappear relatively early.

6. Auditory Symptoms: Impairment of hearing is not a common symptom in pure concussion without associated inner ear injury. The presence of unilateral deafness should lead one to suspect physical injury to the auditory apparatus. However, the complaint of ringing in the ears is not unusual.

It can no longer be reasonably assumed that the characteristic residual symptoms of cerebral concussion are all to be dismissed as "post-concussion neurosis" or malingering.

POST-TRAUMATIC EPILEPSY

Convulsions are more likely to occur when the covering membranes of the brain are penetrated and, more frequently, if the surface of the brain or cortex is lacerated. It is rare for convulsions to follow a simple concussion. The length of time before convulsions appear depends upon the location of the injury in respect to the motor strip, the severity and extent of the injury, and the reparative process of the surrounding tissue. Post-traumatic epilepsy may occur within a short period of months or even several years following a penetrating injury to the brain, or severe bruising of the brain.

N. Injuries To The Female Genital System

Any injury to a pregnant woman frequently raises a liability problem to both the expectant mother and the child. Generally speaking, this problem can be broken down into five phases, as follows:

1. *Abortion,* which means the loss of a baby prior to the period of viability
2. *Premature labor,* meaning the onset of labor prior to the expected time and after the fetus can be saved; this is generally considered about twenty-eight to thirty weeks of gestation
3. *Abnormal labor,* which refers to breech presentations, transverse presentations, hand presentations
4. *Caesarean section,* meaning the operation through the abdominal wall to deliver the baby
5. *Toxemia of pregnancy,* which is a condition wherein the metabolic processes of pregnancy have interfered with normal functions of the body, resulting in high blood pressure, albumin in the urine, swelling of the hands and feet, all of which may culminate in convulsions.

FIGURE 6-6

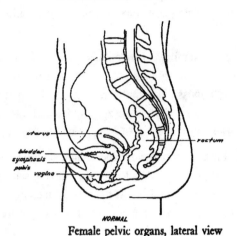

Female pelvic organs, lateral view

FIGURE 6-7

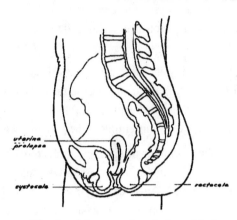

Female pelvic organs, lateral view with abnormalities

1. Abortion: Frequently patients contend that an abortion came about because of an injury that may have occurred regardless of the type of severity of the injury. Actually, abortion is rarely caused by an injury and medical statistics generally conclude that the trauma is improbable[4] as a principal cause of abortion. One major study done by Hernig and Shelton, for example, showed that there was only 1 case out of the 1,000 cases examined where abortion following an automobile accident was associated with a normally developed egg or embryo. [Account as cited in Thurber, Claims Medical Manual, (4th ed.) p.88.]

The prerequisites for ascribing abortion to a specific injury have been outlined by medical experts as being the following:

1. The course of the pregnancy before the accident must have been normal.
2. Pathological examination of the fetus and membranes must reveal no evidence of abnormal development.
3. The time interval between the alleged injury and the onset of bleeding or other signs of inevitable abortion must have been a matter of minutes, or at the most a few hours.

2. Premature Labor: Premature labor is the onset of labor in an individual before the normal nine months has elapsed. Labor must begin soon after the alleged injury, and there must be physical evidence of the cause — such as a blood clot behind the placenta, bleeding, or a physical separation, or early rupture of the bag of waters. In most instances there would be external contusions or bruises (visible injury marks) if the injury was severe enough to bring on labor. True, spontaneous premature labor (meaning premature labor that has begun without any known cause), is common even among women who have taken the maximum precaution against this accident. However, it should be recognized as well that premature labor sometimes is induced by severe abdominal injury or violent jarring. In such cases labor follows shortly after the accident, and it is accompanied by signs and symptoms of uterine contractions or bleeding. Unless these symptoms subside promptly, evidence follows of opening of the mouth of the uterus cervix, which is called dilatation. Once the dilatation begins, it is unusual for the labor not to progress to the expulsion of the fetus.

[4]A case on record is the case of a 19 year old girl who was beaten, choked, and thrown from an automobile. She had several injuries, including multiple fractures and even serious cerebral hemorrhages. When she died five days later, an autopsy was done and the afterbirth was observed to be normally attached; the amniotic fluid, which is the liquid in the uterine cavity, was clear; there was no evidence of bleeding within the uterus; and the male fetus, which was about 2 inches long, showed no evidence of injury. Although this girl had been severely injured, there was no injury to the product of this uterus in conception. (Account, as given by Robert J. McNeil, in "Injuries to the Female Genital System," edited by Thurber, Claims Medical Manual, pp.88-89).

3. Abnormal Labor: Abnormal labor and its complications include the following conditions:

    a. Placental abruption, which means breaking off or tearing away of the afterbirth from the wall of the uterus

    b. Placenta previa, which means the afterbirth lies in front of the baby over the opening of the uterus

    c. Abnormal fetal presentations, which would be breech presentation, or hand presentation or transverse presentation, and prolapse of the umbilical cord.

Of these conditions, **placental abruption** is the most likely to follow accidental injury. The symptoms suggesting this condition starts immediately after the injury and at delivery there should be substantiating evidence, such as a blood clot behind or accompanying the afterbirth.

Placenta previa, on the other hand, is a predetermined condition which cannot be altered by trauma from any accidental injury. Painless bleeding, which is indicative of this placenta previs condition, must occur at a certain period of pregnancy complicated by placenta previa, irrespective of the coincidence of accidental injury. Likewise, abnormal fetal positions obviously cannot be a result of external injury!

Intra-uterine fetal death. Intra-uterine fetal death may be caused by external injury, but to ascribe it to that cause, there must be real evidence of severe injury to the mother. In addition, there must be intra-uterine evidence of the cause of fetal death.[5]

4. Caesarean Section: Caesarean section, which means abdominal operation for delivery of a child, is almost never indicated as the result of trauma unless external injury is of such extent that the uterine muscle of the afterbirth is damaged. Bleeding within the uterus is almost the only indicating for a Caesarean delivery after traumatic accident.

5. Toxemia of Pregnancy: Toxemia of pregnancy is a metabolic toxic condition and is not caused or influenced by external trauma.

Gynecological problems.

In a non-pregnant woman there are many more conflicting problems. Often it is difficult to determine whether a pain in the back is due to injury of the pelvic organs, or due to orthopedic or urological problems. In general, however, if the pelvic organs are normal and freely movable they can be absolved as the cause of the backache. The back pains that follow automobile accidents, or other injuries, are usually orthopedic in origin, but can be psychologically transferred to the pelvic organs by simple suggestion. Once a patient has associated such pains with her pelvic organs, it is difficult to convince her that all of the problem does not stem from, for example, a "tipped uterus", meaning a uterus that lies backwards, contrary to the common position. These convictions are true even though she may have been aware of a tipped uterus for many years.

It is true that a uterus may be tipped backwards, or retro-displaced, as a result of trauma, but in order to ascribe this condition to trauma the following conditions should be met:

    1. The symptoms must follow immediately after the accident.

    2. Vaginal bleeding must be present.

    3. There must be pelvic pain and pressure.

    4. The uterus must be felt deep in the cul-de-sac; the symptoms must be relieved when the uterus is replaced to the anterior position; and recovery must follow directly thereafter.

The injury that is most likely to cause a retro-displacement or a tipping of the uterus, is a fall on the buttocks or abdominal blow while the patient is in the squatting position, or with a full bladder.

---

[5]A decision of the Superior Court of Los Angeles established a fair precedent in denying a claim of accidental injury and fetal death due to injury that had been based simply on the argument that "there was no other reason for the fetus to die." It is accepted that approximately 11 percent of all pregnant women do not deliver normal, healthy, live babies at the end of their confinement. Within this 11 percent, somewhere between 1 and 2 percent of these percentage of cases, is the group that experiences intra-uterine fetal death for no cause that can be demonstrated. It has been reported that 4 of 8 women who had penetrating wounds of the uterus while pregnant delivered normally from 4 to 5 months after the accident. (Account as cited in Claims Medical Manual, p.91).

Vaginal bleeding after injury.

Abdominal blows from moving parts of machines do cause injury to the female genital organs, but such injuries are temporary in nature. Vaginal bleeding is quite common following injury. This bleeding is not related to the severity of the injury. The injury may either be *physical or psychological*. Physical injury, of course, refers to a blow or impact by some object; psychological injury refers to the traumatic impact of a severe emotional upset. A profound experience that creates fright or an emotional impact, such as the death of a relative, may initiate vaginal bleeding or cessation of vaginal bleeding. The exact mechanism of the psychological, or mental, affectation of the pituitary, ovarian, and uterine components is not known. The recognition of the problem is based on clinical experience, rather than experimental evidence. It is very common for a woman to complain of having received some form of injury and then having a heavy vaginal flow of blood and mucus immediately following. Upon pelvic examination, under such circumstances, no considerable pathological change may be noted. Bleeding in such situations usually clears spontaneously, although occasionally some medical treatment is necessary for a short period of time. This irregular menstrual bleeding, which is called **menometrorrhagia**, may last through two menstrual cycles. If bleeding lasts beyond 60 days, further diagnostic studies are indicated to rule out organic disease. If infectious disease or the residual effect of infection is present, then trauma is eliminated as a causative factor.[6]

Uterine prolapse, cystocele, and rectocele.

The problems of **uterine prolapse**, which means falling of the uterus into the vaginal tract, **cystocele**, which means falling of the bladder, and **rectocele**, which means falling of the rectum, have become a part of the insurance picture. Of the 500 gynecologists surveyed on the question, all of whom were recognized specialists in the field throughout the United States, 277 of them replied, and only 17 of these felt that uterine or vaginal prolapse, as well as bladder prolapse, or cystocele, could be caused by abdominal or vaginal injuries. It was the opinion of several of those who answered that these injuries were by definition not possible. What is safe to assume, is that in most instances, cystoceles or prolapses are noticed only some time after the injury and there is no evidence at the examination of an acute injury, and that it is with respect to such cases that the opinion of the majority of the gynecologists who replied in the questionnaire is overwhelmingly valid that uterine prolapse, cystocele, and rectocele, are not caused by sudden intra-abdominal increase in pressure. It is accepted that these conditions arise, rather, as a result of weakness in the structures and tissues that give support to the bladder and rectum. It is not logical to assume that such a rupture can occur as a result of a single insulting traumatic blow, *unless there is evidence of real tissue damage to the anterior and posterior vaginal vault.*

Along with this same consideration of vaginal prolapse, one occasionally encounters the claim wherein **stress incontinence** has developed following some abdominal or vaginal injury. Stress incontinence refers to the involuntary expulsion of urine upon coughing or sneezing. Here again, the burden of proof should be placed upon direct and conclusive evidence of tissue damage in the area as the result of trauma. It is known that about 40 percent of young women in college, who have never had children, experience stress incontinence frequently.

Pelvic pain.

Abdominal hysterectomy and/or **oophorectomy** means removal of the uterus, and/or ovaries. Sometimes this is done in cases where the patient complains of pain in the pelvis following abdominal or vaginal injury, but in the experience of one medical expert[7] who studied this issue, the cases that have been studied almost never showed a pathological indica-

---

[6]In a questionnaire answered by 277 gynecologists, all the doctors reported only 5 cases of intra-abdominal bleeding as a result of injury to a women. This indicates the rare necessity for surgical intervention in cases of abdominal injury, even though such injury is followed by vaginal injury. According to the replies from this questionnaire, most physicians observe relief from the injury within two weeks. In only one case was bleeding that lasted more than one month reported. Here again, it must be concluded that if the abdominal blow is severe enough to cause serious injury to the internal organs, there must be external evidence of the extent of this injury on the abdominal wall or about the body. (Cited from Thurber, ed., <u>Claims Medical Manual</u>, p. 93).

[7]View of Robert J. McNeil, M.D., Diplomate, American Board of Obstetrics and Gynecology, as reported in Thurber, ed., <u>Claims Medical Manual</u>, p. 97.

tion from the laboratory tissue report which would substantiate the claim that the injury necessitated the operation. This expert contended that, while the usual claim places great stress upon intra-abdominal adhesions, and frequently places great blame upon adhesions to the abdominal wall which lie at the site of a previous operation, a careful and impartial review of the operative records and pathological findings will usually reveal obvious and apparent evidence of an old infection or of a previous inadequately performed operation. Hence, it is contended, it is difficult to outline or imagine a logical cause that would create intra-abdominal adhesions as a result of an injury to the abdominal wall, and that the most common cause of intra-abdominal adhesions is either previous infection, or previous surgery.

Summary

To summarize, injuries to pregnant women do not usually cause an obsterical crisis. When such an event does occur, if there was such a relationship, there is positive medical evidence that relates to the accident.

Menorrhagia and metrorrhagia (irregular menstrual bleeding) are common sequelae of physical and psychological injury, but they are of temporary nature in cases in which there is no demonstrable pathological condition upon pelvic examination. Uterine prolapse, cystocele, and rectocele (i.e., falling of the uterus, the bladder, and the rectum, respectively, into the vaginal tract), are not caused by a single injury, except in extremely rare instances. When the vaginal vault injury has occurred as a result of a single injury, there is clinical evidence of severe tissue damage.

O. Medical Disability:
The Definition & Types

Disability, defined simply as an "interruption of functions which diminishes the individual's capacity for physical and mental activity,"[8] may be either physical when it results in the impairment of a physical bodily function, or emotional. Damages for disability are a separate element for which compensation is payable in a claimant's personal injury damage award, separate and apart from damages for lost earnings, impaired earning capacity, lost medical expenses, and pain and suffering.[9]

(A) PERMANENT VERSUS TEMPORARY DISABILITY; TOTAL VERSUS PARTIAL DISABILITY

In discussing the concept of disability, it is first important to develop a thorough understanding of the relevant terminologies. Commonly, personal injuries are classified as either **"permanent" or "temporary."** *The two terms are used basically to describe the anticipated <u>duration</u> of an injury, and not its degree of severity.* Thus, if an injury is conceived as one which would continue throughout the remainder of an individual's lifetime, it is said to be "permanent" in nature. And conversely, if it is reasonably probable that the claimant will attain a full or complete recovery within some reasonable future period, the injury is classified as temporary, regardless of how severe or extensive the injury might otherwise appear.

Another common classification of disabilities relate to whether they are considered to be **"total"** or only **"partial."**

---

[8]Lanzet v. Greenberg, 222 N.J. Super. 540, 537. A.2d 742.744 (1988).

[9]Note, however, that in those jurisdictions which also permit the recovery of separate damages for the plaintiff's "Loss of Enjoyment of Life," or "disfigurement," additional damages for permanent disability is not always separately compensable, since such components may be overlapping. [See, generally, Annotation, Loss of Enjoyment of Life as a Distinct Element or Factor in Awarding Damages For Bodily Injury, 34 A.L.R. 4th 293 (1984)).] Secondly, note also that, as a rule, to be compensable, a DISFIGUREMENT normally must be severe, such as extensive scarring, or physical deformity or the noticeable physical abnormality caused by amputations or severe burns; and minor scars and other blemishes resulting from an accident usually are not regarded as disfiguring injuries. [See, for example, Martinez v. Bullock, 535 p.2d 1200 (Alaska 1975), where an 11-year-old injured in an automobile accident was awarded only $500 for stitches received following accident; 243 Kan. 249, 757 p.2d 279 (1988); and Smith v. Marshall, 225 Kan. 70, 587 p.2d 320 (1978), where a 1.5 inch scar on plaintiff's leg, even though permanent, was ruled as not being a serious disfigurement.]

These terms refer to the actual EXTENT of the plaintiff's injuries, regardless of whether they are permanent or temporary in duration. For example, an injury that causes one to lose an arm and one that causes another person to become a total quadriplegic, may both be considered **permanent** in nature, since both are probably certain to continue throughout the future. However, most courts would not consider the loss of an arm to constitute a "total" functional disability when compared with the quadriplegic injury. Conversely, the victim of a serious automobile accident who was hospitalized for two weeks following the accident, but thereafter made a complete recovery with no residual permanent injury, would still be considered to have been totally disabled during the two-week period of hospitalization. *Thus, partial disabilities are distinguishable from total disabilities in that partial disabilities are not as extensive in scope nor as disabling in nature.* With a partial disability, ordinarily the plaintiff does continue to retain substantial, although perhaps reduced, bodily function.

(B) THE FOUR SPECIAL CATEGORIES OF DISABILITY OFTEN USED

The classification of an injury as either permanent, temporary, partial, or total, as suggested in the above passage, does not always accurately describe the true nature of particular disability, since many injuries are not actually disabling in any real economic sense. (For example, the loss of a toe, although definitely a permanent injury, would probably not be considered disabling to any significant degree by most people.)

Many courts, looking for a system that will better distinguish among these different conditions of disabling injury, have found it more useful to use a disability classification scheme which, in addition to classifying each injury as either "permanent" or "temporary", also gives an indication of whether the injured person has been rendered completely or only partially disabled by the injury. *Thus, the following four special categories of disability are often utilized in personal injury litigation: (1) temporary partial disability, (2) temporary total disability, (3) permanent partial disability, and (4) permanent total disability.*

(1) TEMPORARY TOTAL DISABILITY is symbolized by a seriously injured person who initially is temporarily hospitalized or otherwise completely impaired, although expected to eventually regain full function. *This is perhaps the most common category of disability in personal injury cases,* and one which is most easily proven inasmuch as the injured party can usually establish the fact of hospital confinement during the period of the disability.

(2) TEMPORARY PARTIAL DISABILITY is symbolized by that period when, following the initial period of complete impairment of the seriously injured party (the period of temporary total disability), the party recovers and is able to resume some but not all former activities. Similarly, a less seriously injured person who is merely treated in an emergency room following an accident but is not hospitalized or otherwise totally restricted from performing his daily activities for any significant period of time, may also be said to be in a state of temporary, partial impairment or disability during the period of the treatment in the emergency room. The disability during the period is categorized as "temporary partial" because it is only partial in extent and a full recovery is still anticipated at some future time.

(3) PERMANENT TOTAL DISABILITY describes a condition, usually applicable in the most severe cases, in which the injury produces a nearly **total** impairment to the body as a whole, again placing the emphasis both on the **extent** of the functional impairment, and its **duration.**

(4) PERMANENT PARTIAL DISABILITY describes a condition where the injured party, even after sustaining a permanent injury, still retains some substantial body function or earning capacity, with the emphasis being the *extent* of the functional impairment itself.

NOTE: For further medical information of relevance in personal injury cases, refer to Appendices D, E and F. Those Appendices deal on aspects like medical words and terminology, common roots, pre-fixes and suffixes used in the medical world, and principal abbreviations and short hands employed in medical reports and practice, and are primarily intended to further aid you in being able to read and interpret your medical records.

CHAPTER 7
THE LAW OF FAULT, NEGLIGENCE & ACCIDENT LIABILITY, VERSUS HOW THE LIABILITY SYSTEM ACTUALLY WORKS IN THE REAL WORLD OF CLAIMS SETTLEMENT

A. Defining Negligence & Fault

Negligence, for the purposes of an auto insurance claims settlement, can be defined in one of two ways: Either that the motorist being held at fault for an accident did that which he should not have done, resulting in harm or injury ("damages") to the claimant, or that he (the motorist at fault) failed to do that which he should have done, again resulting in harm or injury to the claimant.

The concept of **"negligence"** is based on a legal doctrine called the **"reasonable man's"** doctrine under the common law. By that doctrine, it is held that a person of ordinary prudence — a "reasonable man" — has a standing natural obligation to exercise a certain degree of care and diligence in certain situations, and that if and when he fails to uphold that duty, and if it should result in any harm or injury to another (or his property), it is a legitimate cause for the harmed or injured party to be "made whole" again—i.e., to be monetarily compensated for his "damages" — by the party. *In short, the term "negligent," as it is applied in "tort" situations, in general, and auto accident claim cases, in particular, refers basically to a level of conduct or behavior that is deemed to fall below the acceptable standard established by law for the protection of others against reasonable risk of harm.*

Thus, in auto accident liability situations, for example, the determination, through the settlement process or the jury system, of whether a given motorist is "negligent" relative to another motorist in an accident, is made based on the judging party's assessment of this fundamental question: 'Did the given motorist do what a reasonably prudent person would have done and would have been expected to do in a similar situation as the one at issue?" And could such a prudent person, acting with due care, have avoided the accident and/or injury that occurred here?'

B. How the Concept of Negligence Affects Your Ability to Collect on Damages

What is the significance of the concept of negligence (or fault) to you as a claimant? A lot! Under the prevailing law governing auto accident matters in most states (i.e., except in the few "true" no-fault states), the concept of negligence is of critical significance since the amount of your recovery—in deed, whether you are to be entitled at all to any recovery, in the first place—will depend on the degree of your contribution of fault to the accident; how much of the accident you are judged to be responsible for!

H. Laurence Ross, a leading authority on the subject, summed it up this way in his seminal 1980 study:
> "Although the science of traffic safety is unwilling to place responsibility [as to who is to blame for an accident] on any single component of the system, the law—both civil and criminal—has made a choice. It blames the driver. An important assumption of the tort law—which governs the remuneration of the injured accident victim—is that an accident represents harm done by one person to another through carelessness.
>
> The fundamental concept on the law relevant to accidents is negligence, which may be defined as an omission or commission of an act that is unreasonable, as judged by the standard of the ordinary prudent person under the circumstances prevailing and that creates a risk of harm to others. Negligence is a question of fact...In other words, the decision as to whether there had been negligence [and who is at fault] involves careful consideration of the particular circumstances of a given accident, and of what an ordinarily prudent person would do."[1]

C. Are You in a 'Contributory' or 'Comparative' Negligence State?

Under the formal law, the basis upon which the determination is made as to one's role on the issue of negligence or liability, and the nature and degree of that role, depends on the state of the occurrence of the accident, and the legal rule—the "doctrine" or philosophy—adopted by that state. The legal doctrines by which states operate in auto negligence cases fall into these two basic categories:

    1. The Doctrine of Contributory Negligence; and

    2. The Doctrine of Comparative Negligence.

1. CONTRIBUTORY NEGLIGENCE

Under the Contributory negligence rule, the underlying philosophy ("doctrine") is that **if you contributed to the cause of the accident in any way at all** (say, even up to 5%), you can be ineligible to receive any compensation for your claims. To put it another way, under this doctrine, if by your negligence you caused (or largely caused) the occurrence of an accident, but the other driver involved happens to have "contributed" to the occurrence of this accident even if in a very minor way, you yourself may be relieved of liability for the accident altogether, the underlying theory being that the other party helped cause ("contributed" to) the accident under such a circumstance. And likewise, if on the other hand, you "contributed," even if as little as 5% or so, to an accident largely caused by another party, you are barred from recovering any claims at all from the other party.

In essence: WHEN <u>BOTH</u>— i.e., YOU AS WELL AS HIM OR HER—ARE NEGLIGENT, <u>NEITHER</u> CAN RECOVER!

EXAMPLE: Mr. Benson, not thinking what he is doing, starts across the street in the middle of the block and is hit by a speeding car making far more than the 55 miles-per-hour limit posted for that road, fracturing Mr. Benson's leg. Under the doctrine of contributory negligence, Mr. Benson would have no legal grounds to bring a legal suit or win damages against the driver in this case. The driver, though clearly more negligent and irresponsible for speeding far beyond the permissible speed limit when he hit Mr. Benson, is relieved of liability in the accident by Mr. Benson's "contribution" by negligently jaywalking!

---

[1]Ross, <u>Settled Out of Court</u>, p. 15.

See Table 7-A below for a listing of Contributory Negligence States.

2. COMPARATIVE NEGLIGENCE

To put it in plain terms, the doctrine of comparative negligence replaces the "all or nothing" system involved in contributory negligence with what might be termed a "little-of-something" system. Within the past two decades or so, most states which previously were contributory negligence states have adopted the comparative negligence system as there seems to have been a general surge in recognition across the nation that the contributory negligence doctrine can often lead to unfair and inequitable results.

As the name suggests, under the "comparative negligence" rule, the underlying philosophy ("doctrine") is that if you are <u>PARTIALLY</u> at fault in causing the accident, the insurance company will merely reduce your compensation by the assessed percentage of your fault. In other words, RESPONSIBILITY AND LIABILITY FOR DAMAGES ARE ASSIGNED IN DIRECT PROPORTION TO EACH PARTY'S RELATIVE FAULT AND NEGLIGENCE in bringing about the damages. For one thing, the doctrine of comparative negligence recognizes — and this writer dares say, quite appropriately so — the reality that in any given case or situation one party to an accident may very well be more negligent and at <u>greater</u> fault for the happening of the accident than the other party!

D. The Two Basic Forms Of Comparative Negligence

There are two basic forms which the comparative negligence rule have taken in most states:

1. Pure Comparative Negligence or The 100% Type.

Under this form, injured parties may collect for damages up to the amount of their damages, minus the percentage by which they were at fault. For example, suppose the insurance company and the claimant came to an understanding, after due negotiations, that a driver who fails to sound her horn or to brake to avoid a collision with a car that had ran a stop sign was just 15 percent at fault. Assuming her damages were $5,000, she would collect 85 percent of that, which is $4,250.

2. Modified Comparative Negligence (50% Type or 49% Type).

Under this form of comparative negligence, which is the prevailing version in most states, drivers can collect damages from the other party's insurance carrier only if they are at fault <u>LESS THAN A SET PERCENTAGE</u>, usually 49 percent or 50 percent, and what they'll collect will only be in the same percentage as their level of fault. (Thus, in effect, a driver who is 51 percent or more responsible cannot generally collect anything.)

The states with modified system fall generally under two categories. One group of states, termed the **"50% type"** and constituting the overwhelming majority of the whole, fixes the permissible level of claimant's fault at 50% — meaning that a claimant may collect ONLY IF he is 50% at fault or better. And the other group, on the other hand, the so-called **"49% type,"** fixes the permissible level of claimant's fault for eligibility to collect at 49 percent — meaning that a claimant may collect only if his negligence or fault is determined to be <u>LESS</u> than the other party's; or, to put it another way, only if claimant's negligence or fault constituted at most 49 percent or less, relative to the other party's negligence or fault.

EXAMPLE: Suppose you are in a **"49% Type"** modified system state, and that following due negotiations you and your insurance company conclude that your accident was 45 percent your fault. Assuming your damages were fixed at $20,000, you would be entitled to 45 percent of the $20,000, or $9,500. However, supposed, on the other hand, that in that same case you were found to have been 50 percent (anything more than 49%) at fault in the accident? In that event, you would be entitled to nothing—you collect absolutely zero in damages!

[See pp. 96 for a listing of Comparative Negligence States]

Table 7-A
COMPARATIVE NEGLIGENCE STATES

STATE	TYPE[1]	AUTHORITY
ALASKA	1	Kaatz v. State, 540 P.2d 1037 (1975)
ARKANSAS	3	Ark. Stat. Ann. §16-64-122
CALIFORNIA	1	Li v. Yellow Cab Co., 532 P.2d 1226 (1975)
COLORADO	3	Colo. Rev. Stat. §13-21-111
CONNECTICUT	2	Conn. Gen. Stat. Ann. §52-572(h)
FLORIDA	1	Hoffman v. Jones, 280 So.2d 431 (1973)
GEORGIA	3	Ga. Code Ann. §51-11-7
HAWAII	2	Haw. Rev. Stat. §663.31
IDAHO	3	Idaho Code §6-801
ILLINOIS	2	Ill. Ann. Stat. Ch. 110, Para. 2-1116
INDIANA	2	Ind. Code Ann. §34-4-33-4
IOWA	2[2]	Iowa Code Ann. §668.3
KANSAS	3	Kan. Stat. Ann. §60-258a
LOUISIANA	1	La. Civ. Code Ann. Art. 2323
MAINE	3	Me. Rev. Stat. Ann. Title 14, §156
MASSACHUSETTS	2	Mass. Gen. Laws Ann. Ch. 231, §85
MICHIGAN	1	Placek v. Sterling Heights, 275 N.W.2d 511 (1979)
MINNESOTA	2	Minn. Stat. Ann. §604.01
MISSISSIPPI	1	Miss. Code Ann. §11-7-15
MONTANA	2	Mont. Code Ann. §27-1-702
NEBRASKA	3	Laws 1991, LB 88, effective 1/1/92
NEVADA	2	Nev. Rev. Stat. Ann. §41.141
NEW HAMPSHIRE	2	N.H. Rev. Stat. Ann. §507.7-d
NEW JERSEY	2	N.J. Stat. Ann. §2A:15-5.1
NEW MEXICO	[3]	City of Albuquerque v. Redding, 605 P.2d 1156 (1980)
NEW YORK	1	N.Y. Civ. Prac. L.& R. §1411
NORTH DAKOTA	3	N.D. Cent. Code §32-03.2-02
OHIO	2	Ohio Rev. Code Ann. §2315.19
OKLAHOMA	2	Okla. Stat. Ann. Title 23, §13
OREGON	2	Or. Rev. Stat. §18-470
PENNSYLVANIA	2	42 Pa. Cons. Stat. Ann. §7102
PUERTO RICO	1	P.R. Laws Ann. Title 31, §5141
RHODE ISLAND	1	R.I. Gen. Laws §9-20-4
SOUTH CAROLINA	[4]	Marley v. Kirby, 245 S.E.2d 604 (1978)
SOUTH DAKOTA	[5]	S.D. Codified Laws Ann. §20-9-2
TENNESSEE	[6]	Garner's Masonry Contractors v. St. Louis-San Francisco Railway Co., 470 S.W.2d 945 (1971).
TEXAS	2	Tex. Civ. Prac. & Rem. Code Ann. §33.001
UTAH	3	Utah Code Ann. §78-27-38
VERMONT	2	Vt. Stat. Ann. Title 12, §1036
VIRGIN ISLANDS	2	V.I. Code Ann. Title 5, §1451
WASHINGTON	1	Wash. Rev. Code §4.22.005
WEST VIRGINIA	3	Bradley v. Appalachian Power Co., 256 S.E.2d 879 (1979)
WISCONSIN	2	Wis. Stat. Ann. §895.045
WYOMING	2	Wyo. Stat. Ann. §1-1-109

Source: 1992 Summary of Selected State Laws & Regulations Relating to Automobile Insurance (AIA Law Publications)

1. **Type 1**-So-called "Mississippi" or "pure type" permits recovery regardless of the degree of plaintiff's negligence
   Type 2- "50% type" permits recovery where plaintiff's negligence was not greater than defendant's.
   Type 3- "49% type" permits recovery where plaintiff's negligence was not as great as defendant's.
2. Contributory negligence mitigates damages in actions by employees against railroad corporations.
3. Although contributory negligence is still the rule in New mexico, it is generally a question of fact rather than a matter of law.
4. Declared S.C. Code Ann. §15-1-300 unconstitutional as violative of equal protection because statute only applied to motor vehicle accidents.
5. Contributory negligence not a bar where it was "slight" in comparison to the negligence of the defendant.
6. Recovery reduced, based on plaintiff's "remote" contributory negligence.

E. How the Law of Negligence or Fault Actually Works in Practice in Auto Claims Cases

To put it simply, there is a direct connection between the level of your 'negligence' and 'liability' and your level of compensation or right to be compensated. The doctrine of negligence or fault, largely sketched in the preceding passages of the chapter, is fundamental in auto accident claims settlements (or any other tort-oriented or liability-based claims settlements, for that matter). This is so, precisely for the reason that the concept of "negligence" or "fault" lies at the very heart of the legal basis upon which determination of claims and related matters are ostensibly made.

The fundamental theory underlying auto accident claims is rooted in traffic law. The governing premise in the context of an auto accident is that the motorist found to be in relative violation of the prescribed traffic laws and regulations are presumptively "at fault" or "negligent," and is therefore the "liable" party — the one to make payment of damages to the other motorist, the supposedly non-negligent or less negligent party.[2] Where there has been problems or difficulties in the settlement of auto accident claims, it has usually been where substantial issues exist concerning determination or attribution of the fault or negligence. Most contested cases of liability, in or out of court, have generally centered around the question of the "negligence" of the respective parties. In deed, if you were to take away the negligence and fault issue in driving behavior among motorists, you would have taken away the only ostensible rationale for the participation of lawyers and the courts in the handling of accident claims cases! In sum, the legal doctrine of negligence and fault— the belief that the reckless and negligent vehicle operator can, and should, be differentiated from the careful, traffic-law-abiding operator, and be somehow monetarily penalized for his driving conduct — is at the very heart of automobile liability laws, which are, in turn, the very essence of the rules governing how and why auto accident damages are awarded.

F. Forget What "The Law" Says. What Actually Happens?

BUT HERE'S THE POINT OF RELEVANCE HERE FOR YOU, THOUGH: all of that portrait that we have presented in this chapter so far—i.e., the portrait of "the law"—is only a portrait of the law as it operates or should operate, *in theory;* the theoretical law, if you like!

What we have so far described in those preceding passages is the way the formal law is *supposed to work* in theory, the desired or ideal aims and objectives it is *supposed* to attain. The real question though, the one that is really of practical relevance for you, as an accident claimant, is this: HOW DOES THE SYSTEM ACTUALLY OPERATE IN THE REAL WORLD OF THE DAY-TO-DAY PRACTICES OF THE INSURANCE CLAIMS ESTABLISHMENT!? Putting it another way, to what extent, if any, are the purposes and principles purported by the formal, theoretical law— the goal, for example, of fostering safe transportation and deterring reckless driving and rewarding good driving— a prime consideration in the work of the insurance claimsman or the negligence lawyer in the claims settlement process? The simple answer to all of that, according to experts and available data, is.: VERY LITTLE, IF AT ALL!

---

[2]"Tort law shifts accidental loss from one party to another only upon proof that defendant's negligence causes plaintiff's injuries, and then only if plaintiff withstands a defense of contributory or comparative negligence. Negligence law is thus based upon a fault principle: absent wrongdoing, losses should lie where they fall." (Daniel D. Caldwell, "No-fault Automobile Insurance: An Evaluation Survey," Rutgers Law Review 30: 909, 1977, pp. 914-915).

Another expert opinion put this way: "Liability is the formal legal basis for any claim, and thus for any payment by an insurance company under a liability policy. A claim without liability is formally a claim without any value at all." (Ross, Settled Out of Court, p. 122).

G. The Major Differences Between 'The Law' and How the System Actually Works

The study by the University of Denver's Professor H. Laurence Ross, whose sociological study of the institutional environment in which tort claims settlements operate still remains the classic in the field, sheds a very helpful light on the world of tort law as it is actually practiced. Ross' classic study compares and contrasts what he terms the "law in action" with the "formal tort law" and the high ideals and principles the formal law is meant to promote, and finds that, on each score, the way the **"law in action"** is actually practiced by claimsmen and lawyers drastically differ from the literal provisions of the **"formal law."**

Among the findings established by Ross, are the following:

- That a fundamental premise of the formal law of tort, namely, that an accident is caused by carelessness on the part of a driver, is diametrically at odds with the findings established by the science of traffic safety and the scientific literature in that the science of traffic safety holds, rather, that traffic accidents are failures of several components in the system rather than just of any single component.

- That while in States with 'contributing negligence' system, the formal law holds that a person is either totally liable to another for injury or harm, or not liable at all, this, however, is totally at variance with what the claims adjusters experience in the practical world. A claims adjuster, Ross found, is seldom able to proceed in accordance with the contributory negligence model. For one thing, he often finds that the black-and-white 100%-liability-or-zero-liability model of the formal law is directly contradicted by what he sees in his daily experience: bodily injury claims are of grey shades of questionable liability and all have some value of sorts. Hence, the way the adjuster typically deals with this is that, whether he is operating in a contributory negligence or comparative negligence state, he generally treats cases of questionable liability as a fact by which to merely lower his evaluation of the damage award, but not to totally eliminate or deny it.

- That even when there's a clear, total absence of liability on the part of their client, adjusters would nevertheless often make payments to claimants in spite of what the formal law would have mandated—based, that is, on practical and pragmatic considerations and on the impact of certain informal pressures operating on the adjusters in settlement negotiations. Thus, for example, adjusters would often authorize what is termed "danger value" payments—payments made anyway as a "compromise" primarily to avoid or reduce the possibility ("danger") that a seriously injured party may be chased into the hands of an attorney, thereby possibly resulting in a kind of lawsuit which, even if lacking in merit, has the potential of winning a large 'sympathy' damage award from the typical jury, aside from long and expensive litigation. Then, in situations involving routine claims but of questionable liability with respect to the claimant, adjusters would also often make a like payment to claimants for similar reasons—a so-called 'nuisance value' payment. Such payments are again made under the rationale that, as one adjuster stated, "from an economical standpoint...it might pay you to pay $25, $50, maybe even several hundred dollars, to settle a claim that is highly questionable [rather] than be faced with $750 in legal expenditures to defend that [small claims] case."[3]

---

[3]Ross, <u>Settled Out of Court</u>, p. 205.

● That the single, most powerful and most persistent organizational pressure that drives the claims adjuster, it turns out, is not to keep payments low or even to deny them. Rather, it is to close the claims cases quickly. And, the principal effect that such pressures have on claims settlement process is that it has caused the average adjuster to simplify and routinize their claims investigation, evaluation and settlement procedures in favor of shortcuts and approximations — contrary to the presumption of elaborate, and time-consuming procedures espoused by the textbooks of the formal tort law.[4]

● That whereas the formal tort law is concerned with issues of reasonableness and prudence in driving, such issues seldom arise in the routine claims settlement process. Rather, in claims evaluation and investigations, the primary focus is on such mundane issues as these: the vehicle's speed and position, what is seen as opposed to what was done or what actually happened. The fine weighing of evidence for the purpose of determining 'negligence' on the part of one motorist or the other, as envisioned by the formal law, does not in fact generally take place.

● That, true, the heart of the negligence issue in claims settlement concerns whether one party or the other violated a traffic law. However, in the practical world of claims settlement, largely because of the necessity for masses of cases to be handled in a fast and efficient manner, automobile claims cases are generally resolved on the basis of routine *"mechanical considerations"*—such as who was to the rear or to the left of the vehicle, whether the traffic light was red or amber, and the like.

● That the rules of the formal law of negligence are not, in fact, generally applied, even at the level of the courts, as differentiated from the level of the 'law in action,' where they are even far less applied or hardly ever applied [Research widely demonstrate, for example, that in a large number of cases (66% of them) where there is strong indication of liability on the part of the claimant, the claimants still made recovery notwith standing their apparent negligence.][5]

● That in the routine claims cases, the evaluation and investigation process rarely concerns the motorist's experiences regarding such critical issues as the amount of pain, suffering, and inconvenience experienced by the accident victim because of an injury. Rather, the pain or injury evaluation process consists almost entirely of medical and other bills collected, not the recounting of pain, injury and distress.

● That, by and large, the supposedly all-important issue of "liability" is understood in mechanical terms, rather than in terms of morality and the high ideals envisioned in the formal law, inasmuch as the overwhelming number of claim cases must, of necessity—and are, in practice—settled by negotiations, which necessarily employs tactics, skills and facilities that are different from those required in litigation.

Ross, contrasting how the model tort law (the "formal law") is supposed to work in theory, with how the true tort system (the "law in action") actually works in the real world of insurance adjuster and claimsmen, sums up his findings this way:[6]

> "The formal law of negligence liability, as stated in casebooks…deals with violation of a duty of care owed by the insured to the claimant and is based on a very complex and perplexing model of the "reasonable man," in this case the reasonable driver…
> *It is not with this intellectual model, however that claims men must deal. In their day-to-day work,*

---

[4]Ross, p. 235-6. See, generally, also, Ross, Chaps. 2 and 3.
[5]Ross, <u>Settled Out of Court</u>, pp. 199-201.
[6]Ross, p. 235-6. See, generally, also, Ross, Chaps. 2 and 3.

the concern with liability is reduced to the question of whether either or both parties violated the rules of the road as expressed in common traffic laws. Adjusters tend to define a claim as one of liability or of no liability depending only on whether a rule was violated, regardless of intention, knowledge, necessity, and other such qualifications that might receive sympathetic attention even from a traffic court judge. Such a determination is far easier than the task proposed in theory by the formal law of negligence.

To illustrate, if Car A strikes Car B from the rear, the driver of A is assumed to be liable and B is not. In the ordinary course of events, particularly where damages are routine, the adjuster is not concerned with *why* A struck B, or with whether A violated a duty of care to B, or with whether A was unreasonable or not. These questions are avoided for practical reasons not only because they may be impossible to answer, but also because the fact that A struck B from the rear will satisfy all supervisory levels that a payment is in order, without further explanation. Likewise, in the routine case, the fact that A was emerging from a street governed by a stop sign will justify treating this as a case of liability, without concern for whether the sign was seen or not, whether there was adequate reason for not seeing the sign, etc.

In short, in the ordinary case the physical facts of the accident are normally sufficient to allocate liability between the drivers. Inasmuch as the basic physical facts of the accident are easily known—and they are frequently ascertainable from the first notice—the issue of liability is usually relatively easy to dispose of. In fact, many adjusters claim to be able to predict the matter of liability with considerable accuracy from the moment they receive the notice of the accident. I interpret this as evidence of the mechanical and superficial way in which liability is determined; and if endless squabbles and large numbers of court cases are to be avoided, mechanical and superficial formulas are a necessity here as elsewhere for the vast bulk of routine cases...

In other words, although the formal law may put the question of negligence in difficult terms, the law in action finds that the basic diagrammatic facts of the accident are usually sufficient to answer the question... ***Those who believe that some more traditional understanding of fault is meaningful in the automobile insurance system [are simply grossly mistaken]"***

TRANSLATION OF ALL OF THAT: In the real world of actual claims adjustment and settlement, simply throw out of the window all those fancy talks and high ideals of the written law about how the "negligent" party is supposed to be determined or how "fault" or "liability" in an auto accident is supposed to be assigned or determined! And, instead, rather do exactly what professional claimsmen and negligence lawyers in such situations usually do: SIMPLY EMPLOY THE "STANDARD MECHANICAL AND SUPERFICIAL FORMULAS"[7] AND "MECHANICAL ASSUMPTIONS" used in the trade — routinized insurance industry rules-of-thumb and short-cuts employed by the adjusters and claims lawyers in the handling of claims and liability matters!

H. The Short-Cuts & Rules-of-Thumb Used by the Insurance Industry in Making A Determination of Parties' Negligence and Liability

Listed below are some of the major , more common, rules-of-thumb and short-cut formulas — the "standard mechanical formulas and assumptions" — used by the insurance claims industry and lawyers in assigning the liability of

---

[7]Ross, for example, finds demonstrably from statistical analysis of the actual cases undertaken by select insurance company adjusters he studied, that there's a very "strong support to the adjusters' claims that the eventual decision as to liability can be predicted from the minimal information [the adjusters had] concerning the accident configuration"—as symbolized by these "mechanical presumptions" and "superficial formulas." Thus, by and large, these "mechanical presumption" are, for all intents and purposes, a fairly reliable measure of 'apparent liability' of the respective parties involved in an auto accident case. [See Ross, Settled Out of Court, pp. 100-6, esp. Tables 3.1 and 3.2 on pp. 103-4]

parties in auto accident cases. [And, what is even more important to emphasize, you had better be sure, yourself, to employ these same formulas in your own dealings with the insurance adjuster, since they are essentially the formulas the claimsmen you'll deal with in your claims case (adjusters, lawyers, etc.) would probably use and rely upon, especially when your case is a so-called 'routine' case!][8]

Here they are:

- If your accident involves a REAR-END COLLISION (and this kind of accidents alone generally constitutes close to 50% of all auto accident claims), you should probably make a strong presumption that the rear driver is the liable party.

- If your accident involves a COLLISION IN A CONTROLLED INTERSECTION situation, you should probably make a presumption of innocence or lack of fault in favor of the driver favored by a stop sign or a green light. (Be ready to resist possible claims by the other motorist that you were speeding, especially in serious types of cases.)

- If your accident involves COLLISION IN THE MAKING OF AN ENTRY INTO A MAIN HIGHWAY FROM A DRIVEWAY OR SIDE ROAD, you should make a presumption of innocence or lack of guilt in favor of the driver favored by the stop sign or a green light, but be ready to defend against a potential claim by the other driver that you were speeding.

- If your accident involves the MAKING OF A U-TURN, OR A LEFT TURN IN FRONT OF ON-COMING TRAFFIC, you should generally assume liability on the part of the driver who made the turn.

- If your accident involves COLLISION IN AN UNCONTROLLED INTERSECTION, typically under state laws the car on the right should be presumed to have the right-of-way and to the car first to get into the intersection is presumed to be the innocent or less liable party.

[You should note that, as a rule, this kind of accident situation is the principal kind in which the liability question is often most troublesome and most difficult to resolve—often involving elaborate investigations, grossly conflicting testimonies by the parties and issues about the speed of the vehicles. (The speed of the vehicles, as established and proven by or for the respective parties, is probably the most important factor in this type of accident, in that it affects the issue of liability directly in terms of helping to single out the probable "negligent" motorist and helping to sort out the meaning of the configuration of vehicle damage for the purpose of answering the question of who arrived first in the intersection).]

Nevertheless, here's the 'rule-of-thumb' to use: generally, presume fault on the part of the driver who hit the rear of another with the rear of his car. (Regard the one who sustains damage anywhere forward from the center line of his vehicle as the one at fault).

- If your accident involves either HEAD-ON COLLISION OR SIDE SWIPES, but involves disputes as to where on the road the accident took place, providing there's no adverse testimony by the police or a bystander or witness, you should simply stick as strongly as possible to your own particular version (whatever it may be!) of what spot exactly the accident supposedly took place, and do the same with respect to other factors in the accident. For, in such a disputed situation, for reasons of "previously established trust" and because it is deemed to be in the insurance company's interest, adjusters will often side with the insured!

---

[8]A 'routine' case will be largely whiplash or neck sprain types of injury, while the 'serious' case is distinguished by residual impairment and disfigurement of some sort, such as scarring, amputations, and prosthesis, the use of braces, limping, impairment of sight or other senses, and similar residuals. There is one simple way of measuring whether a case is 'routine' or 'serious' one: simply determine that by the size of the cost of medical services involved for the injuries.

TABLE 7-B

Improper Driving Reported in Accidents, 1990

Kind of Improper Driving	Fatal Accidents			Injury Accidents			All Accidents		
	Total	Urban	Rural	Total	Urban	Rural	Total	Urban	Rural
Total	100.0%	100.0%	100.0%	100.0%	100.0%	100.0%	100.0%	100.0%	100.0%
Improper driving	65.8	64.6	67.9	77.8	79.5	76.8	77.8	78.6	75.4
Speed too fast or unsafe	24.9	24.1	25.9	20.2	19.5	26.0	16.3	15.7	22.4
Right of way	14.0	18.9	11.6	25.7	30.1	17.3	24.1	27.1	16.8
Failed to yield	9.6	12.2	8.2	18.3	20.1	13.7	18.2	19.5	13.7
Passed stop sign	2.5	2.6	2.4	2.4	2.6	2.0	1.9	2.0	1.7
Disregarded signal	1.9	4.1	1.0	5.0	7.4	1.5	4.0	5.6	1.4
Drove left of center	8.1	2.5	9.5	2.7	1.1	5.1	2.4	1.3	4.6
Improper overtaking	3.8	3.1	5.1	1.8	1.6	2.6	2.3	2.2	2.9
Made improper turn	0.4	0.4	0.3	1.6	1.6	0.9	2.6	2.7	1.4
Followed too closely	0.7	0.6	0.5	7.6	7.4	3.8	8.7	7.6	4.5
Other improper driving	14.0	15.1	15.1	18.3	18.2	21.1	21.3	21.9	22.8
No improper driving stated	34.2	35.4	32.1	22.2	20.5	23.2	22.2	21.4	24.6

Source: Based on reports from 15 state traffic authorities. As cited in Accident Facts, 1991

I. Determining the Negligent (Liable) Driver in Situations of Doubtful Liability

Many cases often arise where it is not at all clear-cut as to who is the negligent, and therefore, liable party (or parties) for the accident among the parties involved — the so-called cases of *doubtful or questionable liability*. In such cases that are not too clear-cut, where, for example, the claimant and the insured driver say grossly different things about the facts of the accident, or their versions are not confirmed by reliable witnesses, and the physical facts (the pattern of damage to the vehicles, skid marks, etc) are ambiguous or not in conformity with the claimant's version, opposing versions of the accident naturally lead to different liability conclusions—that is, to different conclusions as to who among the parties is the one liable for the accident.[9] The following are the relevant guidelines followed by insurance claims adjusters and professional claimsmen in their actual, day-to-day work in situations involving varying degrees of 'doubtful liability':

- In typical situations of "slight" degree of doubtful liability (where, for example, the insured party makes a left turn and collides with a vehicle headed straight through the intersection in the opposite direction), the typical charge by adjusters in such situations, which usually is that the claimant driver was exceeding the speed limit, is generally not expected to reduce the payments they will have to make to the claimant. Rather, such a charge is usually seen and used only as a "negotiating tool."

---

[9]Ross proposes a useful model of "three zones of doubt" (degrees of doubt) as one way of handling this type of cases of questionable liability: The first zone, involving when there's a "slight" degree of doubt, should merely serve as a "talking point" that should not significantly affect the adjuster's (or your) evaluation; the second zone, the zone of "moderate doubt," should have the effect of reducing the case to one of "compromise," to agree to award the claimant something reasonable, something amounting, to say, only the special damages but short of the "full value" of what the claim is worth; and the third zone, the zone of "severe doubt," would make the case one of "nuisance," possibly justifying payment is relations to the potential costs of mounting a legal defense against the claimant, rather than in relations to injuries sustained. (See Ross, Settled Out of Court, p. 129).

• Another category of typical situations would be one of "moderate" degree of doubtful liability. This would be exemplified, for instance, by the uncontrolled intersection accident where neither driver has a stop sign or a traffic light and the parties collide in the middle of the intersection with both cars possibly hitting the front end. In this kind of situation, there is almost always a strong likelihood of negligence on the part of <u>BOTH</u> drivers. As one adjuster put it, "It's usually a 50-50 proposition" — i.e., a compromise situation on the award, amounting to, say, at least the special damages value.

Vehicle movement in accidents

In both urban and rural areas, collision between vehicles is the most common type of fatal accident, as well as the most frequent kind of accident overall. "Other collisions" (fixed objects, pedalcycles and railroad trains) are the next most important type for both locations.

• Then there's the third category, situations of "severe" degree of doubtful liability. This category, by the way, is the hardest and rarest ones of all to find in practice, according to experts. This would be the kind of situation that arises, for example, when the chances of the insurance company winning the case if it were litigated in court is below, say 50 or 75 percent, where there's no possible liability or doubt on the part of the potential defendant (the other party who is being defended by the insurance company) and the facts of the accident are clear that the accident was caused SOLELY by the negligence of either somebody else that you (the claimant) can't sue, or SOLELY by your (the claimant's) negligence.

<u>NOTE:</u> It's worth noting that most experts who possess practical working experience in this matter, commonly agree that this type of cases—i.e., those in which the facts of the accident are absolutely clear-cut as to who is at fault or liable, and where you can clearly attribute negligence or liability to only one side—is generally very rare to find, even non-existent, in practice. As one Harrisburg, Pennsylvania negligence attorney put it, the kind of cases "where it's quite clear that there's no fault on the part of the potential defendant or defendants, where you don't have any possible liability…are very hard to find. Very often you can come up with some sort of an argument that the potential defendant had some degree of fault." (As cited in Ross, <u>Settled Out of Court</u>, p. 130).

SUMMARY

To sum up what has so far been discussed on the all-important issue of LIABILITY in auto accident cases, the central reality is that the way things work in the ACTUAL, daily, practical experience of the insurance adjusters involving actual claims negotiations and settlements, is vastly different from the stipulations in the "formal law"—the law as it is written or supposed to work, in theory. As Ross elegantly but accurately put it, what emerges is that "The black-and-white, liability-or-not model of the law means very little in the world of the claims man. Most bodily injury claims are of the grey shades of questionable liability and nearly all have some value."[10]

Consequently, in the real world of claims settlement, "compromise" and compromising is the general order of the day, in practice, as it is commonly accepted among claims professionals that in any given case there is almost always a strong likelihood of negligence applying to BOTH sides, rather than solely to one driver. WHAT THIS BOILS DOWN TO, IN PRACTICAL TERMS, IS THIS: that in the real world of claims settlements, practically no claims whatsoever is without merit or is totally lacking in some value of some sort[11] — a very comforting piece of information for you to know as a claimant! It's just that you have to be well aware of, and knowledgeable, though, about the way the claims "system" actually works; and then, you have to be also willing to go out and actually but aggressively demand your entitlements under that system!!

As Ross, again, put it, "Compromise, then, is the order of the day [even] in cases of questionable liability…Moderate or severe degrees of doubt [as to your own liability for an accident] will be used by the claims man to attempt denial of the claim, and often he will succeed. *It is only when faced by a determined claimant that the adjuster will make compromise payments…[for] the adjuster will make some payment [only because it dawns on him that he had better get the claim resolved by settlement] rather than allow the claim to go to litigation.*"[12]

Figure 7-C

Numbers of Accidents, Total, and by Selected Movement, 1990

Vehicle Movement	Fatal Accidents			All Accidents		
	Total	Urban	Rural	Total	Urban	Rural
Total Accidents	41,200	14,700	26,500	11,500,000	7,740,000	3,760,000
Pedestrian	7,200	4,200	3,000	70,000	50,000	20,000
Two-vehicle collision total	15,800	5,700	10,100	9,160,000	6,840,000	2,320,000
Angle collision	5,200	2,200	3,000	2,440,000	1,920,000	520,000
Head-on collision	4,600	1,000	3,600	280,000	160,000	120,000
Rear-end collision	1,800	700	1,100	2,200,000	1,570,000	630,000
Other two-vehicle collision	4,200	1,800	2,400	4,240,000	3,190,000	1,050,000
Other collision total	13,400	4,400	9,000	1,560,000	780,000	780,000
Noncollision total	4,800	400	4,400	710,000	70,000	640,000

Source: Based on reports from state traffic authorities. Procedures for estimating deaths and injuries for certain accident types were changed for the 1990 edition and are not-comparable to those in previous editions.

As cited in Accident Fact, 1991

---

[10]Ross, Settled Out of Court, p. 129.

[11]Statements such as the following, the first two by experienced, practicing insurance adjusters, and the third by a practicing negligence attorney, adequately makes the point: "I don't think there is any case that doesn't have some value to it." Or, "I would venture to say that [even] most questionable cases are paid. Some of them aren't, most of them are…" Or, "I guess the only time that a case drops to zero is where it's quite clear that there's no fault on the part of the potential defendant or defendants, where you don't have any possible liability…[but such] cases are very hard to find." (Ross, Settled Out of Court, p. 130.

[12]Ross, Settled Out of Court, pp. 130-1.

J. A Cautionary Note: Avoid Talking to The Adjuster to Minimize Complicating Your "Liability Position"

Claims adjusters and negligence lawyers have long been aware that one of the major ways by which lawyers have typically been able to make a difference in the handling of claims for their clients, is by the fact that they exert "control" over the appearance of liability (and of damages) on the part of the claimant they represent. Principally, the lawyer does this simply by not allowing his client to talk to or give statements to the adjuster, thereby shielding the client from possibly giving "incriminating" statements to adjusters that could later be interpreted as admissions of contributory negligence or liability on the part of the client. Instances abound when ill-informed claimants with no legal counsel or knowledge of the way the system works, have forfeited recovery of damages merely because they unwittingly made statements to an aggressive adjuster that can later be construed as incriminating or implicating, often involving written statements signed and placed in the case file.

In deed, because of this danger alone, claims lawyers and strategists are almost unanimous in advising that the best strategy for the claimant—any claimant—is simply to avoid talking to or giving any statement of any sort to an adjuster, or to any insurance or defendant's representative. One expert[13], a lawyer, put it this way, sounding his caution rather dramatically:

> "If the other driver (involved in an accident) had insurance, it's likely that the company adjuster will come bounding up your front porch that evening with a big smile and an offer of $25 for a release (unless you're in a state with the new "no-fault" insurance). *Don't sign anything!* In fact, the best advice at that point is don't even talk to him. Tell him politely but firmly that you're not ready to discuss the claim, and that you'll be in touch with him at some future time.
>
> He probably won't give up that easily and will want to take a statement from you. It's dangerous and foolhardy for you to give him one, at least at that time. Most adjusters are honest, but many have a charming, if unintentional, habit of slanting the story, at best, and putting down some of the information inaccurately, at worst.
> "Oh," you say, "I'll correct any mistakes when I read it over." But all too often you won't catch thesubtle slanting. Or you'll miss the mistake. Or you might not realize you've given him some incorrect item. Or you may not be sure of a "small" detail (such as speed or distance or time of day), which the adjuster will "prompt" you into estimating, often adversely to your claim.
> So rule one, do not—(REPEAT!)—do not give any statement to the adjuster, at the beginning.
>
> It's wise for you to write out your own version of the facts, for yourself, while the accident is still fresh in your mind; but giving the adjuster a statement without thinking it out — and without understanding the law involved— can be devastating to your claim.
> The adjuster may agree to your "no statement" desire, but then start pumping you with questions anyway. Often he'll have a tape recorder in his coat pocket. Don't discuss the claim with him. Again, tell him courteously that you'll contact him later.
>
> He may even imply that you must have something to hide if you're "afraid" to talk to him. Don't be fooled. You have plenty of time to talk to him, at your convenience.
> By not giving the adjuster a statement, you'll accomplish the following: 1) Save yourself from botching the claim at the very beginning, and 2) Give the adjuster some worries, and put him on the defensive."

THE FOLLOWING STATEMENTS OFTEN MADE TO THE ADJUSTER BY CLAIMANTS, ARE THE KINDS OF STATEMENTS WHICH HAVE BEEN FOUND TO BE INCRIMINATING AGAINST CLAIMANTS:

> Question to claimant (by adjuster): "When you first saw the other car for the first time, how far away was the front of your car from the other car?" State in feet, yards, car lengths.

---

[13]Siegel, How to Avoid Lawyers, p. 2-3. One adjuster interviewed by a researcher conceded that the 'no-talk' attitude by a claimant had, in deed, often worked in favor of the claimant to the disadvantage of the adjuster: "Where I can get a good, strong statement from the claimant, this is enough to turn him down. If I can never get a statement from him I have to begin negotiation without this, and [if] I don't feel that I have a strong enough investigation to warrant a turn-down, then I will make a compromise settlement. Now, this effect, it works better for the claimant in that he comes out to the advantage, he at least gets some payment on the claim" (Ross, Settled Out of Court, p. 118).

Claimant: "I saw the car a pretty good distance away" or "I didn't see the other car until the collision occurred"
Question: Why?
(The implication of this exchange from the claimant's answer, is that he wasn't looking or paying attention when the accident occurred.)

The 'I assumed' statements: "I assumed that he was going to stop" or "I assumed that because I had a green light I could proceed on it" (You can't "assume" in an uncontrolled intersection, for example, where there's no absolute right of way!)

"I didn't see the other car." (Then why? Motorists often think that if they didn't see the other party then it's a help to them, that this gives them excuse to have proceeded. Not so, though! In truth, the fact of not seeing the hazard is generally taken as an admission of negligence—an admission that you weren't quite looking.)

Making wild, fixed estimates. Example: "I was going 35 miles an hour" (A better answer is to give a broad range: "I was going between 25 and 40 miles…")

"I made a left turn in front of somebody"
"I hit somebody in the rear end"
"A car stopped in front of me. I couldn't stop and I hit him"
"I failed to see the red light"
"I'm new in the area, the bushes were hiding the stop sign and I went through the stop sign".

CHAPTER 8

Do You Have An Auto Insurance Coverage? What Type(s) And What Compensations Does It Entitle You To?

Which Insurance Company Do You File Your Claim Against?

Out of every $10 that Americans spend every year for all property and casualty coverages, over $4 of that goes to pay the premium for insuring motor vehicles. Of the total net premium of $217.8 billion written by all property/casualty insurance companies in 1990, for example, $95.4 billion of that was written for auto insurances, representing 44 percent of the total premium.

The Coverages That Are Typically Included In Auto Insurance Policy

An auto insurance policy is a package of six different types of coverage, each with it's own premium. A motorist can eliminate certain types of coverage, although most states require that at least the coverage for bodily injury and property damage be carried. The six types of coverage are:

      a) Liability Insurance (Bodily-injury and Property-Damage Liability insurance)

      b) Collision Insurance

      c) Comprehensive Coverage Insurance

      d) Medical Pay (or Expense) Insurance

      e) Uninsured-Motorist and Underinsured-Motorist Insurance

      f) No-Fault Insurance System

      g) Personal-injury Protection (PIP) under No-Fault

A. Liability Insurance Coverage

Liability insurance covers the owner of a vehicle against any damage or legal wrong he or she may cause from his negligent operation of the vehicle. Liability coverage is regarded as the most important policy of all auto policies, and is the only "compulsory" auto coverage in most states, i.e., the only auto coverage which, by law, the motorist must carry in most states. Thus, for example, of the total of $95.4 billion worth of premiums paid for all auto insurance policies in 1990, liability coverage alone (personal and commercial) accounted for $60 billion or 63 percent that, while collision and comprehensive coverage accounted for $35.3 billion or 37 percent, according to figures by New York's Insurance Information Institute. [See Table 8-A below]

And even in those handful of states which do not have the "compulsory" auto insurance law[1] that makes it compulsory to maintain an automobile liability insurance, there generally exists, instead, financial-responsibility laws which, along with the ever present threat of a financially crippling judgement award in the event of an accident, has had the effect of

---

[1]There are only 8 such states in 1989: Alabama, Mississippi, New Hampshire, Rhode Island, Tennessee, Virginia, Washington, and Wisconsin.

TABLE 8-A PRIVATE PASSENGER AUTOMOBILE INSURANCE, 1981-1990

($1,000)

Year	Liability			Collision and comprehensive		
	Premiums written	Annual % change	Combined ratio*	Premiums written	Annual % change	Combined ratio*
1981	$19,649,912	+5.7	108.9	$14,033,870	+7.2	98.6
1982	21,487,468	+9.4	110.1	15,292,070	+9.0	101.4
1983	23,343,939	+8.6	111.0	16,974,304	+11.0	96.3
1984	24,809,382	+6.3	112.8	18,497,769	+9.0	100.6
1985	28,243,882	+13.8	118.9	21,180,583	+14.5	98.9
1986	32,972,920	+16.7	117.9	24,198,891	+14.3	93.6
1987	37,449,134	+13.6	116.1	26,838,193	+10.9	89.7
1988	40,812,744	+9.0	115.9	28,676,435	+6.8	92.0
1989	43,976,575	+7.8	117.0	29,585,442	+3.2	95.5
1990	47,830,741	+8.8	117.7	30,561,903	+3.3	93.9

*Before dividends to policyholders.
Source: A.M. Best Company, Inc., Best's Aggregates & Averages.

COMMERCIAL AUTOMOBILE INSURANCE, 1981-1990

($1,000)

Year	Liability			Collision and comprehensive		
	Premiums written	Annual % change	Combined ratio*	Premiums written	Annual % change	Combined ratio*
1981	$4,745,262	+0.3	117.5	$2,713,919	-1.2	99.8
1982	4,738,978	-0.1	125.6	2,713,417	0.0	106.0
1983	4,736,128	-0.1	132.0	2,773,199	+2.2	105.9
1984	5,407,281	+14.2	142.4	3,268,035	+17.8	110.9
1985	7,842,789	+45.0	126.3	4,066,138	+24.4	97.1
1986	11,108,002	+41.6	111.6	5,106,615	+25.6	82.1
1987	11,755,444	+5.8	107.1	5,157,198	+1.0	79.4
1988	11,707,484	-0.4	107.5	5,182,808	+0.5	80.4
1989	12,047,151	+2.9	111.5	5,253,759	+1.4	85.4
1990	12,211,706	+1.4	113.7	4,762,688	-9.3	90.4

*Before dividends to policyholders.
Note: The $95.4 billion in premiums written for auto insurance in 1990 breaks down into $78.4 billion (82 percent) for private passenger auto and nearly $17 billion (18 percent) for commercial. Source: As cited in The Fact Book, 1992

making the purchase of liability insurance a virtual necessity for the overwhelming majority of motorists.

Liability insurance consists of two basic components — the "bodily-injury" liability part, and the "property-damage" liability part.

1. WHAT THE BODILY-INJURY PART OF LIABILITY INSURANCE COVERS

The bodily-injury liability coverage is the part that pays for you (the insured party) for any bodily injury related damages you may become legally obligated to pay to a person injured or for someone killed in an accident involving your vehicle. People you injure can collect against this coverage to pay for their medical expenses, their pain and suffering from resultant bodily injuries suffered, and for lost wages, and other miscellaneous expenses.[2]

2. WHAT THE PROPERTY-DAMAGE PART OF LIABILITY INSURANCE COVERS

The property-damage part of your auto liability insurance policy (which is generally combined with the bodily-injury part in your premium payments), is the part that pays for you (the insured party) if you damage someone else's property, usually a vehicle. In other words, this part of the coverage is concerned with compensation for **property-related aspects** of the damages you may become liable for, as differentiated from the bodily-injury part of the coverage which, on the other hand, is concerned with the *injury-related* aspects of the damages.

---

[2]The bodily injury liability coverage also pays for the compensation or expense for: liability brought about by relatives and friends who drive your (i.e., the insured party's) vehicle with your (the owner's) permission; first aid costs to the other parties; investigation expenses; court costs; bail bond; attorney's fees; and lost-wages, even if it's incurred for your being needed in court.

3. OTHER TYPES OF LIABILITY POLICIES

A motorist could have taken out what is called a **"single limit of liability"** coverage. (You can tell what the policy holder has by simply looking at the cover sheet, or "deck" sheet, of the policy — the paper that lists the vehicle's insured, the serial number, coverages, etc.) A single-limit-liability policy is a policy which pays one amount per accident, regardless of how many individuals are involved. Thus, instead of stating the figures $25,000/$75,000/ $50,000, your policy would simply show the single limit of $55,000. And this will mean that the most your insurance company will pay out for the accident is $55,000, whether it's for bodily injury or property damage, or is to be paid to one accident victim or to more.

Another type of auto liability insurance policy which a motorist could take out, is known as an **"umbrella insurance policy."** This type of policy is a "supplementary" kind of insurance, meaning that it is an insurance meant to add additional coverage to the basic liability coverage already possessed. Thus, a motorist having a basic minimum policy of, say, 20/40/10 can supplement his liability coverage with an "umbrella" policy that provides, say a $50,000 protection.

Umbrella policies are said to be "floats" above your other coverage, meaning that the insured motorist must carry the underlying basic liability coverage before he can buy the umbrella. As a rule, umbrella policies are usually purchased by people who have assets worth far more than the normal-limit liability coverage.

B. Collision Insurance Coverage

Next to liability insurance, collision insurance is the second largest coverage in auto insurance, accounting for 30 percent of the insurance premium on new or older model cars. Collision coverage is that category of insurance policy which is concerned with paying for any loss or damages to the insured party's car caused by upset of the car or collision with another object, whether or not the insured party is at fault, and whether or not another vehicle is involved.

In other words, claims for collision damages (as with damages for fire and theft) of your insured motor vehicle, are made under YOUR OWN insurance policy, and it doesn't matter if the accident is your fault, subject to a "deductible" amount. It is also the collision insurance that covers hit-and-run accidents, as well as your deductible if you are in an accident involving another car and you are at fault.[3]

For example, let's say you (the insured party) have a collision coverage in your policy and that you accidentally slide off the road into a telephone pole or that you run a red light and hit another vehicle. Or, let's say your packed car is struck by another driver whose identity is unknown to you. In each of these cases, it is YOUR OWN insurance company that will pay you for the expenses of fixing your own car—providing, of course, you have purchased and did have in force a collision insurance coverage (or a comprehensive coverage.)

(Note; however, that the collision coverage is always limited by, and subject to, a "deductible" amount, meaning that the amount the insurance company will pay you for any given damages or expenses will only be an amount over and above your applicable "deductible" amount. The available deductibles in this regard are $50, $100, $250, $500, and $1,000.)

What Are Your State's Liability Insurance Limits?

Most states have laws, commonly known as FINANCIAL RESPONSIBILITY LAWS, requiring that a person involved in an automobile accident must furnish proof of financial responsibility—usually in the form of auto liability insurance—up to a certain minimum dollar limits. Thus, many states require car owners to have a minimum amount of bodily-injury and property-damage liability insurance (either in lieu of, or in addition to other types of "financial responsibility" protections). A typical state minimum would be a bodily injury coverage that pays up to $20,000 for each person hurt in an auto accident, but not more than $40,000 in total per accident for all persons involved in each accident, and $10,000 for property damage per accident. (See the table below. Notice, for example, that the state of Alabama has exactly these three above-stated minimum requirement limits of $20,000, $40,000 and $10,000.)

---

[3]The way this works is this: you use your collision coverage, less the "deductible" amount, to pay for the damage to your car and then let your insurance company try to collect the money back from the other party.

TABLE 8-B

AUTOMOBILE FINANCIAL RESPONSIBILITY/COMPULSORY LIMITS			
State	Liability limits*	State	Liability limits*
Alabama	20/40/10	Montana	25/50/5
Alaska	50/100/25	Nebraska	25/50/25
Arizona	15/30/10	Nevada	15/30/10
Arkansas	25/50/15	New Hampshire	25/50/25
California	15/30/5	New Jersey	15/30/5
Colorado	25/50/15	New Mexico	25/50/10
Connecticut	20/40/10	New York	10/20/5
Delaware	15/30/10	North Carolina	25/50/10
District of Columbia	25/50/10	North Dakota	25/50/25
Florida	10/20/10	Ohio	12.5/25/7.5
Georgia	15/30/10	Oklahoma	10/20/10
Hawaii	15/35/10	Oregon	25/50/15
Idaho	25/50/15	Pennsylvania	15/30/5
Illinois	20/40/15	Rhode Island	25/50/25
Indiana	25/50/10	South Carolina	15/30/5
Iowa	20/40/15	South Dakota	25/50/25
Kansas	25/50/10	Tennessee	20/50/10
Kentucky	25/50/10	Texas	20/40/15
Louisiana	10/20/10	Utah	20/40/10
Maine	20/40/10	Vermont	20/40/10
Maryland	20/40/10	Virginia	25/50/20
Massachusetts	10/20/5	Washington	25/50/10
Michigan	20/40/10	West Virginia	20/40/10
Minnesota	30/60/10	Wisconsin	25/50/10
Mississippi	10/20/5	Wyoming	25/50/20
Missouri	25/50/10		

The first two figures refer to bodily injury liability limits, and the third figure to property damage liability. For example, 10/20/5 means coverage up to $20,000 for all persons injured in an acicdent, subject to a limit of $10.000 for one individual, and $5,000 coverage for property damage.
Source: The Fact Book, 1992, pp. 100-101.

Experience has shown, however, that the size of court settlements in auto accident cases are frequently far in excess of the minimum limits mandated by state laws. Consequently, insurance companies, consumer publications and other experts generally recommend that automobile owners purchase higher levels of liability insurance than the state minimum laws require. More commonly mentioned figures are at least $100,000 of bodily injury protection per person and $300,000 total per accident. People who own a house or other assets, for example, particularly need minimum of at least such magnitudes in order to protect their assets from potential large court awards.

NOTE: In each combination, the first two figures refer to bodily injury liabilities, and the third figure to property damage liability; the first figure is the monetary protection unit you have in case you injure or kill one person in an "at fault" accident or are otherwise considered to be in the wrong, the middle figure is the protection limit you have if one or more persons are injured or killed in an accident, and the last figure is the protection limit you have for all property damages you cause in an accident. For example, 10/20/5 means coverage up to $20,000 for all persons injured in an accident subject to a limit of $10,000 for an individual, and $5,000 coverage for property damage.

C. Comprehensive Insurance Coverage

This type of policy is carried by about 70 to 80 percent of all auto accident insurance policyholders. As the name implies, comprehensive personal liability insurance coverage is a catchall coverage that pays for damages resulting from just about everything — except collision with another car or a solid object, or upset. It's coverage is, in short, sweeping—"comprehensive." It provides personal liability coverage for members of the insured's family, and it also offers other persons protection for their own liability arising out of their use or care of the insured's vehicle, and further provides medical payments (without regard to who is negligent or at fault) for persons who are injured in an accident involving the vehicle or the insured, and even pays transportation allowance if the insured's car had been stolen.

The specific damages covered by comprehensive insurance include the following: damages to the insured's car resulting from causes like floods, hail storms, explosions, theft, vandalism, wind, falling objects, fire, riots, collision with animals or birds, and glass breakage.

Note, however, that as with the collision insurance, described immediately above, the comprehensive insurance is also usually subject to "deductibles" which range from $50 to $500.

D. Medical Pay (or Expense) Insurance Coverage

Auto medical-expense coverage is not the same as liability coverage. Rather, it is an *optional* coverage and not a required one, on the auto policy, primarily meant to pay the medical expenses of the insured and his passengers. Basically, the so-called **"med-pay"** coverage pays the insured and his passengers up to a certain amount (usually $1,000, but sometimes as high as $5,000) for medical expenses incurred by them within a year, and pays them regardless of who's at fault.

This coverage is not usually required or necessary in no-fault states, and many people who already have family health insurance forgo buying a duplicate coverage in an auto policy, while even among those people who choose to purchase the auto medical insurance coverage, most of them purchase only a small coverage of about $1,000 to $2,000 of it.

Medical expense coverage on your auto policy pays for the following:
- the medical expense you or others may incur up to the policy limits for you (the insured party) or any person injured "in, on, around, above, and below" your car, regardless of who's at fault.
- The medical expenses of any relative in the insured's household who doesn't own a car, if they are injured either while riding in other cars, or are struck by another car.
- Costs of an ambulance ride from the accident scene, and for the funeral of the insured person involved in a fatal car accident.

Only medical expenses incurred **within** one year from the date of the accident, is payable by this policy, however.

E. Uninsured & Underinsured Motorist Insurance Coverage

1. UNINSURED COVERAGE

Uninsured-motorist insurance coverage has been called "the most misunderstood coverage in the field of car insurance."[4] Hence, let us be very clear on its definition before we proceed. Uninsured-motorist insurance coverage will usually reimburse you (i.e., the insured party) for any bodily injury, and medical expenses or death (but NOT for any **property damage**) that you or anyone in your vehicle may sustain from an auto accident — in accidents caused by a hit-and-run driver, or a driver of a stolen car, or a driver who has no insurance. In other words, as its name would seem to imply, uninsured motorist coverage provides you protection you probably would not have otherwise, against any bodily injury you sustain from an accident with a motorist who is underlined.

The way this works is this: say you have an accident with a hit-and-run or an uninsured motorist, the only place you can turn to for compensation for all bodily injuries and medical expenses, is YOUR OWN coverage. In such a situation, assuming, of course, that you yourself have insurance coverage, you'll get reimbursed by your own insurance company, rather than having to look to the other motorist's policy to do so!

How, though, do you make a claim from your uninsured motorist benefits? The particular practice and details may differ in terms of particular insurance companies. But, generally, your insurance company would want to have some sort of proof or verification that the other motorist did not, in fact, have an insurance coverage (i.e., that he was , in deed, uninsured as of the date of the accident). While some companies may independently do its own verification to obtain this information, others may ask you, the claimant, to obtain and file such proof or verification with your insurance company. [See Chapter 3, Section I (pp. 50-1), for more on the uninsured motorist and how to secure necessary processing information about or from him]

2. UNDERINSURED COVERAGE

Underinsured coverage is usually (though not always) offered as part of the uninsured motorist coverage. The difference between the uninsured coverage and the underinsured coverage is simple: whereas the UNINSURED case is concerned with providing protection for bodily injury if the other driver doesn't have any insurance at all (a "no insurance" situation), the UNDERINSURED coverage case is concerned with providing such protection if the other driver doesn't have enough insurance to cover all of your bills ("insufficient insurance" situation). To put it briefly, if the other driver's bodily-injury insurance happens not to be enough in terms of covering your bills, your UNDERINSURED-motorist coverage is to pay the balance up to the limit on the policy.

---

[4]Jeff O'Donnel, Insurance Smart, p. 47.

F. The No-Fault Insurance System

If your state is a "no-fault" insurance state (see pp. 113 & 116-125 below, for a list of no-fault states), many of what we have described or the comments we made in the preceding passages of this whole chapter as to your rights to collect the damages outlined, or the procedures thereof, may not apply.

What is a "no-fault" insurance system, to begin with? Simply put, no-fault is a relatively recent concept by which YOUR OWN INSURANCE COMPANY is required to pay you for your losses for bodily-injury, without regard to who is at fault in the accident. No-fault encompasses damages for your medical and hospital expenses growing out of an auto accident, and your loss of earnings thereof, requiring them to be reimbursed by YOUR OWN insurance company, without regard to fault.

No-fault also encompasses property damages, in the sense that insured motorists in no-fault states can buy collision insurance coverage to pay for damage to their own cars and only enough property-damage-liability coverage to protect them when driving outside their states.

No-fault system requires, however, that in exchange for being able to count on almost automatic payment for damages from your own insurance company without haggling about who is "at fault," you give up your right to recover anything for "pain and suffering" from injuries in an accident. You will not have to give up the right in all situations, however. Rather, you'll (generally) give up this so-called "right to sue" only with respect to less serious cases, but still retain the right to sue on cases involving demonstrable extraordinary injuries. (The law in a given state, for example, may require that the motorist must sustain injuries amounting to, say, more than $500 in medical bills, before he can ask or sue for compensation for pain and suffering.)

As of this writing in 1992, there are 22 no-fault states in the nation, but of these 22 states, only 14 of them are considered "true" no-fault states, according to New York's Insurance Information Institute, an authority on the subject — meaning states which have strong no-fault laws that strictly limit law suits in auto injury cases, allowing suits only when injuries are serious enough. See p. 113 for a list of no-fault states in the nation.

Personal-Injury Protection (PIP) Under No-Fault

Of particular interest to motorists in states with no-fault insurance system, is what is known as the Personal Injury Protection (PIP) automobile insurance plan. In plain language, PIP is simply the type of insurance policy which the state laws require motorists to buy in no-fault states. It is a more comprehensive form of medical payments coverage. PIP not only covers medical and hospital bills, but generally covers lost wages during the period of incapacity to work due to injuries, replacement of services while the injured party is unable to perform routine or household work, and some funeral expenses.

The no-fault insurance system basically provides that payment is made by the injured party's insurer, regardless of who was at fault. In general, no-fault coverage porvides for you (i.e., the policyholder or the injured person) to be reimbursed by YOUR OWN insurance company for medical bills and lost wages — up to certain dollar amounts — for injuries sustained in an accident, regardless of who was at fault for the accident, and in exchange for that quick, certain, and faultless compensation, you'll ordinarily forego any lawsuits and any claims for injuries and "pain and suffering." You (i.e., the injured party or parties) may, however, sue for injuries and pain and suffering, but ONLY in extraordinary situations — i.e., if and when the case meets certain conditions("threshholds"). These conditions, known as "thresholds," relate basically to severity of the injury.

In the event a passenger is injured, the insurer of the car in which the passenger was riding pays. If the driver isn't insured, then the insurer of any other driver in the accident pays. Pedestrians are paid by the insurer of the car that struck them. If none of the parties is insured, your only alternative, as a victim, is to sue the party you believe to be at fault, *unless* you were driving and carried uninsured-motorist coverage, in which event your insurer pays you but only if the other party, in fact, was at fault.

No-fault benefits are always limited to economic damage (the so-called Special Damages), i.e., compensation for medical bills, lost wages, and in some states, funeral expenses, cost of hiring replacement labor (such as a housekeeper), and physical rehabilitation or job retraining courses. In other words, *payments for pain and suffering and other noncash expenses (General Damages) are not usually covered by no-fault.*

Sometimes the insurer will refuse to pay benefits or cut them off prematurely, in the victim's judgement. Should that happen to you, you may have to go to court to gain or regain the benefits.

In most states, the no-fault insurer pays the injured party's medical bills up to a set statutory maximum (see Chart on pp. 116-125), and payments by Blue Cross/Blue Shield or similar private medical insurance plans begin only after the permitted maximum has been reached. However, in some states (e.g., Connecticut, Kentucky, Pennsylvania, and South Dakota) the injured party is permitted to collect both from the no-fault insurer and from the private medical plan for the same item of medical expense.

As stated above, in one way or another, the right to sue is retained, however, in every no-fault state. It's just that the victim may sue ONLY WHEN his or her medical expenses exceed a specified "threshold" limit. A typical figure is $2,000 to $2,500, but in a number of states there is no limit, while in still others ("add-on" states) you must prove certain specified "serious" injuries, a definition that usually includes death, before suit is permitted. (See Summary Chart on pp. 116-125).

STATES WITH NO-FAULT SYSTEM

The following 22 states, plus the District of Columbia and Puerto Rico, have some form of no-fault auto insurance system:

Arkansas	Kentuckey	Oregon
Colorado	Maryland	Pennsylvania
Connecticut	Massachusetts	Puerto Rico
Delaware	Michigan	South Dakota
District of Columbia	Minnesota	Texas
Florida	New Jersey	Utah
Hawaii	New York	Virginia
Kansas	North Dakota	Washington

No-fault coverage will only pay for medical bills and lost income within the PIP benefits limits of your policy. No-fault does not generally apply at all to VEHICLE DAMAGES, for claims concerning that, you may still file a liability claim against the party who is responsible for the accident. And, in some states, after you file under the no-fault insurance claim — often referred to in the insurance policy as PERSONAL INJURY PROTECTION or PIP — you may still also be able to file a liability claim against the person at fault. Such a liability claim will permit you (the injured motorist) to file a liability claim, and a lawsuit if necesssary, against another driver who was at fault in an accident to obtain compensation for medical and income losses over and above whatever PIP benefits that have been paid, as well as compensation for pain, suffering, emotional distress and inconvenience, the same as in a liability claim in a state having a fault insurance system. (Look to the provisions of your individual insurance policy, as well as the specifics of the no-fault law of your state of the accident — Summary chart on pp. 116-125 below — for a determination of that.).

STATES HAVING "ADD-ON" BENEFITS

Of the 22 states which are listed as no-fault, some of them — Arkansas, Delaware, Maryland, Oregon, South Dakota, Texas, Virginia, and Washington — have what is called "add-on" benefits that allow motorists to file a liability claim against the person at fault for an accident, in addition to ("added on to") making a PIP claim under their no fault coverage. In other words, in those 9 states you do not have to meet any injury or monetary "threshold" before you may file for compensation for economic damages (medical and other out of pocket expenses) and/or noneconomic damages (pain and suffering, and the like.).

In these so-called "add-on" coverage states, a liability claim is filed and processed exactly the same way as a regular claim would be filed and processed in a state without no-fault, as there are no restrictions on lawsuits.

"VERBAL" AND/OR "MONETARY" THRESHOLD

The term 'verbal threshold' describes the point in each no-fault state above which the tort restriction does not apply, when it is expressed either in terms of severity of injury, or in terms of length of disability caused by injury. In other words, once you have reached that specified injury or disability level ("threshold"), you are then free to file a regular liability claim or lawsuit against the parties at fault for your accident.

Each state also has a <u>monetary</u> threshold, meaning the limit, expressed as dollars of medical expenses (e.g., "damages recoverable if medical expenses exceed $4,000") above which you are permitted to file a liability claim or lawsuit.

The types or levels of injury or medical or other expenses that count towards reaching the prescribed 'threshold' under each state's laws, differ from state to state. To find out what exactly is counted towards such threshold in your state, simply read carefully the definitions of the injury, medical expense and monetary thresholds in your own no-fault (PIP) insurance policy.

> <u>NOTE:</u> Note that notwithstanding even the best efforts of a state law to expressly define what exactly constitutes a "threshold" under each state's no-fault law, as practical matter, the working definition of the term is essentially subjective. Frequently, there is no definite determination of that issue; hence, it is essential always for you to remember that the issue of whether your injury meets the threshold standard of your state is something that is subject to negotiation with the insurance company of the person at fault.

"CHOICE" NO FAULT STATES

Of the no fault states, there are three so-called "choice no-fault" states among them — New Jersey, Pennsylvania, and Kentucky. Here, a motorist has a "choice": he may elect either to reject the lawsuit threshold and maintain an unrestricted right to sue for both economic damages and pain and suffering, <u>OR</u> choose to limit his right to sue — i.e., to retain the ability to sue for recovery of economic damages (medical expenses, wages, and the like), while limiting the ability to sue with respect to pain and suffering.

G. WHICH INSURANCE COMPANY DO YOU FILE YOUR CLAIM AGAINST?

The first place, and often the only place, a person injured in an auto accident needs turn to for compensation is to the other driver's insurance company, as just about every state requires that every motorist or registered vehicle carry some kind of accident liability insurance coverage. If you have a no-fault auto insurance coverage, however (see p.112), you will primarily file your claim with your own insurance company, but may, in many instances, also be able to file a claim against the other driver's insurance comsany, especially when the injury and medical expense "threshold" shall have been surpassed under your state law's provisions (see Chart on pp. 116-125).

What happens when you are involved in an accident with more than one vehicle? In such a situation, you should simply file your claim for damages with the insurance companies for each of the motorists involved. In a situation such as that, it's customary for the insurance to get together and decide among themselves on who will provide the "primary" coverage for your claims, depending on the percentage of "comparative" fault assigned to each party — that is, the party who will take the main responsibility for your compensation. The other company or companies will be required only to provide the **"excess" coverage,** meaning to make up for any excess in damages that you may incur over and above the limits available under your primary policy, if that should become necessary.

If you are a passenger injured in an accident (though not a relative who's living with the driver), you should file a claim with both the insurance company of the driver or owner of your vehicle, and of the driver or owner of the other vehicle or vehicles. This way, you can be sure that you will be able to collect for your damages from one party or the other even if a driver or owner of the vehicles is either uninsured or underinsured for the amount of your total damages.

If the vehicle you are driving which is involved in an accident is someone else's, you should file your claims for damages against the other driver; if the other vehicle happens to be uninsured, then file your claim primarily with the uninsured motorist coverage of the owner of the car you were driving and, secondly, with your own uninsured motorist coverage.

If you are involved in a situation where the driver of the other vehicle involved in an accident is not the owner of the vehicle, you should file your liability claims primarily with the owner's insurance company, and only secondly with the driver's insurance company. And if neither the other driver nor the owner of the vehicle is insured, you should consider filing your claims with your own uninsured insurance motorist coverage (see pp. 50-51 & 111).

EXPLANATORY NOTES TO NO-FAULT STATES' CHART

The following notes explain the Headings and other information provided in the No-Fault summary chart on pp. 116-125.

NO-FAULT AND ADD-ON BENEFITS

There are three types of no-fault automobile insurance policies: Policies with verbal thresholds, policies with monetary thresholds, and choice no-fault policies.

Verbal Threshold: The point in each no-fault state, above which the tort restriction does not apply, expressed in terms of definitions describing seriousness of injury, or in terms of length of disability caused by injury.

Monetary Threshold: The point in each no-fault state above which the tort restriction does not apply, expressed as dollars of medical costs (e.g. "damages recoverable if medical expenses exceed $4,000").

Choice No-Fault: States which may elect either to maintain an unrestricted legal ability to seek financial compensation for both economic damages and noneconomic damages, or choose to limit the ability to sue (i.e., retain the ability to sue for recovery of economic damages while limiting the ability to seek noneconomic damages).

Add-On: A no-fault policy wherein a motorist can file a liability claim against the person at fault for an accident in addition to making a claim under his no-fault coverage.

Vehicles Included: Designates the types of vehicles required to maintain no-fault and first-party benefits coverage. Most states exclude motorcycles from mandatory coverage requirements.

Complying Coverage For Out-Of-State Vehicles In State: The majority of states requiring first-party benefits also require insurers writing automobile policies in the state to provide the same minimum coverage in any policy they write (in any state) so that such policies will provide the required no-fault benefits when the insured vehicle is in the state.

Priority Of Policies: Designates the order in which different policies apply to a claim where more than one policy could be involved.

Persons Entitled To Benefits: Indicates which persons may receive first-party benefits under a no-fault policy when the accident occurs in the state of vehicle registration [I.S.] and when the accident occurs out-of-state of registration [O.S.]. In most states, the named insured, relatives, vehicle occupants and pedestrians suffering loss in an in-state accident are entitled to benefits. In out-of-state accidents, most states exclude pedestrians other than insureds and family members from first-party benefits.

Persons Excluded: Indicates specific persons who "may" (i.e., at the insurer's option) or "must" (i.e., by statutory provision) be excluded from first-party benefits upon the occurance of an accident. Persons intentionally causing injury, vehicle converters, and persons committing felonies, are commonly excluded.

General Damages (Noneconomic): Indicates the specific injury or medical expense required to permit the victim or survivors to sue in tort for noneconomic loss.

Specific Damages (Economic): Refers to specified injury, medical rehabilitation, or uncompensated loss thresholds necessary to permit the victim or suvivors to sue in tort for economic loss.

Medical Benefits: Generally include doctor, hospital, and rehabilitation expenses. Most states have a maximum limitation on medical benefits receivable. Such limits are either specified or subject to the limitations on total benefits receivable.

Wage Loss Benefits: Refers to benefits received for loss of income the victim would have received were it not for the injury. In most states, the amount of wages recoverable is limited to a percentage of lost wages, wages which would have been earned in a fixed time period, and/or the total amount of first-party benefits receivable.

Replacement Services Benefits: Benefits received for expenditures for services the victim would normally perform without pay for the benefit of family members were it not for the injury. Maximum limits are set by liquidated amounts over specified time periods and/or by limitations on total first-party benefits receivable.

Survivors'/Funeral Benefits: Generally, survivor benefits refer to compensation to dependents of the deceased victim for lost wages and replacement services. In most states, maximum limits are set by liquidated amounts and/or limits on total benefits receivable. Funeral benefits refer to amounts recoverable by the victim's survivors for burial expenses. The amounts set forth in the summary chart are maximum limits.

Required Optional Coverages/Required Deductibles: Designates additional coverages and deductibles, which insurers must offer and the insured may accept.

Subrogation: Indicates general nature of subrogation rights. Refers to the right of your insurance under some no-fault policies, to recover your Personal Insurance Protection (PIP) benefits directly from the liable person's insurance company. In other words, rather than you first recovering the damages from the liable person's insurance company and then reimbursing your own PIP insurance company for the amount it paid you, your PIP company may directly recover your PIP benefits directly from the liable party's insurance company, but the damages you yourself collect from the liable person's insurance company would be "net" any amounts your PIP coverage paid you.

Assigned Claims: Refers to whether a state has an assigned claims plan in effect and whether benefits are limited to persons suffering injury while in the state. Generally, under an assigned claims plan, benefits are available if there is no applicable or identifiable insurance, or if an insurer is insolvent. Benefits are not generally available to owners of uninsured vehicles.

Miscellaneous: Includes arbitration provisions and other pertinent information.

CHART — NO-FAULT STATES, SUMMARY OF THE LAWS

ARKANSAS — DISTRICT OF COLUMBIA

STATE	Types of Vehicles included in coverage	Complying Coverage for Out-Of-State Vehicles In State	Priority of Policies	Persons Entitled to Benefits (in state [I.S.] and out of state [O.S.] accidents)	Persons [1] Excluded May or Must Be Excluded	TORT EXEMPTION/LIMITATION	
						General Damages (Noneconomic)	Special Damages (Economic)
ARKANSAS [Add-on benefits state]	All excluding government vehicles, motorcycles, mopeds, commercial and fleet vehicles	No provision	No provision	I.S. - Insured and family, occupants, pedestrians [2]	Intent, Felony, Evade/may	None	None
COLORADO [monetary threshold]	All excluding government vehicles, farm equipment, motorcycles, minibikes, snowmobiles or any vehicle designed primarily for off-road use	Yes	(1) Nonowner operator's policy (except motor carrier employees); benefits applicable to operator only (2) Victim (3) Vehicle	I.S. - Insured and family (unless in own uninsured vehicle), occupants, pedestrians [9,3] O.S. - Insured and family (unless in own uninsured vehicle) [[3]	Intent, Conv., Named driver, Resident relatives, Accident O.S., grounds approved by Commissioner/may; Unins./must	Damages recoverable only if injury results in death, dismemberment, permanent disfigurement, permanent disability, medical and rehabilitative expenses in excess of $2,500, loss of uncompensated earning capacity for more than 52 consecutive weeks, or where damages are in excess of first party benefits.	
CONNECTICUT [monetary threshold]	All private passenger excluding motorcycles, large trucks and vehicles used as public and livery conveyances only	Yes	(1) Employment passenger vehicle (2) Victim (3) Vehicle	I.S. - Insured and family, occupants, pedestrians [8] O.S. - Insured and family, occupants	Intent, Conv., Unins./must	Damages recoverable only if medical expenses exceed $400 or injury is permanent or consists of fracture, permanent "significant" disfigurement, permanent loss of bodily function, loss of member, or death [12]	
DELAWARE [Add-on benefits state]	All excluding farm tractors	No provision	(1) Vehicle, if accident in Delaware (2) Victim	I.S. - Occupants, pedestrians [3], insured and family occupying or struck by non-Delaware vehicle O.S. - Same except no pedestrians except insured or family	None	None. Persons eligible for benefits precluded from pleading or introducing into evidence damages for which benefits are available, regardless of elective reductions in coverage or whether benefits are actually recoverable.	
DISTRICT OF COLUMBIA' [Not a truly no-fault or add-on law state. Has a compulsory liability law with no-fault option]	All excluding commercial vehicles and taxicabs	Yes	(1) Victim (2) Vehicle (3) Uninsured motorist fund	I.S & O.S. - Insured or occupant of insured's vehicle or vehicle which insured is driving	No provision	A person who elects to receive PIP benefits may recover if: (a) the injury results in substantial disfigurement, permanent impairment which prevents the injured person from performing substantially all the material acts that constitute normal activity for more than 180 days; (b) the PIP benefits are exhausted; or (c) death of victim (see miscellaneous column). A person who elects not to receive PIP benefits is not subject to any lawsuit restrictions.	

[1] **Persons Excluded Intent** — person intentionally causing injury, **Felony** — person committing felony; **Influ** — person under influence of alcohol or drugs; **Conv.** — converter; **Named Driver** — any specified driver; **Unins** — owner of uninsured vehicle; **Stolen** — occupant of stolen vehicle; **War** — person injured during war; **Explosion** — person injured due to nuclear explosion; **Evade** — person evading arrest; **Race** — person involved in races; **Consent** — user without consent.

[2] Pedestrians struck by secured vehicle.

[3] Any pedestrian injured in accident involving secured vehicle.

Source: 1992 Summary of Selected State Laws & Regulations Relating to Automobile Insurance (AIA Law Publications)

FIRST PARTY BENEFITS						SUBROGATION	ASSIGNED CLAIMS	MISCELLA- NEOUS
[8] Medical	Wage Loss	Replacement Services [8]	Survivors'/ Funeral Benefits	Required Optional Coverages / Required Deductibles	Primacy of Benefits	Insurer: (1) has direct right of action; (2) reimbursed out of tort recovery; (3) reimbursed by tort feasor's insurer.	Plan / Applicable to in-state accidents or all accidents	
$5,000 if incurred within one year	70% of loss up to $140 per week for 52 weeks; 8 day waiting period	Up to $70 per week payable to non-income earner for one year	$5,000 to personal representative if death caused by injury, sickness or disease resulting from accident within one year/Funeral: limited by medical benefits total	None/None	No provision	(2)	No provision	Any or all portions of coverage may be rejected in writing.
$50,000 if incurred within five years; $200,000 overall maximum on first party benefits	1st $125-100%, 2nd $125-70%, remainder-60% ($400, 52 week maximum)	$25 per day for one year	$1,000 paid to victim's estate/ Funeral: None	Unlimited medical; 85% of work loss to $100,000; No-fault collision/ Medical - $100; Collision - $50, $100, $150, $200, $250	Benefits primary except workers' compensation deducted	(1) In excess of $2,500 and limited to tort-feasor's liability coverage, (3)	No provision	Insurer of person who is or would be liable reimburses insurer paying benefits; amount determined by binding intercompany arbitration. No reimbursement from liability insurance of a tortfeasor so as to reduce amount available to compensate a victim. The prevailing party shall be awarded attorney fees in proportion to the amount by which the claiming party was successful in the arbitration.
Limited only by total benefit limit; $5,000 overall maximum on first party benefits	85% of "work loss," maximum $200 per week; [6] "Work loss" defined to include expenses incurred for replacement services; $5,000 overall maximum on first party benefits	Up to $200 per week for lost income and replacement services [11]/ Funeral: $2,000; $5,000 overall maximum on first party benefits	All insurers offering comprehensive coverage must offer glass damage coverage without regard to any deductible or minimum amount.	Benefits primary except workers' compensation deducted	(1), (2) The assigned claims plan shall be considered an insurer for subrogation purposes. Reimbursement under (2) shall be reduced to reflect claimant's attorney's fees;	Yes/In-state accidents	Basic and added reparations benefits exempt from garnishment, income withholding, attachment, execution and other process or claims to the extent that wages or earnings are exempt under any applicable law except for court orders of support.
Limited only by total benefits limit but must be incurred within 2 years [4]; 15/30 overall maximum on first party benefits	Net loss, no weekly maximum; includes self-employed persons; 15/30 overall maximum on first party benefits	Limited only by total benefits limit; 15/30 overall maximum on first party benefits	None/Funeral: $3,000; 15/30 overall maximum on first party benefits	None/None	Benefits excess over similar insurance as to non-resident passengers injured out of state.	(1) Up to the maximum amount of tortfeasor's liability insurance coverage; subrogation rights include claims under any workers' compensation law	Yes/All accidents	Claims for benefits or vehicle damage must be arbitrated if insured so requests in writing.
$50,000	80% of gross wages; maximum not less than $12,000	Loss for reasonable expenses incurred obtaining ordinary and necessary services during first three years after accident	None/Funeral: actual costs up to $4,000	Medical - $100,000; wage loss and replacement services $24,000. Insured may obtain one or any combination of the three PIP coverages	Benefits primary except workers' compensation benefits shall be deducted from temporary non-occupational disability insurance required by a state or the District government.	(3)	Yes/All accidents	A victim must notify the PIP insurer within 60 days of an accident of the victim's election to receive PIP benefits. When insurers disagree on the entitlement to, or amount of, reimbursement, the issue shall be settled by intercompany arbitration.

[4] If necessity for medical, dental, or surgical procedures is verified in writing by a qualified medical practitioner within a two year period, the cost of such procedures shall be covered.

[5] For expenses incurred within three years of the accident.

[6] Medical expenses shall be presumed reasonable and necessary unless the health care provider is given notice of denial of the charges within 60 calendar days after the insurer receives notice of claim from the provider. Within 50 calendar days after the insurer receives notice of the claim, the provider shall, within 10 business days, answer in writing questions from the insurer regarding the claim.

[7] The $2500 limit is the mandatory overall maximum on the first-party benefits. However, the State Board of Insurance provides additional limits up to $100,000.

NO-FAULT LAW SUMMARY

FLORIDA — MASSACHUSSETTS

STATE	Types of Vehicles included in coverage	Complying Coverage for Out-Of-State Vehicles In State	Priority of Policies	Persons Entitled to First-Party Benefits (in state [I.S.] and out of state [O.S.] accidents]	Persons [1] Excluded May or Must Be Excluded	TORT EXEMPTION/LIMITATION	
						General Damages (Noneconomic)	Special Damages (Economic)
FLORIDA [verbal threshold]	All excluding motorcycles, mopeds, mobile homes, taxicabs and limousines	Yes, after vehicle has been in the state for 90 days	(1) Victim [9] (2) Vehicle	I.S. - Insured and relatives not owning uninsured vehicles, occupants and resident pedestrians O.S. - Insured and resident relatives not owning uninsured vehicles occupying secured vehicle	Intent, Unins., Consent, Felony/may	Recoverable only if injury results in significant and permanent loss of an important bodily function, permanent injury within a reasonable degree of medical probability (other than scarring or disfigurement); significant and permanent scarring or disfigurement; or death.	Victim may plead and prove all his special damages (including those for which PIP payments have been or will be made) but he may not recover them in the suit.
HAWAII [monetary threshold]	All excluding motorcycles, motor scooters, and government vehicles	Yes	(1) Vehicle (any involved vehicle for pedestrian except where vehicle on temporary loan from repair shop; policy on vehicle being repaired or serviced is the primary coverage) (2) Victim	I.S. - All persons suffering loss in accident involving vehicle O.S. - All persons suffering loss, except pedestrians other than insureds and persons injured in or by fleet or uninsured vehicles	Intent, Conv., Occupying vehicle while committing crime punishable by more than one year/must	Damages recoverable only if injury results in death; significant permanent loss of a part or function of the body; permanent and serious disfigurement subjecting insured to mental or emotional suffering, or if the amount paid or accrued exceeds the "medical rehabilitative limit" computed by the commissioner.	
KANSAS [monetary threshold]	All excluding government vehicles, farm tractors, vehicles operated on the highway merely for crossing and motorized bicycles	Yes	(1) Vehicle (2) Any applicable policy; reimbursement of insurer paying benefits by other liable insurers	I.S. - Insured and family, resident occupants not owning uninsured vehicles O.S. - Insured and family occupying insured vehicle	Named insured and resident relatives while occupying vehicle owned by named insured and not insured under the policy; Consent, Intent, Conv., Injury occurring while loading or while in the business of repairing vehicle/may	Recoverable only if injury results in permanent disfigurement, fracture to a weight-bearing bone, a compound comminuted, displaced or compressed fracture, loss of a body member, permanent loss of a bodily function, death or medical expenses in excess of $2,000.	No provision
KENTUCKY [choice] — i.e., motorist may reject lawsuit threshold and retain the right to sue for any auto-related injury.]	All excluding farm tractors, motorcycles, construction equipment, mopeds	Yes	(1) Vehicle (2) Victim	I.S. - All persons suffering loss and not having waived tort limitations	[2] O.S. - Same, except pedestrians other than insureds injured in or by fleet or government vehicles	Conv., Intent/must	Recoverable only if injury results in permanent disfigurement; a fracture to a bone; to a compound, comminuted, displaced or compressed fracture; loss of a body member; permanent injury within reasonable medical probability; permanent loss of bodily function; death; or medical expenses exceeding $1,000. Limitation not applicable to motorcycle passengers.	Exempt from liability to extent of first party benefits payable without regard to deductible. However, this exemption applies "except to the extent noneconomic detriment qualifies" pursuant to the general damages tort exemption provision; no limitation on the right to recover if no first party benefits payable [17]
MARYLAND [Add-on benefits state]	All except taxicabs, mopeds, buses, farm equipment and vehicles operated to only cross highways	No provision	(1) Vehicle (2) Victim	I.S. & O.S. - Insured and family, occupants, pedestrians [3]	Intent, Felony, Evade, Stolen, Persons occupying motor-cycles/occupying or struck by own uninsured vehicle/may	None	None
MASSACHUSETTS [monetary threshold]	All excluding motorized bicycles	No provision	(1) Vehicle (2) Victim	I.S. & O.S. - Insured and family, occupants pedestrians	Intent, Felony, Evade, Influ./may	Recoverable only if in-state accident and medical exceeds $2,000 or injury causes death, dismemberment, disfigurement, loss of sight or hearing or consists of a fracture	For in-state accidents, to extent of first party benefits

[8] Replacement services benefits payable for services performed by persons other than family.

[9] Insureds and family injured on motorcycles or eligible for benefits.

[10] If victim unemployed at the time of injury, at least the equivalent of any unemployment compensation benefits victim would have received, if eligible during the period of his disability had he not been injured.

[11] Payable only to spouses or I.R.S. recognized dependents.

	FIRST PARTY BENEFITS						SUBROGATION	ASSIGNED CLAIMS	MISCELLA-NEOUS
Medical	Wage Loss	Replacement Services [8]	Survivors'/ Funeral Benefits	Required Optional Coverage / Required Deductibles	Primacy of Benefits	Insurer: (1) has direct right of action; (2) reimbursed out of tort recovery; (3) reimbursed by tort feasor's insurer.	Plan / Applicable to in-state accidents or all accidents	
80% of all reasonable expenses; $10,000 overall maximum on first party benefits. The insurer may provide an option to an insured to use a preferred provider at the time that medical services are sought.	60% of gross income loss, no weekly maximum; $10,000 overall maximum on first party benefits	Limited only by total benefits limit; $10,000 overall maximum on first party benefits.	$5,000/none; $10,000 overall maximum on first party benefits	Fault and no-fault collision/First party - $250, $500, $1,000, $2,000; Collision - any amount requested; deductible for comprehensive coverage or combined additional coverage not applicable to windshield damage	Benefits primary except workers' compensation and medicaid shall be deducted	(3) But only if insured was an occupant of a commercial vehicle or was struck by a commercial vehicle while not an occupant of a self-propelled vehicle.	No provision	Every insurer shall include in its policy for personal injury protection benefits for binding arbitration of any claims dispute involving medical benefits arising between the insurer and any person providing medical benefits if that person has agreed to accept the assignment of personal injury protection benefits. The prevailing party shall be entitled to attorneys fees and costs. [14]
Limited only by total benefits limit [15]	100% up to $900 per month; $15,000 overall maximum on first party benefits	$800 per month; $15,000 overall maximum on first party benefits	Maximum wage loss and replacement services amounts/ Funeral: $1,500; $15,000 overall maximum on first party coverage	Collision: excess no-fault benefits/Collision - $250 and as established; First party - $100, $300, $500, $1,000; Motorcycles - $500, $1,500, $3,000	Benefits secondary to workers' compensation (This provision is inapplicable if the benefits are payable to surviving spouse or dependent).	(2) No-fault insurer reimbursed by person who receives the duplicate benefits	Yes/All accidents	
$4,500 plus $4,500 for rehabilitation	85% up to $900 per month for one year	$25 per day for one year	Minimum of $900 per month for lost income and $25 per day for replacement services, less disability payments received, for up to one year/ Funeral: $2,000	None/None	Benefits primary except workers' compensation deducted	(1) after 18 months if insured, dependents or personal representative fail to commence an action (to extent of benefits only), (2), (3)	Yes/In-state accidents	
Limited only by total benefits limit [[16]	85% (more if tax advantage is less than 15%) up to $200 per week. $10,000 overall maximum on first party benefits	Included in $200 per week wage loss total; $10,000 overall maximum on first party benefits	Up to $200 per week for lost income and replacement services/ Funeral: $1,000; $10,000 overall maximum on first party benefits	Excess first party benefits in increments of $10,000 to the lesser of $40,000 or excess of liability coverage over minimum limits/First party - $250, $500, $1,000	Benefits primary except workers' compensation benefits deducted	(1), (2), (3)	Yes/All accidents	Kentucky Insurance Arbitration Association established - insurers reimburse each other on basis of tort law. Insureds may reject tort limitations, but rejection must be written and filed with the Department of Insurance prior to an accident. Such objection is effective until revoked by insured.
Limited only by total benefits limit; must be incurred within three years; $2,500 overall limit on first party benefits; [5]	85% of loss; no weekly maximum $2,500 overall maximum on first party benefits [6]	Limited only by total benefits limit; only for services usually performed by non-income earners; $2,500 overall maximum on first party benefits [5]	None/Funeral: limited by total benefits limit; $2,500 overall maximum on first party benefits[5]	Collision/Collision - $50, $100, $150, $200, $250	Benefits primary except workers' compensation deducted.	Prohibited	No provision	
Limited only by total benefits limit; all PIP benefits subject to a two year limit; $8,000 overall maximum on first party benefits	75% of loss; no weekly maximum; all PIP benefits subject to a two year limit; $8,000 overall maximum on first party benefits	Limited only by total benefits limit, payments made to non-family members; all PIP benefits subject to a two year limit; $8,000 overall maximum on first party benefits	None/Funeral: Limited only by total benefits limit; all PIP benefits subject to a two year limit; $8,000 overall maximum on first party benefits	No-fault and partial no-fault collision/First party - $100 and up to cash value of vehicle less deductible; collision and limited collision; $500 collision/comprehensive deductible; $100 glass deductible	Benefits primary except work-loss reduced by amount payable under wage-continuation program[18] benefits precluded if entitled to workers' compensation.	(1), (2), (3)	Yes/In-state accidents	Personal injury protection policy effective January 1, 1993.

[12] Non-economic detriment may include economic loss from interference with work.

[13] Insurance providing coverage for a lessee, renter, or driver may be primary if the leasing or renting driver consents.

[14] In any claim filed for personal injury in an amount of $10,000 or less, or a property damage claim in any amount, either party may demand mediation of the claim prior to litigation.

[15] Medical expenses and wage loss benefits to be made available on a deductible basis at the option of the insured (deductible not applicable to compensation for pedestrians or death or permanent injury.)

NO-FAULT LAW SUMMARY

MICHIGAN — NEW JERSEY

STATE	Types of Vehicles included in coverage	Complying Coverage for Out-Of-State Vehicles In State	Priority of Policies	Persons Entitled to Benefits (in state [I.S.] and out of state [O.S.] accidents)	Persons [1] Excluded May or Must Be Excluded	TORT EXEMPTION/LIMITATION	
						General Damages (Noneconomic)	Special Damages (Economic)
MICHIGAN [Verbal threshold] * Sunsets 1/1/92 unless extended before such date.	All excluding farm tractors, motorcycles and mopeds (but first party medical benefits must be offered to motorcycle owners)	Yes, after vehicle has been in state more than 30 days	(1) Vehicle transporting passengers as a business [[19] (2) Employment vehicle (3) Victim (4) Vehicle (5) Vehicle operator Pedestrians: (1) Vehicle (2) Vehicle operator	I.S. - Insured and family, occupants, pedestrians [2] relatives domiciled in same household O.S. - Insured and family, occupants	Consent, Unins./must	Recoverable only if injury results in death, serious impairment of body function, permanent serious disfigurement	No recovery to extent of first party benefits
MINNESOTA [monetary threshold]	All excluding motorcycles and mopeds [22]	Yes	(1) Employment vehicle [23] (2) Victim (3) Vehicle (4) Any involved vehicle for pedestrians	I.S. - All persons suffering loss [24] O.S. - Insureds and occupants of an insured vehicle except commercial vehicles transporting persons or property which are fleet vehicles or government vehicles (other than this state or its subdivision)	Intent, Conv., Race/must Persons 14 or younger may be in assigned claims plan even if they converted a vehicle. Unins. may not be in assigned claims plan.	Recoverable only if injury results in permanent disfigurement, permanent injury, death, disability (for 60 days or more) or medical expenses exceeding $4,000	Economic loss to the extent of basic or optional first party benefits paid or payable without regard for deductibles must be deducted from tort recovery prior to reduction of claimant's damages under contributory fault
NEW HAMPSHIRE [Add-on benefits state]	All excluding fleet and commercial vehicles, large trucks, mopeds, motorcycles and persons with equivalent medical coverage	Yes	No provision	I.S. & O.S. - Occupants of secured vehicle	Conv./may	None	None
NEW JERSEY [[choice] — i.e., motorist may reject lawsuit threshold and retain right to sue for any auto-related injury.	All excluding commercial vehicles, large trucks, motorcycles and mopeds	No provision	1) PIP policy 2) Reimbursement of insurer paying benefits by other liable insurers	I.S. & O.S. - Named insured and family, occupants with permission of insured, pedestrians struck by secured vehicle or projectile from vehicle	Felony, High Misdemeanor, intent, Unins., Consent/may	Named insured required to maintain PIP protection coverage. Must elect one of two tort options: no threshold (i.e., unrestricted ability to seek damages for noneconomic loss) or limited threshold (i.e., damages for noneconomic loss recoverable only if accident results in death, dismemberment, fracture, loss of fetus, permanent loss of use of body organ or member, significant limitation of use of body function or impairment of a non-permanent nature which prevents the injured person from performing substantially all of the material acts which constitute that person's usual and customary daily activities for not less than 90 days during the 180 days immediately following the occurrence of the injury or impairment.	Uncompensated economic loss recoverable by injured party from tortfeasor.

[16] Not payable to public assistance recipients receiving free insurance.

[17] Any person may reject the no-fault system grant of a limited tort exemption and its limitation on the right to receive in tort. Rejection bars recovery of no-fault benefits.

[[18] Insurers reimburse wage-continuation programs for amounts paid to insured (up to 75% of loss), and if work-loss benefits are reduced, must make benefits available for one year should wage-continuation benefits be exhausted.

[19] Excepting school buses, common carriers certified by public service commission, government program buses, buses for non-profit organizations, and taxicabs.

FIRST PARTY BENEFITS						SUBROGATION	ASSIGNED CLAIMS	MISCELLA-NEOUS
Medical	Wage Loss	Replacement Services [8]	Survivors'/ Funeral Benefits	Required Optional Coverage / Required Deductibles	Primacy of Benefits	Insurer: (1) has direct right of action; (2) reimbursed out of tort recovery; (3) reimbursed by tort feasor's insurer.	Plan / Applicable to in-state accidents or all accidents	
Unlimited [20]	85% up to $3,077 per 30 day period for three years. (Maximum adjusted annually by CPI; current maximum in effect until 9/30/92)	$20 per day for three years	Survivor: wage loss and replacement services up to $3,077 per 30 day period for three years (adjusted annually to reflect cost-of-living increases.) Funeral: Policy amount but not less than $1,750 nor more than $5,000	May offer deductibles and exclusions, subject to prior approval by the commissioner, up to $300 maximum	Benefits primary except as to benefits provided under state or federal law.	(2) [21]	Yes/in-state accidents. Also has Motor Vehicle Accident Fund for unsatisfied judgement claims.	
$20,000	85% up to $250 per week; $20,000 maximum for first party benefits other than medical	All expenses reasonably incurred to maximum of $200 per week; replacement services loss commences after eight day waiting period; $20,000 maximum for first party benefits other than medical	Wage loss and replacement services, each up to $200 per week/ Funeral: $2,000; $20,000 maximum for first party benefits other than medical	No provision	Benefits primary except workers' compensation deducted. No entity may coordinate benefits unless it provides an appropriately reduced premium rate.	(1), (3) where commercial vehicle involved. No subrogation for non-commercial vehicles unless negligence causing injury occurred outside of state. Subrogation only to extent necessary to prevent double recovery by insured. "Commercial vehicle" must weigh more than 5500 pounds curb weight.	Yes/All accidents	Arbitration determines amount of reimbursement by insurer of negligent commercial vehicle. Medical benefits shall include the expenses incurred in traveling to receive such benefits. Stacking of PIP is optional, but insurer must notify insured of this option.
$1,000 if incurred within one year	No provision	No provision	None/None	No provision	No provision	Prohibited	No provision	
$250,000	100% up to $100 per week for one year with lifetime maximum of $5,200	$12 per day to maximum of $4,380	Maximum wage loss if income producer; maximum replacement serices/ Funeral: $1,000	Excess wage loss, replacement services survivors' and funeral benefits, 75% of difference beween $5,200 and income loss (to $35,000 income); medical expense benefits deductibles $500, $1,000, $2,500; minimum $500 deductible must be offered for collision and comprehensive coverages	Benefits primary except for health insurance coverage (elected in lieu of PIP medical expense benefits) and workers' compensation, employees' temporary disability benefits, medicare and benefits under Federal law to active and retired military personnel which are in fact collected	(1) Insurer paying PIP benefits may recover within two years from uninsured tortfeasor or tortfeasor not required to maintain PIP or medical expense benefits (other than for pedestrians), (3) if tortfeasor insured (by agreement or arbitration)	No plan, but unsatisfied claim and judgement fund provides coverage for qualified victims of uninsured motorists.	Rate increases without prior approval under 1988 flex rating provisions must be submitted to Public Advocate. Public Advocate may challenge flex rate change; if rate reduced or resinded, insurer pays costs. Commissioner will promulgate plan implementing statutory and non-statutory rating factors no later than 1/1/92. New Jersey Auto Insurance Guaranty Fund created in 1990; special non-lapsing fund to satisfy financial obligations of New Jersey Full Insurance Underwriting Association. Guaranty Fund funded by assessments imposed on auto insurance premiums, surcharges collected by DMV and other sources.

[20] Amounts paid in excess of $250,000 will be reimbursed by the Michigan Catastrophic Claims Association

[21] Reimbursement is not permitted from that portion of tort recovery attributable to non-economic loss or to allowable expenses, work loss and survivors loss in excess of payments made by the insurer.

[22] Coverage shall also extend to any motor vehicle while being rented by named insured, except for antique and recreational vehicles.

NO-FAULT LAW SUMMARY

NEW YORK — PENNSYLVANIA

STATE	Types of Vehicles included in coverage	Complying Coverage for Out-Of-State Vehicles In State	Priority of Policies	Persons Entitled to Benefits (in state [I.S.] and out of state [O.S.] accidents)	Persons [1] Excluded May or Must Be Excluded	TORT EXEMPTION/LIMITATION	
						General Damages (Noneconomic)	Special Damages (Economic)
NEW YORK [verbal threshold]	All except motorcycles and government vehicles [25]	Yes	(1) Vehicle (except school buses or buses - victim's policy is primary) (2) Victim	I.S. & O.S. - All persons suffering loss except occupants of other vehicles. (Persons who are not owners or their families residing in the same household are only covered for O.S. through the purchase of optional additional coverage.)	Intent, Felony, Influ., Evade, Race, Stolen, Unins., Pedestrian struck by own vehicle which is uninsured, and Injury while repairing or servicing vehicle if in course of business and on business premises/may	Recoverable only if injury results in death; dismember-ment; significant disfigure-ment; loss of a fetus; a fracture; permanent loss of use of a body organ, function or system; permanent consequential limitation of use of a body organ or member; significant limitation of use of a body function or system; or a medically- deter-mined injury or impairment of a non-permanent nature which prevents the injured person from performing substantially all the material acts which constitute normal activity for at least 90 of the 180 days immediately following the accident.	No recovery to extent first party benefits are payable (or would be but for exclusions or deductibles); tort remedy retained in death cases.
NORTH DAKOTA [monetary threshold]	All excluding motorcycles and mopeds	Yes	(1) Workers' Compensation (2) Vehicle (except buses and ridesharing arrangements) (3) Victim (4) Bus (5) Ridesharing vehicle	I.S. - Owner and family, occupants, pedestrians O.S. - Same, except no pedestrians other than insured and family	Intent, Race, Unins., Consent/must	Recoverable only if injury results in death, dismember-ment, serious and permanent disfigurement, disability beyond 60 days or if medical exceeds $2,500	No recovery to extent of first party benefits.
OREGON [add-on benefits state]	All excluding motorcycles, mopeds, farm tractors and commercial vehicles	Yes	Occupants: (1) Vehicle (2) Victim Pedestrians: (1) Vehicle (2) Victim	I.S. - Insured and family, occupants, pedestrians [2] O.S. - Same except pedestrians other than insured and family excludeable	Intent, Race/may	None	None
PENNSYLVANIA [choice] - i.e., motorist may reject threshold and retain the right to sue for any auto-related injury]	All insured by a natural person excluding motor-cycles, mopeds, recreational vehicles, or vehicles owned by the United States	No provision	(1) Victim (2) Vehicle [29]	I.S. Insured and family	Intent, Felony, Evade, Conversion of motor vehicle, Unins./must named driver/may	Customers may choose limited tort option (no legal ability to seek damages for pain and suffering or other non-economic damages unless serious injury but may seek recovery of all medical and other out of pocket expenses) or full tort option	None. Consumers may choose limited tort option or full tort option.

[[22] Coverage shall also extend to any motor vehicle while being rented by named insured, except for antique and recreational vehicles.

[23] Occupants of commuter vans, Minnesota residents on buses in Minnesota, children in school buses, and children being transported to a family day care facility paid by policy under which they are insured before vehicle policy. Employment vehicle coverage includes relatives in same household.

[24] Includes pedestrians struck by motorcycles

[25] Motorcycles shall provide and be liable for payment of first party benefits to pedestrians for loss arising out of the use or operation of the motorcycle within the state.

FIRST PARTY BENEFITS						SUBROGATION	ASSIGNED CLAIMS	MISCELLA- NEOUS
Medical	Wage Loss	Replacement Services [8]	Survivors'/ Funeral Benefits	Required Optional Coverage / Required Deductibles	Primacy of Benefits	Insurer: (1) has direct right of action; (2) reimbursed out of tort recovery; (3) reimbursed by tort feasor's insurer.	Plan / Applicable to in-state accidents or all accidents	
Limited only by total benefits limit [26]; $50,000 overall maximum on first party benefits	80% up to $1,000 per month for three years; $50,000 overall maximum on first party benefits	$25 per day for one year; $50,000 overall maximum on first party benefits	$2,000 [27]/ Funeral: none	"Family" deductible; collision; coinsurance and deductibles as prescribed by the Superintendent	Benefits primary except Social Security, disability, workers' compensation, and medicare deducted	(1), (2) against unsecured person, (3) [28]	No plan, but the Motor Vehicle Accident Indemnification Corporation (MVAIC) provides no-fault benefits to qualified victims of uninsured motorists.	Insurers of persons who would be liable reimburse insurers paying benefits - amount determined by arbitration.
Limited only by total benefits limit. Charges must be reasonable.	85% up to $150 per week; $30,000 overall maximum on first party benefits	$15 per day; $30,000 overall maximum on first party benefits	Survivor's income loss up to $150 per week; survivor's replacement services loss up to $15 per day. Funeral: $3,500; $30,000 overall maximum on first party benefits	Excess no-fault benefits up to $80,000/No required deductibles.	Benefits primary except workers' compensation deducted	(1), (2), (3) if injury was "serious" or vehicle weight exceeds 6,500 pounds	Yes/All accidents. Also has Unsatisfied Judgement Fund for unsatisfied judgement claims.	Injured uninsured owner not eligible for benefits through the assigned claims plan except where such individual has requested temporary suspension of insurance and was injured by or in a motor vehicle not owned by him. Stacking of benefits is not permitted.
$10,000, if incurred within 1 year[6]	70% up to $1,250 per month for 52 weeks; only if victim disabled 14 days or more	$30 per day for 52 weeks payable only to non-wage earners; only if victim disabled 14 days or more	None/Funeral: $2,500	None/None	Benefits primary except workers' compensation or other medical or disability benefits deducted.	None (1), (2), (3)	No provision	Disputes between insurers as to liability and amount of reimbursement decided by arbitration.
$5,000 [30]	80% of actual loss of gross income; five working day waiting period	Reasonable expenses actually incurred	Death benefit if injury causes death within 24 months of date of accident. Funeral expenses directly related	Medical: up to at least $100,000; extraordinary medical from $100,000 to $1,100,000 in $100,000 increments; income loss up to at least $2,500 per month to maximum of at least $50,000; accidental death benefit up to at least $25,000; Funeral benefits $2,500. First Party Benefits may be purchased in combination package subject to total limit of $177,550.	Benefits primary except for workers' compensation	Prohibited	Yes/In-state accidents	Insurers must provide $500 deductible for collision coverage unless insured signs statement indicating awareness that purchase of a lower deductible is permissible and that there is an additional cost of purchasing a lower deductible. A person or institution providing treatment to an injured person may not require payment in excess of 110% of the prevailing medicare rate charged for treating injuries covered by liability uninsured/- underinsured motorist coverage and first party medical benefits (including extra-ordinary medical benefits.)

[26] No time limit for medical expense benefits if, one year after accident, it is ascertainable that further expenses may be incurred as a result of injury.

[27] In addition to any first party benefits for economic loss.

[28] Only if at least one of the vehicles involved weighs more than 6,500 lbs. unloaded or is used principally for the transportation of persons or property for hire. No reimbursement is permitted from the insurer of a bus or school bus.

NO-FAULT LAW SUMMARY

PUERTO RICO — WASHINGTON

STATE	Types of Vehicles included in coverage	Complying Coverage for Out-Of-State Vehicles In State	Priority of Policies	Persons Entitled to Benefits (in state [I.S.] and out of state [O.S.] accidents)	Persons [1] Excluded May or Must Be Excluded	TORT EXEMPTION/LIMITATION	
						General Damages (Noneconomic)	Special Damages (Economic)
PUERTO RICO [monetary threshold]	All excluding farm tractors, highway construction equipment, and vehicles operated solely on private property	No provision	No provision	I.S. - All	Intent, Race, Influ., Consent, Injured while committing criminal act/must [31]	Recoverable if damages in excess of $1,000	Tortfeasor relieved from liability to extent of no-fault benefits except where damages exceed $2,000.
SOUTH DAKOTA [Add-on benefits state]	All four-wheel passenger motor vehicles owned by natural persons including trailers, excluding motorcycles	No provision	No provision	I.S. & O.S. - Insured and family, occupants, pedestrians[2]	No provision	None	None
TEXAS [Add-on benefits state]	All except government vehicles and farm vehicles	No provision	No provision	I.S. & O.S. - Insured and family, occupants	Intent, Felony, Evade/must	None	Tort recovery by guest from owner reduced by amount of first party benefits
UTAH [monetary threshold]	All excluding motorcycles, trailers, semi-trailers, and farm vehicles	Yes, after vehicle has been in state more than 90 days	(1) Vehicle (2) Victim	I.S. - Insured and family, occupants, pedestrians [3] O.S.-None	Intent, Felony, Unins., Consent/may	Recoverable only if injury results in death, dismemberment, permanent disability, permanent disfigurement, or if medical exceeds $3,000	No provision
VIRGINIA [Add-on benefits state]	All	No provision	No provision	I.S. & O.S. - Insured and family, occupants	No provision	None	None
WASHINGTON [Add-on benefits state]	All except motorcycles, mopeds, motor carriers, and government vehicles	No provision	No provision	No provision	No provision	None	None

[[29] A person who suffers injury arising out of the maintenance or use of a motor vehicle shall recover first-party benefits against applicable insurance coverage in the following order of priority: (1) For a named insured, the policy on which he is the named insured; (2) For an insured, the policy covering the insured; (3) For the occupants of an insured motor vehicle, the policy on that motor vehicle, and (4) For a person who is not the occupant of a motor vehicle, the policy on any motor vehicle involved in the accident. For the purpose of this paragraph, a parked and unoccupied motor vehicle is not a motor vehicle involved in an accident unless it was parked so as to cause unreasonable risk of injury.

[30] First-party medical benefits required by law, wage loss, replacement services survivor and funeral benefits are optional.

[31] Benficiaries of such persons may collect any benefits applicable to them.

FIRST PARTY BENEFITS						SUBROGATION	ASSIGNED CLAIMS	MISCELLA-NEOUS
Medical	Wage Loss	Replacement Services [8]	Survivors'/ Funeral Benefits	Required Optional Coverage / Required Deductibles	Primacy of Benefits	Insurer: (1) has direct right of action; (2) reimbursed out of tort recovery; (3) reimbursed by tort feasor's insurer.	Plan / Applicable to in-state accidents or all accidents	
Unlimited if incurred within two years. (Benefits may be extended beyond 2 year period in certain cases.)	50% up to $100 per week for first 52 weeks; up to $50 per week for next 52 weeks; no benefits for first 15 days	$25 per week for 16 weeks	$10,000 to primary dependent; $1,000 to each secondary dependent, to maximum of $5,000; additional benefits to children under 19 (up to 21 if student) pursuant to schedule to a maximum of $10,000 for all/ Funeral: $1,000	None/None	Benefits secondary to all other sources except certain commonwealth-provided programs; duplicative recovery of amounts available under social security	None, but state fund has right of indemnity.	No provision	Benefits for dismemberment: fee schedule ranges from $2,500 to $10,000 under first party benefits.
$2,000 if incurred within 2 years	$60 per week for 52 weeks for disability extending beyond 14 days from day of accident	$30 per week for 52 weeks for disability extending beyond 14 days; benefits payable only if named insured is not gainfully employed at time of accident	$10,000 death benefit if death occurs within 90 days of accident/Funeral: None	None/None	Wage loss and replacement services benefits not reduced if workers' compensation or similar benefits are available; not reduced if collateral benefits are available from any other source.	No provision	No provision	Any or all portions of coverage may be rejected. Coverage must be offered.
Limited only by total benefits limit if incurred within 3 years; $2,500 overall maximum on first party benefits [[7]	100% of loss; no weekly limit; $2,500 overall maximum on first party benefits	Limited only by total benefits limit; payable only to non-wage earners; $2,500 overall maximum on first party benefits	None/Funeral: Limited only by total benefits limit, $2,500 overall maximum on first party benefits	None/None	Benefits primary	Prohibited	No provision	Coverage applicable unless insured rejects in writing.
$3,000	85% up to $250 per week for 52 weeks; need not be paid for the first three days	$20 per day for 365 days; benefits are not payable unless such expenses are actually incurred	$3,000 to heirs/ Funeral: $1,500	None/None	Benefits primary except workers' compensation or any similar statutory plan and benefits for active U.S. military service deducted	(3)	No provision	Insurer of person who is or would be liable reimburses insurer paying benefits; amount determined by arbitration.
$2,000 if incurred within three years (includes chiropractic expense)	100% up to $100 per week for up to 52 weeks	No provision	None/Funeral: Included in medical	PIP benefits are required "optionals" for BI or property damage liability insurance policies	Benefits primary except workers' compensation, amounts recoverable under Federal Tort Claims Act, or similar legislation.	No right of subrogation to recover medical payments made on behalf of an injured person from any third party.	No provision	Insured has option of purchasing either or both medical and work loss benefits.
$10,000 if incurred within one year	85% of weekly income to $200 per week; total loss of income benefits $10,000; beginning 14 days after accident; up to one year	Up to $12 per day, up to one year	None/Funeral: Included in medical	No provision	Insurer can elect to make income continuation benefits secondary to any employer-provided wage loss plan (exclusive of sick leave and vacation benefits).	No provision	No provision	Voluntary plan promulgated by Washington Insurance Department Bulletin.

CHAPTER 9

EVALUATING THE WORTH OF YOUR CASE. HOW TO FIGURE OUT WHAT AMOUNT YOU'RE TO ASK FOR

A very important aspect of your claims action, in deed probably the most crucial aspect of the whole process, is the EVALUATION of your claim — determining, by way of "an educated rather than an uneducated guess," the realistic dollar amount you are to ask for or realistically expect to receive as compensation. *The need to have a realistic and credible estimation of the value of your damages cannot be emphasized enough. Such estimation, especially if competent, forms the basis of your demand, and the centerpiece around which to conduct your settlement negotiations and discussions subsequently.*

Briefly put, evaluation of the worth of your claim (your "damages") in a personal injury or auto accident claim case basically boils down to this: estimating the total sum, expressed in dollars, of the harm and losses—financial, physical, and emotional — which you claim your accident and injuries caused you. Put another way, evaluation of your claim basically means doing an evaluation of your "damages."

A. Various Valuation Methods Used in the Claims Industry

Experts and professionals engaged in the field of claims settlement—insurance adjusters, personal injury lawyers, and others—have devised a number of methods by which they estimate the claimant's reasonable damage award. These methods range from fairly simple mathematical formulas to fancy multidimensional equations[1] of varying usefulness and efficiency.

Such claims evaluation methods include the following:

1. Simple Multiplier or Rule-of-Thumb Formula. This calls for the amount of the claimant's actual monetary loss to be multiplied by a variable, (X), which relates to the claimant's assessment of the strength of his case. Thus, if a claimant's case is considered to be weak, in terms of say, his liability position, the case could typically be assigned a multiplier variable of 2 or 3, and up to 10 or more in a strong case.

2. Percentage of Disability Method, which attempts to determine the injured person's actual "percentage of permanent disability." Here, each percentage point is allocated a particular dollar amount derived, in turn, from, say, a survey of recent jury verdicts in cases of similar type from similar jurisdictions.

3. Point Allocation Method, which allocates points to specific factors like liability, degree of injury, age of the claimant, etc., and compares them to a hypothetical "perfect" damages award to produce an estimated amount of

---

[1]For a summary of the various methods used in the claims industry, see generally Charfoos & Christensen, "Measuring Damages." 72 A.B.A. Journal 74 (Sept. 1, 1986). For the fancier, more complex models, see for example, Victor, "How Much is a Case Worth? Putting Your Intuition to Work to Evaluate the Unique Lawsuit," 20 Trial 48 (July 1984); Nagee, "Lawyer Decision Making and Threshold Analysis," 36 U. Miami Law Review, 615 (1982), and Otto, "Lawsuit Evaluation and Outcome Prediction: A More Objective, Dimentionalized and System Approach," 52 Insurance Counsel Journal, 634 (Oct 1985).

damages in the case at issue.[2]

4. Use of Specialized Valuation Handbooks. These are several specialized publications (Valuation Handbooks) which purport to predict probable damage awards in a given personal injury case by comparing the claimant's injuries with reported jury verdicts involving similar injuries in comparable jurisdictions.[3]

B. Here are the Two Methods Preferred for Readers of this Manual

For the purposes of the readers and users of this manual, however, we shall only illustrate two methods of claims evaluation in this manual: One method, **the Rule-of-Thumb or Special Damages Multiplier method** (or, SDM for short) is intended for use by the reader in routine, less serious types of cases; and the second method, the **Modified Sindell Method** or MSM formula, for short (pp. 134-154), is for use in more serious types of cases involving disabling injuries and high stake level of claims.

We shall first illustrate in the later part of this chapter, the SDM (Rule-of-Thumb) method and the way it works (see pp. 130-3). But before we go into that, let us first say a few things about this method and why it is preferred by the author for the users of this manual.

C. Why We Like the Special Damages Multiplier Method

There are, of course, many other more sophisticated evaluation methods in the field that we could have chosen, some presumably more "accurate" than the Special Damages Multiplier method recommended herein, and we are fully aware of that. But, for our purposes—for the specific needs of the type of readers for whom the manual is primarily meant, namely, ordinary lay people and non-experts with largely routine, smaller size, less-serious injury types of cases—this method presents, in our estimation, several advantages that make it preferable for use by the broad readership of this self-help guidebook.

First, and perhaps foremost, this method's prime beauty and attractiveness lies in its extreme simplicity and straight-forwardness.

Secondly, and by far more importantly, is the fact that this method is not only one of the most simple, but that it is, in truth, also probably the single most commonly used method of claims evaluation in the claims industry, one that enjoys widespread but "secret" preference and popularity among claims adjusters and claims lawyers alike, particularly in the assessment of "routine" types of claims. Strangely, though, the evidence reveals one interesting phenomenon about the claims professionals' employment of this method: frequently, these same professionals would evaluate their claims with this method in their daily practice, but would just as often disavow and malign, in public, the use of the method as over simplistic—largely for reasons of public relations and image-making!

---

[2]Probably the best known formula which utilizes a system of points allocation, is the so-called Sindell method. And most other methods in this category are generally based on some variation of the Sindell formula, often using several different variables.. See, Sindell, "What Price Personal Injury?" 3 Prac. Law. 37 (Feb 1957); Personal Injury Settlement Evaluation (Matthew Bender & Co., Inc. 1963); and Swafford, "Evaluating Damage Claims," 412 Insurance Law Journal 273 (May 1957), and Baldyga, How to Settle Your Own Insurance Claim (MacMillian & Co., 1968) pp.. 118-126.

[3]See, for example, the following: Personal Injury Valuation Handbook, Vols. 1-12 (Jury Verdict Research Inc. 1986); R. Harley, What's it Worth?: A Guide to Current Personal Injury Awards and Settlements (1985) (Containing a detailed listing of recent personal injury cases tabulated according to the type of injury and amount of verdict or settlement). See also The National Jury Verdict Review Analysis, which reports national jury verdicts in personal injury cases together with detailed summaries of selected individual cases; Verdicts & Settlements, which are monthly reports of jury verdicts and settlements in personal injury cases; West's Personal Injury News, which provides a biweekly summary of all personal injury cases reported within the West National Reporter System and indexed by headnote topics and case names.

D. How and Why Claims Lawyers and Adjusters Commonly Use the SDM Method But are Hypocritical About It!

University of Denver's Professor Laurence Ross' findings in his authoritative sociological study of the "law in action"—the law as it actually operates in real life—in the insurance claims industry, is typical. Ross observed that, particularly with respect to the evaluation of the routine types of cases involving less serious injuries (e.g., whiplash, or neck sprain, and generally cases with no residual impairments and disfigurement), insurance adjusters and claims lawyers do commonly employ the Rule-of-Thumb formula method, a formula that is directly equivalent to this book's Special Damages Multiplier method. Lawyers as well as claims adjusters, Ross notes, readily take to this method of evaluation because, he states, there is an "understanding common to both adjusters and attorneys concerning an appropriate relationship between settlement and the degree of injury as measured by medical bills."[4] Yet, Ross notes, such "formula method is by no means always avowed. It's legitimacy in the abstract is frequently challenged by both attorneys and adjusters."

Why do the lawyers and adjusters use the SDM (Special Damages Multiplier) formula but frequently disavow using it? Ross found this answer: The trouble, Ross found, was that both the adjusters and the lawyers often find it necessary to deny their use of the method primarily for image-making reasons—for fear of being perceived in the eyes of the other as being "non-professional"!

The following contrasting statements by two claims professionals interviewed by Ross, one a lawyer, and the other an insurance adjuster, is revealing:

By the lawyer: "I had an adjuster practically stand on his head trying to impress me with the fact that he doesn't use the [formula method] rule of thumb, three and a half times expenses. But every time I looked at his lump offer on the case I came out with this three and half times expenses, and this is wrong. I think they should be taught and impressed with the fact that you can't analyze a case in that direction."

By the adjuster: "Generally, in this area here, if you talk to an attorney, you can talk to an attorney until he's blue in the face and he won't admit that he's [using the formula of], say, four or five times the specials. He talks the type of injury and things like this, its true. But still, when you've got a little claim and he evaluates it in numbers, he takes medical bills, he multiplies them by four or five times. Generally, that's what you end up settling for."

Said Ross, whose empirical study of the insurance claims industry remains one of the most authoritative research works on the subject, "In my opinion, both 'accusations' [by the lawyer and the adjuster] are correct."

Other experts in the field find a similar pattern of conduct particularly among lawyers, noting that while frequently disavowing the rule-of-thumb formula method or denying its use, the lawyers would just as frequently employ the method, nevertheless, in their daily claims valuation work. **John Guinther,** a nationally acclaimed author and personal injury insurance claims expert, notes the following in his epic 1980 study:

"Although many lawyers deplore it and try to avoid it when they can, a system has developed for calculating settlements that is in use across the country...The system is predicated on the assumption that—even though no one knows what any individual jury will do—the average jury, in making an award, will take the probable special damages and multiply them by some figure in order to come up with the total award...and insurance-company actuaries [also think the same]."[5]

---

[4]Ross, Settled Out of Court, p. 107. Ross elaborated (p.161): "Dependence on formulas is virtually always denied in the abstract by both adjusters and attorneys...In practice, formulas are used very often, not only for evaluation, but also for purposes of negotiation. Where a range of possible agreement points exists, and there is need for singling out one of them, the artificial and conventional formula is one of the means available and suitable...Their major and crucial value is as a way to point the parties to a bargain..."

[5]Guinther, Winning Your Personal Injury Suit, p. 110. In the same vein, witness the rather ambivalent statements for and against the use of this method coming from one claims lawyer: "How much should you ask for, and how do you decide what your injuries are worth? This is tough even for experienced lawyers, since there's no accurate yardstick to measure pain and suffering. But there are certain guides or formulas that are helpful. One such rule-of-thumb, used successfully by many insurance companies is that a claim is worth three or four times the amount of the 'out-of-pocket' expenses [specials]...Don't believe it! This so-called 'rule' is strictly an insurance company gimmick. It's arbitrary and illogical and shouldn't be used as a guide. In many cases, the amount of the "specials" has no reasonable relationship whatsoever to pain and disability suffered...On the other hand, the value of a claim necessarily does have some relationship to the amount of your bills." [Siegel, How to Avoid Lawyers (Ballentine Books, 1989 ed.), at p.9.]

Ironically, Siegel, having offered and then condemned the formula almost in the same breath, never provides any alternative formula that could, in his view either work better or is preferable. Furthermore, if the rule-of-thumb formula is, in fact, "arbitrary and illogical and shouldn't be used as a guide," why offer it at all, in the first place? And why offer it as an example (in deed his only example) of "certain guides or formulas that are helpful"!?

Guinther had made a rather fascinating discovery when he conducted a small survey of four different negligence lawyers. He had separately asked each of the four lawyers to evaluate the settlement value (damages) of two separate personal injury cases—for a Ms Barber and a Ms Martin. Hypothetical facts of the cases: No contributing negligence was to be assumed on the part of either party, and both parties regained full recovery from their injuries; $4,500 damages in medical bills and lost income for Ms. Barber's injuries (fractured ankle and wrist), and $3,000 damages in medical bills and lost income for Ms Martin's injuries (minor back injury, superficial cuts, and broken ankle).

And the results from the Guinther survey? With respect to Ms. Barber, each one of the four lawyers (all of whom had, of course, worked independently without knowing of each other), evaluated her case as being worth between $15,000 and $20,000, and each said that he would recommend that she accept a settlement of "around" $15,000. THE BIG REVELATION: *The result was more than just a coincidence, Guinther found!*

All of these lawyers, it turned out, had actually used the standard 'rule-of-thumb' or 'multiplier' formula! They had each used the typical multiplier of between three and five times the total damages—the standard norm in the claims industry for the area!!

Then, with respect to Ms. Martin, one of the four lawyers valued her case at $15,000, while the other three gave a $20,000-$25,000 range as the appropriate settlement.

How come, Guinther asked the lawyers, they didn't seem to have strictly applied the "common multiplier" (of between 3 and 5 times the "special damages") in Ms. Martin's case, as they clearly seemed to have done in Ms. Barber's case? Guinther discovered that EVEN THERE, TOO, THE LAWYERS HAD, IN FACT, USED THE MULTIPLIER FORMULA AS WELL! "It turned out each attorney did, in fact, use the multiplier for his basic figure but then added to it" to compensate for the "special circumstances" of her own case, Guinther said. The four lawyers respectively gave as their main reason for assigning in Ms. Martin's case some extra value over and above the normal multiplier factor, the fact that there was an element of "special circumstances" in her case—primarily, that her case had a "target defendant" (i.e., the railroad authority, since she had fallen in a railroad platform, as opposed to Ms. Barber, who fell on a private sidewalk). It was each lawyer's position that Ms. Martin's case was worth the extra money because, in their calculation, jurors would likely view the railroad's "negligence" much more seriously than they would that of an ordinary citizen (the private householder) like themselves, if the case were to go to court.[6]

In sum, the point is that the multiplier or rule-of-thumb formula method, a method prescribed for readers in this guidebook, is a claims evaluation tool that is widely and routinely employed by claims adjusters and attorneys across the United States in their daily work [7]; that it is just as good a method for you to use as any other in the industry in working out your own claim evaluation!

---

[6]In fact, one of the lawyers was noted to have lamented: "The only problems is the size of her [Ms. Martin's] specials. If I could get them up to $6-7,000, I don't think I'd settle for a penny under $30,000" (Guinther, <u>Winning Your Personal Injury Suit</u>, p. 112).

[7]In deed, the multiplier evaluation method is commonly endorsed in the relevant practical literature, generally, but often with just the proviso that it be used with some qualifications or under certain prescribed conditions. Witness the following:
  "Most lawyers will seek five to seven times the specials depending, of course, on the amount presented. A good rule of thumb for the claims man when dealing with the claimant directly is one to two times the specials...Lawyers should be offered approximately one to two-and-one-half times the true special damages [Jack R. Artstein, "Analyzing Special Damages," <u>Insurance Law Journal</u> 496:261, 1964, p. 265].
  Or, witness this:
  "Despite the inadequacy of 'rule of thumb' settlements in cases of insured liability, a settlement of 2 to 3 times the medical expenses added to the special damages is usually a desirable settlement, and is usually equitable in cases where no permanent partial disability or future medical care is anticipated. It is obvious [however] that this type of settlement is inadequate and rarely effected in cases of serious injuries resulting in permanent disability, unexpected complications regarding the injuries." [John R. Foutty, "The Evaluation and Settlement of Personal Injury Claims," <u>Insurance Law Journal</u> 492:5, (1964), p. 101.]
  Or, witness this from a 40-year insurance claims veteran:
  "How do you place a value on personal injury or death?...Knowing the extent of the plaintiff's medical bills and lost wages and of the plaintiff's permanent disability, an experienced adjuster or personal injury lawyer can make a fairly accurate prediction...[they] employ various rules of thumb to calculate the likely value...For instance, if the victim completely recovered from his injuries, an adjuster might predict that the jury would award the victim as compensation for pain and suffering an amount equal to twice the total of the victim's medical bills and wages. On the other hand, if the accident left the victim in a state of permanent discomfort, the multiple would go up...the evaluation of personal injury claims is an art, not a science..." (Dumas, <u>Claim Paid</u>, pp. 156-7)

As Ross summed it up, in deed the ultimate reality is that:

> "[It's inevitable that attorneys and adjusters would embrace the multiplier formula method of evaluation because the reality is that] the key to simple and rapid agreement on the part of attorneys and adjusters is that both sides understand that, in a routine case, a multiple of medical bills that appear to be in proper relation to the claimed injury forms a reasonable basis for evaluating the total claim. The formula method is mechanical and artificial, but it is efficient as a means of disposing of a large workload of claims…[In deed], even when some aspects of a claim are unusual… the formula method [still] provides a starting place for negotiation. It indicates a general standard with which a specific settlement may be compared and from which a planned deviation may depart… in a situation in which ordinary men, albeit specialists, have to handle large numbers of rather routine claims, the formula method provides a simple, efficient evaluation that does not seem unjust. To a party who denies the validity of this method, the negotiator may reasonably put the question, 'If not this, then what?'"[8]

E. Now, Let's Actually Work Out A Case Evaluation Using The Special Damages Multiplier Method

All right. So you now know — you are "in good company" with "the best and brightest" of the claims industry, the lawyers and the adjusters, when you use the Special Damages Multiplier (SDM) method to make an evaluation of your claim! How is this method applied, though? How does the method actually work, in practice?

Basically, the formula calls for you to take your (i.e., the claimant's) "special damages", meaning the amount of your actual, out-of-pocket monetary loss and damages— medical expenses, lost wages, etc... — and to multiply it by a **"multiplier"** or **"variable,"** (X), which relates to your assessment of your bodily injuries and the strength (or weakness) of your case. (In other words, this "multiplier" is used instead and in place of an exact measure to gauge the "intangibles" of the case — the pain and suffering from your injuries, the disability, disfigurement, and the like). Next, after having multiplied the Special Damages figure by the designated MULTIPLIER, you add all property damage costs or values to that product to get a final gross figure as your settlement figure.

How do you pick the appropriate "multiplier" number or factor to use? The multiplier factor to use will depend on your view and assessment of the degree of the "intangible damages" in your particular case (the nature and degree of your injuries, of the pain and suffering and inconvenience involved, or of disability, disfigurement, etc), and your subjective but realistic assessment of the strength (or weakness) of your case, such as your liability position, the thrust of the evidence, your possible vulnerability vis-a-vis the opposing driver (are you a "sympathetic" personality, or is the defendant-driver a "target" defendant, for example?). Generally, however, the multiplier variable typically ranges from a factor of 3 or 4 to 5, in cases of weak to moderately strong liability and moderate degree of injuries and intangible damages. It could, however, go as high as 6 or 7 or even 10 (or more), in strong cases involving significant injuries, pain and suffering or inconveniences, disability, disfigurement, etc.

Here are some two principal variations of this formula used.[9] The first one we shall call the **3X** multiplier system, and the other the **5X** multiplier system.

THE **3X** SYSTEM: Under this version, to determine the acceptable settlement value, you simply multiply your <u>entire</u> special damages by a factor of 3. Then, add to this the uncompensated total property damage value, if any.

THE **5X** SYSTEM: First, you multiply your <u>medical</u> damages alone (and <u>not</u> the entire special damages) by a factor of 5; then add all the other Special Damages (your wage loss, etc) to that figure. Next, add the uncompensated property damage figure, if applicable.

---

[8]Ross, <u>Settled Out of Court</u>, pp. 110-111

[9]Advocates and users of this formula often employ differing multiplier factors or variables. A recent work on the subject, for example, uses this basic formula: Medical Specials is multiplied by a factor of anywhere from 1.5 to 5, and the claimant's lost income is then added to that. [See Matthew, <u>Win Your Personal Injury Claim</u> (1992), pp. 5/3-5/4]. However, after having surveyed and studied the various variations employed by various authorities and users, the author of the present manual opts for the variant used in this manual for reasons of greater flexibility, wider applicability and inclusiveness, among others. The formula in this manual is similar to that preferred by John Guinther, as cited in p. 129 of the manual.

PREREQUISITES: Note that we do not promise or present this to be a magic formula of any sort. The point is that, **FIRST**, before you even begin to apply this formula (or, for that matter, the one illustrated on pp. 134-154) — or ever hope to be able to understand or properly use it — you must have a few basic background "tools" in hand. Basically, *you must have thoroughly done your homework and read practically the entire guidebook (and not just skimming or browsing through it, either!) in advance of using this formula. You must be competently familiar with these essential elements:* the basic facts and information of your case, and the necessary documentations thereof (see pp. 25-51 & 52-57); the basic law and doctrines regarding negligence, fault and liability (pp. 93-106); a working knowledge of the nature and extent of the injuries you sustained, and of the associated treatments, pain and suffering and inconvenience thereof (see pp. 54-57; 41-43); facts about your doctor's medical report (see, especially pp. 41-43, 54-57, & Chapter 6); your wage loss and other "special damages" items (pp. 53-54); data about your auto body damages and other property damages or losses (pp. 44-45); and other pertinent facts and information outlined in this manual.

And then, only thereafter may you — should you — fruitfully do an actual evaluation of the settlement value of your case, using this formula method (or any other method)!

AN EVALUATION WITH THE SPECIAL DAMAGES MULTIPLIER (SDM) METHOD

AN ILLUSTRATIVE EXAMPLE

Assume these facts:

1. Special Damages (See Chapter 3, pp___; & Chapter 4, pp.___):

Doctor bills	$500
Hospital charges	750
Telephone & TV expenses during hospital stay	50
Diagonostic tests(X-rays, CT scan, etc.)	120
Prescription Drugs	90
Emergency room care	100
Physical Therapy	210
Private nursing care	150
Rehabilitative care	150
Future Medical Expenses (estimate)	400
Prosthetic devices & equipment	200
TOTAL MEDICAL EXPENSES 2,720	

Lost wages & earnings	900
Lost vacation time & sick leave	400
Other lost earnings (from deprived opportunity for advancement or promotion due to injury)	300
Travel expenses (car rentals, public trans., etc) to doctor or hospital	20
Household help & housekeeping during disability	100
Babysitting expenses	75
TOTAL, ALL OTHER (i.e. NON-MEDICAL) SPECIAL DAMAGES 1,795	

TOTAL SPECIAL DAMAGES 4,515

2. <u>Property Damages</u> (See Chapter 2, Section D, at pp. 44-45 & Chapter 4):

Auto repair cost	$1,300
Damaged clothing	130
Broken glasses	95
Loss of use of vehicle (cost of substitute car rentals)	200
Vehicle towing & storage	50
TOTAL, PROPERTY DAMAGES	**1,775**

Under the 3X Multiplier System

Total Special Damages	4,515
multiplied by 3	x 3
	13,545
Add: Total, Property Damages	1,775
TOTAL:	**$15,320**

Under 5X Multiplier System

Total Past Medical Expenses	2,720
multiplied by 5	x 5
	13,600
Add: All Other (i.e. non-medical) Special Damages	1,795
	15,395
Total, Property Damages	1,775
	$17,170

INTERPRETATION: We interpret this to mean that the approximate "Settlement Range" for this case is:

A value of from $15,320 to $17,170

(3X)   (5x)

Note the Following:

• First, you should bear in mind that although we have in this manual adopted the multiplier factors of 3 and 5 as generally typical or customary in the insurance claims industry (or, at least, "reasonable" for the purposes of the average reader), nothing that we know of either in the law or the insurance industry practice would prohibit or preclude a given claimant from using a higher multiplier factor in a given case, depending on the facts of the case.[10] As stated above,

---

[10]See, for example, State vs. Hipkiss, 174 Ind. App. 337, 367 N.E. 2d 1137, 1139 (1977). Here, the court, responding to defendant's argument that a $10,000 award by the jury was excessive in light of proven pecuniary losses of only $1,000, stated that: "no authority is cited, and we know of none, in support of the State's position that damages for pain and suffering which are nine times the amount of the pecuniary loss are necessarily indicative of passion or corrupt motive by the jury"

depending on your subjective but realistic assessment of the nature and degree of your injuries, the strength of your particular case[11], and the "special circumstances" of your particular situation, you can well apply a higher multiplier factor — as high as 6 or 7 or even 10 or more, where, for example, the injuries are significant, or severe pain, disfigurement or disability is involved.

• The next point worth noting, concerns how the multiplier technique may be applied in states which employ the **"comparative negligence"** doctrine in determining auto accident liability. (See chapter 7 pp. 95-96). With respect to such states, the only thing that will be different in that instance is that, upon the parties having an understanding in regard to the percentage of negligence for which you are responsible (say it's 20 percent), the entire settlement amount, as determined by the multiplier method, will simply be reduced by the same percentage of negligence imputed to you (i.e. the same 20 percent).

• Finally, the third point to note is that in no way should it be concluded that the figure arrived at by the SDM formula (or by any other valuation method, for that matter), is necessarily the "must" amount to be ultimately settled for in the case. Bear in mind that, rather, all that has been accomplished here is that there has been created a "BALLPARK FIGURE" that is probably known to both sides, a figure reasonably within the "SETTLEMENT ZONE" and which you can work with. For, as experts have been quick to acknowledge, this formula, like each and every other formula used in the claims industry, "is no more or less than an educated guess"[12], for "there is no exact value of personal injury claim, only an approximation."[13]

Auto Accident Claims Costs

The table below shows that the value of insurance claim settlements and court awards resulting from auto accidents have risen steadily in recent years. From 1981 through 1990, the average paid bodily injury claim rose 124.9 percent from $4,453 to $10,013; the average paid property liability claim climbed about 90 percent from $889 to $1689.

TABLE 9-A
AVERAGE PAID CLAIM COSTS,*
LIABILITY INSURANCE, PRIVATE PASSENGER CARS

Year	Bodily injury	Property damage	Year	Bodily injury	Property damage
1981	$4,453	$889	1986	$7,396	$1,298
1982	5,041	958	1987	7,847	1,410
1983	5,699	1,020	1988	8,736	1,535
1984	6,163	1,125	1989	9,338	1,646
1985	6,815	1,217	1990	10,013	1,689

* For all limits combined and including all loss adjustment expenses. For bodily injury liability, dollar averages exclude Massachusetts (for all years) and most states which have no-fault automobile insurance laws. For property damage liability for 1981-1989, dollar averages exclude Massachusetts, Michigan and South Carolina. For 1990 property damage liability, dollar averages exclude those three states plus New Jersey. **Source:** Insurance Services Office. Source: The Fact Book, 1992, p. 80.

---

[11]The relevant factors and indicators of strength of a case would include: the size and composition of the special damages, especially the medical bills component; the type and nature of severity of injury (are they, for example, subjective or objective? Can they be demonstrably proven, as say, the loss of a limb or by an x-ray?); existence of a "target" type of defendant (e.g., a government body, a corporation, particularly a railroad, transit, trucking, or insurance company); the nature and extent of pain and suffering, and the treatment procedures accompanying the injuries; and the extent of permanency or disability of injury. Is the injury an occupational handicap or disability? How powerful is the expected medical testimony for and against you (as indicated, for example, by the graphic nature and comprehensiveness of your doctor's report)? The circumstances of the other driver's negligence or fault in the accident (e.g. was he drunk? Was it "gross and Wanton" kind of negligence on his part, or simply "a little bit" of negligence?) Degree of your own "contributory" or "comparative" negligence in the accident, and so on. In general, look for the same types of factors and considerations as are outlined in the discussion of the Modified Sindell Method of case evaluation (pp. 134-154).

[12]Swafford, "Evaluating Damage Claims," Insurance Law Jr., 412:273 (1957), p. 285

[13]Foutty, "The Evaluation Of Settlement Of Personal Injury Claims,"Insurance Law, Jr., 492: 5 p.6.

CHAPTER 10
EVALUATION OF THE SETTLEMENT VALUE IN MORE "SERIOUS" CASES: THE MODIFIED SINDELL METHOD

A. "Serious" Claims Or Injury Cases Defined

Experts are almost universally of the opinion that claimsmen and claims attorneys and other professionals approach the claims evaluation task in two different ways, based on the degree of "seriousness" of the case.[1] While the evaluation of the settlement value in "routine" or less serious cases is largely based on the size and nature of the medical expenses incurred by a claimant, the estimation of the worth of the case in "serious" cases, the experts say, is based on an entirely different array of considerations, considerations which could be summed up as being the "jury value" of the case, the assessment as to the likelihood of substantial recovery by the claimant in a jury trial.

For our purposes here, more serious types of cases could be broadly defined as those involving bodily injuries that involve residual impairment, disability, and/or disfigurement — e.g., serious scarring (involving, perhaps, a large number of stitches preferably in a conspicuous part of the body, or possibly plastic surgery), amputations and prosthesis, the use of braces, limping, impairment of sight or other senses, and similar "residuals", or in extreme cases, even death. Equally important, "serious" cases are also distinguishable from "routine"cases by the fact that serious cases are of such nature that, if they are not settled by negotiation, they have a more realistic chance of being litigated in court. [Routine cases, on the other hand, would usually be worth so little "trial value" (in terms of the court costs, the attorney's fees and time expenditure, etc., relative to it's "settlement value") as to rule out use of litigation in such cases.].

B. The Modified Sindell Method (MSM)

In light of the belief common among claims professionals that a wholly different set of factors and considerations should apply in the evaluation of serious claims cases, we have picked out for our use in this guidebook one specific method of evaluation which addresses many of the customary concerns involved in assessment of serious cases. We shall call this method the MODIFIED SINDELL METHOD (MSM formula, for short). [Or, it could also be called the Modified BALDYGA PROBABILITY STATISTICS formula of claims evaluation].

---

[1]See, Ross, Settled Out Of Court, pp. 106-7, 111-116.

In the studied opinion of the present writer, this method has two compelling advantages for the specific purposes of the typical claimant doing his own claims settlement himself: it is relatively simple, straightforward and efficient; and it's calculations, aimed essentially at estimating the likely jury value of a case, is "sensitive" to (i.e. takes into account) the major variables and considerations believed by claims professionals to be of concern and influence to typical jurors in judging the worth of a case before them. [The original Sindell formula, from which the "modified" version presented in this manual is derived, was based essentially on allocation of evaluation "points" to six specific factors which ranged from liability and degree of claimant's injury to claimant's personality and out-of-pocket expenses, based on surveys of juries'opinions by Sindell concerning the factors they viewed as most important in awards of damages.[2]]

As with almost every other method of claims evaluation employed in the trade, this method, too, is often a source of controversy among claims experts and professionals. However, highly experienced claims professionals and legal practitioners who use this method on a day-after-day basis in their work have pronounced it a "most advantageous"[3] method of evaluation. And, in any case, as with any other evaluation formula in use in the trade today, "[the Sindell method] is no more or less than an educated guess, but at least it is one based upon a principle of operation and which at least gives one a starting point."[4]

The point is that claimants who use this evaluation method (or for that matter, the so-called rule-of-thumb method outlined in the preceding Chapter 9) to arrive at a reasonable settlement value for their claim, can rest assured that their result is at the very least no less valid or defensible as any that is tossed around by the professional claims lawyer or adjuster, whatever the nominal "sophistication" of the alternative method used.[5]

C. Description of the Structure of the MSM Formula

First, we shall discuss the structure of the formula and it's different components, and explain how the formula works. And next (from p. 143), we shall do an actual rating or evaluation of some typical claims cases wherein we assign specific settlement values to cases using the MODIFIED SINDELL METHOD.

D. The MSM Formula

Basically, the formula works this way: six (6) specific elements or factors which are considered to influence the award of damages in lawsuits or claims are allocated rating "points" by the evaluator. A maximum of 100 points is allocable to the theoretical "perfect" claims case or lawsuit — that is, the higher the claimant's case can score in terms of possessing more of each of the various elements or qualities designated, the closer its score will get to 100 points.

---

[2]See, for example, the following:Sindell, "What Price Personal Injury?," Practising Law. 37(Feb. 1957); The Sindell Negligence Folio (Lawyers and Judges Publishing Co.); Swafford, "Evaluating Damage Claims," Insurance Law Jr.,412:273, 1957; and Baldyga, How To Settle Your Own Insurance Claim, pp. 118-126.The model presented in this manual represents a modified version of the original Sindell formula by the present writer, and incorporates elements of Daniel G. Baldyga's "Probability Statistics Formula"which is, itself, a version of the Sindell formula. Hence our term, the "modified" Sindell formula. The areas of modifications relate primarily to the dollar amount of the actual loss or out-of-pocket expenses which has been upgraded to account for the inflation factor since the original Sindell formula in 1953, and the incorporation of elements of the calculation procedure from Baldyga's version, for reasons of practicality and relative simplicity of computations.

[3]Swafford, "Evaluating Damage Claims," p.282. See also comments by Baldyga, How To Settle Your Own Insurance Claim, pp. 3-4, 118-9. It's important to note that numerous variations of the Sindell formula are employed by various claims practitioners in essentially the same manner, but often using several different variables [See, for example, Personal Injury Settlement Evaluator (Matthew Bender & Co., 1963), which uses an adaptation of the Sindell formula with 7 instead of 6 variables; and Otto, "Lawsuit Evaluation and Outcome Prediction: A More Objective, Dimensionalized and System Approach," 52 Insurance Counsel Jr., 634, (Oct. 1985), which illustrates a Sindell type point-of-allocation formula based upon 40 instead of 6 variables.]

[4]Swafford, op. cit. p. 285.

[5]Analysts have noted, for example, that lawyers and insurance adjusters, even as they claim or pretend to employ supposedly "objective" or "rational" procedures in arriving at their settlement figures, are often unable to provide rational or coherent explanations of how they obtained their values. This attitude by a lawyer is typical, who, when asked for an explanation of how he arrived at a settlement figure he had given, retorted: "Don't ask me why I picked that number out; I just know — from experience, intuition, whatever.." (Guinther, Winning Your Personal Injury Suit, p.112). And another analyst noted this of insurance adjusters he observed in his study: "[there's] difficulty {in the ranks} of the adjusters themselves in describing how they obtained their ideas of value...some of them, no matter how pressed, could not explain how they reached the figure [they arrived at on claims]."(Ross, Settled Out Of Court, p.97).

The "points" are allocated in terms of the 6 ELEMENTS, as follows:

       I. Degree of Liability On Defendant's Part .... 1 to 50 points
       II. Nature Of Injury .... 1 to 10 points
       III. Your Age .... 1 to 10 points
       IV. Type Of Person You Yourself Are .... 1 to 10 points
       V. Type Of Person the Defendant Party Is .... 1 to 10 points
       VI. Your Actual Loss (Special Damages) .... 1 to 10 points

NOTE: The Property Damages part of the claims (for auto repair or replacement cost, loss or damages to personal effects, etc.) if any, is a separate matter; it's usually separately calculated and then added to the settlement final demand, as illustrated at the ends of the worksheet on p. 154.

For the purposes of this discussion, for each of the above 6 ELEMENTS or factors, we shall outline the important considerations that an evaluator takes into account in his assessment as to how many "points" (the value) he or she is to allocate to the factor in a given case.

I. Degree of Liability on the Other Party's Part:

As could be seen from the table above, from 1 to 50 points can be allocated to this category alone, meaning that this element alone could represent as much as 50 percent of the whole value of the case. We interpret this to mean that in cases where there is a clear case of "perfect" liability on the defendant's part — which is to say, where the other party (motorist) in the accident is 100 percent negligent and at fault, or where the other party might even be held to be "gross and wanton" in his negligence — you may allot the entire 50 points in the case. And, by the same token, where there is, on the other hand, a serious doubt as to whether there is a "jury question" (where there's serious doubtful liability or little or no potential for liability on the part of the other party), an allocation of 1 point may be made to this element in the case.

Of course, in point of fact, the reality about the average claim would often probably be somewhere between these two extremes! *The important point to stress is that in all instances, each claim must be studied individually along with the facts in the file and as they relate to the law [see below, as well as Chapter 7 (pp. 93-106) especially Sections G and H therein] before making any such allocation as to the liability of each party.* Thus, the number of points allocable for the overall degree of the defendant's (the other party's) liability — up to the maximum 50 points — may be adjusted upwards or downwards according to your estimate of the variety of factors outlined below which directly relate to the liabilty issue.

[POINTERS: Thoroughly read and review Chapter 7 of this manual, dealing with the issues of injuries, negligence, liability, the insurance industry rules-of-thumb, and short-cuts for assignment of liability, etc.].

Some factors to be considered which are to be directly related to the issue of liability are as follows:

   (1)   The circumstances of the negligence of the defendant. — Was the defendant violating a particular statute or ordinance you know of? Was he (she) drunk? Are there possible basis reasonably for the charge of gross and wanton negligence, or was he just "a little bit" negligent?

   (2)   What possibility, if any, of contributory negligence (or comparative negligence) is there on your part? Look at the table on p. 96 . If your state is a "contributory negligence" state, some degree of negligence on your part, no matter how minor, may be an absolute defense by the defendant which could bar any recovery by you. Or, if the situation is such that the proof of the negligence clearly favors neither party, (a serious case of "doubtful liabitlity"), a liability factor of only 25 points may be more appropriate. In most states in the nation (see p. 96), the rule of "comparative negligence" governs. In such states, on the issue of liability and allocation of points under this formula, you should seriously try to view, objectively and critically, your actions as they bear upon the basic liability of the defendant.

(3)   Did you possibly answer any questions put to you by the insurance company or its adjusters that might possibly have a bearing on attribution of liability — the sort of questions mentioned on pp. 105-6 of this manual, for example? If so, what questions and how did you answer them?

(4)   Possible psychological impact of liability facts. — These are matters which do not deal with the personalities of the parties (hereinafter discussed), but are facts which make a claim attractive or unattractive to the jury from a liability standpoint. An example of unattractive facts, in the stated experience of one Kansas city attorney, is that the average jury does not like the idea of teenagers in automobiles late at night. (Accordingly, your allocation of points under this section in evaluating your claim should take such factors into account as they relate to you, regardless of the circumstances of the accident.)

(5)   Known or possible opposition. — Considered under this section will be the element of the known probable or possible opposition which you will encounter in establishing before a jury the liability facts. Certain lawyers have a reputation of being thorough in their preparation both of facts and law, aggressive in the trial and full of ingenuity. Others are not. Hence, in considering the evaluation on the subject of liability, this is a factor which is often strongly considered in the light of statements and so forth you may have made (or will make) on the matter of liability. An effective cross-examiner, for example, could devastate, in certain cases, a claimant committed to a bad liability fact.

(6)   Venue and forum.— To be considered under this category is the locale of a possible trial, the community in which you may ultimately have to contest the liability facts, the judge before whom you will try the case and the type of jury which you can reasonably be expected to draw.

(7)   Proof. — Your estimate of the proof, the availability and credibility of witnesses, and a variety of other factors directly relating to the issue of liability.

II. Nature of Your Injuries (See especially Chapter 6):

The range of points that can be alloted to this element is from 1 to 10 points, depending on the degree of severity of the injury. Thus, slight or minor injuries (e.g., if you were only bruised or "shaken up" or lost little or no time from your employment), might be assessed only 1 to 2 points; moderate injuries 3 to 5 points; and severe injuries (if, for example, you were to have been permenently or totally disabled or disfigured involving, say, serious scarring requiring surgery and stitches, amputations and prothesis, loss of limb or brain injury, the use of braces, limping, impairment of sight or other senses, and similar residuals) such will merit an allocation of anywhere from 6 to 10 points, depending on the nature and degree of severity. For "multiple" type of injuries, the points should be allocated for each individual injury and added up to obtain the final point total for the injury category — for example, a broken leg (2 points), bruised ribs (1 point), and disfiguring facial scar (6 points), would amount to nine points for injuries. Here again, the average case would fall somewhere between the two extremes.

Each case must be studied and analyzed in the light of competent and honest medical advice. In this connection, you should note that insurance adjusters are often suspicious of doctors who, on one hand, exaggerate and "blow up" injuries, or, on the other hand, doctors who never find anything wrong with anybody. To make an honest evaluation on the matter of injuires, a prerequisite is that you have honest medical opinion.

Some factors which are considered are:

(1)   The nature of the injury. — You consider whether your complaints are objective or subjective; whether they are demonstrable as in the case of loss of a limb or observable by X-rays; whether they are disfiguring or disabling.

(2)   The nature and extent of the pain and suffering accompanying such injury. — Juries are sympathetic to pain, as they should be.

(3)   The nature and extent of medical treatment. — Under this category you do not consider this in relation to the expense involved, but in terms of the discomfort, inconvenience, painful operations or procedures, and similar compensable experiences you might have had.

(4)   Permanency.— This, of course, should always be considered. There can be minor and painless permanent results of an injury, and there can be painful and substantial permanent injury; or there can be no permanent injury.

(5)   Occupational handicap. — Injuries, whether permanent or not, frequently create an occupational handicap in the claimant's particular line of work, and if such exists, this factor should also be considered.

(6)   Past medical history. — Previous injuries are a factor which should always be considered, and aggravation of pre-existing disability or disease is a factor which should increase the injury value of a case. You should avoid ever trying to "forget" your medical history in the hopes that it will not be brought out. This is disastrous since the insurance company defense attorneys always dig it up!

(7)   Expected medical testimony. — Under this heading you consider the personality, background and ability of the doctors involved. As we all know, some are good testifiers and some are miserable ones. If you don't know who's who, you just make it a point to personally interview the doctors involved on your side and make some kind of an investigation as to the doctors involved on the other side. What are the doctor's credentials, and his reputation with insurance companies? Has he been (or does it look like he will be) difficult to work with in court? Or has he, on the other hand, been forthcoming and elaborate in his medical report for you?[6]

POINTER: Thoroughly review the following sections of the manual, among others: Chapter 3, Section C; Chap. 4, Sections IV & V; Chap. 6; and Appendices D, E, & F.

III. Your Age (Claimant's Age):

In this category, the range of allocable points is from 1 (one) to 10. Sindell originally based his age rating on the American Life Mortality Tables[7] as follows:

AGE	POINTS
1 to 7	10
8 to 15	9
16 to 23	8
24 to 31	7
32 to 39	6
40 to 47	5
48 to 55	4
56 to 60	3
61 to 65	2
66 and over	1

IV. Type of Person You Are:

The formula allocates from 1 to 10 points in this category. Of course, everybody knows (at least we've all heard it said) that the personality of a person in the trial of a lawsuit before a jury is invariably most imporant. Some call this "jury appeal." In essence, you will have to rate yourself and in order to do so correctly, you have to be brutally honest. Thus, if you are an argumentative or disagreeable person, or you have a criminal record or a record of antisocial behavior

---

[6]As one negligence lawyer put it, "Some doctors can minimize a very serious injury before a jury by giving them a lot of mumbo-jumbo that they don't understand." — exactly the kind of doctor that you would want to avoid as a claimant!

[7]Note that point values allocated according to a claimant's age may also be based on standard mortality tables.

that is of the sort likely to prejudice a jury against you, then allot to yourself some 1 or 2 or 3 points. But if you are an above average person in terms of character and behavior, an attractive, articulate, sympathetic and amiable person who would present an excellent courtroom appearance, allocate to yourself the most points.

[**POINTER:** Under ordinary circumstances you would be on the safe side to simply give yourself a minimum of 5 points!]

Some of the factors you are to consider in applying points in this category are:

(1) Your Appearance and Demeanor.

(2) YourRace or Color. — If we are to be realistic, we must accept that these are factors that juries consider. [Research consistently shows that if you are a member of a minority group (blacks in parts of the south, especially, and other minorities elsewhere), your claim is likely to be "down-graded".]

(3) Your Mentality. — Like claims attorneys you may practice having someone (a friend or whatever) "examine" and "cross-examine" you in the privacy of your home so that you may gauge your ability to take care of yourself, your alertness and your general comprehension of facts.

(4) Your Occupation. — It is a well recognized 'open secret' among claims experts that certain occupations work an advantage or disadvantage to a claimant. For example, the average jury is sympathetic to a housewife (although they will not grant her as much money as a working person) or a nurse or one engaged in a charitable or humane occupation. On the other hand, the average jury dislikes policemen or gamblers. These are factors which should be considered.

(5) Your Demeanor and Temperament. — Honestly try to analyze your temperament. Are you one that could be goaded into an angry display or are you calm and unemotional? Do you think, honestly speaking, that if you were to go before the jury the jurors would consider you some sort of crank, someone who, as one lawyer put it, is the type of person "with very genuine injuries who cannot make anyone believe it hurts"? Analyze yourself as a trial lawyer must, indeed, analyze his client in this category! Be brutally frank with yourself.

(6) Your History and Record. — Obviously, your history, personal and physical, is of great importance. Cases abound where a claimant has tried to repeatedly sell the same injury or where he has denied a past criminal felony conviction. Unsually when those matters occur, that ends the claim or lawsuit! On the other hand, a client's civic history in the community may be of great benefit to him if he has been active in charitable, religious or political endeavor.

V. Type of Person the Defendant is:

Under this category, the formula allocates 1 to 10 points. Here, though, note that you are to allocate the points **in reverse order** to the way you did it above when it was yourself that you had to rate. That is, here, the better and more atractive the defendant (the other motorist) looks, then the LESS points he (or it) gets, and the worse his character and reputation, the MORE points he gets: [For example, the highest points, say all 10 points, would go to a known bookie or drunk driver defendant, or a large impersonal, corporate defendant with a "deep pocket," whereas the lowest points would go to the same defendant if he were well known and well loved and behaved. A construction worker might be allocated only 3 to 5 points in this category, and an elderly school teacher or housewife might receive only 1 point.] You are, in a word, to attempt to categorize the defendant both economically as well as sympathetically.

The things which you consider here are not much different in principle from those which you considered with reference to yourself, if the defendant is an individual.

If, however, the defendant is a corporation, particularly a railroad, transit, trucking or insurance company, you usually allocate a more liberal point evaluation. Whether this is justified or not, we must recognize the fact that most juries are prone to "stick it" to corporations and big companies — in other words, juries are not as reluctant to bring in a substantial verdict against such defendants as they are against an individual. [**Pointer:** Once again, under ordinary circumstances, you would be on the safe side to simply give the defendant a minimum of 5 points!]

VI. Your Actual Loss or Out-Of-Pocket Expenses (Special Damages):

Under this category, points from one to 10 are to be allocated for elements of your actual money losses, such as medical expenses, lost wages, etc. Here again, an arbitrary position must be taken. The formula calls for the allocation of 1 point for no loss to $1,000, up to 10 points for $9,000 or over, under the following "scale of loss evaluation."

Loss	Points
$ 00 - $1,000	1
$1,001 - $2,000	2
$2,001 - $3,000	3
$3,001 - $4,000	4
$4,001 - $5,000	5
$5,001 - $6,000	6
$6,001 - $7,000	7
$7,001 - $8,000	8
$8,001 - $9,000	9
$9,001 - $10,000	10

NOTE: You are to add 1 point for every $1,000 worth of Special Damages — but only up to $10,000. (Round off to the nearest $1,000, if the amount falls in-between two levels in the scale). But what if your special damages are in excess of (i.e., is over) $10,000? Then, what you do is this: allot the case a "perfect" 10 points, but later on when you're ready to calculate the rating of the case, you add back the excess amount to the final calculations. (See example, line 10 of worksheet, on p. 144, for illustration).

THE MSM FORMULA WORKSHEET

PART I. POINTS ALLOCATION PART

POINTS ALLOCATED

1. Liability (1 to 50 Points)... _____

2. Nature of Injury (1 to 10 Points) .... _____

3. Your Age (1 to 10 Points, see chart on p. 138)................................... _____

4. Type of Person You Are (1 to 10 Points) .... _____

5. Type of Person (or Entity) the Other Party is (1 to 10 Points, in reverse) .... _____

6. Your Special Damages (1 to 10 Points, round off to nearest $1,000)* .... _____

7. TOTAL POINTS ALLOCATED .... _____

* Add any excess over $10,000 to Line 10 of Part II below.

PART II: CASE RATING PART

1. Enter Your Total Special Damages Amount: $ _____

2. Line 1, multiplied by 2 (i.e., doubled) .... $ _____

3. Add Allowance for Total Disability [@ $1,500 per week of Total Disability]** .... $ _____

4. Add Allowance for Partial Disability [@ $750 per week of Partial Disability]** .... $ _____

5. Total (Add Lines 2, 3, and 4) .... $ _____

6. Line 5 rounded Out to the nearest $1,000 .... $ _____

7. Line 6 Divided by 100 (This is called the "CASE RATE FIGURE") .... $ _____

8. Enter Total # of "Points" Allocated to Case [Line 7 of Part I above].............. _____

9. Line 8 Multiplied by the dollar amount on Line 7 .... $ _____

10. Add   Excess over $10,000 in Special Damages, if any .... $ _____

11. TOTAL (Add Up Lines 9 & 10).. $ _____

This figure (on line 11) is the **"Mean Settlement Value"** (MSV) of your case—i.e., the figure that best reflects the true value of your claim

---

**Note: Note that these allowances (allowance for Total or Partial Disability) are separate and apart from, and have nothing to do with, wages or the medical bills. For purposes of this formula, whether you're employed or unemployed, you're to simply assign yourself $1,500 per week for any periods of Total Disability you had, and $750 per week for any periods of Partial Disability. Estimate the type of disability (total or partial) from the contents of your doctor's report. If your doctor's report didn't make specific statements about your disability status, this may be one time when it may be necessary for you to go to him and request a proper update or correction of the report along the lines suggested elsewhere in the guidebook. [Refer to pp. 55-56 of book, among other sections]

12. Line 11 Divided by 4 (i.e., take ¼ or 25% of Line 11) .... $ ———

13. Add the Resultant Line 12 Amount to Line 11 .... $ ———
This is the **"High Settlement Value"** (above the mean) of the case

14. Subtract the Resultant Line 12 Amount from Line 11 .... $ ———
This is the **"Low Settlement Amount"** (below the mean) of the case

YOU NOW HAVE: The High Settlement Value (Line 13) .... $ ———
(Add the Total Property Damages, if any)* .... $ ———

The Mean Settlement Value (Line 11) .... $ ———
(Add the Total Property Damages, if any)* .... $ ———

The Low Settlement Value (Line 14) .... $ ———
(Add the Total Property Damages, if any)* .... $ ———

THE SETTLEMENT ZONE OR AREA

NOTE: Ordinarily, under normal circumstances involving no special circumstances in a case, the estimated "Mean Value" should generally suffice as a reasonable basis upon which and around which to formulate a settlement. However, the SETTLEMENT ZONE OR AREA is designed, additionally, to make allowance for situations involving given cases which may have extraordinary or special circumstances which a claimant may feel should give his case more value, or for which, on the other hand, the insurance adjuster (or even the claimant) may feel that lesser value on the claims could be acceptable. In effect, the entire range of the "Settlement Area," as opposed to just on particular figure, provides the broad "area" within which to negotiate — THE ZONE OF NEGOTIATION.

*The Property Damages part of a claim is generally reimbursed in full, dollar-for-dollar. So, with regard to any property damages you might have incurred (for auto repairs or replacement, damaged or lost personal or other property, towing or storage, cost of substitute car rentals to work, etc.), providing you are not otherwise being compensated for it, simply add the total of that amount to your final demand figure, or add the "deductible" amount, if applicable.

E. Illustrated Examples of Four Hypothetical Cases, Using the MSM Formula Worksheet*

Actual Rating of Case with the Sindell Technique

Now, let's rate some cases in terms of setting the settlement values for each claim using the Modified Sindell Method (or Probabilty Statistics) Formula.

For the purposes of providing practical illustration of the way the Modified Sindell Method formula is applied, we shall work out below, four separate hypothetical claims cases. By using the author's exclusive WORKSHEET provided in this manual (pp. 144-145), you should find the whole valuation calculation process a relatively simple exercise.

ILLUSTRATIVE EXAMPLE A:

Facts of the Case: Mr. A, a 43-year old average citizen, was an employed college professor earning $1,000 per week when, while driving to work his car was hit on the rear end by Mr. X, who clearly was speeding and at fault, but was also a decent average citizen. Mr. A was hospitalized with a broken leg. Upon being discharged from the hospital, he went home to recuperate. While at home, he was still confined. The leg injury took 6 weeks to heal, and he was in a cast this whole period and was therefore totally disabled for the period. Once out of the cast, he was able to get back to normal life quickly. He only saw the doctor once more for a routine checkup so his partial disability was zero. His total hospital & medical bills were $5,000. Mr. A filed claims.

---

*These four hypothetical cases are taken from samples cited in <u>How To Settle Your Own Insurance Claims</u>, pp. 123-126.

THE MSM FORMULA WORKSHEET

PART I. POINTS ALLOCATION PART

POINTS ALLOCATED

1. Liability (1 to 50 Points) 50

2. Nature of Injury (1 to 10 Points) 10

3. Your Age (1 to 10 Points, see chart on p. 138) 5

4. Type of Person You Are (1 to 10 Points) 5

5. Type of Person (or Entity) the Other Party is (1 to 10 Points, in reverse) 5

6. Your Special Damages (1 to 10 Points, round off to nearest $1,000)* 10

7. TOTAL POINTS ALLOCATED 85

* Add any excess over $10,000 to Line 10 of Part II below.

PART II: CASE RATING PART

1. Enter Your Total Special Damages Amount: $11,000

2. Line 1, multiplied by 2 (i.e., doubled) .... =$ 22,000

3. Add: Allowance for Total Disability [@ $1,500 per week of Total Disability]** .... $ 9,000

4. Add: Allowance for Partial Disability [@ $750 per week of Partial Disability]** .... $ _____

5. Total (Add Lines 2, 3, and 4) .... $ 31,000

6. Line 5 rounded Out to the nearest $1,000 .... $ 31,000

7. Line 6 Divided by 100 (This is called the "CASE RATE FIGURE") .... $ 310

8. Enter: Total # of "Points" Allocated to Case [Line 7 of Part I above] 85

9. Line 8 Multiplied by the dollar amount on Line 7 .... $ 26,350

10. Add: Excess over $10,000 in Special Damages, if any .... $ 1,000

11. TOTAL (Add Up Lines 9 & 10) .... $ 27,350

This figure (on line 11) is the **"Mean Settlement Value"** (MSV) of your case—i.e., the figure that best reflects the true value of your claim

---

**Note: Note that these allowances (allowance for Total or Partial Disability) are separate and apart from, and have nothing to do with, wages or the medical bills. For purposes of this formula, whether you're employed or unemployed, you're to simply assign yourself $1,500 per week for any periods of Total Disability you had, and $750 per week for any periods of Partial Disability. Estimate the type of disability (total or partial) from the contents of your doctor's report. If your doctor's report didn't make specific statements about your disability status, this may be one time when it may be necessary for you to go to him and request a proper update or correction of the report along the lines suggested elsewhere in the guidebook. [Refer to pp. 55-56 of book, among other sections]

12. Line 11 Divided by 4 (i.e., take ¼ or 25% of Line 11) .... $ 6,837.50

13. Add the Resultant Line 12 Amount to Line 11 .... $24,187.50
This is the **"High Settlement Value"** (above the mean) of the case

14. Subtract the Resultant Line 12 Amount from Line 11 .... $20,512.50
This is the **"Low Settlement Amount"** (below the mean) of the case

YOU NOW HAVE: The High Settlement Value (Line 13) $34,187.50
(Add the Total Property Damages, if any)* .... $_____

The Mean Settlement Value (Line 14) .... $ 27,350.00
(Add the Total Property Damages, if any)* .... $

The Low Settlement Value (Line 14) $20,512.50
(Add the Total Property Damages, if any)* .... $_____

THE SETTLEMENT ZONE OR AREA

> **NOTE:** Ordinarily, under normal circumstances involving no special circumstances in a case, the estimated "Mean Value" should generally suffice as a reasonable basis upon which and around which to formulate a settlement. However, the SETTLEMENT ZONE OR AREA is designed, additionally, to make allowance for situations involving given cases which may have extraordinary or special circumstances which a claimant may feel should give his case more value, or for which, on the other hand, the insurance adjuster (or even the claimant) may feel that lesser value on the claims could be acceptable. In effect, the entire range of the "Settlement Area," as opposed to just on particular figure, provides the broad "area" within which to negotiate — THE ZONE OF NEGOTIATION.

EXPLANATION OF THE PROCESS (Example A)

On allocation of points in the case, liability is clearly clear-cut in Mr. A's favor (the claimant), so he gets a perfect score of 50 points. He gets another perfect 10 points for injury since his injury was obviously of serious and disabling nature. He's 43 years of age so he merits 5 points on the age category. He's an average citizen with no serious blemish on his past, and so also is Mr. X who hit him — thus, each is assigned 5 points on each of the two categories. The total Special Damages is $11,000 ($5,000 is medical/hospital bills, $6,000 in wage loss), and so fetches another perfect score of 10 points, but leaves an excess of $1,000 above the maximum score of $10,000 amount allowed. (This $1,000 is added back in Line 10 of the Case Rating Part of the Worksheet.) The total of 85 points awarded to this case is what we enter on line 8 of the Case Rating Part of the WORKSHEET. The final calculations exercises carried out in lines 12 thru 14 of the case rating part of the worksheet, is merely meant to provide an "area" or range of the "zone in which to negotiate," — as opposed to just one single, rigid figure — a range which could be very useful in tailoring the ultimate settlement to the particular facts and circumstances.

---

*The Property Damages part of a claim is generally reimbursed in full, dollar-for-dollar. So, with regard to any property damages you might have incurred (for auto repairs or replacement, damaged or lost personal or other property, towing or storage, cost of substitute car rentals to work, etc.), providing you are not otherwise being compensated for it, simply add the total of that amount to your final demand figure, or add the "deductible" amount, if applicable.

ILLUSTRATIVE EXAMPLE B:

Facts of the Case: You are a 37 years old 'Average Joe' and were a passenger on a motor scooter when it was struck by Mr. Y's car, also an "Average Joe' type of fellow, causing you only a bad sprained finger. Following your initial examination by your doctor (which included X-rays of your finger, among other things), you saw him three more times within a period of 4 weeks. No time was taken off from your work, but you had continual pain in the injured finger for a month, which significantly curtailed your daily activities. Your doctor gave you 4 weeks of partial disability only. Your total medical bill amounted to $500.

Example B
THE MSM FORMULA WORKSHEET

PART I. POINTS ALLOCATION PART

POINTS ALLOCATED

1. Liability (1 to 50 Points) .... <u>50</u>

2. Nature of Injury (1 to 10 Points) .... <u>5</u>

3. Your Age (1 to 10 Points, see chart on p. 138) .... <u>6</u>

4. Type of Person You Are (1 to 10 Points) .... <u>6</u>

5. Type of Person (or Entity) the Other Party is (1 to 10 Points, in reverse) ..... <u>5</u>

6. Your Special Damages (1 to 10 Points, round off to nearest $1,000)* .... <u>1</u>

7. TOTAL POINTS ALLOCATED .... <u>73</u>

* Add any excess over $10,000 to Line 10 of Part II below.

PART II: CASE RATING PART

1. Enter Your Total Special Damages Amount: $<u>500</u>

2. Line 1, multiplied by 2 (i.e., doubled) .... =$ <u>1,000</u>

3. Add: Allowance for Total Disability [@ $1,500 per week of Total Disability]** .... $ <u>-0-</u>

4. Add: Allowance for Partial Disability [@ $750 per week of Partial Disability]** .... $ <u>3,000</u>

5. Total (Add Lines 2, 3, and 4) .... $ <u>4,000</u>

6. Line 5 rounded Out to the nearest $1,000 .... $ <u>4,000</u>

7. Line 6 Divided by 100 (This is called the "CASE RATE FIGURE") ..... $ <u>40</u>

8. Enter: Total # of "Points" Allocated to Case [Line 7 of Part I above] ..... <u>73</u>

9. Line 8 Multiplied by the dollar amount on Line 7 .... $ <u>2,920</u>

10. Add: Balance over $10,000 in Special Damages, if any .... $ <u>0</u>

11. Total (Add Lines 9 & 10) .... $ <u>2,920</u>

This figure (on line 11) is the **"Mean Settlement Value"** (MSV) of your case—i.e., the figure that best reflects the true value of your claim

---

**Note: Note that these allowances (allowance for Total or Partial Disability) are separate and apart from, and have nothing to do with, wages or the medical bills. For purposes of this formula, whether you're employed or unemployed, you're to simply assign yourself $1,500 per week for any periods of Total Disability you had, and $750 per week for any periods of Partial Disability. Estimate the type of disability (total or partial) from the contents of your doctor's report. If your doctor's report didn't make specific statements about your disability status, this may be one time when it may be necessary for you to go to him and request a proper update or correction of the report along the lines suggested elsewhere in the guidebook. [Refer to pp. 55-56 of book, among other sections]

12. Line 11 Divided by 4 (i.e., take ¼ or 25% of Line 11) .... $ __730__

13. Add the Resultant Line 12 Amount to Line 11 .... $ 3,650
   This is the **"High Settlement Value"** (above the mean) of the case

14. Subtract the Resultant Line 12 Amount from Line 11 .... $ 2,190
   This is the **"Low Settlement Amount"** (below the mean) of the case

YOU NOW HAVE: The High Settlement Value (Line 13) $3,650

(Add the Total Property Damages, if any)* .... $ ____

The Mean Settlement Value (Line 11) .... $ 2,920

(Add the Total Property Damages, if any)* .... $ ____

The Low Settlement Value (Line 14) .... $ $2,190

(Add the Total Property Damages, if any)* .... $ ____

}

THE SETTLEMENT ZONE OR AREA

NOTE: Ordinarily, under normal circumstances involving no special circumstances in a case, the estimated "Mean Value" should generally suffice as a reasonable basis upon which and around which to formulate a settlement. However, the SETTLEMENT ZONE OR AREA is designed, additionally, to make allowance for situations involving given cases which may have extraordinary or special circumstances which a claimant may feel should give his case more value, or for which, on the other hand, the insurance adjuster (or even the claimant) may feel that lesser value on the claims could be acceptable. In effect, the entire range of the "Settlement Area," as opposed to just on particular figure, provides the broad "area" within which to negotiate — THE ZONE OF NEGOTIATION.

Explanation of the Process (Example B)

On allocation of points in the case, liability is clearly clear-cut in this instance in your (i.e. the claimant's) favor, so you can assign a perfect score of 50 points. Your injury is average, nothing too serious or spectacular, nor objectively provable, so you get assigned the average points on that — 5 points. For your age, you score 6 points on that. You are a "nice guy" with nothing particularly bad or derogatory about your background, so you get a slightly above average score of 6 points on personality, out of the 10 points allowed. The fellow who hit you, a Mr. Average Guy as well, gets assigned a score of 5 points on personality. The total special damages of $500 being less than $1,000, gets the minimum score of 1 point. The total points awarded to this case amount to 73, and that's what is entered on Line 8 of the Case Rating Part of the worksheet.

---

*The Property Damages part of a claim is generally reimbursed in full, dollar-for-dollar. So, with regard to any property damages you might have incurred (for auto repairs or replacement, damaged or lost personal or other property, towing or storage, cost of substitute car rentals to work, etc.), providing you are not otherwise being compensated for it, simply add the total of that amount to your final demand figure, or add the "deductible" amount, if applicable.

ILLUSTRATIVE EXAMPLE C

Facts of the Case: You are a 39 year-old full-time housewife who, though not "employed" in the conventional sense, is fully busy and employed 'inside the home' with a husband and minor children to care for. While crossing the street, you were struck by a car driven by Mr. Jones who was clearly at fault. You injured your shoulder and had a slight headache which lasted for 24 hours. Your total medical bills amounted to $1,630 (consisting of hospital emergency room $60, drugs $120, x-rays $200, doctor's charges for examination and visits $1,250). You were not completely confined to bed but were only able to "get up and about" the house for half of the days during the next 4 weeks. (According to your area's Local Department of Labor, the "minimum wage" rate paid generally, and the wage rate paid to non "live-in" domestic servants in your own area at the time, was $5.00 per hour.) The doctor's report gave you 4 weeks of partial disability only. You figured the lost earning capacity you incurred as a housewife, to amount to $400 — i.e., at 20 hours per week (half of regular 40 hour work week) for 4 weeks of partial disability. Hence, by your calculation your total Special Damages amounted to $2,030 ($1,630 + $400).

Example C

THE MSM FORMULA WORKSHEET

PART I. POINTS ALLOCATION PART POINTS ALLOCATED

1. Liability (1 to 50 Points) .... <u>50</u>

2. Nature of Injury (1 to 10 Points) .... <u>4</u>

3. Your Age (1 to 10 Points, see chart on p. 138) .... <u>6</u>

4. Type of Person You Are (1 to 10 Points) .... <u>6</u>

5. Type of Person (or Entity) the Other Party is (1 to 10 Points, in reverse) .... <u>5</u>

6. Your Special Damages (1 to 10 Points, round off to nearest $1,000)* .... <u>2</u>

7. TOTAL POINTS ALLOCATED .... <u>73</u>

* Add any excess over $10,000 to Line 10 of Part II below.

PART II: CASE RATING PART

1. Enter Your Total Special Damages Amount: $<u>2,030</u>

2. Line 1, multiplied by 2 (i.e., doubled) .... =$ <u>4,060</u>

3. Add Allowance for Total Disability [@ $1,500 per week of Total Disability]** .... $ <u>-0-</u>

4. Add Allowance for Partial Disability [@ $750 per week of Partial Disability]** .... $ <u>3,000</u>

5. Total (Add Lines 2, 3, and 4) .... $ <u>7,060</u>

6. Line 5 rounded Out to the nearest $1,000 .... $ <u>7,000</u>

7. Line 6 Divided by 100 (This is called the "CASE RATE FIGURE") .... $ <u>70</u>

8. Enter Total # of "Points" Allocated to Case [Line 7 of Part I above] .... <u>73</u>

9. Line 8 Multiplied by the dollar amount on Line 7 .... $ <u>5,110</u>

10. Add Excess over $10,000 in Special Damages, if any .... $ <u>0-</u>

11. TOTAL (Add UP Lines 9 & 10) .... $ <u>5,110</u>

This figure (on line 11) is the **"Mean Settlement Value"** (MSV) of your case—i.e., the figure that best reflects the true value of your claim

---

**Note: Note that these allowances (allowance for Total or Partial Disability) are separate and apart from, and have nothing to do with, wages or the medical bills. For purposes of this formula, whether you're employed or unemployed, you're to simply assign yourself $1,500 per week for any periods of Total Disability you had, and $750 per week for any periods of Partial Disability. Estimate the type of disability (total or partial) from the contents of your doctor's report. If your doctor's report didn't make specific statements about your disability status, this may be one time when it may be necessary for you to go to him and request a proper update or correction of the report along the lines suggested elsewhere in the guidebook. [Refer to pp. 55-56 of book, among other sections]

12. Line 11 Divided by 4 (i.e., take ¼ or 25% of Line 11) .... $ 1,277.50

13. Add the Resultant Line 12 Amount to Line 11 .... $ 6,387.50
This is the "High Settlement Value" (above the mean) of the case

14. Subtract the Resultant Line 12 Amount from Line 11 .... $ 3,832.50
This is the "Low Settlement Amount" (below the mean) of the case

YOU NOW HAVE: The high Settlement Value (Line 13) $6,387.50

(Add the Total Property Damages, if any)* .... $_____

The Mean Settlement Value (Line 11) $5,110.00

(Add the Total Property Damages, if any)* .... $_____

The Low Settlement Value (Line 14) $3,832.50

(Add the Total Property Damages, if any)* .... $ _____

THE SETTLEMENT ZONE OR AREA

NOTE: Ordinarily, under normal circumstances involving no special circumstances in a case, the estimated "Mean Value" should generally suffice as a reasonable basis upon which and around which to formulate a settlement. However, the SETTLEMENT ZONE OR AREA is designed, additionally, to make allowance for situations involving given cases which may have extraordinary or special circumstances which a claimant may feel should give his case more value, or for which, on the other hand, the insurance adjuster (or even the claimant) may feel that lesser value on the claims could be acceptable. In effect, the entire range of the "Settlement Area," as opposed to just on particular figure, provides the broad "area" within which to negotiate — THE ZONE OF NEGOTIATION.

Explanation of the Process (Example C)

On allocation of points in the case, since liability is clearly clear-cut in your (the housewife's) favor, you assign a perfect score on this element — 50 points. The injury is somewhat minor, certainly nothing major or serious, so you assign 4 points to that category. Your age, in terms of the age chart, merits 6 points for that. You are a nice, lovable housewife dutifully catering to a husband and minor children, so assign 6 points to your personality. Mr. Jones, the "defendent" person who hit you, is a person of average character and background, so he gets a score of 5 points on personality. The total Special Damages is $2,030 ($1,630 in medical bills plus $400 in lost earning capacity), which merits 2 points. The total of 73 points awarded to this case is what we enter on line 8 of the Case Rating Part of the work sheet.

---

*The Property Damages part of a claim is generally reimbursed in full, dollar-for-dollar. So, with regard to any property damages you might have incurred (for auto repairs or replacement, damaged or lost personal or other property, towing or storage, cost of substitute car rentals to work, etc.), providing you are not otherwise being compensated for it, simply add the total of that amount to your final demand figure, or add the "deductible" amount, if applicable.

ILLUSTRATIVE EXAMPLE D

Facts of the Case: You are 47 years of age and employed, and while driving home from work, you and another vehicle, a commerical tow truck, collided head-on in the middle of an intersection. The intersection was uncontrolled with neither a stop sign nor a traffic light for either driver. You are an average person with no particular blemish in your background or driving record; the driver of the other vehicle was found to be intoxicated by the police on the scene. You were bumped and bruised and shaken up by the experience; but, in addition, the accident aggravated an old shoulder problem you had and caused you about 4 or 5 days of pain and discomfort. You were away from your job for 1 week; your regular pay, is $1,250 per week. Your doctor's report gave you 1 week of total disability, and 3 weeks of partial disability. Your total medical bills (for x-rays, hospital emergency room treatment, drugs, etc.) were $1,530.

The total property damages you incurred in the accident (for repairs or replacement costs of your vehicle, value of damaged personal and other property, expense for substitute car rentals, vehicle towing and storage expenses, etc.) was $2,000.

Example D

THE MSM FORMULA WORKSHEET

PART I. POINTS ALLOCATION PART   POINTS ALLOCATED

1. Liability (1 to 50 Points) 38

2. Nature of Injury (1 to 10 Points) 7

3. Your Age (1 to 10 Points, see chart on p. 138) 5

4. Type of Person You Are (1 to 10 Points) 5

5. Type of Person (or Entity) the Other Party is (1 to 10 Points, in reverse) 9

6. Your Special Damages (1 to 10 Points, round off to nearest $1,000)* 3

7. TOTAL POINTS ALLOCATED 67

* Add any excess over $10,000 to Line 10 of Part II below.

PART II: CASE RATING PART

1. Enter Your Total Special Damages Amount: $2,780

2. Line 1, multiplied by 2 (i.e., doubled) .... =$ 5,560

3. Add: Allowance for Total Disability [@ $1,500 per week of Total Disability]** .... $ 1,500

4. Add Allowance for Partial Disability [@ $750 per week of Partial Disability]** .... $ 2,250

5. Total (Add Lines 2, 3, and 4) .... $ 9,310

6. Line 5 rounded Out to the nearest $1,000 .... $ 9,000

7. Line 6 Divided by 100 (This is called the "CASE RATE FIGURE") .... $ 90

8. Enter: Total # of "Points" Allocated to Case [Line 7 of Part I above] 67

9. Line 8 Multiplied by the dollar amount on Line 7 .... $ 6,030

10. Add: Excess over $10,000 in Special Damages, if any .... $ -0-

11. TOTAL (Add Up Lines 9 & 10) .... $ 6,030

> This figure (on line 11) is the **"Mean Settlement Value"** (MSV) of your case—i.e., the figure that best reflects the true value of your claim

---

**Note: Note that these allowances (allowance for Total or Partial Disability) are separate and apart from, and have nothing to do with, wages or the medical bills. For purposes of this formula, whether you're employed or unemployed, you're to simply assign yourself $1,500 per week for any periods of Total Disability you had, and $750 per week for any periods of Partial Disability. Estimate the type of disability (total or partial) from the contents of your doctor's report. If your doctor's report didn't make specific statements about your disability status, this may be one time when it may be necessary for you to go to him and request a proper update or correction of the report along the lines suggested elsewhere in the guidebook. [Refer to pp. 55-56 of book, among other sections]

12. Line 11 Divided by 4 (i.e., take ¼ or 25% of Line 11) .... $ 1,507.50

13. Add the Resultant Line 12 Amount to Line 11 .... $ 7,537.50
   This is the **"High Settlement Value"** (above the mean) of the case

14. Subtract the Resultant Line 12 Amount from Line 11 .... $ 4,522.50
   This is the **"Low Settlement Amount"** (below the mean) of the case

YOU NOW HAVE: The High Settlement Value (Line 13) $7,537.50
(Add the Total Property Damages, if any)* $2,000.00

The Mean Settlement Value (Line 11) $6,030.00
(Add the Total Property Damages, if any)* $2,000.00

The Low Settlement Value (Line 14) $4,522.50
(Add the Total Property Damages, if any)* $2,000.00

} THE SETTLEMENT ZONE OR AREA

> **NOTE:** Ordinarily, under normal circumstances involving no special circumstances in a case, the estimated "Mean Value" should generally suffice as a reasonable basis upon which and around which to formulate a settlement. However, the SETTLEMENT ZONE OR AREA is designed, additionally, to make allowance for situations involving given cases which may have extraordinary or special circumstances which a claimant may feel should give his case more value, or for which, on the other hand, the insurance adjuster (or even the claimant) may feel that lesser value on the claims could be acceptable. In effect, the entire range of the "Settlement Area," as opposed to just on particular figure, provides the broad "area" within which to negotiate — THE ZONE OF NEGOTIATION.

Explanation of the Process (Example D)

On allocation of points in this case, first, regarding liability, this is a typical situation of "moderate" degree of doubtful liability — a situation where the evidence is not quite clear-cut as to who exactly is liable and one in which there's almost always a strong likelihood of BOTH sides being just as negligent. (See Section I on pp. 102-3). Ordinarily, the pure situation of moderate doubtful liability would normally have merited a 50-50 split — that is 25 points on the liability factor. However, here there are a few "strikes" against the defendent from the liability standpoint (and other standpoints); he was intoxicated at the time of the accident, and he's a classic "target" defendent (commercial tow truck company). Hence, for these considerations, he loses more points on liability thereby raising your score to 38 (out of a possible 50) on liability. On injury, sure, the injuries sustained in the accident were not major; however, the fact of the aggravation of an old shoulder condition makes you deserving of a higher score of 7 on injury. Your age, at 47 gets an automatic 5 points from the age chart on p. 138. You are an average guy in terms of character and background, so you get a score of 5 out of a possible 10 on personality. The defendent party, on the other hand, gets, in reverse, a score of 9 points - being that he was intoxicated at the accident scene. From the incomes chart (p. 140), your total Special Damages of $2,780 ($1,530 in medical bills and $1,250 in wage loss) is assigned an automatic 3 points. The total of 67 points awarded to this case is what is entered on Line 8 of the worksheet's Case Rating Part.

*The Property Damages part of a claim is generally reimbursed in full, dollar-for-dollar. So, with regard to any property damages you might have incurred (for auto repairs or replacement, damaged or lost personal or other property, towing or storage, cost of substitute car rentals to work, etc.), providing you are not otherwise being compensated for it, simply add the total of that amount to your final demand figure, or add the "deductible" amount, if applicable.

CHAPTER 11
CONDUCTING YOUR OWN FINAL SETTLE- MENT NEGOTIATIONS: THE ANOSIKE 8-STEP STRATEGIC PROGRAM OF SETTLEMENT NEGOTIATIONS (ASPON)

This chapter brings to a head all that this whole manual is all about, the central issue of our whole exercise in the guidebook — GETTING THE MONEY INTO YOUR POCKET! IT PROVIDES YOU A PROGRAMMATIC SYS- TEM BY WHICH TO NEGOTIATE A SETTLEMENT WITH YOUR ADJUSTER AND BE ABLE TO WALK AWAY WITH A FAIR COMPENSATION WHEN IT'S ALL DONE.

For convenience and simplicity of comprehension, the chapter is divided into two main Sections. The first section (Section A), gives an analysis of the structure of the insurance company and how the Claims Department and Claims Adjusters, with whom you'll have to do the negotiations, generally work; it summarizes for you the basic skills and knowledge — the negotiating "tools" — you must first possess and master in order to undertake the task of claims negotiations. And Section B gives you an 8-step systematic, programmatic formula to successfully negotiate and secure a fair settlement — the author's exclusive *Anosike 8-Step Strategic Program of Negotiations or ASPON.*

SECTION A

With respect to automobile-related accidents, settlement terms are subject to negotiations in the following contexts:

A. In "Fault" Insurance States

1. For all personal injuries resulting from auto accidents in "fault" states.
2. For all personal injuries resulting from an auto accident caused by an uninsured motorist.

B. In "No-Fault" Insurance States

1. For some personal injuries resulting from an auto accident caused by an uninsured motorist.
2. For all such personal injuries resulting from an auto accident that are not compensated for under your own no-fault auto policy, where and when that is allowed under the state's no-fault law

C. How An Insurance Company Works: Its Internal Operations

Knowing a little about how an insurance company, particularly its claims apparatus, operates—what happens when you make a claim, who makes the major decisions to deny or pay a claim, etc.—is a very helpful preparation for under- standing the claims settlement process and the way settlement negotiations work in the insurance industry.

All insurance companies consist of at least two main departments—the underwriting department and the claims department. Larger insurance companies have other departments, such as marketing, finance departments, etc., as shown in Figure 11-1 below). The underwriting department essentially issues policies for which policyholders would pay premiums, while the claims department settles claims made by claimants on the insured persons. For our purposes in the manual, the UNDERWRITING and CLAIMS departments are the two most important departments of relevance, but of more immediate relevance for our discussions in this chapter is *the claims department.*

Fig 11-1 below shows the structure of a typical large insurance company.

FIGURE 11-1

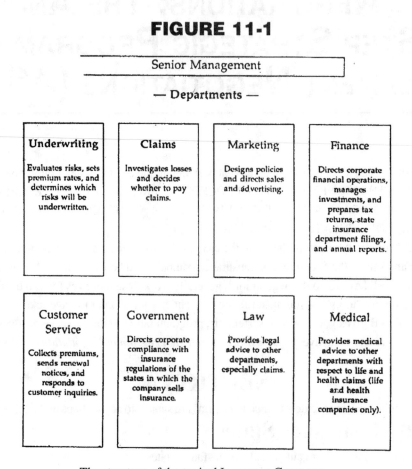

The structure of the typical Insurance Company

It is from THE CLAIMS DEPARTMENT of the insurance company that the payoff is made to you on the claim you file. Shown below, in Fig 11-2 is the structure of typical claims department, while Fig 11-3 (p. 157) shows the structure of a typical branch claims office.

The branch claims office is merely the local claims office to which your claim is referred after you report it to the insurance agent. It is the personnel in the branch office to which your claim is referred, that will handle and supervise your claim, and issue the check to settle your claim.

FIGURE 11-2

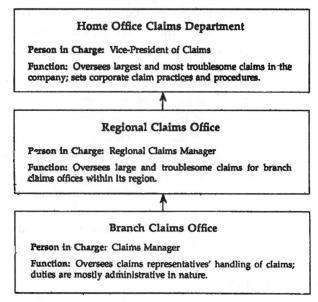

The structure of the typical claims department

FIGURE 11-3

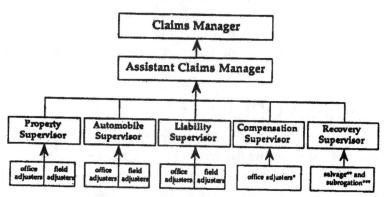

The structure of the typical branch claims office

D. The Branch Claims Office

The key personnel in the local branch office claims office, for your purposes as a claimant, are the following: the adjuster, the line supervisor, and the local claims manager.

1. THE ADJUSTER

The primary agent assigned to handle a claimant's claim, is the insurance ADJUSTER. Upon your filing a claim with an insurance company, the insurer will usually assign your claim to a **field adjuster**, and it is that adjuster who will usually contact you either personally or by phone or letter, and it is he or she who will perhaps come to your home and personally handle the details concerning your claims.

Your adjuster could be either a **"Staff Adjuster"** (salaried employee of the insurance company,) or an **"Independent Adjuster"** (self-employed, usually state-licensed adjuster hired by the insurance company to handle your claim on the company's behalf), or a **"Public Adjuster"** (a self-employed adjuster who may be hired for a fee by a claimant to work for the claimant, as opposed to the insurer company).

The role of the insurance adjuster, in particular, in the claims process is of direct and major relevance as a background material for the discussion of the primary topic of this chapter—the procedures of claims settlement negotiations and adjustments. One analyst put it quite directly this way: "The insurance adjuster is the porthole portfolio through which the insurance company views its claims. For this reason, he has a tremendous influence on the evaluation, settlement or denial of your claims."[1]

Another analyst is even more explicit in portraying the pervasive, if dominant role, of the adjuster:[2] "Besides the agent who sold you your policy, the adjuster is probably the only person you will ever meet from your insurance company. Unless your claim is very large or particularly complicated or troublesome, you will seldom have contact with anyone else in the claims department…[he's] the eyes, ears, and voices of the company…[he] make[s] the decision whether the company will pay or deny your claim. You will negotiate the settlement of your claim with an adjuster."

2. THE LINE SUPERVISOR

Overseeing the adjusters, are the line supervisors. Each line supervisor specializes in the claims of a particular "line," or type, of insurance — automobile collision claims, fire and theft claims, personal injury claims, liability claims, and so on. Such a line supervisor involved in your category of claim will, under normal circumstances, have the final word on whether the insurer will pay or deny your claim.

3. THE LOCAL CLAIMS MANAGER

The claims manager is in charge of the branch claims office. The line supervisors report to the claims manager or line assistant. In the handling of insurance claims, the key role is played by this official, in that he is generally an important executive to whom the line supervisors report directly on a daily basis and such line supervisors' work is subject to the claims manager's review and instructions. However, especially in many claims offices where thousands of claims are reported each month, however, the claim manager can only keep track of the large or troublesome claims and rarely involves himself with routine claims.

E. The Regional Claims Office

The regional claims office is the next step up the claims department hierarchy above the branch claims offices. The regional claims offices perform purely administrative functions (e.g., the overseeing of the branch offices' handling of large claims over a certain threshold amount and certain categories of high exposure claims, such as those involving death or permanent injuries) and usually do not have direct contact with claimants. As a claimant, the regional claims office will usually not be a concern of yours unless you get involved with litigation in your case. And, *if you cannot get satisfaction from your branch claims office, the place to go to is straight to the top, to the home office—not the regional office.*

F. The Home Office Claims Department

The home office claims department is located at the insurance company's corporate headquarters. The top claims executive in most insurance companies, called the **Vice President in Charge of Claims**, is located in the home office, and here, under the leadership of such a vice president, claims examiners, claims supervisors and senior claims executives would review claims submitted by the branch and regional claims offices. In most companies, the home office

---

[1]Baldyga, How to Settle Your Own Insurance Claims, p. 127
[2]Dumas, Claim Paid, A Consumers Guide Through the Insurance Claims Maze, p. 33.

claims department oversees only the very largest claims—those of $50,000 or more—and almost never has direct contact with claimants.

In addition to overseeing the largest and most sensitive claims, the home office establishes the company's overall policies for handling claims, as well as its overall claims philosophy.

G. Before You Negotiate A Claim with An Adjuster, Be Aware of Certain Clear Advantages Enjoyed By the Adjuster

Studies on the subject have established that the vast majority of "unrepresented" auto accident claimants — meaning claimants who file on their own without an attorney — are grossly "unsophisticated", that they are simply not knowledgeable in the claims settlement and negotiation procedures. And, even more relevant, that this frequently results in the "unrepresented" claimants receiving settlements that are less in amounts than claimants who are either represented by an attorney, or are unrepresented but "sophisticated"[3]

Admittedly, part of this apparent effect of legal representation is directly attributable to the fact of the lawyers' selectivity in picking the claimants they represent—the fact that the lawyer would typically select the "top of the cream" types of claimants, in the first place, meaning those having more serious injuries, bigger sized claims, and better legal merits to win in court.

But, for our purposes in this manual, what is even much more relevant and revealing is what the studies found as to the **REASONS behind this difference** between the awards received by the "unrepresented" claimants and those received by the "represented" ones. *What the studies show is that this difference is attributable, not to any presumed superior legal skills or knowledge the lawyer might have possessed or brought to the case, but largely to lack of NEGOTIATING SKILLS ON THE PART OF THE AVERAGE CLAIMANT! Many self-represented claimants, the studies found, are naive; they have only a vague knowledge concerning their rights to recover and what exactly they are entitled to; and they are unfamiliar with the basic rules and tactics of negotiation employed in the insurance claims industry.*

Professor H. Laurence Ross who conducted an extensive field study of the way claims professionals interact with claimants both in instances when they are represented by an attorney as well as in instances when they are not, attributes the discrepancy in the amounts received by the attorney-represented and self-represented claimants largely to the "deficiency of the claimant in negotiating skills." Ross found that when it comes to dealing with a claimant who is not represented by an attorney, the adjuster's negotiating approach and tactics are typically different—he either plays the negotiation "game" very badly, or replaces the normal mode of negotiations with a different "game" altogether.

It was found, for example, that whereas the adjuster almost never used this approach when the settlement negotiations were between "professionals" (i.e., between adjusters and claimants' lawyers), the adjuster dealing with a claimant who was unrepresented and was acting for himself, would typically make the claimant an offer on a "take-it-or-leave-it" basis; the adjuster would simply make a single offer to the claimant and rigidly stick to it. Or, as another example of the tactic uniquely used by the adjuster when dealing with an unrepresented claimant, the adjuster would simply demand of the claimant that he "document" his losses and damages as a basis for discussion and settlement, and would then hurry to add up the specific items listed by the claimant, after which he asks the claimant: "Is there anything else?" And if the claimant mentions nothing more, the adjuster would simply offer the claimant the claimant's designated total figure by immediately commencing to fill out a **"Draft and Release"** form which he will then invite the claimant to sign. *No mention, in other words, would be made to the claimant by the adjuster of the fact that the claimant may possibly be*

---

[3]See, Ross, pp. 70, 166-170, 193-8, and 209; Conard et. al., Automobile Accident Costs and Payments: Studies in the Economics of Injury Reparation (Univ. of Michigan Press, 1964), p. 226.

entitled to a good deal more than merely the claimant's medical expenses and wages— some big,additional entitlements, such as awards for pain and suffering, for example!

Ross sums it up this way, at once describing how the unrepresented is typically treated at the hands of the adjuster and why:[4]

> "The techniques [of negotiation employed by adjusters when dealing with unrepresented claimants] hardly qualify for the designation of negotiation. In deed, they may be thought of as replacing negotiation when dealing with a party who is unable to play the "game" [of negotiation]. The unrepresented claimant [is treated the way he is treated in negotiations because the adjuster perceives that he] has a less precise idea of the ultimate value of his possible recovery, and thus is less able to make appropriate demands....[because] he is ignorant of the accepted principles according to which his demands can be rationalized....[or] which, if any, threats may be effective [for him to use to get concessions]..."

HERE'S THE POINT. Let's keep our eye and mind on the central point of relevance for the underlying purposes of the present analysis. *The point to remember here is this: that, to the extent that the claimant who is represented by a lawyer (or, for that matter, represented by a public adjuster hired by the claimant to represent him) enjoys an apparent advantage over the self-represented claimant in settlement negotiations with the adjuster, that advantage comes about by virtue of (i.e., is primarily owing to) the better NEGOTIATING SKILLS AND KNOWLEDGE possessed by the lawyer, and not necessarily because of any superior legal knowledge the lawyer might have preumably possessed or employed at the negotiation tables!*

Ross put it this way:[5]

> "[the advantage of the represented claimant] is understandable, less in the light of the attorney's knowledge of the formal law than in the light of his negotiation power...knowledge of formal law [is not] the key to the attorney's advantage....Negotiation power, on the other hand, is present throughout the range of liability and injury combinations [in claims settlements]. The attorney, as compared with the unrepresented claimant, understands the rules of negotiation."

H. The Basic Tools You Must Have as a Self-Representing Negotiator

In sum, as a claimant, the KEY to your faring well in claims negotiations with the adjuster, or being able to come away from the negotiating session with a fair and reasonable settlement, is simply this: possessing the requisite basic knowledge and information! You've got to be reasonably informed and knowledgeable, not so much on any sophisticated doctrines of law governing accidents or claims settlement, as on the basic procedures and some essentials of claims settlements — the nature of your rights, a reasonable idea of the value of your possible recovery, the nature and extent of your bodily injuries and of your special as well as general damages, the basic rules and tactics involved in claims negotiations and the like.

Such knowledge is, in a word, the requisite and indispensable "tools" you'd need to have in order to undertake the central phase of this chapter next discussed below for the rest of the chapter—CLAIMS SETTLEMENT NEGOTIATIONS.

---

[4]Ross, Settled Out of Court, pp. 169-170.

[5]Ross, Settled Out of Court, p.195. Ross relates that, on the other hand, when unrepresented claimants who are, nevertheless, "sophisticated" and knowledgeable in claims procedures have confronted adjusters in negotiations, such claimants frequently come away from the encounters with decent settlements, notwithstanding their lack of representation by an attorney: "Frequently, the somewhat knowledgeable claimant will challenge an offer of special damages only [that is made to him by the adjuster]. He will refuse to sign the release tendered [to him by the adjuster], or he will ask,...'How about something for myself?' On occasion, the terms of art, 'pain and suffering', will occur. In a clear liability case, the adjuster will not resist an additional payment...the demand is usually accepted..."(Ross, Ibid. p. 169).

SECTION B

What follows below, outlined systematically in an orderly, step-by-step format, are the 8 basic steps of the "ASPON" formula to a successful   negotiation of your auto accident claim. *For maximum effectiveness, you __MUST__ follow and do these steps in EXACTLY the same sequential order in which they are listed below. Do not skip around or jump around.*

ASPON CAUTION: There are two things (among others) you must __NOT__ do. First, do not enter into the actual settlement negotiation until __AFTER__ all your special damage items are in, for only then could you have done some fair assessment concerning the value of your claim and thereby be in a position to discuss such a value with an adjuster. And secondly, but most importantly, whatever you do, __DO NOT__ (REPEAT, __DO NOT__) begin to discuss anything whatsoever with the adjuster at this time (or at any time earlier), until it's the proper time to do so much later on. Answer no questions. Say nothing. Just tell him 'thank you' and that you'll get back to him shortly. [See chapter 2, Section 5 (pp. 21-22), and chapter 7, Section J (pp. 105-6)]

The Anosike 8-Step Strategic Program Of Negotiations, ASPON. The Principles

STEP ❶: HAVE THE FACTS OF YOUR CASE, AND YOURSELF AS WELL, READY

This is an absolutely vital and indispensable necessity; negotiation is all about knowledge and information, how much of it each side possesses and can trade back and forth. If you lack knowledge about your case, you can't, in effect, "negotiate" — there will be nothing for you to negotiate with or on or about! *Use of the ASPON principles to negotiate one's claim is fundamentally predicated on the premise that the claimant shall have thoroughly done his background homework.*

So, the __FIRST__ thing you had better done—you __MUST__ do—even before you ever get into any serious discussions (negotiations) concerning the settlement of your claim is: HAVE THE NECESSARY FACTS AND INFORMATION READY, AVAILABLE, ORGANIZED, AND RIGHT AT YOUR FINGER TIPS! Assemble your facts and information and the documentations to back them up; and arrange and put them together in an organized, orderly format for your easy reference at any time during the negotiation process.

In deed, as has been amply emphasized in various sections of this manual (see for example, pp. 18 & 25) , *the point cannot be emphasized enough that the ultimate key to a successful or favorable claims settlement is adequacy of pertinent information and documentations.* As one insurance claims expert put it, "[in insurance claims adjusting work] all that supervisors and claims examiners look for is whether the claim is 'documented.' That means that the more paper in the file,...the more likely that the supervisor or claims examiner [will approve the claim]."[6]

So, Here Are the Questions You Must First Answer In The Affirmative

- Have you thoroughly prepared yourself __both__ on "the facts" as well as on "the law" of your case—on the law and concept of negligence, fault, and liability, for example; on the nature and extent of your bodily injuries; details about your accident, about your special damages, and about your actual physical pain and suffering, etc.? [Read the following sections of the manual, for example: Chapters 2,3, 4, 6 & 7.]

---

[6]Dumas, Claim Paid, p. 9

- Have you thoroughly assembled all the necessary proofs, documentations, and supporting evidence for your case—police and accident reports, signed or recorded statements of eye witnesses, newspaper clippings, doctors' and hospital reports (even for the ones paid or to be paid by Blue Cross or other insurance), prescription drug bills, car repair estimates or bills, employer's statement of time and wages lost from job, doctors' and medical bills, receipts and/other proofs of payments or expenditures made, and the like, to the extent available? [Refer to the following sections of the manual: Chapters 3, 4 & 5]

- Have you made a thorough evaluation of the reasonable settlement value of your claim? [Refer to chapters 9 & 10, pp. 126-133 & 134-154].

- Have you educated yourself as to whether you have a 'Fault' or 'No-Fault' insurance coverage? And have you determined which insurance policyholder(s) and company (or companies) are appropriate for you to file your claims against [See chapter 8, Section F thereof at pp. 112-125]

IN SHORT, YOU HAVE TO HAVE READ, STUDIED AND MASTERED VIRTUALLY THIS WHOLE MANUAL, CERTAINLY THE VITAL PARTS OF IT, __IN ADVANCE__ OF GOING INTO ANY NEGOTIATIONS WITH YOUR INSURANCE CLAIMS PEOPLE!

Step ②: ENTERING THE ACTUAL NEGOTIATIONS: A PRELIMINARY STAGE

NOTE: Be sure not to enter into the actual settlement negotiations until AFTER all of your medical and special damages items are in, for only then could you have done some fair assessment concerning the value of your claim and thereby be in a position to discuss such a value with your adjuster.

A. Making the Initial Contact with the Insurance Company

There is no single way or pattern in this. Settlement negotiations may be handled by telephone or by letter, or by face-to-face meeting and discussion. Usually, however, because of the insurance adjuster's heavy caseload and the dedication of the insurance company to controlling costs, the negotiations are often done by telephone. In deed, in modern times, it is said that "the majority of claims are handled on the telephone by office adjusters"[7]—a process euphemistically called **"telephone adjusting."**

Whatever the communication method used, however, settlement negotiations would generally involve a round of personal contacts (by phone, letter and/or in person) between yourself and the insurance adjuster. These contacts, which may possibly be a long drawn out affair, is often felt necessary and helpful by both sides as it provides a useful "feeling out" time to both sides and thereby helps them understand and deal with each other better.

B. Assemble Your Facts and Documentations

So, now you are finally ready to submit the claim? What you do are these: make a photocopy of each of the supporting documents and proofs you shall have accumulated in support of your claim and put away the originals for now. Then, put together the **photocopies** of only those documents you'd need to initially establish your claim to the insurance company, without necessarily going into too much details or every little bit of detail yet—police and accident reports, statements of eye witnesses, doctors' and hospital reports giving your bodily injuries and medical condition, employer's statement (or other proof) of time and wages lost from job, car repair estimates or bills (or a tabulation thereof), doctors' and medical bills (or a tabulation thereof), other bills and expenditures, or a tabulation thereof, etc.

---

[7]Dumas, Claim Paid, p. 9.

Now, organize these papers in order—primarily, the papers dealing with each aspect of the case (e.g. the accident and its occurrence, the hospital & medical treatments, the lost wages, the car damage or repairs, the pain and suffering, and the like) should be put in a separate set and be properly labelled, and all the papers are then packaged into a complete set.

C. Draft a Good Claims Demand Letter

Next, you are to draft, and preferably have it type written, a CLAIMS DEMAND LETTER wherein you summarize your case as to how the accident occurred, who you contend is at fault for it and why, what your injuries and other damages are, and above all, your case for being entitled to compensation.

It should be strongly emphasized that this letter is an instrument of the utmost importance in the entire negotiating process. Often, such a letter will be the actual instrument around which the negotiating discussions are conducted. How well the letter is constructed — its contents, what it says and how it says it, what facts and information it lays out, and how it does it, etc.—tells the insurance company a great deal about how well prepared and informed you are, and how organized and coordinated you have formulated your case or arguments concerning your claims.[8] Hence, IT IS HIGHLY IMPORTANT THAT YOU TAKE THE NECESSARY TIME AND TROUBLE AND MAKE SURE THAT YOU DRAFT A GOOD LETTER.

Here are some important ASPON pointers on writing a good claims demand letter:

•Provide, in a brief summary fashion, the "FACTS" of the accident: how it happened and who and who were involved; what injuries and medical examinations and treatments you received (and how much they cost,) including the pain and disability you suffered, the length and difficulty of your recovery, and any long-term or permanent effects of your injuries on your daily life. [Refer to and consult your medical records, doctors' reports, and daily "pain diary," and chapter 6 and the Appendices in the manual for medical terms, among other information sources.]

•Sum up why, from your own vantage point, the other party (or parties) was "negligent" and at fault for the accident and therefore should bear legal responsibility or "liability" for it [what and what the other party did wrong, what the police report showed about the carelessness of the other parties, photographs, eye witness accounts, etc.]

•Sum up why you qualify to make a third party claim under no-fault, if that's applicable to you.

•Include a summary of each and every category of expenses, costs and losses you suffered (use the same figures from the official billing record); the amount of time missed from work and income losses thereof; medical expenses from all medical providers; cost of car damages sustained and any other damages suffered. [Get these figures directly from your evaluation calculations of the settlement worth of your claim—Chapters 9 and 10 and the Checklist in chapter 5 (pp. 63-68)].

•On the important issue of "liability," merely raise the issue in your letter just so that the insurance company will know that you are aware of that matter, but categorically deny that you were at all in any way negligent; do not admit to any fault, even if partly, on you part, even if you believe otherwise; dwell only on the facts and why you were not at fault.

•In describing events of the accident in the letter, don't be shy about saying what actually happened and how important these things are to you. You can, for example, use the power of carefully chosen "strong words" to a good effect in getting across to the adjuster the personal or emotional side of the accident and

---

[8]One informed report put it this way "The demand letter is the centerpiece of the negotiation process...[it] not only sets out your theory of the case and the range of the demand, but it can also demonstrate to the insurance company your understanding, organization, and preparation of your claim. In other words, a good demand letter—clear, organized, including all useful information—sets the tone for a good settlement." Joseph L. Mathews, "How to Win Your Personal Injury Claim," (Nolo Press), pp. 6/12-6/13.

injury you sustained where you might not have been able to do that by use of ordinary day words. But don't over-exaggerate or be too "colorful" in your claims. Be honest and to the point; be clear and organized, and include the essential information.

- In a word, all that your Demand Letter is about, is to briefly sum up your strongest arguments to the effect that the accident in question was mostly the other party's fault and that you suffered some distress or permanent effects, and incurred loss of income, medical expenses, etc. as a result of that for which you deserve and demand due compensation.

- **Important:** Finally, <u>DO NOT</u> include in this letter, the dollar figure you are demanding as your compensation or settlement value for your claim. Invite the insurance adjuster to, and leave it to him to, make you the first offer [see p. 177 for the reasons for this]

Joseph L. Matthews, a lawyer and author of a personal injury claims manual provides some helpful insights into what the structure and contents of good demand letter should look like, which bears some repeating here:

"A demand letter begins by describing how the accident happened and why the insurance company's insured was at fault: *'I was driving north in the right-hand lane along 4th Avenue at about three o'clock in the afternoon. When I was more than halfway through the intersection with Broadway, your insured entered the intersection in the center eastbound lane on Broadway and slammed into the passenger side of my car.'*

Include all points that might indicate that the insured was at fault for the accident. Put your strongest argument first:
'I clearly had the right of way at the intersection. The insured had a stop sign on Broadway and I had no stop sign on 4th Avenue.'

And add other facts that might lead to an even stronger case against the insured:
'Furthermore, since the insured struck my car on the rear side panel, it is obvious that I was already well into the intersection when he entered. Also, the extent of the damage to my car indicated that your insured was moving at a substantial rate of speed, which would mean that he never stopped at the stop sign.'

If you have any outside support for your theory, make sure to include it here. In a vehicle accident case, repeat any helpful remark in a police report. In a premises liability case, quote a building code section which has been violated. Information received from any source about similar accidents should be included. Although you do not have to give the identities of your sources at this stage. If you have information that the other driver has a bad driving record, mention it here.

If you have any witnesses who support your version of the accident, let the insurance company know how many of them back up your story. If you have a good written statement from a witness, quote the best part of the statement. You do not have to reveal the identity of a witness in the demand letter; instead, write that you will make the identity of the witnesses known to the insurance company "at the appropriate time." Be sure to let the insurance company know that you are aware of other information, or intangibles, that could help you should the case ever get to court. For example, if there was any evidence that another driver's breath smelled of alcohol, or there was an empty beer bottle in the car, even if he or she was not cited for drunk driving, mention it in your demand letter.
'From the beer cans on the floor of your insured's automobile, observed by my passenger as well as by me, it also appears that your insured may have been drinking and driving.'

Another intangible may be how gruesome your damaged car looked. If it was badly smashed, describe that. And include a photo if you have one, to highlight how serious the collision was. If the car was spun all the way around, mention it. If it had to be towed away, mention that. Likewise, if you have a photo of a hole you tripped in or a dangerous-looking object that injured you, include the photo and refer to how obviously dangerous it is just from looking at the picture...*"*

[See pp. 184-5 & 186-8 for 2 sample CLAIMS DEMAND LETTERS illustrating the form a typical claims letter should take, tailored of course, to the facts of one's particular accident, injuries, and other relevant circumstances.]

D. Send the Demand Letter, Along With The Initial Documentations, to the Insurance Company

Now, you are to mail (or otherwise submit) one set of the documentations you've put together in STEP 2, Section B above, to the claims office of the appropriate insurance company. SEND ONLY THE PHOTOCOPIES (not the originals) of the documentations. Attach to this, though, the original of the Demand Letter, but retain a copy of the letter for your files.

Which insurance company or companies do you send your claims demand papers to? As a person injured in an auto accident and filing a claim, very often the only insurance company you'll ever need to send your claims paper to is the other driver's insurance company. Or, if you have a no-fault insurance policy, you'll primarily file your claim with (send your papers to) your own insurance company, but may, in many instances, also be able to file a claim against the other driver's insurance company where the injury and medical "threshold" shall have been surpassed under your state's legal provisions. [Refer to pp. 112, 114 and 20-21, for more specifics on where to file your claims.]

In any event, typically even by the time you're ready to formally file your claim or draft your demand letter, you will probably have received a notice from the appropriate insurance company involved, especially if you had, as advised in Section 4 of chapter 2 [see pp. 20-21], taken the pains to send notification letters to all potentially connected parties immediately upon the occurrence of the accident. If more than one company is involved in a given situation, they shall have indicated to you which one among them is to provide the "primary" settlement for the accident and which one will be responsible for a **"secondary"** or **"excess"** compensation, if that should become necessary (Section G of Chapter 8). The company you need to send your demand letter to is only the one that serves as the **primary** company. However, if by chance you have not received from the companies a notice of which of them is to provide the primary coverage by the time you're ready to file your claims, here's what you do: prepare and send demand letters to the insurance company of each of the parties you hold liable for the accident (with the contents of each letter tailored, of course, to the facts of the given insured party), and you should thereafter expect to get a response from the companies indicating which one assumes the primary responsibility.

Now, assuming you've mailed your demand letter (and the accompanying documentations thereof) to the required insurance company, typically an adjuster of the company will usually try to contact you within a short period thereafter upon receipt of your package. However, if after mailing your package to the insurance carrier you have not heard from an adjuster in 20 days or so, contact the adjuster or insurance company by phone and arrange for an immediate face-to-face meeting with him for direct discussion of your claim, unless you have a different preference for your own personal reasons.

> ASPON CAUTION: WHATEVER YOU DO, WHENEVER YOU HEAR FROM OR TALK TO THE INSURANCE PEOPLE, DO NOT YET DISCUSS ANYTHING WHATSOEVER WITH THEM AT THIS POINT! Answer no questions. (Begin to talk, to some extent, only in STEP 3 and then STEP 4, below.) AND, FURTHERMORE, DO NOT REVEAL (OR EVEN ADMIT) TO THE ADJUSTER, CERTAINLY NOT YET, THE SOURCE OF YOUR INFORMATION OR KNOWLEDGE, OR ABOUT THE SOURCE OF THE ASPON PRINCIPLES OF CLAIMS NEGOTIATIONS OR EVALUATION YOU ARE USING. (As a rule, the adjuster will usually never tell you the source of his own knowledge and information, and that's simply because that gives him some tactical edge over you!)

Step ❸: BE READY & GET IN THE MOOD TO PLAY THE NEGOTIATION 'POWER GAME'

A. Claims Negotiation is a "Power Game." Here's How & Why

Claims adjusters, attorneys, and experts vastly experienced in the negotiation practices of insurance companies invariably view and approach the process of insurance claims negotiations as a "power game."[9] And, even a few others who do not quite characterize the process in those exact terms, have tended to describe it, nevertheless, in terms conveying the same image that the process is a power game.[10] What is important to note, is that in this negotiation "game," the central bone of contention—the central issue being fought over—is "control": which of the two sides would control the other, or, to put it another way, which side would set and dictate the terms of settlement—would it be the insurance side, or the claimant's side!?

One former claims adjuster with many years of practical negotiating experience with a major insurance company was brutally frank about it:[11]

> "Negotiating an accident claim is not a situation where one side pays an honest debt to the other. Instead, it's a power game in which both sides fight for control. The insurance adjuster begins with all the advantages. He is a skilled negotiator who knows the law; he has prior information on just how much his company will pay; he chooses the time and place of each negotiation; and he controls each session. The only way a claimant can counter all of this is [for the claimant] to gain control [himself]"

THE MESSAGE: TO STAND A CHANCE IN YOUR NEGOTIATIONS WITH THE INSURANCE COMPANY REPRESENTATIVE, YOU'VE GOT TO BE THE ONE THAT GETS TO BE "IN CONTROL" OF THE NEGOTIATIONS!

B. The ASPON Ways of Being 'IN CONTROL' of the Negotiations At The Initial Stages

Here are some of the major ASPON ways to initially take (and retain) control in the negotiations process with the adjuster:

1. You Set the Negotiation Agenda

When you decide it's time to begin the settlement discussion, <u>YOU</u>, the claimant, should be the one who calls the adjuster and schedules the first appointment. Tell the adjuster something like: "I expect a few more doctor visits, but I'm willing to begin discussions" (As much as it's realistically possible, always avoid admitting or creating the impression that you're fully recovered!)

2. You Set the Date and Time for the Meetings

If any meetings are to be had, you should be the one who **sets** the date and time. But do this: schedule them during the normal working hours of the normal work days, even if weekends and evenings would be more convenient for you or the adjuster. (If questioned by the adjuster as to your rationale for this, simply say to him that you just want all dealings with him to be "official" and "business like," and that there are certain "consultants" you may have to phone or call upon during business hours for some guidance during the negotiations. As you will see from Paragraph # 6 below, there are certain phone calls you just may or may not make during the negotiations!)

---

*[9]Saadi, <u>Claim if Yourself</u>, p. 17; Ross, <u>Settled Out of Court</u>, pp. 169-170.

[10]Compare these two statements by the same writer, an insurance claims manager: "The amount of settlement usually depends as much on the claimant's expectations as on the adjuster's expertise. Unfortunately, it is the claimant who is difficult to deal with and has an exaggerated conception of the value of his claim who commands a larger settlement than the cooperative individual who will accept almost any offer." Foutty, The Evaluation & Settlement of Personal Injury Claims," Insurance Law Jr. (Jan. 1964), p. 10.
"When negotiating a personal injury settlement with a claimant's attorney, a different approach should be taken than in discussing settlement directly with the claimant...the adjuster should realize that he is now dealing with someone who probably has a general idea as to the value of the claim, and further, that an attorney seldom realizes a profit in handling a claim settled for less than $1,000 [read $10,000 in 1992!] As this is the case, an offer of payment [which seems small or unreasonable]...[may] often be a bar to further negotiations." [Foutty, 1 bid, p. 14.]

[11]Saadi, <u>Claim It Yourself</u>, p. 77.

3. Take Some Witnesses With You

Take an adult friend or relative with you to the negotiation sessions to serve as an observer and/or for moral support. (Choose someone who can attend each meeting). Don't ask the adjuster's permission for this or inform him of the plan in advance of the meeting. Just introduce the person(s) as a friend or relative who you simply want to sit in on your discussions but will not participate in the discussions. (**ASPON Pointer:** Having this witness will keep the adjuster guessing and on the edge and may come in handy for you later if the adjuster shall have lied to you on any aspect of the terms of the settlement or use high handed or unethical tactics!)

4. Tape Record the Discussion and/or Take Copious Notes

You should bring either a tape recorder or a pen and notebook with you to the negotiations, preferably a tape recorder. Insist from the outset on recording the discussions (preferably on a tape recorder but otherwise on a notebook) and openly do so to the knowledge of the adjuster. Let the adjuster know that you plan to check out everything he tells you.

5. As Negotiations Begin, Demand FULL Payment For FULL Wage And Other Losses

Most negotiating sessions usually begin with the adjuster and the claimant comparing the amounts and figures listed for the bills, costs and expenses from the accident—the (special) damages on wage loss, the medical expenses, etc. Typically, the adjuster will probably pull out the CLAIMS DEMAND LETTER you had sent him (p. 165) and begin to read out to you the figures from that.

For you, HERE'S THE ASPON POINT: Don't agree or accept otherwise from the adjuster; demand to be given **FULL** compensation for the totality of each and **every** category or type of losses and expenses you incurred—the full gross wage loss amount (permit no deductions to be taken out of it, for, say, sick leave benefits, even if you have been paid your wages by your employer or another insurance company);[12] full amount of your transportation cost to and from the treatment clinics or hospitals, or for hiring a baby-sitter or a housekeeper, or renting a substitute car, etc. etc. [Chapters 3, 4, & 5].

> **ASPON POINTER:** The adjuster may come up with a psychological ploy; he may accuse you of being "greedy" or of trying to "profit" from the accident. Your response to him? Resist giving in to any disguised attempts to blackmail or intimidate you; respond with something like: "Yes. Call it what you wish. But I plan to get every penny and cent that is legally owed me and nothing more, since no amount of money could ever really compensate for the pain and suffering I've been caused by this accident. I've already been victimized by a negligent driver and I don't intend to be victimized a second round by his insurance company!"

6. Demand to have the Adjuster's Legal Authority & Threaten to Call the Insurance Commissioner

If your adjuster still insists on taking out from your gross wage loss amount certain kinds of payments you might have received from other sources, or insists on disallowing you certain kinds of wage-related out-of-pocket expenditures you might have made (or will make), then here's what you do. Demand of the adjuster to cite you his "legal authority" for this stance. Ask him to cite you chapter and verse (or produce for you to see) specific court decisions, or legal precedents or statuatory texts in your state which permit him to so to convince you that he truly has legal justification for doing this and is not really trying to cheat you out of your legitimate entitlement. And, secondly, also tell the adjuster that (if he persists) you're going to call your state insurance commissioner's office (or his local office in your area) to verify the standard practice and the legality of his proposed deductions from your gross wage amount to settle the matter of its permissibility for both sides. At this point, ask that the negotiation session be temporarily stopped so that you can

---

[12]Under the laws of many states, time lost from your job are compensable as damages, even if you have had no actual loss of wages, as, for example, when your salary is in part or in whole paid by your own insurance, or by taking sick leave, or some other such employee wage plan. In such states, such payments received by an employee are said to come from a "collateral source," which therefore can still be claimed by you as damages even though you are paid for them otherwise. Unfortunately, though, the practice is not universally applied in all 50 states, in general.

make this call. (See Appendix A, pp. 193-6 for the addresses and phone numbers of each state's insurance commissioner's office in the state capital. Similar information for the local branch office in your location, especially for those in the the large cities, can be obtained by calling the local telephone directory or information operators.)

You will not, however, usually have to actually make that call! Why? Because no adjuster would want a personal complaint lodged against him with the state officials or during a negotiation. He'll probably agree to pay the FULL gross wage loss amount, or to otherwise compromise with you.

> ***BUT HERE'S EVEN THE MUCH LARGER ASPON SIGNIFICANCE OF THIS:*** BY HOLDING YOUR OWN GROUND AND NOT READILY YIELDING ON THIS LITTLE "SKIRMISH" SO EARLY IN THE GAME, YOU SHALL HAVE ACTUALLY "WON" A VERY IMPORTANT TACTICAL VICTORY, AS YOU SHALL HAVE SET A PRECEDENT AND THE TONE THAT WILL SURELY INFLUENCE THE REMAINDER OF THE NEGOTIATIONS! THE BIG MESSAGE THAT SHALL HAVE COME LOUD AND CLEAR TO YOUR ADJUSTER IS: THIS CLAIMANT IS NO "PUSHOVER"; HE (SHE) KNOWS EXACTLY HIS RIGHTS AND ENTITLEMENTS AND HE (SHE) IS NOT AT ALL SHY TO FIGHT FOR THEM!!

7. Demand FULL Inclusion Of ALL Your Medical Bills

BE FOREWARNED. Be alerted to the fact that, typically, adjusters would often disallow (or at least try to disallow) a substantial part of the claimant's total medical expenses that supposedly do not quite qualify as "medical" in character.

How does the adjuster do this? Basically, the adjuster would divide your medical costs into two arbitrary parts — **"diagnostic"** and **"treatment."** In the "diagnostic" category, will be included items such as these: ambulance and emergency room costs, costs of X-rays, and other diagnostic procedures, and visits to specialists. And the rest, principally costs of the hospital and regular office visits to doctors, physical therapy and medication, will be termed "treatment." The items that are categorized as "diagnostic" expenses are the part the adjuster would want to disallow as not being really "medical" types of activities, proper!

The adjuster would want to be able to make this differentiation basically for two reasons. First, because with this differentiation between what is "diagnostic" and what is supposedly the true medical "treatment," the basic worth of your claim shall have been drastically reduced, as the size of your "special damages" shall have been, in the first instance, curtailed. That is, he would have in effect, dismissed as inapplicable one whole half of the total medical expenses, the diagnostic aspect, which could at times constitute as much as 50 percent or more of an accident victim's total medical bills. And, secondly, with this differentiation recognizing only the "treatment" expenses (if it were to be allowed to be made), he can then go ahead to base his calculation of your "general damages" (i.e., the 'pain and suffering' part of your award) on the "treatment" amount only. The adjuster will simply argue that the "treatment" portion of your medical bills is the part that is "directly related" to the severity of your injury, and, hence, is the part that truly reflects or measures your "pain and suffering", or the General Damages portion of your claims.

The point here is that, as a claimant involved in claims negotiations, you should not automatically let the adjuster arbitrarily divide your medical expenses into some arbitrary categories like "diagnostic" and "treatment" without at least a strong challenge and resistance on your part, since such a move by an adjuster will directly reduce the worth of your claim, often drastically.

HERE IS WHAT SHOULD BE YOUR ASPON TACTICS. Demand FULL inclusion of ALL medical bills, as well as all medically related bills, in the calculation of the total medical expenses for your injuries. Ask the adjuster: Does he accept all the medical bills as authentic, genuine and arising from the accident, in the first place? And if he says he does, then your position should be to demand, over and over and over again, to know why — on what rational, logical, reasonable, or even legal basis — should he then divide these same bills into two different categories?

ASPON POINTS; HOW TO COUNTER THE ADJUSTER:
- "Mr. Adjuster, if the so-called 'diagnostic' expenses are unimportant or less important, or of a really different category than 'treatment,' then why was it that your company (meaning the insurance company) went ahead and paid {or will pay} the providers of these services the full amount of each of such bills charged?"
- "The only reason I ever incurred the so-called "diagnostic" bills, in the first place, is because the accident occurred — only because YOUR driver, the driver insured by YOU, injured me, Mr. Adjuster. If the accident hadn't occurred, in the first place, would I have sustained the injuries, and would I have had these "diagnostic" medical expenses, in the first place?"
- "It's absurd and illogical to separate medical expenses into two arbitrary categories and designate one aspect as "diagnostic," and the other "treatment," since each aspect works hand-in-hand with the other in medical practice. One cannot get treated (or at least properly treated) without being diagnosed, nor can one get diagnosed without being treated!"
- "Diagnostic bills are just as much a pertinent and objective standard of measuring how badly one is hurt, and are just as important as the actual treatment procedure. If it were not so, why is it that people who are involved in clearly minor auto accidents rarely generally get carted off to the hospitals or sent to specialists, Mr. Adjuster?"
- "By what specific legal authority or judicial precedents have you got the right to do this, Mr. Adjuster? What's your legal authority or medical expertise to distinguish between the medical items covering my injuries and to arbitrarily pick and choose which ones you should compensate?" (Any specific laws or any specific court decisions in this state to back this up? Then cite them, show them to me.)
- "I'm the party that's injured here; you're only the insurance adjuster. Don't I, shouldn't I, even, have a say, some say, at least, in the matter?"
- By what *objective* criteria do you decide which items to pick and choose to throw into the 'diagnostic' category? I mean, why and how, for example, does treatment received in an ambulance or the emergency room or from a specialist qualify, but not the treatment of exact nature received in a regular doctor's office or a hospital?"

STEP ❹: BE PREPARED AND READY TO CALL THE ADJUSTER'S BLUFF ON HOW REALLY SERIOUS YOUR INJURIES ARE

A. A Critical Issue: Are Your Injuries "Routine" or "Serious"?

As a rule, the principal issue in the majority of settlement discussions or negotiations, often centers on whether your case ought to be considered a "routine" or a "serious" one. This will usually arise by way of discussion of your injuries. The adjuster's basic tactic is typically to try to convince you that your injuries really are minor and does not warrant the disability period you had or are claiming. *For the adjuster, this matter is one of tremendous tactical as well as substantive importance since proving that (or, actually, convincing you that) you were not seriously hurt is his best weapon for decreasing the GENERAL DAMAGES portion of your claim, that is, the "pain and suffering" part.*

How this issue is resolved could be of great, indeed crucial, importance to both sides in terms of determining which side ultimately gets the "better" settlement — that is, whether it's going to be you, the claimant, on the one hand, or the insurance company, on the other hand. One keen analyst summed up the centrality of this question this way:

> "The importance of this distinction [as to whether a case is to be branded a "routine" case, or a "serious" one] is that cases defined as routine are acknowledged by both sides to warrant a relatively small settlement... Having obtained the concession that a case was routine, an adjuster would then argue [that a given multiplier of the medical bills and other 'specials' should be a fair settlement award in the given case]. On the other hand, a case defined as serious would be further discussed in terms of previous settlements or of jury awards in similar cases, as well as specific injuries and impairments,..."[13]

B. Adjuster's Typical Tactics For Downgrading Your Injuries

Basically, the adjuster's tactic will be to overwhelm you with his apparent "superior knowledge" of medicine, medical jargon, and physical trauma. Presumably, he shall have been generally familiar with basic medical terminology and some elementary ability to interpret medical reports and to relate them to alleged or suspected disability; he shall have presumably been familiar with hospitalization and disability, and the types of treatment necessitated by various injuries; and he shall have probably had at his disposal a chart depicting the length of hospitalization and degree of disability normally caused by various types of injuries. And, with apparent intent to capitalize on his presumed "superior knowledge" about your medical condition to gain advantage over you, the adjuster will primarily attempt to sway you to the viewpoint that your injuries are of the "routine" type rather than of "serious" type, or that the degree of 'pain and suffering' you had is actually less than what you claim. The adjuster will attempt to do this in a variety of ways, employing varying tactics.

For example, using your doctor's medical report, the adjuster may attempt to show (or merely contend) that your extended disability is not compatible with the injury involved [he may , for example, cite "independent information" he supposedly gathered from informants such as your neighbors and business associates in regard to your home or social or business activities since the accident; or cite reports of supposedly independent medical examination he supposedly obtained from a "reputable" physician, or even cite the showings of photographs or movies depicting you engaging in physical activities that are incompatible with your injury.]

Or alternatively, the adjuster would just compare the disability your doctor expressly granted you in your medical report with the actual time off you took from work. And if the time off you actually took happens to be more than the disability time specifically allowed in the doctor's report, the adjuster's reaction would be both to downgrade the seriousness of your injuries and to use that piece of discrepancy also to argue that he owes you lost time and wages only for the initial disability period specifically designated in your medical report. [It's common for doctors to initially give the claimant two weeks off for disability but to then forget to enter in the records and in writing an extension of the original time, even though the patient (claimant) has not recovered — a mere clerical error or omission that could end up costing you much money!]

With the "mission" of downgrading your disability accomplished and out of the way, the adjuster now will describe your injuries in seemingly impressive, fancy medical language and then compare and contrast them to more extreme, often extraordinary and ominous sounding types of medical problems or conditions as a way of "proving" that what you

---

[13]Ross, <u>Settled Out Of Court</u>, p.154.

had is a relatively less serious or less real physical damage. He will read out the statements and medical opinions and analysis that might have been contained in your doctor's report and attempt to "wring the water out of them" — meaning, to create an impression that if the report were really properly read or interpreted, they really mean that you were just a little sore and not really seriously damaged.

For example, if you had a so-called whiplash injury, the adjuster would compare this to fractures or nerve damage and tell you that this is the most insignificant type of injury an accident victim can have. And, if you happen to be younger than 60 years of age, the adjuster would further claim that a person of your age should recover rapidly and without any painful "residuals" (after effects)![14]

Here's an excerpt of a true, actual discussion between an adjuster and a claimant's lawyers, centering on the degree of seriousness that a claimant's injuries ought to be accorded:[15]

Adjuster: We are looking at a hell of a lot of damages here for what may be bruised hip as opposed, say, to a broken hip...

Lawyer: She of course did not have a broken bone, but yet did complain quite bitterly, and she did everything short of surgery — that she would not go through... Although you seem to feel that this $1,000 in specials is a bit too high for what you are calling a bruise, as far as I am concerned, my knowledge of this woman which is extensive — I've known her for many, many, many years, goes way, way, way back — from my own personal knowledge, this woman is not a complainer — just exactly the contrary... As a comparison I've got an accident case where there is a broken hip and a rather severely broken hip in three or four places, if I remember rightly. That woman has healed up completely and she had no residuals[after effects], nothing, with the breaks. And here we have one where there are no breaks and yet she still has residuals and I believe her sincerely when she says, "It hurts; it bothers me." I don't call it a mere bruise...

Adjuster: I think about the only thing we have is a demonstration of tenderness and pain upon palpitation which seems to be compatible with the type of injury she has described.

C. ASPON Response To Adjuster's Tactics: Temporarily Cut Off Negotiations

The relevant question for you is: How do you counter the above described tactics of the adjuster and his efforts to downgrade and downvalue your injuries? Here are your ASPON response. First, right from the onset as soon as the adjuster begins to discuss your doctor's report (or any medical report at all about you), insist on his giving you a copy of the report he's reading from or referring to, if you don't already have one. Tell the adjuster to allow you some time to study it. Take your time and personally read and check it carefully for accuracy. (Contrary to common belief, doctors are human who can make mistakes just as well! For an accident victim who suffers a broken thumb and sprained fingers, for example, the doctor could mistakenly list only sprains in his medical report). It's possible that you'll come across some inaccuracies or omissions upon your examination of the report — say, in the doctor's diagnosis or prognosis, or in the period of time allowed you for disability, etc., as the case may be. If so, the thing to do is simple. Don't waste your

[14]Saadi, a former adjuster, relates this tactic as one that she herself specifically and regularly used with claimants she dealt with during her claims adjusting days. (See Saadi, Claim It Yourself, p.81.)

[15]As cited in Ross, Settled Out Of Court, pp. 153-4.

time arguing with the adjuster. Simply phone (or visit) your doctor's office and ask for a written correction or verification, as is necessary.

In any event, even if your adjuster's criticisms of your doctor's report or of the nature of your injuries are mild, but especially when they seem significant or to have some substance, *a better tactic — the ASPON tactic — would almost always be for you to cut off the ongoing negotiation at this stage and request a brief postponement.* What you do is, allow the adjuster to finish 'playing the doctor' with your medical report or injuries. Let him reel and rail all he wants about it (or about other issues he cares to raise). Let him be the talker this time, you be the listener. Allow him all the time he needs. Pay close attention and take down or record all he has to say. Take notes. When he's done, politely ask him a few probing questions just so he'll clarify for you his exact positions. (No arguing with him or any sarcasm, just simple, direct questions).

Once you feel the adjuster has substantially made all the points he wanted to make, here's what you do. At that point, jump in and announce something to this effect: "Your points about my injuries (or about my wages, or whatever the case may be) are interesting. I would just like to discuss them in detail with my doctor. May we break off and resume these negotiations, say, a week from today, on the (day) of (month) 199_, to allow me time to consult with my doctor?"

And, with that declaration, get up and start packing, and promptly close all further conversations. Be firm but polite. The adjuster, unlikely to welcome your tactic and probably taken by surprise by it, would probably try to make some last ditch effort to get you to agree to a continuation of the negotiation session. Firmly but politely resist such efforts. At this point, watch out. The adjuster, probably boiling inside for your "pulling an ASPON" on him, may come up with some psychological ploys. He may accuse you of being "difficult" or "afraid" to talk or of having "something to hide." He may also try to give you some "potential settlement" figures for you to "just think about" in the meantime pending the next meeting.

Again, you should firmly but politely tell the adjuster that you've made your decision; refuse to accept from him any figures or offers and get out of the negotiation room as fast as possible! (If the adjuster can't leave you with a specific dollar figure 'to think about,' that means he would now not be able to tie you or your injury to specific amount, and that, in turn, means that when you get down to making your claim's evaluation, you would have to think of it NOT in terms of the adjuster's sense of the value, but of YOURS!

The Great Tactical Value Of The ASPON Move Of Temporarily Breaking Off Negotiations

HERE'S THE ASPON POINT. Having the negotiations closed, however temporarily, may seem to the uninitiated mind like a radical or even improper move to make, since it's common knowledge that most claimants (in deed, even the insurance companies as well) want to complete negotiations and get their settlement money paid as fast as possible. However, in the opinion of many skilled and experienced claims negotiators, *A DELAYING MOVE SUCH AS THIS IS OF GREAT TACTICAL VALUE FOR THE CLAIMANT: it's a vital part of the continuing negotiation "power game" designed to tip the psychological edge in your favor once again!* In deed, experienced and seasoned claims negotiators strongly recommend this tactic of temporarily closing the initial negotiations in all situations, even when the adjuster has been completely forthcoming or "generous" in his offers or in the negotiations. As one analyst, a former claims adjuster herself, put it, "[Even] if an adjuster has given you no problem about your lost wages, medical bills, and medical report, you should not settle on his first visit. *No matter how much money an adjuster offers you in the first negotiation, it is never the full amount he has to spend on a claim.* It may seem tiresome, and it requires extra work, but prolonging these sessions will mean hundreds or even thousands more settlement dollars for you."[16]

In deed, it's a rather open secret within the insurance claims industry that insurance companies have a great love and preference for what they fondly call "first call" settlements — i.e., settlements quickly concluded, preferably on the first meeting — because it invariably results in lower settlement payments to claimants owing to what could be termed the "impulse effect" of rushed negotiations on claimants, and because first call settlements directly reduce or eliminate, to

[16]Saadi, Claim It Yourself, p.81.

the company's benefit, the expenses the company would have had to make on such undertakings as investigation, evaluation, and negotiation of a claim before settling it.[17] ***To put it another way, the reality is that in the world of actual claims negotiations, it will frequently pay you better when you foster an image, and an impression, of being a "tough and difficult" fellow in the negotiating process!*** Insurance claims professionals have found that, as one of them put it, it is a "truism" in the claims industry — a practical fact of life— that it is the "difficult" claimant that usually commands bigger settlements than the "cooperative" ones. Consequently, by avoiding a "quickie" or easy settlement, and employing, instead, the let's-put-it-off-till-another-day tactic against the adjuster, you shall have greatly increased your chances of getting a higher settlement amount in the end.

> ***BUT HERE'S THE ULTIMATE ASPON STRATEGIC VALUE YOU SHALL HAVE ACCOMPLISHED BY THIS MOVE OF DEFERRING THE NEGOTIATIONS TO ANOTHER DAY:*** (1) YOU SHALL HAVE, IN EFFECT, SEIZED THE BARGAINING 'MOMENTUM' (CONTROL) FROM THE ADJUSTER; (2) SERVED NOTICE UPON THE ADJUSTER ONCE AGAIN THAT <u>YOU</u>, AND NOT THE ADJUSTER OR THE INSURANCE COMPANY, WILL CALL THE SHOTS IN THE NEGOTIATION "POWER GAME"; (3) GIVEN THE ADJUSTER SOME WORRIES AND PUT HIM ON THE DEFENSIVE; AND (4) IMPRESSED ON THE ADJUSTER THAT THE SETTLEMENT WOULD BE DONE ON <u>YOUR</u> OWN TERMS, AND NOT ON THE ADJUSTER'S!

STEP ❺: NOW, PURPOSEFULLY UTILIZE THE BREAK PERIOD TO RE-STUDY & RE-DO YOUR CASE

A. Re-check, Then Firm-Up The Facts On Your Injuries And Losses

The act of delaying the settlement negotiations for a short while will be at its greatest tactical, as well as practical usefulness to you, though, only on one condition: if you make sure that you utilize that delay time to make further preparations that might have become warranted in light of your discussions with the adjuster and his analysis and criticisms at the previous meeting. In a word, you are basically to use that time to deliberate on the comments and arguments the adjuster shall have made in that initial negotiation session — on the size, nature or appropriateness of your various expenses, your wage loss claims, the type, nature, and extent of your injuries, etc. And, you'll then take a critical "second look" at your facts and your claims in light of these comments and arguments (to the extent that they may be valid, if at all), and then formulate your rebuttal and your own final arguments and counter arguments and position.

If warranted by the circumstances of your particular case — if, for example, the adjuster had made what frankly appears to you to be a reasonable or a strong or damaging case against your doctor's report or the nature of your injuries — you would probably have to (in deed, it's highly advisable to) contact your doctor during this period and inform him about the questions raised by the adjuster. In doing this, your approach should be simple: ***aim basically at playing your doctor against the adjuster!*** How do you do this? It's simple. Just describe to your doctor in detail, preferably in the

---

[17]One insurance company claims manager summed it up this way: "As the insurance company is engaged in the business of making money, the function of claim department is to 'save' the company money, nobler sentiments to the contrary... First call settlements are always desirable... It should always be kept in mind that the value of a personal injury claim often increases in proportion to the time elapsed since the date of the injury... Claims are usually settled most advantageously to the company during the initial negotiations." (Foutty, The Evaluation & Settlement Of Personal injury Claims," Insurance Law Journal, Jan. 1964 pp. 7-14.) The claims manager added: "Unfortunately, it is the claimant who is difficult to deal with and has an exaggerated conception of the value of his claim who commands a larger settlement than the cooperative individual... (This is) a truism which the adjuster must recognize." (Foutty, Ibid., p.10.)

adjuster's exact words, how the adjuster had belittled and downplayed the doctor's report or analysis, how exactly (or approximately) he had defined and interpreted the medical terms in the doctor's report, and his arguments and opinions about the doctor's diagnosis, treatment and prognosis about your injuries. (Assuming that you had tape recorded or taken down a detailed written note during that first discussion session with the adjuster, giving your doctor such an account should pose no problem for you.) Then, after giving your doctor these facts, ask him his opinion of the adjuster's opinions and analysis. Are they valid? Could the adjuster have had a point? And if not, what then are the correct positions?

YOUR ASPON STRATEGY: To try to stir up something between your doctor and the adjuster; to get your doctor as mad and upset against the adjuster as possible for "challenging" the doctor's professional integrity and expertise! The idea, in fact, is to get your doctor so mad and upset that he will (you'll hope) go out of his way to more readily cooperate with you in supplying you the necessary medical information you'll need both to counter the adjuster's arguments and to successfully press your case with the adjuster. (By the way, you should know that you have a right, substantially as a matter of law, to have any reasonable questions you may have about your injuries answered or clarified for you by your doctor. So, don't be bashful in asking questions of your doctor, or demanding answers or clarifications thereof.)

B. Re-Check, Then Firm-Up Your Evaluation Of Your Claim's Worth

Another piece of important information you should use the break period to refine and finalize, is the settlement value to accept for your claim. Re-do the valuation. But, this time, seek to determine how much the claim is realistically worth *in light of the adjuster's points and arguments* — to the extent to which you have become convinced (from talking to your doctor, re-verifying the facts, etc.) that the adjuster's points are either valid on the one hand, or without merit, on the other hand. To what extent, at this particular point, are the adjuster's arguments or points on the parties' negligence and liability, for example, valid or lacking in merit? Or, his position on your injuries, your "diagnostic" medical bills, your wage loss? And what is your final re-assessment of the worth of your claim after taking into consideration those arguments or positions — to the extent that you realistically find them to be relevant, valid and convincing? [Refer to Chapters 9 & 10 for the detailed discussion of claims evaluation procedures.]

You should note, however, that this does not mean that you necessarily or automatically have to change or modify your figures (upwards or downwards) in every instance whenever the adjuster has raised objections. That is to say, that it is possible —- in deed, probable — that in a given case, even after you have duly considered the adjuster's objections and arguments and re-checked the adjuster's points against your own set of facts and figures, and even after you shall have talked anew to your doctor and made other verifications, you may still find no real justification to change or modify your original figures downwards; you may still find that the adjuster's points or figures just "don't add up" and that there's no legitimate reason to justify your modifying your original figures. In such a case, you should simply leave your original figures as they are and present them when the negotiations resume just the way you originally had them.

STEP **6**: 'TAKE CONTROL' OF MATTERS WHEN THE NEGOTIATIONS RESUME

A. ASPON Plan: This Time, It's Your Turn To 'Take Control'

Now, recall the situation when you closed the first official negotiation session with the insurance adjuster and postponed the negotiations (STEP 4, Section C). Recall that on that occasion it was the adjuster that did all the talking — he was the dominant figure who had all the questions and arguments and raised all the objections about everything from your employment time loss to your disability, the nature and extent of your injuries, your doctor's medical report, and so on and on. That first session was, in other words, one in which the adjuster had the "control" of the deliberations.

This time around, though, at the resumption of the negotiations, let there be no mistake about this: IT'S YOUR TURN AND OCCASION NOW TO TAKE "CONTROL" — AND, ONCE TAKEN, TO MAINTAIN IT FOR THE REST OF THE SETTLEMENT NEGOTIATIONS!

B. First, Answer All Charges & Arguments Made By The Adjuster In The Prior Meeting

How do you do this? The ASPON formula calls for you to do it in a combination of ways. Firstly, by addressing the major points and arguments raised by the adjuster at the first meeting, and fully "rebutting" (answering) each of them. At this resumed session, begin with a detailed, organized, orderly but carefully thought-out discussion of the adjuster's arguments and analysis. Take it one topic and one point at a time. Refute or answer them point-by-point — his major points or arguments on your lost wages and lost time from work, on your medical bills, your disability, the nature or extent or seriousness of your injuries, his interpretation of your doctor's medical report or his diagnosis, etc., etc.

On the adjuster's arguments or opinions about your injuries or your doctor's report, for example, you could make your ASPON counter argument as follows:

> *"No offense is meant, sir. But, certainly you are not a doctor. You are no medical expert or authority to know better than or second-guess my doctor. He's a fully qualified and reputable physician. Look. You claim my injuries are only a 'mere bruised hip' as opposed to a broken hip. I just consulted my doctor on that question, once again, during this break. If anything, after going over my medical condition and injuries, once again, my doctor remains even more firm and absolute about the accuracy if his original diagnosis that it's definitely a broken hip.*
>
> *But, even apart from my doctor's (any doctor's) analysis, I'm probably the best judge in the world of my own injuries — of how serious and painful and bothersome they are to ME; the suffering I have gone through from them. You call it a 'mere bruise.' But how is it, sir, that it has been over three months since I had this accident and I still suffer excruciating pains? How is it that I can't sit up or lift things or even get up the stairs like I used to? Even to this date! Constant pains! The truth is: it hurts; it bothers me, it disables me. It is me that's been enduring it — NOT YOU! It's not a 'mere bruise' to me, sir. Neither does my doctor think it is. My doctor is an expert on this. And what does he say? THAT IT WILL TAKE AT LEAST MONTHS TO CLEAR UP, IF AT ALL!."*

ASPON POINTERS:

* As much as possible, formulate your responses in such a way as to pit the adjuster against **your doctor**, rather than against you; put the adjuster in the position of arguing with or disputing the opinion of **your doctor,** and not with you. This way, it will be more difficult — and somewhat odd — for him to downplay, belittle or dismiss your injuries.

* Answer each and **every** major point the adjuster made; do not leave out any unanswered. (Refer to your notes at the meeting to get a complete picture as to the major points he made).

* The idea is to strongly impress it upon the adjuster that you are a serious and averagely knowledgeable student of your medical condition and your just entitlements and must be taken seriously by the adjuster; that you do not accept his major objections, conclusions, or arguments.

* Use the kind of style, of whatever nature, that you feel most 'natural' with, the one that you're most comfortable and at ease with — polite and friendly or angry and assertive, but without ever being insulting or disrespectful.

* Your central approach should be to be fair but firm, aggressive but not hostile or belligerent: to make a thoughtful and documented presentation of a claim which relies on the power and persuasiveness of a "sound demand adequately documented and properly communicated to the adjuster."[18]

---

[18]Baldyga, <u>How To Settle Your Own Insurance Claim</u>, p.132. As another analyst put it, "Your approach with the claims adjuster ought to be that of a salesperson — familiar with your product, aware of what it's worth and able to communicate this information to the adjuster in a friendly, but businesslike way. Bring the adjuster over to your side" (Kaplan and Benjamin, <u>Settle It Yourself</u>, p.49).

C. Second, Raise The Dollar Question With The Adjuster: 'How Much Will You Pay Me For My Damages?'

Next, when you are finished with the phase involving the refuting of the points made by the adjuster in the first session (or in his initial document submission to you, if no face-to-face meetings had been involved), now it's time for you to talk about the specific dollar figures for your claim — MONEY!

You shall have, of course, first reviewed your original valuation of the settlement value of your claim to take into consideration any valid or reasonable mitigating factors (if there are any) the adjuster might have raised in your first meeting, as advised in the preceding STEP 5 above (pp.173-4). You should have with you, confidentially tucked away in your folder, a copy of your final evaluation calculation which gives you the absolute 'bottom line' settlement figure you can accept for your claim.

I. Present Summary Dollar Figures For Your Losses & Expenses, Then Demand An Offer For Your Damages

To kick off the negotiations on money, start by presenting to the adjuster your newly reworked summary figures for each item of your special damages — the gross wage loss items, medical bills, miscellaneous out-of-pocket expenses, etc. Of course, in the preceding sections above [Section B5, B6, & B7 of STEP 3], you and the adjuster had hotly argued out much of these figures for your special damages, including your permissible medical, "diagnostic" and "treatment" expenses, and the permissible disability time and/or wage loss from employment, etc. And, in Section B above, you have rebutted each and every major point of argument or objection that had been raised by the adjuster on the major items of costs and expenses. The adjuster himself had presented his own version — what he thinks should be the proper figures — of your special damages costs and expenses (pp. 167-9). So, here, at this point, it's your turn to formally present before the adjuster for negotiation, your own final summary figures on your items of SPECIAL DAMAGES AND PROPERTY DAMAGE.

EXAMPLE:

Special Damages

My wage losses are	$2,000
My wage expenses are	$3,000
My future medical expenses (estimate) are	$1,000
Miscellaneous drugs (estimate)	$ 300
Miscellaneous out-of-pocket expenses (baby-sitter, transportation to and from your doctor, housekeeper, nursing care) are	$ 900
TOTAL SPECIAL DAMAGES	$7,200
Car damage ($100 deductible)*	$ 100
Damage to eye glasses in accident	$ 100
	$7,400
Disability and pain and suffering (General Damages)	?

Now, be sure to be alert. Immediately after you have completed your presentation of the above figures to the

---

*NOTE: See pp. 44-45 for details on procedures for gathering your data on auto body and other property damages.

adjuster, put these three questions to him: NOW, HOW MUCH WILL YOU GIVE ME AS A FAIR SETTLEMENT FOR MY SPECIAL DAMAGES, MR. ADJUSTER? HOW MUCH WILL YOU GIVE ME FOR MY DISABILITY AND PAIN AND SUFFERING? (This is also called the General Damages). HOW MUCH WILL YOU GIVE ME FOR MY AUTO AND OTHER PROPERTY DAMAGES?

II. Insist On The Adjuster Making You An Offer First

Predictably, the adjuster would probably not give you a 'straight' answer to the above questions. In deed, he would probably not give you an answer to the questions at all. Rather, most predictably, he would probably sidestep the question by asking you a question of his own. Something like: "What do you yourself think your claim is worth?" Or, "What do you yourself think you should be paid for general damages....?" Such a reaction from the adjuster is somewhat predicable because adjusters are generally known to fondly prefer the claimant to be the one who makes the offer FIRST. Why? Because, experts say, such a format is one that best affords them the best opportunity to maintain "control" of the claims negotiating process! As one analyst explained, such tactic is "a trick [employed by adjusters] to get you to undervalue your claim by asking, first, [say] $1,500, for an accident that is worth [say] $5,000."[19]

One claims professional, a claims manager, advised claims adjusters as follows, concerning why it's to their advantage to get the claimant to make the first offers:

> "It's normally best [to the adjuster for him] to allow or suggest that the claimant present a settlement demand before an offer is made [by the adjuster, because] often a claimant will make a demand which is less than the adjuster was preparing to offer. Also, if the claimant makes an excessive demand, the adjuster will not have committed himself to an offer which has left little room for further negotiations."[20]

TRANSLATION*: The adjuster is at his best position to exercise "command and control" over the manipulation and setting of the dollar amount to be paid a claimant when it is the claimant that makes the offer first, rather than the adjuster!*

The adjuster prefers that you, the claimant, make the offer first, because that allows him to come in with his own offer after you. From his professional experience in the claims field, he is fully aware that the average accident victim hasn't got the foggiest idea of the true settlement value of his claim. Hence, he sees the ploy of having you make the offer first, as a gauge by which to determine the general degree of your knowledge about the settlement value to which you are entitled. *He intends that tactic, in other words, as a ploy by which to be "in control" in the negotiation "power game" on the all-important issue of money valuation.*

Given the above described reality, what then do you, the claimant, do? What should be your ASPON reaction or strategy when confronted with an adjuster who demands (as adjusters invariably do) that you first make the settlement offer or demand? The ASPON answer is simple: DON'T! DON'T ACCEPT THAT. Rather, insist on the initial offer — a realistic, good faith one — coming from the adjuster first, before you may make yours. And continue to insist and insist on that until you finally get one. REMEMBER: IT'S ALL ABOUT THE ALL-IMPORTANT QUESTION OF WHO GETS TO 'CONTROL' YOUR CLAIMS VALUATION DETERMINATION — YOU, OR THE ADJUSTER!

But here's an important point to watch out for in this connection, though: the adjuster should not just make you a FIRST offer — just any offer at all. It would not be sufficient for the adjuster merely to come up with any offer — a phoney offer. You must be sure to persistently insist on, and to hold out until you find that he makes you the *first*

---

[19]Saadi, <u>Claim It Yourself</u>, p.84.

[20]Foutty, "The Evaluation and Settlement of Personal Injury Claims," Insurance Law Journal (Jan. 1964) p. 11.

REALISTIC offer.[21] And, only then — and then alone — should you now respond with your own first counteroffer.

D. Negotiating With the Adjuster: Here's the Actual 'Haggling' Process and Procedure

Here is the negotiating scenario and tactics given by one expert, Michele Saadi, a widely experienced former insurance claims adjuster, for commencing and holding actual negotiations with the adjuster (Saadi, Claim It Yourself, 85-6):

> "Insist that he [the adjuster] give you a figure [first] and *refuse to continue the negotiations until he does.* When the adjuster makes his first offer, do not accept. This is always a ridiculously low figure that he hopes you will be stupid enough to accept.[21]
>
> Tell him you realize he must make a low first offer, but you now expect a realistic figure. His next one will be a few dollars more, but still far below your claim's true value. This time, you can answer.
>
> The figure you present should be an exact one [based, for example, on what your research from a local law or reference library tells you is the average jury award for general damages for your type of injury in your geographic area,[22] or based on commonly used claim's valuation methods or formulas]…
>
> Make your first demand in dollars and cents, without rounding off. This is important since most claimants begin by asking for $5,000 or $10,000. You want to stand apart as someone who knows exactly what he wants. The adjuster, of course, will refuse this demand, claiming your accident is not worth that much money. Tell him that this is what claims similar to yours are worth and introduce your research on jury awards [and/or your calculations from a commonly used valuation method or formula] to support your demand.
>
> Finding and using jury awards [or employing other valuation methods used in the industry], is a tactic that few accident victims ever use. Your adjuster would expect this from an attorney, but never from a claimant. For this reason, he might try to reject your examples as being different from your accident or he might try to tell you that all claims are judged on individual basis. Tell the adjuster that your samples are both similar to your accident and a good cross-section of jury awards for your area [or that the valuation method you used is widely used by lawyers and insurance adjusters alike]. Also, point out that you know his company uses jury awards [or the valuation method you used] as the standard for awarding general damages. If he were negotiating with an attorney, the lawyer would use this argument. *It is no less valid coming from a claimant.*
>
> The adjuster may reject all of this. If he does, stand firm. Insist that he accept your examples and begin to negotiate in the range of your figures. *Threaten to close the session* so you can check on his assertion that jury awards [or your valuation method] play no part in the evaluation of a claim. Tell the adjuster that you know he is lying to you and you will prove this to him and the executives of his company [and/or threaten to take the case to an attorney]. In other words, that you will file a complaint with the home office of the insurance company. Since no adjuster wants to lose control of a negotiation, he probably will raise his offer to the point where you can seriously negotiate."

Saadi offers the following tactics on the actual give-and-take and back-and-forth trading of dollar figures in the practical negotiations of claims settlement:[23]

> "The next part of the session is where you and the adjuster trade figures. He will try to stay at one offer and force you steadily to decrease your demand. *Make the adjuster understand that you will not*

---

[21]In deed, insurance industry claims negotiators and strategists, because they have become generally aware that claimants and claimants' attorneys do not generally take the adjuster's initial offers seriously, any way, expressly advise the adjuster not to put forth realistic offers in their initial offers to claimants. Witness these words from a claims manager: "No matter what amount the claimant demands, the adjuster should have a maximum settlement offer in mind and refrain from offering this amount unless he is certain [that] settlement cannot be consummated below this figure...Most claimants and claimants' attorneys feel that the adjuster will make an offer below what the claim is worth, and therefore will expect the original offer to be increased. As such is the case, the adjuster should not make his initial offer his maximum." (Foutty, "The Evaluation & Settlement of Personal Injury Claims," Insurance Law Jr. Jan. 1964, p.12).

Furthermore, even as the adjuster is compelled, against his will, to make the initial offer first, you should be diligent to guard against a practice often resorted to by adjusters trapped in such a situation: the practice of making the claimant a phony or "trick offer." The "trick offer," most commonly employed by adjusters in dealings involving "unrepresented" claimants with little or no knowledge of the procedures of claims settlement, works this way, in the words of one insurance claims adviser and strategist: "If the claimant will not [first] make demand before an offer is made [by the adjuster], one method of extending the first offer [on the adjusters' part] is the "rounding off" method, wherein the adjuster totals the claimant's special damages [less collateral source benefits], and makes an offer of an even amount slightly over the total. [In other words], this method omits any mention of [award for] the claimant's inconvenience [for pain and suffering] and any explanation...The adjuster merely states: 'Your out-of-pocket expenses are $___. Does $50 sound fair?' It is surprising how often this method succeeds, especially claims involving minor injuries." (Foutty, Ibid., p.12. See, also, Ross, Settled Out Of Court, pp. 168-9, for further description of the use of this method.)

[22]Saadi's specific prescription for valuation of the settlement worth of a claim, is determination by the claimant of the "average amount a jury awards in your area" for a comparable type of injury and expenses — information which, she suggests, a claimant can readily obtain simply by visiting a local law library or the nearest city reference library and requesting the librarian to give him some of the "several publications that give this information in short, easy-to-understand articles...[and contain] recent examples of settlements in auto accident cases." Saadi, Claim It Yourself, pp. 82-3.

[23]Saadi, Ibid, p. 86.

bid against yourself.[24] ***Never decrease your figure unless he raises his offer.*** Always tie your numbers to the facts of the accident. When you decrease your demand, never subtract a larger amount than the adjuster is willing to add to his. [For example], if you come down $100, do not let him raise his offer by only $25. Maintain parity as you negotiate, reminding the adjuster that this is the only fair way to arrive at a figure for your accident.

Trading figures may only take a few minutes, or several hours, or even more sessions while the adjuster checks with his supervisors. He may need extra authorization to pay you the money you want, or make a reasonable offer that both of you can live with. If this happens, accept it, sign the release, and close the claim..."

AND HERE'S ANOTHER EXPERT PERSPECTIVE, THIS ONE FROM A CLAIMS LAWYER, ON THE PRACTICAL MECHANICS, TACTICS AND STRATEGIES BY WHICH YOU MAY NEGOTIATE YOUR SETTLEMENT WITH YOUR ADJUSTER:[25]

"It's also a universal rule that insurance companies do not pay the amount you 'ask for.'...

Since the company will ordinarily not pay your opening demand (even if it's reasonable), it's necessary to ask more than a claim is actually worth to give both sides some "bargaining" room. *It's something like a poker game, with the better bluffer winning the pot even though he may not hold the stronger hand. And don't be afraid to bluff. You have a strong trump card: the threat of turning the case over to a lawyer for litigation.* When this happens, [i.e., if you were to hire a lawyer, adjusters are fully aware that] it means new expense to the insurance company — for court costs, depositions, and legal fees — and they'd like to avoid that. If they think you mean business, they'll settle with you, if they can get out for a reasonable figure.

It would be nice if you could give a 'take-it-or-leave-it' one-shot figure to the adjuster, and not have to haggle... but such a tactic will [not generally] work...

Most insurance companies will not give you their "top" offer the first time around. Occasionally an adjuster will do this, but it happens infrequently. [Consequently], when the initial offer is given to you, it's usually advisable to tell the adjuster politely that you're not willing to settle for that amount, but that to save litigation you might consider a little less than your first figure. At this point, he'll probably ask you what you'll "really take." Reduce your offer between 10 and 15 percent. Usually he'll offer more, or he'll re-submit your proposal to his supervisor and report to you later...

A great many adjusters, after receiving your demand, will tell you that you're asking so much, and [that] you're so far "out-of-line" on your demand, that there's no use their even making an offer until you "come down." This is a clever attempt to make you bid against yourself. The adjuster has a pretty good idea, of course, of the value of the claim, and there is no real reason why he can't submit an offer, regardless of how high your demand is. His tactic, though, is to have you immediately cut your asking price without his having to even make an offer." [Emphasis added by the present writer]

THE EXPERT OFFERS THIS ADVICE ON HOW TO HANDLE THAT KIND OF SITUATION:

"You should handle such an approach in one of two ways. The best method is to stand firm, and to tell him that you feel your offer is fair, and that you are unwilling to "cut" your claim. He may try to "out bluff" you and tell you that there is no use negotiating any further.

If the conference ends at this stage, it's usually advisable to let about two weeks pass, in the hope that he'll call you. If he doesn't, then you should write a "final demand letter," telling him that you're turning it over to an attorney for suit, and pointing out that it is evident that the company is not willing to make any reasonable settlement offer [and], that you will hold the claim another ten days on the chance that they may reconsider their position. Such a letter will put some pressure on the adjuster, since his file is being reviewed by a supervisor or claims manager.

The second method to use if the adjuster tries the "you're-asking-too-much-I-can't-even-offer-you-anything" approach, is to cut your demand by 10 to 15 percent. Tell him that you are not willing to accept less than that,

---

[24]Compare the first three sentences in this passage with this by another analyst, describing his field observation of the negotiating technique employed by adjusters when dealing with unrepresented claimants: "[the technique used in such instances is] the Boulwareism technique (named after an officer of the General Electric Company), whereby a single offer is made and rigidly adhered to. This was practically never attempted between the 'professionals' (i.e., adjusters and lawyers) we observed, but it occurred on occasions when adjusters negotiated with unrepresented claimants...no exchange of proposals is involved ... [it's a] 'take-it-or-leave-it' [approach]" (Ross, Settled Out Of Court, p.149. See also Ibid. pp. 169-170.).

[25]Siegel, How To Avoid Lawyers, pp. 11-13.

and that you would like to know his offer. If he repeats the "you're-asking-so-much" routine, then you should terminate the discussion and proceed as previously outlined [with the first approach], eventually writing the 'final demand letter.'"

E. What's Ultimately The "Fair" Offer For You To Accept?

What is a "fair" or acceptable settlement amount for your claim? Or, better still, what should you consider fair and acceptable, personally? It's really simple: *in the final analysis, it's WHAT YOUR OWN FEELINGS TELL YOU IS FAIR AND ACCEPTABLE!* Ultimately, as a practical matter, it doesn't matter what method or formula of evaluation you use, or what amount any formal method or formula might have told you you ought to settle for. It doesn't matter what your little research might have told you is the "jury award" amount for a comparable case like yours for your area. *After all is said and done, the ultimate determining factor should be: what your own gut feelings tell you is the fair and acceptable settlement under the particular circumstances prevailing at the given time in your particular case. To put it simply, if and when you truly feel satisfied that an offer is FAIR, it is a fair offer.*!

Let's say, for example, that at a certain stage late in the settlement negotiations, the adjuster, after having finished with applying the customary your-original-demand-is-out-of-line tactic with you based on certain stated weaknesses in your case, now makes you a counteroffer which then "discounts" (reduces) your own demand because, according to the adjuster, he earnestly finds, from his investigations, that your own actions and inactions materially contributed to causing the accident. In such a situation, all you should do would be simply to listen and pay careful attention to the reasons and rationalizations he advances for reducing your demand or offering you the amount he is offering you, as well as the proof and evidence he advances in support of his stand or arguments. (Ideally, you shall have, as well, probably had some pretty good idea of the absolute "rock bottom" range of values you'll accept in settlement of the claim). Critically consider the adjuster's position (and counteroffer) in light of the surrounding facts — honestly, realistically, reasonably, objectively. Now, let's say that after you carefully verified and gave due consideration to all of that, you find that the adjuster's reasons and rationalizations for his counteroffer actually do reasonably make sense to you, and that the counteroffer seems to be approximately within a settlement range of acceptability in light of the adjuster's reasons and the circumstances of your situation. Then, in such a situation, you should accept the adjuster's offer. To you, under the given circumstances, that offer is — that offer should be considered as being — the "fair" settlement amount for the case![26]

STEP ❼: IF YOU SETTLE, SIGN THE "RELEASE," BUT KNOW WHAT YOU'RE SIGNING AWAY.

At long last, if you and the insurance adjuster are able to come to an agreement on a settlement value for your claims, the adjuster will usually present you a document called a **RELEASE** which he would require you to sign before he may issue you your settlement check. Basically, by signing this document, you (i.e. the claimant) would be giving up your rights to ever make a claim again for the same injury and damages against the other motorist or his insurance company, in exchange for the settlement amount you are accepting.

It's of critical significance that you remember that, ordinarily, once a release is signed a case against the same parties cannot be reopened, and that once you put your signature to the release form, it's for all intents and purposes final and you would almost certainly not be able to get any more money later — even if your injuries turn out to be worse than originally assessed. SO, HERE'S THE MAIN ASPON POINT: BEFORE YOU SIGN THIS FORM, BE ABSOLUTELY CERTAIN THAT YOU ARE SATISFIED THAT YOU ACCEPT TO LIVE WITH THE SETTLEMENT DEAL FOREVER!

The key is to read the release thoroughly and make sure you understand and know exactly what you are signing **before** *you sign it. Read it thoroughly.* And, if it's necessary, read it over and over a few times. If there's anything or any clauses you can't quite understand, ask the adjuster to clarify them for you. There are two questions you want to be

---

[26]For one thing, though, you should bear in mind that there are many intrinsic advantages you stand to reap merely by virtue of accepting a reasonable, even half-way decent settlement, on a timely timetable — avoidance of potential legal fees of one third or more of the settlement amount, potential delays of months or even years of court proceedings before you may actually get paid, court fees and expenses of trials, risk of losing everything in the end if your case were to be litigated since there's never any guarantee that in the end you'll necessarily prevail in a court case, etc.

certain about: Who and who exactly are being released, and what kind of claim against them are you releasing? Is it for personal injuries? Is it for auto damage or other property damage?

For example, never sign a release that releases "all claims" or names "all parties" as the negligent party or defendant being released. Rather, make sure that the specific claims being released are individually designated, (and that the particular negligent parties being released are *specifically* named in the release document. Where more than one party are responsible for the accident or your injuries or damages, then make sure the release document is not in fact releasing all other responsible parties unless, of course, that's your intention. If, for example, the compensation you are receiving is for personal injury only, or for property damage only, or for both, make sure the release says so exactly.

Finally, if you are in a no-fault auto insurance state wherein a settlement has been made under a no-fault policy and an "excess claim right" exists against the negligent party's insurance company, be sure to read the release carefully and make sure that it clearly states that only you are being released, and not the other parties.

STEP **8**: WHAT DO YOU DO IF YOU CAN'T GET A FAIR OFFER FROM THE INSURANCE COMPANY? ASPON RULES

What if, after you have followed, even faithfully and meticulously, all the ASPON negotiation and settlement prescriptions of the preceding passages of this chapter, you find, nevertheless, that the adjuster refuses to yield to reason and would not raise his offer or give you a fair and realistic price for your claim? In such an event, what do you do, then?

Here are a few ASPON tips on dealing with the uncooperative or unreasonable adjuster who refuses to deal with you seriously or to make you a realistic settlement offer:

1. Send Letters To Adjuster's Supervisors

Send a letter, by certified mail, return receipt requested (or, if feasible, pay a personal visit to) the adjuster's superiors and argue your case to them directly. Address the letter to them personally, by their specific names and titles. Politely but firmly demand that the company promptly make a reasonable and fair settlement with you, and make it clear that the insurance executives themselves, as well, and not just the adjuster alone, will have to take responsibility for the potential costs and expenses the insurance company will incur in extra time and legal fees if you should be driven into the arms of an attorney by the unreasonableness of the adjuster. Make the tone of the letter reasonable and factual. [See sample *FINAL DEMAND LETTER* on p. 182]. Always make sure you keep copies of all original correspondence for your own records.

Send that letter by certified mail to the adjuster's supervisor (you can get his full name from either the adjuster or the company's personnel office or telephone operator), and send a photocopy to the head of the home office claims department as well. [Send both by certified mail, return receipt requested.]

2. Re-send Same Letters To Supervisors

If you fail to receive a response within some 10 days or so, mail copies of the same letter again to the same individuals, also by certified mail, return receipt requested, and include a notation that you still have not received any response from them on the letter or the case.

3. Send Letters To Higher Executives

Go up the chain of command. If after another week or so you still have not had a reasonable response or movement on your case, write another letter — a businesslike letter of complaint — to the adjuster's supervisor, and then to the claims manager. Again, the letters should be addressed to these persons by their real names. If that doesn't elicit any reasonable movement, then write to the head of the home office claims department. (This way, you eliminate any possible claim later by the insurance company that the management did not know what might have been going on in the local or branch office!)

4. Lodge Complaint With State's Commissioner Of Insurance

If there's still no reasonable movement from the insurance company, you may next file a written complaint with the

State's Commissioner or Department of Insurance (see Appendix A on pp. 193-6). Send copies of that complaint to both the adjuster and his supervisors as well. Most states' department of insurance, upon receiving a complaint from a complainant about an insurance carrier, will usually write to the company and ask for an explanation of the company's position on the complaint. To be sure, true, there is often not much likelihood that the department of insurance will compel the insurance company to change its position. But the main reason for complaining to the department is to let the insurance company know that if they don't resolve your claim, you are determined to create unpredictable problems for them. In any event, the mere act of lodging this complaint with the department of insurance may help to nudge the insurance company to action, for insurers do not like having to answer to the department.

5. Wait For A While More

What's your next move after you've tried these further measures and you still can't persuade the insurance company officials and operatives to make you a fair offer? It will all depend on how secure you feel you are, both emotionally and financially, at this point. Assuming you still feel emotionally strong enough to continue the fight, and that you are not in dire immediate need for that settlement money, your best choice would probably be this: TO WAIT. You should wait, providing, of course, you are still within the necessary time limit (the "statute of limitations") required for filing a lawsuit in your state. [See Appendix B, pp. 197-8].

FORM 11-1

FINAL DEMAND LETTER (A SAMPLE)

Dear Mr. ......(name of adjuster),

    It has been since your letter (or phone call or personal conversation) of _____ 19 ___ , when I last heard from you on my claim. As you well know, I made it amply clear to you that your offer of $ ___ in settlement of my claim was an absolute insult and was totally unacceptable, and asked that you reconsider your stand and come up with a far, far more reasonable offer.

    It's now _____ weeks/months since then, and there has been no further movement on your part to come up with a realistic, good faith offer to resolve my claim. I am resolutely resolved to do whatsoever I have to do to secure a fair and just settlement that adequately compensates me for my expenses and injuries, for which I still continue to suffer considerable pain and discomfort even now. And if I have to get an attorney to get that fair and just settlement, then that may be just what I'll have to do.

    Please take this letter as my very last attempt. I just want to satisfy myself that I've exhausted all possible efforts to resolve this matter out of court.

    Be hereby advised that I shall hold the claim open for another ten (10) days. Unless I can hear from you with an equitable, realistic offer by the _____ day of _____ , I shall promptly turn the matter over to an attorney to pursue a just settlement.

                                         Signed: _____
                                                  (Claimant)

Copies to:
1. Mr. ...(name of the other driver)
2. Mr. ...(name of the branch manager of the Insurance Co.)

You can put this waiting period to good use in any number of ways. For one thing, typically, insurance adjusters involved in stalled negotiations will often maintain contact with the claimant at least once a month during the duration of the stalemate to further sound out the claimant on his position. Indeed, "negotiations" (usually by phone or letter) may continue in this way between you and the adjuster for a few months. And if, by, say, the third or fourth month your adjuster finds that your demand position still has not changed, the adjuster would by then be convinced that you are truly serious and firm on your stand and would probably make you a more serious or "best" offer possible at that point.

Another use to which you may properly put this waiting time: you may use it to undertake any further medical treatments you may legitimately need or find necessary in the meantime. By continuing to build up such additional medical bills and expenses — and making damned sure, by the way, that you continuously send copies of these new bills to the attention of the insurance company officials — you will further push them into making a serious offer to conclude the case.

6. If All Fails, Consider Getting A Lawyer

Finally, if the insurance company still will not respond to any kind of pressures and still persists in not making you a realistic offer, you probably have no other realistic choice left at that point than this: RETAINING AN ATTORNEY. For more on this, turn to the next chapter, chapter 12.

A FINAL WORD OF GUIDANCE ON USING THE ASPON RULES

This is probably a most fitting note on which to conclude this rather pivotal chapter, an essential reminder on the central principle by which you should be guided even as you go about the task of employing the ASPON tactics and techniques outlined in the chapter to negotiate your claims. *Always bear this in mind: EVERY CLAIM IS UNIQUE AND DIFFERENT, and a settlement offer made by the insurance company, or a negotiating position taken by the adjusters, will vary from company to company, from adjuster to adjuster, and even from region to region.* **What that means, in effect, is that as a claimant your tactics and techniques should be subject to many variations in light of the facts and circumstances of a case.**

The point is that, in the final analysis, the ASPON tactics and strategies represent the most "ideal" scenario involving the ideal situation, and that you may not necessarily have to adopt in every case every ASPON tactic or strategy outlined in the chapter, or to follow them in the exact order given in the chapter. It will all depend on the circumstances of a given case; you are to use particular methods at any stage in the negotiations if, when, and as necessary, and where they seem appropriate to counter the adjuster's tactics or negotiating posture. In short, it is the facts of a given case and the adjuster's attitude and tactics, that will, in turn, largely dictate your own choice of ASPON tactics to counter the adjuster.

FORM 11-2

CLAIMS DEMAND LETTER — SAMPLE I

Accident invoving "Soft Tissue" (mild type) injury having no long term or permanent disability.

TO: Mr/Ms (<u>Name of Adjuster</u>),
    Claims Adjuster
    XYZ Insurance Company
    10 Main Street, Suite 415
    New York, N.Y. 10025

CLAIMANT: John Doe
ADDRESS: 127 Hand Street
New York, N.Y. 10001
DATE: ___ 19__
PHONE # ( ) _____

RE: Insured Party: David Damages
    Insured's License Plate # New York N300-93
    CLAIM NO.: U-925-93
    CLAIMANT: John Doe
    DATE OF ACCIDENT: ___?

Dear Mr./Ms. (Name of Adjuster):

    As I informed you in my notification letter dated ___ 19___, I was involved in an automobile accident with Mr./Ms. _____, a party who is insured by your company, on (date of accident), at the intersection of Accident Street and Apple Street, Brooklyn, New York. I was driving south on Accident Street at about 4 P.M. when I slowed down in the line of traffic at the stop sign at the corner of Apple Street. As I stopped, your insured violently slammed into the rear (back) of my car. The impact was so great, it threw me forward about 20 Feet.

    I was immediately in excruciating pain and agony in my legs, neck, and back, and had severe headaches and dizziness. I went to Dr. John Treatgood for treatment. I was examined and x-rayed, and was diagnosed as having suffered head concussion, torn ligament on my right ankle, and a cervical strain. The doctor fitted me with a cervical collar, and because of the exeruciating pain and severe headaches and dizziness I continued to have, he also prescribed some relaxants and pain relief pills. I was advised to have immediate bed rest.

    I saw the doctor periodically over the next six weeks, as I developed, from time to time, disorientation and nausea from my head injuries, and continued to have constant headaches, dizziness, head pains and soreness in my neck, lower back and ankle. I have also been extremely edgy and nervous and unable to sleep.

    I not only missed 4 weeks of work, but even more painfully, I was also forced, during this period of my disability, to miss the wedding of my younger brother in Los Angeles where I was to have been my brother's best man. I forced myself to return to work on the ____ of ____ 19__, though I was still having head pains, and some soreness and stiffness on my neck, back and leg areas and other medical problems. I'm still having head pains, difficulty sleeping, and I'm still edgy, tense and nervous. I was in excellent health and physical condition before the accident and didn't have these medical conditions.

    My car was also damaged and repaired at Benny's Auto Repairs. I paid $100 under my deductible insurance and my company (ABC Insurance Company) paid the rest.

MY SPECIAL DAMAGES ARE:

Dr. John Treatgood (7 visits) .... $ 700

Dr. John Bread (X-rays) 100

Prescription medications (estimate) 100

Transportation to and from doctor 50

Car rental during period 200

Future medical expense (estimate). 400

Lost wages (4 weeks @ $600 per week) 2,400

Car damage ($100 deductible) 100

TOTAL $4,040

For my GENERAL DAMAGES (for pain, suffering, inconvience, etc) .... ??

Clearly and without question, your insured was grossly negligent and at fault in the accident. His recklessness has caused me all these pain and troubles. I went through a period of excruciating pain, severe headaches and dizziness, and even suffered disorientation and nausea which had lasted now for well over 6 weeks, since a lot of those problems and symptoms still continue. My life and my family's life was shattered, and, on top of all that, I missed the opportunity of a lifetime to be my brother's best man at his wedding. In consequence, I herewith demand compensation for my special damages, as itemized above, as well as compensation for my injuries and all my pain and suffering.

} Summarize your pain and suffering once again

Please respond in writing with your offer for a fair and equitable settlement of this claim. I have made a thorough and competent evaluation of the worth of my claim and you can rest assured that I have a pretty good idea of what a fair and reasonable settlement value ought to be for this case. However, since you're the "expert" on this, I'll defer it to you to set the settlement value in the belief that you'll be fair and professional about it. When you have your offer ready, please write or call me (see above-listed phone #) so that we can arrange to set a mutually convenient date for a meeting and face-to-face discussion of the settlement. Please respond no longer than 30 days from the date of this writing.

Thank you.

Cordially yours,

John Doe

(Claimant)

Supporting documents herewith enclosed:

Police accident report (if available)

Medical record from Dr. Treatgood and medical bills

Doctor's report from Dr. Treatgood

Receipts from the pharmacies

Letter of time lost from job from employer

Written Letter (card) of invitation to brother's wedding

FORM 11-3

CLAIMS DEMAND LETTER — SAMPLE 2

Accident involving a father and infant child and some "hard injuries" with some elements of long term effects, some disfigurement and scarring.

TO: Mr/Ms (Name of Adjuster),
    Claims Adjuster
    Quick Insurance Company
    10 Apple Street, Suite 415
    New York, N.Y. 10025

CLAIMANT: James Claims
                James Claims Jr., an infant
ADDRESS: 127 Handcock Street Apt. 4
              New York, N.Y. 10001
DATE: ___ 19__
PHONE # ( ) _____

RE: Insured Party: David Benson
    Insured's License Plate # _____

    CLAIM NO.: _____
    CLAIMANTS: James Claims; James Claims Jr., an infant
    DATE OF ACCIDENT: ____?

Dear Mr./Ms. (Name of Adjuster):

    As I informed you in my notification letter dated ___ 19___, I was involved in an automobile accident with Mr./Ms. _____, an insured party with your company, on (date of accident), at Fifth Avenue and 30th Street in Manhattan, New York. I was driving south on Fifth Avenue at about 3 P.M. and driving extremely carefully as I had my infant son with me, and as I was more than halfway through the intersection with 30th Street, your insured, going East on 30th Street, ran through a red light and violently slammed into the back of my car, barely missing a direct hit on my two year old infant son, Claims Jr., who was strapped to his sitter in the back seat of the car. The speeding force of your insured was so great that it spun my car all the way around and left it facing north. So gruesome was the damage to my Buick car, only a 1990 model, that upon being towed to the Ever Ready Repair Shop, it was declared a total wreck not worth repairing or having any salvage value.

    Miraculously, notwithstanding the crushing force of the collision, my infant son escaped being smashed to death. But he was obviously terrified and in extreme mental anguish and shock as he moaned hysterically and tightly clung onto me for the rest of the time immediately after the accident. My son and I were taken by ambulance to the emergency room of Bellvue Hospital. I had headaches, pain in the head, neck, hands and back, a deep gash on my forehead and loss of a tooth, as a result of my head smashing into the windshield upon the tremendous impact of the collision. My son and I were x-rayed, I received 10 stitches for the gash on my forehead, we were given some pain relief medication and kept overnight for observation, then released the next morning and advised to see my private physician.

    Upon release from the emergency ward, I continued to experience severe headaches and body pains, and dizziness, soreness in my neck and back, and inability to bend backward. My son remained unusually quiet, nervous, jumpy and sore and cried constantly. Because of this and because my infant son's condition remained largely uncertain and worrisome, my son and I were taken, in the morning of the next day (on the ____day of ____), to see my family doctor, Michael Edson, M.D. My doctor examined us and referred us to Leonard Goodman, M.D., who is an orthopedist and obstetrician. Dr. Goodman examined me and my son and found I had dislocation of my shoulder and elbow, and that my son had cuts and bruises on the hands and face and was seriously traumatized and in shock from the impact of the accident. Dr. Goodman prescribed some relaxants and pain relief pills for both of us, referred me to a physical therapist (or to a chiropracter or acupuncturist, etc., as the case may be) and advised bed rest and continuing close observation of my son. Dr. Goodman also recommended that I see my dentist.

    I saw the physical therapists at the Mayo Therapy Clinic over the next two months, as I continued to have constant head pains and soreness in my neck, hands and back. I also saw my dentist, Dr. Edward Mild, who fitted me with an artificial tooth to replace the one I lost in the accident. My son was taken to see Dr. Goodman periodically; he himself remained extremely sore, traumatized, jumpy, unusually irritable, nervous, and frequently unable to sleep, and still is not fully recovered even today from the shock and trauma of the dark day of the accident.

Upon completion of the therapy prescribed for me by the therapist, I returned to Dr. Goodman for an examination. Dr. Goodman advised me that I will have some pain and discomfort for at least 3 months, maybe longer, and stated that I'll just have to "learn to live with pain for quite a while."

I missed 3 weeks of work as a social worker with the New York Counseling Group as a result of the accident. My car, a 1990 Buick Cutlass, was completely destroyed, and its current book, value per the Blue Book, is $4,500.

MY SPECIAL DAMAGES ARE:

Bellvue Hospital (ambulance, emergency room)	$300
Bellvue Hospital (X-rays)	100
Michael Edson, M.D. (1 visit)	65
Leonard Goodman, M.D. (2 visits)	150
All prescription medications received	190
Mayo Therapy Clinic	500
Dr. Edward Mild (Dentist)	400
Transportation to and from doctors and therapists	200
Payment to housekeepers during period of disability	350
Future medical expense (estimate)	500
Lost wages (3 weeks @ $700 per week)	2,100
	4,855
Car damage ($100 deductible)	100
TOTAL	$4,955
For my GENERAL DAMAGES (for pain, suffering,inconvience,etc).	??

SPECIAL DAMAGES FOR INFANT,J. CLAIMS, JR.:

Bellvue Hospital (ambulance, emergency room),	$300
Bellvue Hospital (X-ray)	100
Michael Edson, M.D. (1 visit)	65
Leonard Goodman, M.D. (4 visits)	300
Prescription medications	60
Transportation to and from doctors, all included 100% in father's damages	-0-
Future medical expense (estimate).	300
TOTAL	1025
For Infant's GENERAL DAMAGES (for pain, suffering,inconvience,etc)	??

Clearly and without question, your insured was grossly negligent and at fault in causing the accident, acting in wanton and reckless disregard for human lives and property and causing me, my little son, and my family all these pain, agony, trauma and anxiety. As stated in the police report of the accident (herewith enclosed), I clearly had the green light and the right of way; your insured was in direct and indisputable violation of my right of way when he ran the red light and plunged into me. The total demolition of my car by the impact of Mr. Benson's car (see enclosed photo) clearly demonstrates the outrageous speed and force with which Mr. Benson rammed into me as he recklessly sped through a red light.

It's apparent that your insured must have been under the influence of alcohol at the time of the accident. He staggered and walked funny and talked incoherently. As one pedestrian, an eyewitness to the accident, stated in her account of the accident, Mr. Benson's "breath smelled of alcohol and he sure looked and walked drunk and out of it." (The written statement from this and other witnesses will be tendered at the appropriate time.)

Because of your insured's reckless driving, I permanently lost a tooth, I am conspicuously disfigured with a gaping gash on my forehead for all the world to see, and I have had to undergo months of excruciating headaches and body pains, and dislocated shoulder and elbow, requiring some two months of tedious physical therapy. According to my doctor, I will have to live with the pain and difficulties for at least 3 months more, and probably even longer than that. And my infant son has been severely traumatized and remains nervous, disoriented and unable to sleep from the impact of the collision. A major source of joy and pleasure in my life and the family's life before the accident, watching my son play and run around the house in infant playfulness and innocence, may have been permanently taken away from me and my family. Several nights, I have myself awakened from sleep in a nightmare, still traumatized and in shock about my son so narrowly missing a direct hit by your insured, which would have been a certain death or crippling injuries for the young life.

} Summarize your pain & suffering once again

In consequence, I herewith demand compensation for my special damages and the special damages of my son, as itemized above, as well as compensation for my injuries and all my pain and troubles and those of my son. Please respond in writing with your offer for a fair and equitable settlement of this claim. I have made a thorough and competent evaluation of the worth of my claim and you can rest assured that I have a pretty good idea of what a fair and reasonable settlement value ought to be for this case. However, since you're the "expert" on this, I'll leave it to you to set the settlement value in the belief that you'll be fair and professional about it. When you have your offer ready, please write or call me (see above -listed phone #) so that we can arrange to set a mutually convenient date to meet for a face-to-face discussion of the settlement. Please respond no longer than 30 days from the date of this writing.

Thank you.

Yours truly,

James Claims

(Claimant)

Supporting documents herewith enclosed:

Police accident report (if available)

Photos and/or diagram of the accident scene (if available)

Medical records from the hospitals (emergency rooms), doctors and physical therapists for the claimant

Bills from the medical personnel and facilities

Letter from employer showing time lost and applicable income thereof

CHAPTER 12
IF ALL ELSE FAILS, HOW TO PICK THE RIGHT ATTORNEY TO PRESS YOUR CLAIM WHILE SQUEEZING THE BEST DEAL OUT OF HIM

A. It May Just Be Inevitable After All To Hire A Lawyer In Certain Instances

It is not at all improbable that a claimant may closely follow, even faithfully and meticulously, the ASPON negotiating formula of Chapter 11 and all the prescriptions of the preceding chapters of this guidebook, and still not get a realistic or reasonable offer in the end from his insurance company. To be sure, the ASPON tactics, strategies, and methodologies outlined in the preceding pages of the book are all tried, tested and proven tools of what have predominantly and consistently worked in the insurance claims trade for purposes of securing settlements for claimants. They should, by and large, work in almost all cases. Unfortunately, though, the brutal truth is that it is in the very nature of the legal system in America, and of the very subjective and prejudicial ways and manner by which auto accident claims are settled, that even a most deserving claims case presented for compensation in the best possible manner may still find itself denied a fair settlement or serious consideration by the insurance establishment. In that instance, then, that will be one situation where the claimant may have no other realistic or advisable option than to seek the services of an attorney to pursue his claim.

One analyst, a former claims adjuster and passionate advocate of self-representation in auto claims settlements, summed up when it may become inevitably necessary to engage an attorney, this way:[1]

> "Although this should be your last resort, it does become necessary when you simply cannot get a fair settlement. You've really done most of the lawyer's work for him [by now] but he can do one more thing you can't — try your case in court. Sometimes, even in the most simple and straightforward injury cases, it comes to that. Claims people themselves don't always understand why their company will pay a fair settlement on one claim and then, a week later, refuse even to approach a fair amount on an identical case.

> After three years as an insurance adjuster, I still have no idea why this happens. In this country, auto accident claims are settled in a subjective way. You can do all [that is necessary or recommended]...and still be forced to retain a lawyer and even go to court...[many a] company have a reputation of denying all reasonable demands, and then handing the claimant's lawyer a check for the amount he wanted, literally on the steps of the courthouse. There is no logic to this, nor is it fair."

---

[1]Saadi, <u>Claim It Yourself</u>, pp.87-88.

B. Criteria For Selecting A Lawyer To Hire

But wait a minute! Hold it. Before you rush out and automatically hire the first man or woman you can find, just so long as he or she is a lawyer, there are some essential background work you must first undertake. First, if the final offer you received from the insurance company adjuster is not in writing, ask the adjuster to give it to you in writing. Thereafter, consult a lawyer[2] — most preferably, one with a good professional reputation for integrity and is a specialist in the personal injury work, rather than a "generalist" — for a legal opinion. Supply him with all the major information and documentations you have assembled. Leave him with only the PHOTOCOPIES and, as in the past, always retain the originals. *Initially, you do not give the lawyer any information or make any mention to him of the offers you had previously received from the insurance company.*

Here are the questions you would want answered for you by the lawyer: What is his estimation of the value of your claim — what he can recover for you on the claim? How long will it take for the case to go through the judical process and for you to receive your compensation in your hands? What will the trial preparation and court costs be? And what is the lawyer's fees?

Go through the same process with at least two different lawyers or even more, who are specialists in the personal injury field. Give each the same information and ask for the answers to the same questions. Thereafter, carefully review their answers and the impressions they make on you and then decide on the one attorney you are to hire among them.

C. What Is The Lawyer's Contingency Fee?

Now, contact that particular lawyer you have selected and discuss with him one very importannt matter: the CONTIN-GENCY FEE ARRANGEMENT he will make with you. The majority of lawyers handling automobile accident cases will usually do so on what is known as a "contingent fee" basis — that is, the fee the lawyer is to get is "contingent" (dependent) upon how much compensation he can get you in claims.

The way this basically works is that the lawyer gets a set percentage of the compensation that is recovered. Some states have now limited the percentage that can be charged. But generally speaking, you can expect the rates to be approximately 33 1/3% (i.e., one third) of the recovered amount, if settled without suit, 40% if the case goes to trial, and as high as 50%, if an appeal is taken in a case. A typical contingent fee agreement ("Authority to Represent") is shown on p. 192.

D. Insist That The Lawyers Fee Be Based Only On Whatever He Can Get You Over The Previous Offer You Had Received

Now, here's the important issue for you to resolve with the lawyer on the contingency fee matter. As you know, you had first negotiated with the insurance company and the insurance company had made you a final offer, which you had

---

[2]One analyst gives the "three best yardsticks" for selecting a competent auto accident attorney as follows: the attorney must qualify as a "Defendent's attorney" — i.e., as one who has had experience "working both sides of the street" in the sense of handling both claimants and insurance company cases; he must still have an <u>active</u> trial practice, and must have a proven successful trial record. (Baldyga, <u>How To Settle Your Own Insurance Claim</u>, p. 134).

rejected as inadequate (Step 6, Section E of Chapter 11).   That offer, in other words, is already "in the pocket, " so to speak — you already had that and could have walked away with that, if you wanted to; you already secured it on your own **without** your lawyer's input. So, when you discuss the matter with the lawyer what you should ask for is for an arrangement — a contingent fee arrangement — that will take into account the efforts you had already separately made and the previous offer you secured on your own. And the way this is done is by limiting the fee the attorney can be paid to only any amount he can get you OVER the insurance company's previous top offer to you. Let's say, for example, that you've already been offered $10,000 by the insurance adjuster. In that event, you should ask that the lawyer may not charge any fee on the first $10,000 he recovers from the company, but only on any <u>additional</u> amounts he may recover OVER and ABOVE the $10,000 amount.

Be aware though, that it's not unusual for the lawyer in such an instance to feel that he should be entitled to a higher than usual percentage in the case — something like 50% — if you're going to use the amount over what you've already been offered. But, according to one source, "generally, though, they'll go along with the usual contingent fee percentage, especially if your case is a good one, and you protest gently."[3] Besides, by the time you go to see the lawyer, you shall have done for the lawyer almost all of the research and evidence gathering work in the case. And that should be one more reason why the lawyer should consider taking a lower percentage contingent fee.

E. Using The Lawyer's Reaction To Figure Out Whether To Go Back & Accept The Adjuster's Offer

Whatever the rate you and your lawyer agree to on your case, whether it be the fairly standard 33 1/3% to 40%, or 50%, the important point is that it has to be agreed that the lawyer has to charge that applicable percentage on only the "net" amount he is able to get you **over** and **above** the offer you had previously gotten from the adjuster. And, finally, there is one further significant piece of fact you should bear in mind in this connection: *if the lawyer should refuse such a contingency fee arrangement with you, this may well be a "sure tip" to you that the original final offer you had gotten from your adjuster on your own was a realistic and fair offer, after all, and you may well be better advised to drop the idea of hiring a lawyer altogether and go back and settle on your own with the insurance company on their offer.[4]* In this connection, it is well that you recall here the advise of insurance claims expert Fred Utz, cited earlier in chapter one of the book: "don't use a lawyer [in a case] to get yourself just a <u>little</u> more money, (15% to 30% more) because his fee will eat up the difference. Use attorney [only] when you must resolve real legal questions."[5]

FOR AN EXAMPLE: Let's say the highest offer you got on your claim from the adjuster was $10,000. But, not being satisfied, you engaged a lawyer to pursue your claim for you. The settlement value your lawyer tells you he'll recover on your case is "at least" $20,000. (Actually, his specific terms are: that you have a "good to excellent" chance of getting $20,000 if the case goes to trial, a "fair" chance of getting $25,000, and the "possibility" of getting up to $30,000.) Expected out-of-pocket expenses by the lawyer if the case is settled without a trial, $1,000, and $2,000 if resolved by trial. His contingency fee percentages: One third (33 1/3%) if suit is settled, and 40% if case goes to trial.

NOTE: We'll assume for all intents and purposes this case will go to trial.

---

[3]Siegel, <u>How To Avoid Lawyers</u>, p.18.

[4]This point is made by Baldyga, <u>How to Settle Your Own Insurance Claim</u>, p.134.

[5]Utz, <u>Collision Course</u>, pp. 17-18.

TRIAL VERDICT SITUATION

Probable Trial Recovery Amount	$20,000
Less: Previous Offer Made To You	10,000
Remainder	$10,000
Less:	
Attorney's Fee @ 40% 4,000	
Attorney's Expenses 2,000	
	- 6,000
Net To You From Lawyer's Effort	$4,000

In this example, it will probably be a wiser move to employ this attorney under these terms; you stand to collect an extra $4,000 <u>over</u> and <u>above</u> the $10,000 offer you previously got from the adjuster — i.e. a 40% increment.

But what if the best recovery the lawyer promised (or actually got) were to be $15,000, rather than $20,000? Then, the lawyer's fee proposition may not be too attractive in such a situation and it may well be more economically beneficial for you to go back to the adjuster and accept his $10,000 prior offer to you. Here's how it works.

Probable Trial Recovery Amount	$15,000
Less: Previous Offer Made To You	10,000
Remainder	$ 5,000
Less:	
Attorney's Contingency Fee @40% 2,000	
Attorney's Expenses 2,000	
	- 4,000
Net To You From Your Lawyer's Effort	$1,000

NOTE: The $1,000 difference you stand to win at trial in this circumstance is not worth the risk and the troubles involved. The jury may possibly give a smaller award, or even none at all — smaller than either the $10,000 offer you previously had, or the $15,000 the lawyer obtained, or even nothing at all!

FORM 11-4

Authority to Reprsent
(Contingent Fee)

I, the undersigned client, hereby retain and employ Mr/Mrs _____ , as my attorney to represent me in my claim for damages against Mr/Mrs. _____or any other person, firm or corporation liable therefor, resulting from an accident that occourred on the _____ day of _____ 19 ___ .

As compensation for said services, I agree to pay for the costs of investigation and court costs, if necessary, and to pay for my attorney from the proceeds of recovery, the following fee:

33-1/3%   if settled without suit
40%   if suit is filed
50%   if an appeal is taken by either side

It is agreed that this employment is on a contingent fee basis, so that if no recovery is made, I will not owe my attorney any amount for attorney's fees.

Dated, this _____ day of _____ 19 ____ .

_____ (Seal)
Client

I hereby accept the above employment.

_____ (Seal)
Attorney

APPENDIX A
STATE INSURANCE COMMISSIONERS IN ALL STATES, D.C. & PR.

Listed below, are the addresses and phone numbers of the Department of Insurance for each State in the nation. Each state's Department of Insurance is headed by a Commissioner. As of this writing in late 1992, the majority of the state commissioners are appointed by the State government and serve at their pleasure, and only twelve states[1] presently elect their commissioners generally to 4-year terms.

According to recent reports,[2] state insurance departments around the country are facing increasing demands from the public for consumer information—on issues like insurance rates, policy options and rates, the financial health of individual insurance companies, record of compensation payment to claimants, and generally, information that the consumer can use to judge companies and policies. You may call, or preferably, write to the address below if you need any help with any issues concerning your claims. Among other things, you can call or write the commissioner's office to lodge a complaint about an insurance company you feel is not reasonable or forthcoming enough in making a "good faith" settlement offer; or to request information as to whether a motorist or a vehicle is insured, and so forth.

State	Title of the Head	Address
Alabama	Commissioner of Insurance	135 South Union St., #181 Montgomery, AL 36130-3401 Tel. 205-269-3550
Alaska	Director of Insurance	P.O. Box "D" Juneau, AK 99811 Tel. 907-465-2515
American Samoa	Insurance Commissioner	Office of the Governor Pago Pago, AS 96797 Tel. 684-633-4116
Arizona	Director of Insurance	3030 North 3rd St., Suite 1100 Phoenix, AZ 85012 Tel. 602-255-5400
Arkansas	Insurance Commissioner	400 University Tower Building 12th and University Streets Little Rock, AR 72204 Tel. 501-371-1325
California	Commissioner of Insurance	100 Van Ness Ave., San Francisco, CA 94102 Tel. 415-557-9624: 800-233-9045
Colorado	Commissioner of Insurance	303 W. Colfax Ave., 5th FLoor Denver, CO 80204 Tel. 303-620-4300

[1]The twelve states are: California, Delaware, Florida, Georgia, Kansas, Louisiana, Mississippi, Montana, N. Carolina, N. Dakota, Oklahoma, and Washington.

[2]"Checking on Insurance Has Risks," The N.Y. Times, March 7, 1992, p. L13.

State	Title of the Head	Address
Connecticut	Insurance Commissioner	165 Capitol Ave., State Office Bldg. Hartford, CT 06106 Tel. 203-297-3800
Delaware	Insurance Commissioner	841 Silver Lake Blvd., Dover, DE 19901 Tel. 302-736-4251: 800-282-8611
District of Columbia	Superintendent of Insurance	613 G. St., NW, 6th Floor Washington, DC 20001 Tel. 202-727-7424
Florida	Insurance Commissioner	State Capitol, Plaza Level 11 Tallahassee, FL 32399-0300 Tel. 904-488-3440: 800-342-2762.
Georgia	Insurance Commissioner	2 Martin L. King Jr. Dr. Floyd Memorial Building 716 West Tower Atlanta, GA 30334 Tel. 404-656-2056
Guam	Insurance Commissioner	P.O. Box 2796 Agana, GU 96910 Tel. 011-671-477-1040
Hawaii	Insurance Commissioner	P.O. Box 3614 Honolulu, HA 96811\ Tel. 808-548-5450: 800-548-5450
Idaho	Director of Insurance	500 S. 10th Street Boise, ID 83720 Tel. 208-334-2250
Illinois	Director of Insurance	320 W. Washington St., 4th Fl. Springfield , IL 62767 Tel. 217-782-4515
Indiana	Commissioner of Insurance	311 West Washington St., Suite 300 Indianapolis, IN 46204-2787 Tel. 317-232-2386: 800-622-4461
Iowa	Commissioner of Insurance	Lucas State Office Building, 6th Floor Des Moines, IA 50319 Tel. 515-281-5705
Kansas	Commissioner of Insurance	420 South West Ninth Street Topeka, KS 66612 Tel. 913-296-7801: 800-432-2484
Kentucky	Insurance Commissioner	229 West Maine St., P.O. Box 517 Frankfort, KY 40602 Tel. 502-564-3630
Louisiana	Commissioner of Insurance	950 North 5th Street Baton Rouge, LA 70802 Tel. 504-342-5328
Maine	Superintendent of Insurance	State House, Station 34 Augusta, ME 04333 Tel. 207-582-8707
Maryland	Insurance Commissioner	501 St. Paul Pl., 7th Fl. South Baltimore, MD 21202 Tel. 301-333-2520: 800-492-6116

State	**Title of the Head**	**Address**
Massachussetts	Commissioner of Insurance	280 Friend St., Boston, MA 02114 Tel. 617-727-7189
Michigan	Insurance Commissioner	611 West Ottawa St., 2nd Floor Lansing, MI 48933 Tel. 517-373-9273
Minnesota	Commissioner of Commerce	500 Metro Square Building, 5th Fl. St. Paul, MN 55101 Tel. 612-296-6848: 800-652-9747
Mississippi	Commissioner of Insurance	1804 Walter Sillers Building Jackson, MS 39201 (P.O. Box 79, Jackson, MS 39205) Tel. 601-359-3569
Missouri	Director of Insurance	301 W. High St., 6 North, P.O. Box 690 Jefferson City, MO 65102-0690 Tel. 314-751-2451
Montana	Commissioner of Insurance	126 North Sanders Mitchell Building Rm. 270 Helena, MT 59620 (P.O. Box 4009, Helena, MT 59604) Tel. 406-444-2040: 800-332-6148
Nebraska	Director of Insurance	Terminal Bldg., 941 O St., Suite 400 Lincoln, NE 68508 Tel. 402-471-2201
Nevada	Commissioner of Insurance	Nye Building, 201 South Fall St., Carson City, NV 89710 Tel. 702-885-4270: 800-992-0900
New Hampshire	Insurance Commissioner	169 Manchester St., Concord, NH 03301 Tel. 603-271-2261: 800-852-3416
New Jersey	Commissioner of Insurance	20 West State St., Trenton, NJ 08625 Tel. 609-292-5363
New Mexico	Superintendent of Insurance	Department of Insurance P.O. Drawer 1269 Santa Fe, NM 87504-1269 Tel. 505-827-4500
New York	Superintendent of Insurance	160 W. Broadway New York, New York 10013 Tel. 212-602-0429; 800-522-4370
North Carolina	Commissioner of Insurance	Dobbs Building, P.O. Box 26387 Raleigh, NC 27611 Tel. 919-733-7349; 800-662-7777
North Dakota	Commissioner of Insurance	Capitol Building, Fifth Floor 600 East Blvd., Bismarck, ND 58505-0320 Tel. 701-224-2440; 800-247-0560
Ohio	Director of Insurance	2100 Stella Court Columbus, OH 43266-0566 Tel. 614-644-2658: 800-282-4658

State	Title of the Head	Address
Oklahoma	Insurance Commissioner	1901 N. Walnut St., Oklahoma City, OK 73105 Tel. 405-521-2828
Oregon	Insurance Commissioner	21 Labor and Industries Bldg., Salem, OR 97310 Tel. 503-378-4271
Pennsylvania	Insurance Commissioner	1326 Strawberry Square, 13th Floor Harrisburg, PA 17120 Tel. 717-787-5173
Puerto Rico	Commissioner of Insurance	Fernandez Juncos Station P.O. Box 8330 Santurce, PR 00910 Tel. 809-722-8686
Rhode Island	Insurance Commissioner	233 Richmond St., Providence, RI 02903-4233 Tel. 401-277-2246
South Carolina	Chief Insurance Commissioner	1612 Marion St., P.O. Box 100105 Columbia, SC 29202-3105 Tel. 803-737-6117
South Dakota	Director of Insurance	Insurance Building, 910 E. Sioux Ave., Pierre, SD 57501 Tel. 605-773-3563
Tennessee	Commissioner of Insurance	500 James Robertson Pkwy., 5th Fl. Nashville, TN 37243-0565 Tel. 615-741-2241: 800-342-4029
Texas	Commissioner of Insurance	1110 San Jacinto Blvd., Austin, TX 78701-1998. Tel. 512-463-6464
Utah	Commissioner of Insurance	160 E. Third St., 300 South, Salt Lake City, UT 84111 Tel. 801-530-6400
Vermont	Commissioner of Insurance	State Office Building 120 State St., Montpelier, VT 05602 Tel. 802-828-3301
Virgin Islands	Commissioner of Insurance	Kongens Gade #18 St. Thomas, VI 00801 Tel. 809-774-2991
Virginia	Commissioner of Insurance	700 Jefferson Building Richmond, VA 23219 (P.O. Box 1157, Richmond, VA 23209) Tel. 804-786-3741; 800-552-7945
Washington	Insurance Commissioner	Insurance Building, AQ21 Olympia, WA 98504 Tel. 206-753-7301; 800-562-6900
West Virginia	Insurance Commissioner	2019 Washington St., East Charleston, WV 25305 Tel. 304-348-3394; 800-642-9004
Wisconsin	Commissioner of Insurance	123 W. Washington Ave., Madison, WI 53702 Tel. 608-266-0102
Wyoming	Insurance Commissioner	Herschler Building 122 W. 25th Street Cheyenne, WY 82002 Tel. 307-777-7401

APPENDIX B
STATUTES OF LIMITATION: YOUR STATE'S TIME LIMIT FOR STARTING A LAWSUIT

The table that follows below is intended primarily for use by parties who know of their injury on the date it occurred. For such persons, the deadline for filing a lawsuit expires in the same date of the injury at the end of the statutory period—that is, a suit on an injury that occurs, say, on October 1, 1992 must be filed by October 1, 1993 in a state with a one-year deadline.

If, on the other hand, you discovered your injury only later after it occurred, the statutory period typically begins from the first day you knew of the injury or from the day a court determines you should have known. There are many variations in late-discovery injuries and the table lists the principal ones; but in late-discovery injuries, it is advised that you always consult an attorney just on that point alone, if nothing else, so as to make sure you protect and preserve your rights. The table gives the general rule for filing most auto related personal-injury suits where the victim survived.

STATUTE OF LIMITATIONS
(Yearly Time-Limits for Starting of Action)

STATE	PERSONAL INJURIES	PROPERTY DAMAGE	STATE	PERSONAL INJURIES	PROPERTY DAMAGE
1. Alabama	1	1	26 Missouri	5	5
2. Alaska	2	6	27. Montana	3	2
3. Arizona	2	2	28. Nebraska	4	4
4. Arkansas	3	3	29. Nevada	2	3
5. California	1	3	30. New Hampshire	6****	6
6. Colorado	6*	6	31. New Jersey	2	6
7. Connecticut	2**	2**	32. New Mexico	3	4
8. Delaware	2	2	33. New York	3	3
9. District of Columbia	3	3	34. North Carolina	3	3
10. Florida	4	3	35. North Dakota	6	6
11. Georgia	2	4	36. Ohio	2	2*****
12. Hawaii	2	2	37. Oklahoma	2	2
13. Idaho	2	3	38. Oregon	3	6
14. Illinois	2	5	39. Pennsylvania	2	6
15. Indiana	2	2	40. Rhode Island	3	4******
16. Iowa	2	5	41. South Carolina	6	6
17. Kansas	2***	2	42. South Dakota	3	6
18. Kentucky	1	5	43. Tennessee	1	3
19. Louisiana	1	1	44. Texas	2	2
20. Maine	6	6	45. Utah	4	3
21. Maryland	3	3	46. Vermont	3*******	3
22. Massachusetts	3	3	47. Virginia	2	5
23. Michigan	3	3	48. Washington	3	3
24. Minnesota	6	6	49. West Virginia	2	2
25. Mississippi	6	6	50. Wisconsin	3	6
			51. Wyoming	4	4

*Colorado - personal injuries two years if against an employer; maximum of 5 years on all late discovery situations. Claim against municipal government must be filed within 90 days.

**Connecticut - personal injuries as well as property damage—one year from date the injury was sustained or discovered, but maximum of 3 years from date of act or omission. (Late discovery, maximum of 3 years.)

***Kansas- personal injuries—action accrues when the act at issue causes substantial injury or the fact of the injury becomes reasonably ascertainable.

****New Hampshire - personal injuries—only one year, if injury is sustained from a skiing accident.

*****Ohio - property damage—personal property 2 years, but 4 years for real property.

******Rhode Island - property damage—4 years for a trespass action, 6 years for action of the case.

*******Vermont - personal injuries—only one year, if injury was sustained from a skiing accident.

APPENDIX C
GLOSSARY OF
LEGAL & INSURANCE TERMS

Accident- An event or occurrence that is neither forseen nor intended.

Accidental Death Clause- A clause in the life insurance policy covering what happens when the policyholder dies as a result of the accident.

Accident and Health Insurance- A type of coverage that pays benefits, sometimes including reimbursement for the loss of income, in case of sickness, accidental injury or death.

Act of God- Legal defense of unavoidable accident; another way of saying there is no negligence involved.

Actual Cash Value- The amount required to replace a damaged property, less depreciation.

Adjuster- A representative of an insurance company who is authorized to investigate, evaluate and settle claims with the claimant.

Adverse Party (or **"Third Party"**)- After the insurancecompany and you, who are the first two parties, this is the next person from whom you seek damages or who seeks them from you.

Allegation- Any charge of misconduct, made by a plaintiff against a defendant, that becomes a basis for a lawsuit; an assertion or statement by a plaintiff or defendant in a lawsuit in which the party sets forth the facts he intends to prove at trial.

Ambulance Chasing- Solicitation of personal injury cases by a lawyer or his agent, in a manner considered unethical and unlawyerly.

ASPON - Short hand for "Anosike 8-Step Strategic Program of Negotiations," the programmatic system of tactics and strategies described in this book for negotiating a fair claims settlement with the insurance company.

Answer- The pleading filed by a defendant in a lawsuit wherein that party sets forth his allegations denying or confirming the plaintiff's charges and states his own defense.

Appearance Loss- An insurance settlement that pays for the degree of damages from a covered loss when the car or other property is not worth repairing. Also called "Loss of Value."

Appraisal- An evaluation or survey of property to determine its insurable value or the amount of loss sustained.

Arbitration- A system mostly used in most jurisdictions to settle minor personal injury claims whereby both sides to a controversy submit their evidence to a panel for a decision; the binding procedure to settle a claim dispute between insurance company and policyholder without suit.

Assets- All funds, property, goods, securities, rights of action, or resources of any kind owned by a person or entity.

Assigned Risk- A means of pooling risks which no insurance carrier wants voluntarily, as required by law.

Assumption of Risk- A ground for defense in a personal injury case that contends that the injured party, by his own acts or negligence, placed himself in a hazardous or dangerous position ("assumed") or intentionally or unreason ably exposed himself to danger ("risk"), and therefore inadvertently participated in the injury's occurrence.

Automobile Insurance Plan- One of several types of "shared market" mechanisms used to make automobile insurance available to persons who are unable to obtain such insurance in the voluntary market.

Automobile Liability Insurance- Protection for the insured against financial loss because of legal liability for car-related injuries to others or damage to their property.

Automobile Physical Damage Insurance- Coverage to pay for damage to or loss of an insured automobile resulting from collision, fire, theft, or other perils.

Automobile Reinsurance Facility- One of several types of "shared market" mechanisms used to make automobile insurance available to persons who are unable to obtain such insurance in the regular market.

Automobile Shared Market- A program in which all automobile insurers in each state and the District of Columbia participate to make coverage available to car owners who are unable to obtain auto insurance in the voluntary market. Except in Maryland, which operates a state-funded mechanism whose losses are subsidized by private insurers, each state uses one of three systems (an automobile insurance plan, a joint underwriting association, or a reinsurance facility) to guarantee the availability of automobile insurance.

Award- Determination made by a judicial body which grants a sum of money to the party that wins.

Bad Faith- An insurer's unreasonable denial of a claim or his unreasonable denial of a third party's settlement offer.

Betterment- The amount by which the value of a depreciated item is enhanced by being replaced new.

Binder- A temporary or preliminary agreement showing the existence of a customer's insurance until the insurer formally issues the actual insurance policy.

Blanket Coverage- Insurance coverage covering more than one item of property at a single location or two or more items of property at different locations.

Bodily-Injury-Liability Coverage- Protection for the policyholder in the event that he or she is held financially responsible for another person's bodily injury, sickness or death.

Book Value- The value placed on a used vehicle by an established guide (NADA, Red or Blue Book, etc.); an average retail price of vehicle.

Captive Agent- An insurance agent who represents only one insurance company.

Carrier- Another name for the insurance company (the one who "carries" the policy or risk.)

Case Law- The body of decisions from the appelate courts of a jurisdiction which partially establish the law of that jurisdiction.

Cash Value- The amount available in cash if an insurance policy holder surrenders or borrows from a policy.

Claim- A demand to recover money for a loss covered by an insurance policy.

Claimant- One who presents a demand for a compensation for loss sustained.

Collateral Source- Any person or entity, other than the defendant in a case, that pays money to an injured person, due to the injury—e.g., payment by Blue Cross/Blue Shield toward a victim's medical bills.

Collision Insurance Coverage- Coverage which insures against any damage to the policyholder's vehicle by collision with another object or upset.

Collusion- An agreement between two or more persons to proceed fraudulently to the detriment and prejudice of an innocent and ignorant third party.

Comparative Negligence- The principle which operates in certain states whereby your award is reduced by the degree of your fault in causing the accident.

Comparative Damages- Any costs or an injury for which payment is permitted in a suit, other than punitive damages.

Comprehensive Coverage- Coverage that insures against any loss or damage to a vehicle except collision or upset.

Compulsory Insurance- Any form of insurance that is required of all parties by law.

Consquential Loss- A loss resulting from, but not caused directly by, an insured peril—e.g., any spoilage of contents resulting from the loss of refrigeration, which was itself caused by a fire.

Constructive Total Loss- A vehicle considered a total loss because the sum of its damage and its salvage value exceeds its total actual cash value.

Contingency Fee- The percentage that the plaintiff pays his lawyer from the money won in a suit or claim.

Contributory Negligence- An act or omission on the part of the damaged party which was a partial cause of the accident.

Coverage- The scope of protection provided under a contract of insurance; any of several risks covered by a policy.

Damages- One's injuries; also the dollar value (compensation) one may recover for loss or injury caused the victim.

'Deep-Pocket' Defendant- A term used by lawyers to refer to a defendant (e.g., an insurance company, a large corporation, or a unit of government) that is financially capable of paying a judgement and is also perceived by the public (and jurors) as having the capacity.

Deductible- The amount a policy holder agrees to pay, per claim or per accident, toward the total amount of an insured loss. Insurance is written at reduced rates depending on how high the deductible is.

Default- Failure of a party to a lawsuit to appear and defend the lawsuit.

Defendant- The party against whom a plaintiff brings his action to recover damages.

Deposition- Oral testimony of a witness taken out of court. The witness swears to tell the truth, a court reporter records the questions and answers, and the whole proceeding is transcribed for later use at trial.

Depreciation- A deduction taken during the valuation of an item of property in order to account for the fact that the property is no longer new.

Double Damages (Prohibition of)- The legal doctrine holding that a defendant cannot be required to pay twice for the same injury.

"Double Dipping"- A practice by which attorneys collect excess fees by taking commissions from both the client and a subrogation claimant.

Economic Loss- The estimated total cost, both insured and uninsured, of mishaps (such as motor vehicle accidents, work accidents, and fires); includes such factors as property damages, funeral expenses, wage loss, insurance administration costs, and medical, hospital and legal costs.

Elimination Period- A specific period of time, beginning at the onset of a disability, that must pass before any policy benefits will be paid. Also known as the "waiting period."

Endorsement- A form attached to any insurance policy to add to, alter, or vary its provisions.

Estimate- An itemized list of visible damages and the cost to repair; a preliminary or inconclusive assessment of damages.

Excess Letter- A letter sent by an insurance company to its insured informing the insured that a suit filed against him seeks damages in excess of the liability coverage provided by his policy.

Exclusion- A provision in an insurance policy that denies coverage for certain perils, persons, property, or locations.

Extended Coverages- Protection against property damage caused by windstorm, hail, smoke, explosion, riot, or civil commotion, vehicle, and aircraft.

Fair-Market Value- The price that other items of this type bring on the open market; what an item can be readily sold for.

Field Adjuster- An adjuster who handles claims by personally inspecting the insured's loss rather than relying on information provided by telephone.

Financial-Responsibility Law- A law under which a person involved in an automobile accident may be required to furnish security up to a certain minimum dollar limits.

First-Party Claim- A claim made by an insured to his own insurance company for a loss he has suffered.

Foreseeability- In negligence law, evidence that indicates that either the plaintiff or the defendant could reasonably have predicted the probability of the injury and taken steps to prevent it. In strict liability, the rule that requires a manufacturer to warn users of a product of dangers arising not only from its proper use but from resonably predictable misuses.

Fraud- A deception or intentional misrepresentation for the purpose of depriving another of property or of denying him something to wish he is legally entitled.

General Damages- Compensation that is permitted for injuries which are the natural or inevitable consequences (the 'intangibles') of an injury, such as pain and suffering and mental anguish.

General Liability Insurance- A form of coverage that pertains, for the most part, to claims arising out of the insured's liability for injuries or damage caused by ownership of property, manufacturing operations, contracting operations, or sale or distribution of products.

Grace Period- A specified amount of time (often 30 or 31 days) after a premium payment is due in which the policyholder may make such payment without incurring a penalty or loss of coverage.

Guaranteed Renewable Contract- A contract that the insurer has no right to change unilaterally as long as the policy is in force, other than to make a change in the premium rate for classes of policyholders.

Hazard- A condition that creates or increases the risk of property damage, bodily injury, or loss of life.

Health Insurance- Insurance that indemnifies an insured for the medical expenses incurred as a result of illness, injuries, and accidents covered by the policy.

Health Maintenance Organization (HMO)- A prepaid, comprehensive health insurance plan, with fixed rates being paid for services by specified medical providers.

Home Office- The headquarters of an insurance company, usually situated in the state in which the firm was incorporated.

Immunity- Protection from suit by statute.

Impact Rule- In negligence cases, the requirement that a plaintiff, to have grounds for suit, must have been touched by the defendant, or by some instrument, such as an automobile, in the defendant's control. The impact rule does not apply to intentional torts.

Indemnify- To pay for another's hurt, loss, or damage.

Independent Adjuster- A self-employed independent contractor who adjusts claims on a case-by-case basis for more than one insurance company.

Informed Consent- The right of a person to receive understandable information about the risks inherent in a service proposed for that person. Commonly used to refer to a doctor's duty to inform a patient of predictable dangers in a course of treatment for an illness; also, the form signed by the patient stating that the risks are undertood and allowing the procedure to take place.

Injury- Legally, any wrongfully inflicted harm, physical or emotional, by one party upon another.

Insurance- Protection by written contract against the financial hazards of specified happenings or fortuitous events.

Insurance Company- Any corporation primarily engaged in the business of selling insurance protection to the public.

Insurance Policy- A written contract between an insurance company and an insured in which the former agrees to indemnify the latter against certain losses for a stated amount of premium.

Insured- A person who is covered by an insurance policy. The term includes not only the specific person named in the policy but also any unnamed persons defined by the policy as being covered, such as members of the named insured's family.

Insurer- Another name for an insurance company.

Intentional Act- A deed done on purpose and not by accident.

Intentional Tort- A ground for a personal-injury suit that occurs when the perpetrator deliberately seeks to harm or does harm to the victim, either by a physical blow, by verbal harassment, by threat, or through any other malicious form of action.

Interrogatories- Questions posed in writing by one side to the other side's witnesses.

Intervening Injury- An injury that occurs after the injury that led to the suit, usually, although not necessarily, at the same site as the original injury. The defense will usually try to prove that the second injury is the reason for all or part of the damages the plaintiff is claiming.

Judgement- The verdict in a case. Also, often used to describe the amount of money a defendant is directed to pay.

Liability- Legal responsibility or guilt for an act. A losing defendant is liable (must pay) the plaintiff for the injury that was caused.

Liability Insurance- Insurance covering the policyholder's legal liability resulting from injuries to other persons or damage to their property.

Liability Limits- The stipulated sum or sums beyond which an insurance company is not liable to protect the insured.

Limitations Period- The maximum time allowed by an insurance policy or statute for a party to file suit on a cause of action.

Litigation- The name given to the entire legal process under which one party sues another.

Loss- The amount of insurance or benefits for which the insurer becomes liable when the event insured against occurs.

Lowballing- Unfair claim settlement practices by which unscrupulous adjusters try to achieve unfairly low settlements with the insureds.

Malicious Mischief- Damage or destruction willfully inflicted on another person's property.

Material Damage Appraiser- An insurance company employee experienced in estimating the cost of repairing automobiles, whose job is to estimate repair costs in automobile accident cases.

Medical-Expense Insurance- A liability coverage in which the insurer agrees to reimburse the insured and others for medical or funeral expenses incurred under specific conditions without regard for the insured's liability.

Mediation- A system for resolving personal-injury suits in which an outside person, a lawyer or a judge, gets the two sides together to help resolve the differences between them. Mediation differs from arbitration in that the mediator makes no binding decision on the case or formal declaration on the merits of the case.

Mental Anguish- A ground for financial recovery in a personal-injury suit; the fear, worry, depression, or loss of life's pleasures arising from the circumstances of an accident or its aftermath.

Miscellaneous Expenses- A category of expenses under hospital insurance, such as for X-rays, drugs, and laboratory tests—i.e., charges other than room and board.

Mitigation- Evidence presented by the defendant to show that the amount of dollar damages claimed by the plaintiff is excessive.

Named Perils- Perils specified in a policy as those against which the policyholder is insured.

Negligence- An act , by one party, arising out of incompetence or carelessness or any failure to perform a known duty properly, that accidentally causes injury to another party; failure to use the degree of care that a person of reasonable prudence would use under given or similar circumstances.

No-Fault Auto Insurance- A form of insurance by which certain financial losses resulting from an automobile accident such as medical expenses and loss of income, are paid by a person's own insurance company without regard to fault.

Nominal Damages- An award, usually no more than one dollar, made to a plaintiff who has shown that a defendant caused a compensable injury, but for which there is not proof of the infliction of substantative harm or monetary loss.

Nonsuit- A declaration by a judge ending a suit in the defendant's favor, following a motion to dismiss it by the defense. Can occur prior to trial or during trial. Commonly, the dismissal is based on a determination that the plaintiff failed to substantiate an allegation of wrongdoing with admissable evidence, or that the plaintiff, through failure to respond to the defense motion, has abandoned the suit.

Nuisance Settlement- A term used mostly by insurance companies to describe a small amount of money paid to a plaintiff to end a claim or suit that is minor in nature and usually of little or doubtful legal merit.

Obvious Total Loss- A vehicle so severely damaged that its repair price exceeds its replacement cost regardless of salvage value.

Office Adjuster- An adjuster who works in a branch claims office, rather than in the field, and who adjusts claims primarily over the telephone.

Old Damage (O.D.)- Any damage which preceded that involved in a current insurance claim and not included in the appraisal total.

Open Items- When parts on an appraisal are suspected of being damaged but not certain, they are listed as "open."

Pain and Suffering- A ground for financial recovery in a personal-injury suit; essentially, the physical agony caused the plaintiff by the injury. It is to be distinguished from mental anguish, which relates to the fear caused by the injury.

Pain and Suffering Award- An amount of cash paid to compensate the victim of an automobile accident for the pain and inconvenience involved.

Partial Loss- An insurance loss which is not total and indicates the vehicle is repairable.

Peril- The cause of possible loss, such as collision, fire or natural disasters.

Plaintiff- The party bringing an action in court.

Pleading- A document in which a party to a civil lawsuit sets forth his allegation regarding the case. In personal-injury cases, usually refers to that part of the suit that states the losses suffered by the plaintiff and the defendant's response to those allegations.

Policy- A contract of insurance.

Policyholders' Surplus- An insurance company's assets minus its liabilities.

Policy Holder- A person to whom an insurance policy has been issued.

Policy Limits Settlement Offer- An offer by a third-party claimant to settle his claim against an insured for an amount that is within the liability limits of the insured's insurance policy.

Policy Term- The period for which an insurance provides coverage.

Precedent- A ruling in an earlier case that is applied to determine the law in a current case.

Premium- The money that na insured pays or has agreed to pay to his insurer in exchange for insurance coverage.

Preponderance of the Evidence- The greater portion of the evidence. Plaintiffs who can show that the preponderance of the evidence favors them will prevail in a personal-injury suit unless contributory negligence on their part rules out a victory.

Proof of Loss- A sworn, written statement made by an insured to his insurer regarding a loss, intended to enable the insurer to determine the extent of its liability under the policy.

Property Insurance- Insurance that indemnifies a property owner for harm to his property caused by a peril covered by the policy.

Proximate Cause- The efficient cause of an insured loss through an unbroken chain of events; the direct or precipitating cause of an injury.

Public Adjuster- A self-employed adjuster who represents insurance claimants against their insurance companies in exchange for a share of the claimant's recovery.

Punitive Damages- An award made in a personal-injury case, in addition to any other award, when the perpetrator of the injury has been shown to have acted in gross disregard for the safety of the victim, either through malice or negligence. Sometimes also called *exemplary* ("to make an example of") *damages or "smart"* (in the sense of "pain") money.

Reasonable-Man Doctrine- The standard required of an individual to determine negligence in many personal-injury trials, by which the jury is asked to decide what a normally prudent person would have done to avoid the injury. Thus, if the jury decides that a "reasonable-man" plaintiff would have acted differently from this plaintiff, the defendant may be found innocent; if a "reasonable man" defendant would have taken steps to prevent the injury that this defendant didn't take, then the defendant may be found liable.

Reduction to Present Value- The legal requirement that the gross amount awarded for a plaintiff's loss of future earnings be lessened to include the amount of interest the plaintiff could earn on the award over the years it is supposed to cover.

Release- An instrument evidencing the discharge of a claim or right to one as against another.

Replacement Cost- The cost to replace your damaged property at today's prices.

Respondent- One who is required to answer charges brought in a suit.

Respondeat Superior- The principle in law which transfers liability to the principal for the negligent act of his agent, with the principal being responsible for the acts of his agent when committed within the scope of the agent's employment. Literally means, "the master is responsible" (for the acts of his servants)

Retainer- The initial fee a client pays to an attorney to secure the attorney's professional services.

Risk- The probable amount of loss foreseen by an insurer in issuing a contract.

Salvage- Property taken over by an insurer after paying a claim to reduce its loss.

Settlement- The resolution of a claim or suit with payment to the plaintiff (claimant) that is arrived at without a trial . Normally, it is the result of private negotiations between the opposing sides, but it can also result from arbitration or the intervention of the judge who has been assigned to hear the case.

Special Damages, (or "Specials.")- Injury-related out-of-pocket costs and expenses of an injury for which a plaintiff may be compensated and which must be proved in specific dollar terms. Specials include both existent costs and those that are reasonably likely to occur in the future. Medical expenses and income losses are the most common form of special damages that result from an injury.

Standard of Care- The degree of responsibility to which a person is legally held for acts that cause harm to others; often used in conjunction with the duty of licensed people, such as doctors or pilots to provide competent services in their field of expertise.

Standard Risk- A person classified by an insurance company as being entitled to protection without extra rating or special restriction.

State Insurance Department- A department of a state government whose duty it is to regulate the business of insurance and give the public information on insurance.

Statute of Limitations- The period of time a person has to file suit after an injury has occurred.

Statutory Law- Any regulation enacted by a legislative body at the local, state, or federal level of government. Some laws controlling personal-injury litigation are statutory, while others are based on the common law.

Stipulation- An agreement between opposing sides in a suit admitting that a certain allegation or statement is true.

Strict Liability- A legal doctrine holding that some situations, activities, animals, and products are by their nature unreasonably dangerous and that those who are in control of them can be held responsible for the injuries they cause even though the controller neither intended the harm nor caused it by a negligent act.

Subrogation- A procedure for collecting on an automobile claim when the other driver was at fault by collecting from your insurance company, minus the deductible, and then letting your insurance collect from the other driver's insurance, hopefully recovering your deductible for you.

Subrogation Claim- A demand for repayment made against a successful plaintiff (claimant) by a party that has paid money on the plaintiff's behalf or directly to the plaintiff as a result of the injury that caused the suit.

Substandard Risk- An individual who, because of health history or driving record, does not measure up to the underwriting criteria of a standard risk.

Suit- A legal document, filed in court and delivered to the defendant, in which the plaintiff sets forth the circumstances of an injury the defendant allegedly caused, and makes a demand for money to rectify the harm done.

Survival Statutes- Laws, varying from state to state, permitting survivors of a person wrongfully killed to be paid for the decedent's pain and suffering, medical bills, funeral bills, and the like. Usually brought in conjunction with a wrongful-death suit.

"Sympathetic" Plaintiff- A term used by lawyers to describe a plaintiff who, because of what he or she is—such as an injured child—is likely to evoke a sympathetic and favorable verdict (and usually a large award) from a jury, even when the evidence in the case doesn't warrant such a result.

"Target" Defendant- A term used by lawyers to describe a defendant that has a poor public reputation and is therefore likely to be found liable by a jury regardless of the merits of the case.

Telephone Adjusting- The process of adjusting claims by gathering the necessary information over the telephone.

Third-Party Claim- A claim made by one person against another, who hopefully has liability insurance covering the claim.

Time Limit- The period of time during which notice of claim or proof of loss must be filed.

Total Loss- Damage to a vehicle or other property which makes it uneconomical to repair.

Tort- An action by which one party wrongfully takes or attempts to take another person's property, infringes on that person's privacy or civil rights or harms or attempts to harm that person's body; a civil injury or wrong that is compensable through a civil lawsuit.

Tortfeasor- One who commits a tort, or wrongful injury. A defendant in a personal-injury suit is said to be a tortfeasor.

Transcript- A document reproducing the testimony given at a trial or deposition, as recorded by a court stenographer.

Trauma- An injury, physical or emotional.

Umbrella Liability- A form of protection against losses in excess of the amount covered by other liability insurance policies. It also protects against many situations not covered by the usual liability policies.

Umpire- In property insurance, the third party to an appraisal process selected by the two opposing appraisers to resolve any differences between the two appraisers.

Underinsured-Motorist Coverage- Insurance that pays the insured's losses when the driver at fault has inadequate liability coverage.

Underwriter- A term that applies to any of the following: (1) a company that receives premiums and accepts responsibility for the fulfillment of the policy contract; (2) a company employee who decides whether the company should assume a particular risk; (3) the agent who sells the policy.

Uninsured-Motorist Coverage- Insurance that pays for your losses when the other driver is at fault but is uninsured or can't be found.

Venue- The judicial district in which the site of an impending judicial proceeding is located.

Vicarious Responsibility or Liability- The imputation of responsibility or liability upon one person for the actions of another. In tort law, if an employee, EE, while in the scope of his employment for employer, ER, drives a delivery truck, and hits and injures P, ER, will be vicariously liable under the doctrine of *respondeat superior,* for the injuries sustained by P.

Waiver- An agreement to give up a legal right.

Wanton Conduct- An injurious action of such recklessness or malice that it becomes grounds for a punitive damage award; also, an action of such magnitude in terms of the degree of misdoing that contributory negligence by the plaintiff need not be considered.

Whiplash- A spinal injury to the neck of the victim, often caused by the impact of a rear-end automobile collision. Because the existence of whiplash is difficult either to prove or disprove medically, it is viewed skeptically by insurance adjusters as an injury that can sometimes be faked, and adjusters, judges and juries often tend, as a result, to be skeptical of it as an injury allegation.

APPENDIX D
A SHORT GLOSSARY OF THE MORE COMMON MEDICAL TERMS USED IN PERSONAL INJURY CASES

Active Motion: A voluntary movement made by a person, or the extent to which he will move a member of his body.

Adhesion: The uniting of one surface with another by scar tissue.

Aneurysm: A dilation, or saccule formation, of an artery. The source may be congenital, luetic, or arteriosclerotic.

Angina: Pain referred to the heart, usually associated with physical effort. It is due, in most instances, to inadequate blood supply to the heart muscle.

Angiography: The visualization of blood vessels by the use of X-ray and the injection of some form of contrast material.

Ankylosis: Complete or partial loss of motion in a joint; the union of bones forming a joint causing a stiff joint.

Anterior - Posterior: Front to back.

Apposition: The fitting together.

Aphakia: Absence of the lens of the eye.

Aphasia: Loss of power of speech; inability to talk.

Arteriosclerosis or atherosclerosis: So-called "hardening of the arteries." A degenerative condition in which the walls of the arteries lose their elasticity and at times become calcified. As a result, there may be some restriction of blood flow.

Arthrodesis: An operative procedure to eliminate a joint and cause fusion of two adjacent bones.

Arthrography: The visualization of the interior of a joint by use of contrast material and X-ray.

Arthroplasty: An operative procedure to restore motion to a joint.

Arthroscope: A surgical instrument that can be inserted into a joint through a small incision, allowing visualization of the interior of the joint, and allowing surgical procedures of certain types.

Cerebral Concussion: A minute and diffuse injury to the brain caused by direct or indirect violence. A diagnostic symptom is a loss of consciousness of momentary to prolonged degree. There is often a transient, or permanent, loss of memory for detail preceeding the accident for a short time. Symptoms of dizziness or headache, known as the "post-concussion syndrome," may persist for some time, without any objective neurological evidence of damage.

Contact Dermatitis: A skin condition secondary to exposure to some substance for which the patient possesses an allergy or sensitivity.

Coronary Heart Disease: A disease process of the arteries that supply the heart causing chest pain or heart muscle damage, which derives from degenerative changes in the tissue of the artery wall. It is believed to bear a relationship to arteriosclerosis.

CT Scan: "CT" stands for "Computerized Tomography." A special X-ray technique which, combined with the computer, allows visualization of the internal parts of the body in better detail than in ordinary X-ray study. At times it is used with injection of contrast materials.

Cystoscope: An instrument to examine the interior of the urinary bladder.

Dislocation: Displacement of an organ or joint surfaces.

Distal: Fartherest away from the body.

Empyema: A collection of pus within the pleural cavity.

Exploratory: In reference to surgery, means that the diagnosis prior to operation is not too definite, and that actual visualization of pathology is necessary to effect a correct diagnosis.

Foot-drop: An inability to dorsiflex or raise the foot, which results in a dragging gait, and is indicative of pathology involving the peroneal nerve.

Functional: In reference to disease, infers that no organic pathology can be found.

Hyperesthesia: Descriptive of an increase in skin sensation.

Hypesthesia (Hypoesthesia): Descriptive of a decrease in skin sensation.

IVP: An abbreviation for "intravenous pyelogram," in which a dye is injected into a vein and the kidney outline is apparent on an X-ray.

Joint-mice: Presence of cartilaginous loose bodies free within a joint cavity.

Laminectomy: A surgical procedure removing part, or all, or the lamina of the vertebrae. The lamina is the bony strut that stands between the body and the spinous process on each side and encloses the spinal canal. The term is sometimes used to indicate the operation for removal of a ruptured, or herniated, intervertebral disc.

Lateral: From the side.

Loose Bodies: This term is used interchangeably with joint-mice.

Lymphadenitis: Inflammation of the lymph glands, secondary to infection.

Meniscus: A small, crescent-shaped piece of cartilage found at the medial and lateral sides of the knee joint.

Myositis: Inflammation of a muscle.

Neuritis: Inflammation of a nerve.

Neurosis: A condition in which mental, or physical, symptoms may occur secondary to some form of subconscious conflict. Although in most cases no organic pathology can be found, the condition may progress to the point where physiological changes occur. A not uncommon condition, it is one that should be distinguished from malingering, that is, situations in which the individual consciously manufactures symptoms for monetary or other gain. A "traumatic neurosis" is the development of neurotic symptoms that have been precipitated by an accident or injury.

Oblique: At an angle, midway between anterior-posterior and lateral.

Opthalmology: The field of scientific information concerning the eye.

Organic: In reference to disease, organic means that there is actual tissue pathology as a source for the condition.

Otology: The field of scientific information regarding the ear.

Paracentesis: To remove fluid from within a cavity by means of a large needle.

Paralysis: This may be *spastic* or *flaccid*. In the flaccid type there is no voluntary control of the muscles involved, and they are in a completely relaxed condition with absence of muscle tone. In the spastic type there is usually no voluntary control, but the muscles remain in a chronic state of contraction and rigidity.

Paresis: This may refer to softening of the brain, such as may occur with syphilis, with a disturbance of mental function. The term is also frequently used to indicate a muscular weakness of neurologic origin, rather than complete paralysis.

Paresthesia: Abnormal skin sensation in the form of itching, prickling, burning, crawling sensations, etc.

Passive Motion: Submissive motion or the extent to which the person will allow the member of his body to be moved by the examiner.

Phlebitis: Inflammation of a vein.

Pleurisy: Inflammation of the covering membrane of the lungs.

Proximal: Closest to the body.

Psychosis: A severe form of mental illness in which the individual loses contact with reality.

Revision: In reference to surgery, to reconstruct or remodel.

Shock: The state of physical collapse.

Spinal Tap: To remove spinal fluid by means of a needle.

Sprain: The result when muscles or ligaments are partially torn, joint fluids may escape,and nerves or blood vessels may be damaged.

Strain: The excessive stretching or overuse of muscles or ligaments.

Tenosynovitis: Inflammation of a tendon and it's sheath.

Ultrasound: High-frequency sound waves which may be used for treatment, or diagnosis, of certain types of pathology.

Varicosity: Refers to varicose veins, meaning abnormal dilatation of certain portions of a vein. This usually leads to failure of valves within the vein and, secondarily, to interference with normal circulation.

Visual Field: An outline of the area of general vision when the eye is kept on a fixed point.

APPENDIX E
COMMON ROOTS, PREFIXES & SUFFIXES USED IN MEDICAL WORDS

Roots

Aden	gland	**Gastr**	stomach	**Path**	disease
Bio	life	**Gynec**	woman	**Ped**	children
Cardi	heart	**Hem** or **hemat**	blood	**Ped**	feet
Cephal	head	**Hyster**	uterus	**Pneum**	lung
Chole	bile	**Kerat**	cornea	**Proct**	anus
Chondr	cartilage	**Leuc**	white	**Psych**	mind
Cost	rib	**My**	muscle	**Py**	pus
Crani	skull	**Neph**	kidney	**Pyel**	pelvis
Cyst	sac	**Oopher**	ovary	**Rhin**	nose
Cyt	cell	**Ophthalm**	eye	**Salping**	tube
Derm	skin	**Oss** or **oste**	bone	**Septic**	poison
Encephal.	brain	**Ot**	ear	**Tox**	poison
Enter	intestine	**Ovar**	ovary	**Trache**	trachea

Prefixes

A- or **An-**	absence of	**Glosso**	relating to the tongue	**Osteo-**	pertaining to bone
A- or **Ab-**	from, away	**Hemi**	half	**Para-**	faulty, related to
Ad-	to, toward, near	**Hetero**	other	**Per-**	throughout
Ambi	both	**Homo**	same	**Peri-**	around
Ante	before	**Hydro**	relating to water	**Phelb-**	veins
Anti	against	**Hyp**	under or reduced	**Poly-**	many
Auto	self	**Hyper**	above or excessive	**Post-**	after
Bi	two	**Hypo**	below or deficient	**Pre-**	before
Circum	around	**In-**	in	**Pro-**	before
Contra	against, opposed	**In-**	not	**Pseud-**	false
Counter	against-	**Infra-**	below	**Pulmo-**	relating to the lungs
Di-	two	**Inter-**	between	**Retro-**	backward
Dis-	the opposite of	**Intra-**	within	**Scolio-**	twisted - bent
Dys-	difficult, painful	**Lipo-**	relating to fat	**Semi-**	half
Ecto-	outside	**Macro-**	large	**Sub-**	under
En-	in	**Micro-**	small	**Super-**	above
Eu-	well	**Mon-**	single	**Supra-**	above, upon
Ex- or **E-**	from, without	**Mult-**	much or many	**Sym-** or **Syn-**	with, together
Exo-	outside	**Odont -**	teeth	**Trans-**	across
Extra-	outside	**Onych-**	nails	**Tri-**	three
				Uni	one

Suffixes

algia	pain	**ostomy**	forming an opening
asis	condition, state	**otomy**	cutting into
asthenia	weakness	**patho**	disease
cele	tumor, hernia	**pathy**	disease
cyte	cell	**penia**	insufficiency
ectasis	dilation	**pexy**	fixation
ectomy	excision (cutting out)	**phagia**	eating
emia	blood	**phasia**	speech
esthesia	feeling, sensation	**phobia**	fear
genic	causing	**plasty**	molding
itis	inflammation	**pnea**	breathing
logy	science of	**ptosis**	falling
oma	tumor	**rhythmia**	rhythm
osis	condition, state	**rrhaphy**	suture of
		uria	urine

APPENDIX F
PRINCIPAL ABBREVIATIONS ("SHORT HAND") USED IN MEDICAL PRACTICE AND REPORTS

Abbreviation	Definition	Abbreviation	Definition
a.	artery	C.	centigrade
abd.; Abd	abdomen	Ca.	cancer
A.B.P.	arterial blood pressure	cap(s).	capsule(s)
abs	absent	car.	carotid
a.c.	before meals	CAT Scan	computerized axial tomography
acc.	accident	CBC	complete blood count
accom.	accomodation	cc.	cubic centimeter(s)
A.C.E.P.	Amerian College of Emergency Physicians	C.C.	chief complaint
		CCU	Cardiac Care Unit
ACG	angiocardiogram	CDC	Center for Disease Control
ACH	adrenal cortical hormone	Cerv.	cervix; or cervical
A.D.A.	American Dental Association	ch	chest
adm.	admission	CHD	coronary heart disease
A/J	ankle jerk	CHF	congestive heart failure
A.M.A.	American Medical Association	Clav.	clavicle
amb	ambulatory	cm.	centimeter
A & P	auscultation and percussion	CNS	central nervous system
AP	anteroposterior	CO	carbon monoxide
Ap.	water	CO_2	carbon dioxide
art.	artery	Coc.	coccygeal
ATP	adenosine triphosphate	contra	against; contraindication
AV	atrioventricular	Cran.	cranial
Bab.	Babinski's sign	Cr. Ns.	cranial nerves
BaEn; BE; BaEnema	Barium enema	CSF	cerebrospinal fluid
Bas.	basal	cu.	cubic
Bic.	biceps	CV	cardiovascular
b.i.d.	twice a day	CVA	cerebrovascular accident; costovertebral angle
b.i.n.	twice a night		
bk.	back	CVD	cardiovascular disease
blad.	bladder		
bld.	blood	D & C	dilatation and curettage
BM	bowel movement	D.D.S.	Doctor of Dental Surgery
BMR	basal metabolic rate	dehyd.	dehydration
BP	blood pressure	depr.	depressed
Brach.	brachial	D.O.	Doctor of Osteopathy
BUN	blood urea nitrogen	DOA	dead on arrival
c̄	with	Dors.	dorsal
		DPT	diphtheria-pertussis-tetanus

Abbreviation	Definition
Dr.	Doctor
DTR's	deep tendon reflexes
Dx	diagnosis
ECG; EKG	electrocardiogram
ECM; EOM	extraocular movements
EEG	electroencephalogram
EENT	eye, ear, nose and throat
Elev.	elevated
EMG	electromyogram
En.	enema
ENT	ear, nose, and throat
ESR	erythrocyte sedimentation rate
extens.	extensors
F.	Fahrenheit scale; or finger
f	female
F.A.C.P.	Fellow of the American College of Physicians
F.A.C.S.	Fellow of the American College of Surgeons
FDA	Food and Drug Administration
fem.	femur; or femoral
f.h.s.	fetal heart sounds
f.h.t.	fetal heart tones
flac.	flaccid
fld.; fl.	fluid
flex.	flexor
fl. oz.	fluid ounces
Fr.; Frx; Fx; frac.	fracture
FSH	follicle-stimulating hormone
Ft.	foot; or feet
G.B.	gallbladder
GI; G.I.	gastrointestinal
gm.; Gm.	gram(s)
gr.	grain(s)
gt; gtt.; Gtt.	drop(s)
G.U.	genitourinary
Gyn.	gynecologic; gynecology; or gynecologist
H.	Hypodermic
H.; hr.	hour
hb; hgb; hg.	hemoglobin
hct	hematocrit
HCI.	hydrochloric acid
Hd.	head
hern.	herniation
h.s.	at bedtime
Ht.	height; or heart
hypo; H.	hypodermically
I & D	incision and drainage
ICU	Intensive Care Unit

Abbreviation	Definition
I.M.	intramuscular
in.	inch
inj.	injection; or injured
IPPB	intermittent positive pressure breathing
I.Q.	intelligence quotient
IRV	inspiratory reserve volume
I.U.	International Unit
IUD	intrauterine device
I.V.	intravenous
IVD	intervertebral disc
IVP	intravenous pyelogram
Jt.	joint
K	Kelvin scale
K.	kidney; or potassium
kg.	kilogram
KJ	knee-jerk reflex
km.	kilometer
K.U.B.; KUB	kidney, ureter and bladder
L.	liter(s)
L & A	light and accommodation
lab.	laboratory
lac.	laceration
lam.	laminectomy
lap.	laparotomy
lb.	pound
lg.	leg; or large
LH	luteinizing hormone
lig.	ligament
liq.	liquid; or fluid
LLQ	left lower quadrant
LMP; l.m.p.	last menstrual period
LP; L.P.	lumbar puncture
L.P.N.	Licensed Practical Nurse
LSK	liver, spleen and kidney
Lt.; lt	left; or light
lumb.	lumbar
M.; m.	meter; or male
MBC	maximum breathing capacity
mcg.	microgram(s)
M.D.	Doctor of Medicine
med.	medical
mg.	milligram(s)
ml.	milliliter(s)
mm.	millimeter(s); or muscle(s)
mol. wt.	molecular weight
MS	multiple sclerosis
M.T.	muscles & tendons
musc.; mm	muscle(s)

Abbreviation	Description	Abbreviation	Description
N.A.D.	No Appreciable Disease	Px.	physical examination
n; Ns	nerve(s)	q; q	every
N	nitrogen	q.h.	every hour
N₂O	nitrous oxide	q.2h.	every two hours
Na	sodium	q.i.d.	four times a day
NaCl	sodium chloride	q.m.; qam	every morning
neg.	negative	q.n.	every night
neur.; neurol.	neurology; or neurologist	qt	quart
no.	number		
noc.	night	R.	respiration; or rectal
norm.	normal	RA	rheumatoid arthritis;
N.S.	Nervous System		or residual air
		rad.	radial
O.	pint	rad	radiation absorbed dose
O₂	oxygen	rbc; RBC	red blood count
O.B.; OB	obstetrics	rehab.	rehabilitation
OC	oral contraceptive	resp.	respiration
Occ.; Occip.	occipital	Rh	Rhesus factor
O.D.	Doctor of Optometry	RLQ	right lower quadrant
O.P.D.; OPD	Out-Patient Department	R.N.	Registered Nurse
OR; O.R.	Operating Room	ROM	range of motion
orth.	orthopedic	Rt.; rt.	right
OT	occupational therapist/therapy	RUQ	right upper quadrant
oz.	ounce	Rx	take; prescription; therapy
P.	pulse	s̄	without
PA	postero-anterior	Sa.	saline
P.A.	pernicious anemia	S.C.; s.c.; S.cut	subcutaneous
P & A	percussion and auscultation	sed. rate; S.R.	sedimentation rate
palp.	palpable; palpate	sero.; serol.	serology
Pap. test	Papanicolaou smear test	Skel.	skeletal
p.c.	after meals	SNS	sympathetic nervous
P.D.	Doctor of Pharmacy		system
P.E.	physical examination	Sod.	sodium
ped.	pediatrics	sp.; spin.	spine; or spinal
pe.	penicillin	sp. cd.	spinal cord
pH.	hydrogen concentration; or degree	St.; stom.	stomach
	of acidity	staph	staphylococcus
P.I.	present illness	stat.	immediately
P.I.D.	pelvic inflammatory disease	S.T.D.	Sexually Transmitted
PMR	Physical Medicine and Rehabilitation		Disease
PKU	phenylketonuria	strep.	streptococcus
pneu	pneumonia	surg.	surgery
p.o.; P.O.	postoperative	SV	stroke victim
polio	poliomyelitis	sys.	system
p.p.d.	permanent partial disability		
ppm	parts per million	T.	temperature
pre-op	preoperative	T & A	tonsillectomy and
p.r.n.; P.R.N.	as needed; or as desired		adnoidectomy
P.T.	Physical Therapy	tab(s).	tablet(s)
pt.; pt.	patient	T.B.; Tbc	tuberculosis
pt.	pint	thor.	thorax; or thoracic
		thromb.	thrombosis

Abbreviation	Description
t.i.d.	three times a day
t.i.n.	three times a night
T.P.R.	temperature, pulse and respiration
T.U.R.	transurethral resection
TV	tidal volume
U.	unit(s)
UHF	ultrahigh frequency
ULQ	upper left quadrant
uln.	ulnar
ung.	ointment
ur	urine
URI	upper respiratory infection
URQ	upper right quadrant
USP	United States Pharmacopeia
UV	ultraviolet
UVL	ultraviolet light
UVR	ultraviolet radiation
v	volt
VA	Veterans Administration
Vag.	vaginal
V.C.	vital capacity
V.D.	veneral disease
vent.	ventral
vol.	volume
w	watt
WBC; wbc	white blood count
W.H.O.	World Health Organization
Wt.	weight
x	Times; power; or multiplied by
XS	excessive
yd.	yard
yr(s).	years

APPENDIX G

BIBLIOGRAPHY

Jack A. Arstein, "Analyzing Special Damages," *Insurance Law Journal*, 496:261 (May, 1964)

Daniel G. Baldyga, How To Settle Your Own Insurance Claim, The MacMillan Company, New York: 1968.

Fred Benjamin and Dorothea Kaplan, Settle it Yourself: Who Needs a Lawyer, Bonus Books,Chicago, 1985.

The Fact Book, 1992, Insurance Information Institute, New York, 1992 ed.

Alfred F. Conard, James N. Morgan, Robert W. Pratt, Jr., Charles E. Voltz, and Robert L. Bombaugh, Automobile
    Accident Costs and Payments: Studies in the Economics of Injury Reparation (Univ. of Michigan Press, 1964).

Frank R. Dumas, Claim Paid: A Consumer's Guide Through the Insurance Claims Maze (Stratton Press, San Francisco
    CA: 1989).

Accident Facts, 1991 ed. National Safety Council, Chicago IL.

John R. Foutty, "The Evaluation and Settlement of Personal Injury Claims," *Insurance Law Journal*, 492:5 (1964).

John Guinther, Winning Your Personal Injury Suit, (Anchor Press/Doubleday: 1980).

James K. Hammitt, Robert L. Houchens, Sandra S. Polin, John E. Rolph, Automobile Accident Compensation Vol. IV:
    State Rules, Rand Institute (1985).

Deborah R. Hensler, Mary E. Vaiana, James S. Kakalik, Mark A. Peterson, Trends in Tort Litigation: The Story Behind
    the Statistics, Rand Inst. For Civil Justice (1986)

Robert L. Houchens, Automobile Accident Compensation, Vol. III: Payments From All Sources,
    Rand Institute for Civil Justice (1985).

The Institute For Civil Justice, Annual Report, April 1, 1990-March 31, 1991 (The Rand Corporation).

Jury Verdict Research, Concise Personal Injury Medical Dictionary, Solon, Oh. Third Edition (1989).

James S. Kakalik, Nicholas M. Pace, Costs and Compensation Paid in Tort Litigation, Rand
    Institute For Civil Justice, Santa Monica, CA: (1986).

Benjamin Lipson, How To Collect More On Your Insurance Claims, Simon & Schuster,
    New York: 1985.

Edward C. Martin, Personal Injury Damages Law and Practice, John Wiley & Sons New York: 1990.

Joseph L. Matthews, How To Win Your Personal Injury Claim, (Nolo Press, Berkley: 1992).

Jeff O'Donnell, Insurance Smart, John Wiley & Sons, New York, 1991.

Wilbur McCoy Otto, "Lawsuit Evaluation and Outcome Prediction: A More Objective, Dimentionalized and System Approach," *Insurance Cousel Journal,* Oct. 1985 pp. 834-7.

John E. Rolph, Automobile Accident Compensation Volume I: Who Pays How Much How Soon?, Rand Institute (1985).

H. Laurence Ross, Settled out of Court: The Social Process of Insurance Claims Adjustment, (Aldine Gruyter Publishers, Hawthorne, New York: 1980).

Michelle Saadi, Claim it Yourself: The Accident Victim's Guide to Personal Injury Claims (Pharos Books, 1987).

Neil T. Shayne, Evaluating & Negotiating Settlement In Personal Injury Cases, Practising Law Institute, NY 1982.

William M. Shernoff, How To Make Insurance Companies Pay Your Claims And What to Do if They Don't, esp. pp. 27-47, (Hastings House Publishers, Mamaroneck, NY (1990).

Edward Siegel, How to Avoid Lawyers, Ballantine Books, New York: 1989.

Ben W. Swofford, "Evaluating Damage Claims," *Insurance Law Journal,* 412: 273 (May, 1957).

Eugene Sullivan, Where Did the $13 Billion Go?, (Prentice Hall, Englewood New Jersey, 1970).

Summary of Selected State Laws & Regulations Relating to Automobile Insurance (American Insurance Association, Wash D.C.: 1992).

Packard Thurber & Packard Thurber Jr., editors, Claims Medical Manual, (4th ed.), Pacific Book Publishers, Palo Alto CA: 1991.

U.S. Department of Transportation Automobile Insurance & Compensation Study, EconomicConsequences of Automobile Accident Injuries Vol. I, Washington D.C.U.S. Gov't Printing Office, April 1970.

U.S. Department of Transportation, Automobile Personal Injury Claims, Vol. I, Washington, D.C. (July 1970).

Fred Utz, Collision Course, Rainbow Books/Betty Wright, Moore Haven, Fl. (1984).

APPENDIX I

PUBLICATIONS FROM DO-IT-YOURSELF LEGAL PUBLISHERS/SELFHELPER LAW PRESS

The following is a list of books obtainable from the Do-it-Yourself Legal Publishers/Selfhelper Law Press of America.

(Customers: For your convenience, just make a photocopy of this page and send it along with your order. *All prices quoted here are subject to change without notice.*

1. How To Draw Up Your Own Separation/Settlement Agreement—Without, Before, Or During Marriage.

2. How To Win Your Tenant' Legal Rights Without A Lawyer (New York Edition)

3. How To Probate, Administer & Settle An Estate Without A Lawyer ($35)

4. How To Adopt A Child Without A Lawyer

5. How To Form Your Own Profit/Non-Profit Corporation Without A Lawyer

6. How To Draw Up Your Own Will Like The Experts Without A Lawyer

7. How To Declare Your Personal Bankruptcy Without A Lawyer ($29)

8. How To Buy Or Sell Your Own Home Without A Lawyer Or Broker ($29)

9. How To File For Chapter 11 Business Bankruptcy Without A Lawyer ($29)

10. How To Legally Beat The Traffic Ticket Without A Lawyer (forthcoming)

11. How To Settle Your Own Auto Accident Claims Without A Lawyer ($29)

12. How To Obtain Your U.S. Immigration Visa Without A Lawyer ($29)

13. How To Do Your Own Divorce Without A Lawyer [Multi-State Regional Editions] ($35 per Volume)

14. How To Legally Change Your Name Without A Lawyer

15. How To Competently Plan Your 'Total' Estate With A Living Trust, Without The Lawyers' Fee ($35)

16. Before Your Say 'I Do' To Him Or Her, Here's How To First Protect Yourself Legally

● **Prices:** Each book, except for those specifically priced otherwise, costs $25, plus $3.00 per book for postage and handling. New Jersey residents please add 6% sales tax. ALL PRICES ARE SUBJECT TO CHANGE WITHOUT NOTICE.

- -

(CUSTOMERS: Please make and send a xerox copy of this page with your orders. DO NOT Tear Off Sheet)

Order Form

TO: *DO-IT-YOURSELF LEGAL PUBLISHERS*
60 Park Place #1013,
Newark, NJ 07102

Please send me the following:

1._____copies of_____
1._____copies of_____
1._____copies of_____
1._____copies of_____

Enclosed is the sum of $_____to cover the order plus shipping. *Mail my order to:*

Mr/Mrs/Ms/Dr._____
Address (include Zip Code please):_____
_____Zip_____

Phone No. and area code: (_____)_____ (_____)_____
(Home)   (Work)

READERS OPINION SHEET

The author (the Publisher as well) is interested in serving **YOU**, the reader, as he's deeply of the view that **YOU,** the consumer, are the KING or QUEEN! He'd love to know: Did this book meet your needs? Did it answer the more general, basic questions that you had; was it to the point? Most importantly, did it get the job done for you—of getting you an accident claim award? If you would like to express your views directly to the author, ***please complete and return this sheet to:*** *the author,* in care of the Publisher. And we'll make sure your opinion promptly gets directly to him. *Please use the reverse side, if you need extra space.* ***[Please do NOT tear out the sheet; just make a photocopy and send that]***

1. The areas (subject matters, chapters, issues, etc.) this book covers that were of interest to me were:
_____

They were _____ were not_____ covered in sufficient depth.

2. Areas not covered by this book that I would like to see are: _____
_____

3. The most helpful chapter(s) was (were): 1 2 3 4 5 6 7 8 9 10 11 12   Appendix A, B, C, D, E, F.

4. The least helpful chapter(s) was (were): 1 2 3 4 5 6 7 8 9 10 11 12   Appendix A, B, C, D, E, F.

5. The organization of the contents and writing style make the manual easy to read and use? Yes__No__
(Explain/Elaborate:) _____
_____

6. What did you like the best about the book? _____
_____

7. The concept of do-it-yourself, self-help law you champion is: An excellent idea _____ A bad
idea_____ *(Please elaborate)* _____

8. How would you improve the manual?_____
_____

9. My job/profession is:_____

10. I have completed 8-12_____ 13-16_____ over 16_____ years of school.

11. My primary reason for reading this book was: _____

12. I learned about the book through this source or medium: _____

13. The book met my primary need in purchasing the book: Yes_____ No_____

14. It saved (will save) me appx. $_____ using the book to process my accident claim without hiring a lawyer.

15. I bought the book, or read it at this bookstore or library (address in full, please): _____
_____

My Name & Address are: _____
_____ Zip _____ Tel. #_____

Send it to: *Dr. Benji O. Anosike, author* • *c/o Do-It-Yourself Legal Publishers, "Tell It To The Author" Program,*
60 Park Place #1013,   *Newark, NJ 07102*

INDEX